SMART BORDER COALITION

SAN DIEGO - TIJUANA

D0423251

PRAISE FOR *EL TERCER PAÍS*

"To fully understand the symbiotic relationship between the United States and Mexico, the view from Washington and Mexico City is insufficient. One has to study the border, the day-to-day movement of goods, services, and people, to grasp the deep interdependence that exists between our two nations. In *El Tercer País*, the San Diego-Tijuana region is expertly examined in surgical detail, with an emphasis on the truly unique character of the region and its people. Crucially, the book provides an insider's view on the bilateral relationship from the perspective of those who live, work, and breathe it every day."

—Duncan Wood, Director, Mexico Institute,
The Wilson Center, Washington, DC

"El Tercer País is a magnificent tale of two sister cities that together form the most dynamic cross-border community in the world. It tells the complete history of the great cities of the San Diego-Tijuana Coastal Plain, which share a common destiny, as well as the world's busiest land border crossing. Interwoven in this tale are the stories of the people who contributed to a major economic success and the construction of a modern, smart, and more secure border."

—Guadalupe Correa-Cabrera, PhD, Associate Professor, Schar
School of Policy and Government, George Mason University

"*El Tercer País* is a fascinating look at the history and future of this mega-region binding Mexico and the United States. It brings history alive with stories from those who lived through the trials and rebirths. The reader learns about the broader relationship between the two nations, as well as the vision and hope that forged cutting-edge partnerships across technology, manufacturing, and culture, despite challenges of crime, migration, and contrary politics. This story of ups, downs, hopes, and determination is well worth the read."

—Earl Anthony Wayne, US Ambassador to Mexico (2011–2015)

"*El Tercer País: San Diego and Tijuana: Two Countries, Two Cities, One Community* presents the essential backstory necessary to understand the importance and the urgency to reimagine our transborder region. Engaging and fair, discerning and challenging, this book guides us through the story of how our two-city region came together, and why it has become inseparable today. It offers us the opportunity to stop, reflect, and relearn what we thought we knew about this binational 'third country,' which has become among the most talked about border regions in the world."

—Adela de la Torre, PhD, President, San Diego State University

"*El Tercer País* is a remarkably comprehensive treatment of the San Diego-Tijuana border metroplex, tracing their intertwined histories from the arrival of the region's earliest European explorers to the present. It provides a well-crafted narrative that makes an important contribution to the literature on US-Mexico relations by drawing attention to the emergence of San Diego and Tijuana as the preeminent twin-city pairing along the US-Mexico border. Importantly, it tells the tale of how San Diego and Tijuana began to work toward a shared binational vision through the efforts of a host of civic organizations, such as San Diego Dialogue, Tijuana Innovadora, and the Smart Border Coalition. All along, *El Tercer País* wraps a long, complex, and compelling story in prose that is remarkably concise and accessible."

—David Shirk, PhD, Chair, departments of political science and international relations, University of San Diego

"Neighbors for centuries, but neighborly for only a relatively short period. For generations, Tijuana and San Diego warily stared at each other, usually reluctant to go beyond mere opportunism—taking advantage of each other as convenience might dictate. Unlike Laredo or Brownsville or El Paso, San Diego never considered itself a border town—tourism and the US Navy were the moneymakers, easier to deal with than Mexico, with its problematic politics and economy. For Tijuana, San Diego offered opportunities for trade, travel, and some education, but it was always tamped down by a certain hesitation based on underlying suspicions of the North. The last twenty-five years have witnessed a profound change. NAFTA altered the economic game, but, more importantly, visionary leaders promoted a new reality—now widely accepted—that the region is much more than a sum of its parts. They recognize that the area has the potential to be an immense economic powerhouse and a unique cultural blend. This is the story of how that change came about."

—Jeffrey Davidow, US Ambassador to Mexico (1998–2002)

"Upon discovering and understanding the complexity of the Cali-Baja Region, centered in Tijuana / San Diego, I implemented a cross-border consular diplomacy to take into account the profoundly binational nature of the community. For those who have not had the opportunity to live on the border, I highly recommend this book which will bring to life the magical dynamic of this mega-region."

—Ambassador Marcela Celorio, Consul General of Mexico in San Diego (2016–2019) and Los Angeles (2019–present)

"Having spent eight years in the Tijuana-San Diego area, I know that both cities, despite their differences, have forged extensive mutual and rewarding connections. *El Tercer País* brilliantly captures the scope and scale of these ties, traces their origin and evolution, and points to a promising future. Discovering this binational cross-border community may be a surprising revelation for more than one reader."

—Remedios Gómez Arnau, Consul General of Mexico in San Diego (2008–2016) and San Francisco (2019–present)

"I highly recommend *El Tercer País* ... for anyone interested in learning the inside story of one of the world's most unique border regions. For decades, Tijuana and San Diego have enjoyed a mutually beneficial symbiosis and a shared fate, joined together by ties of history, family, commerce, and an extraordinary bilingual culture. The principal characters have all played an important role in managing aspects of this cross-border relationship, and this book paints a clear picture of the 'real' San Diego-Tijuana, dispelling common myths and weaving a rich tale of US-Mexican interdependence."

—Steve Kashkett, US Consul General in Tijuana (2009–2012)

"With a clear understanding of what San Diego and Tijuana are individually, *El Tercer País: San Diego and Tijuana* provides an interesting snapshot of its main character: the border region conformed by these two cities. With a diverse, binational cast of individual and institutional stakeholders, and highlighting the importance of soft power to reinvent the relationship's dynamics, the book sheds light on the importance of collaboration and cooperation at the borderlands, both to face common challenges and to take advantage of the many opportunities."

—Carlos González Gutierrez, Consul General
of Mexico in San Diego (2019–present)

"I wish *El Tercer País: San Diego and Tijuana* had been available to me when I first got to Tijuana as a foreign service officer—it would have been a tremendous resource. I recommend it as required reading for all new government officials assigned to the US-Mexico border. Anyone curious about the cross-border movements of people and cargo will find this book an invaluable resource in understanding how modern borders work."

—Andrew Erickson, US Consul General in Tijuana (2012–2015)

"This book fills a hole in the literature about the border region between the two Californias. It's almost impossible to explain to outsiders the binational, bilingual, and bicultural essence of the place. It is something you feel before you understand it. This wonderful book explains much about how the region did not just happen, but evolved, through both accidents and purposeful choices. More importantly, it shines a light on the men and women who are making important decisions and advocating to guide this evolution. This book explains how the border serves as a point of union, drawing us together. The border region, from Ensenada to Torrey Pines, provides a transition between two distinct places, two states of being; but in the middle, *el tercer país*, a special alchemy occurs: neither one nor the other but truly two things at the same time—a mystery. This book reminds me why my family and I fell in love with Cali-Baja and the people who live there."*

—William Ostick, US Consul General in Tijuana (2015–2018)

These views are the author's own and do not reflect the views of the Department of State.

EL TERCER PAÍS

EL TERCER PAÍS

San Diego & Tijuana

Two Countries
Two Cities
One Community

Michael S. Malone
with Cheryl Dumesnil

SILICON
VALLEY
PRESS

Copyright © 2020 by Michael S. Malone

All rights reserved.

No part of this book may be reproduced, or stored in a retrieval system, or transmitted in any form or by any means, electronic, mechanical, photocopying, recording, or otherwise, without express written permission of the publisher.

Published by Silicon Valley Press, Saratoga, CA
Siliconvalleypress.net
Cover design: Riveting River

Front cover photo: Courtesy of Omar Martinez and SEST—Baja California Secretariat of Tourism

Back cover photo: Ariana Drehsler

ISBN (hardcover, English): 978-1-7339591-4-8
ISBN (hardcover, Spanish): 978-1-7339591-5-5
ISBN (ebook, English): 978-1-7339591-6-2
ISBN (ebook, Spanish): 978-1-7339591-7-9

Library of Congress Control Number: 2020909216

To the people of Tijuana and San Diego, who, over the past fifty years, have created a remarkable binational community in the region they share.

And to their children and grandchildren, who will carry this legacy forward to future generations, to treasure, protect, and strengthen.

CONTENTS

ACKNOWLEDGMENTS

This book was born of the desire of leaders—and everyday citizens—in both San Diego and Tijuana to tell the often-turbulent story of their 250-year shared history, especially the transformation of their relationship over the past fifty years. This development has been nothing short of a revolution, a melding together of two great cities from two different countries and cultures into a mutual friendship with significant interdependence and a shared future.

Most remarkably, for the most part, this partnership arose not from the work of governments but out of relationships between private citizens. These were formed in schoolyards and corporate offices, in restaurants, and on the streets. Now, in this age of border crises everywhere, San Diego and Tijuana stand as a model binational community working collaboratively toward a shared destiny.

The driving forces behind the creation of this book were Malin Burnham, arguably one of America's most successful philanthropists and the foremost figure in San Diego over the last half century, and Alan Bersin, the former border czar under Presidents Clinton and Obama, as well as the superintendent of Public Education and the chairman of the Airport Authority in San Diego. Bersin approached Burnham, believing the time had come for a book about the history of the San Diego-Tijuana relationship.

Malin agreed and took two actions. He contacted Joe DiNucci and Atiya Dwyer, owners of Silicon Valley Press, to ask them if they would be interested in publishing such a book and to inquire if I'd like to be the author. I had previously worked with Malin on his own book, *Community Before Self: Seventy Years of Making Waves*, a volume also published by Silicon Valley Press.

Malin, as only he could, then worked with Alan to assemble a consortium of several of the most powerful figures in San Diego and Tijuana to put their support behind the effort and to make themselves available for interviews—among them Lorenzo Berho, Carlos Bustamante, Salomón Cohen, José B. Fimbres, José Galicot, and Steve Williams.

My only stipulations were that I would have complete editorial control of such a book and—given the tight deadline—would be assisted on this book by writer and editor Cheryl Dumesnil, who has often saved my prose from myself. Cheryl not only did a brilliant job editing the manuscript of this book but she also took on the monumental task of interviewing more than fifty figures in both cities, often in great depth. The voices in this book are the result of her hard work and that of veteran San Diego freelancer Roxana Popescu.

Alan Bersin served as the point person for the book. His encyclopedic knowledge of the region's recent history—not to mention his presence at many important historic events involving Mexico and the US during the last few decades—proved absolutely vital to this Northern Californian. He was joined by veteran publisher and cross-border stakeholder James Clark. From his eye-opening initial tour of modern Tijuana, to his introductions to any institution or person we asked for, to his guiding us through the nuances of the languages and cultures of the two cities, James was the perfect Virgil in our journey.

At Silicon Valley Press, Joe and Atiya, as they have many times, cut the path ahead for Cheryl and me, and Molly Vatinel, our ace project manager, kept us on point and on deadline. Their work really began after Cheryl and I were done—and the physical book you hold in your hand is a testament to that work.

Finally, but not least, we want to acknowledge the citizens of both Tijuana and San Diego. This is their story, and a wonderful one it is. We especially want to thank the individuals below for their willingness to share their stories in this era of enormous change. Because of your courage and sense of community, your binational region is working better than any place like it in the world.

In particular, we want to thank these individuals who agreed to sit down and be interviewed in depth:

Isaac Abadi
Alfredo Angeles
Raymundo Arnaiz
Alan Bersin
Malin Burnham
Alejandro Bustamante
Carlos Bustamante
James Clark
Salomón Cohen
Gustavo de la Fuente
Sandra Dibble
Denise Ducheny
José B. Fimbres
Pete Flores
José Galicot
Gary Gallegos
Paul Ganster
Cindy Gompper-Graves
Jorge Goytortua
Mick Hager
Enrique Hambleton
Cheryl Hammond
Jason Heil
Luis Herrera-Lasso

Paul Jablonski
José Larroque
Gastón Luken Aguilar
Gastón Luken Garza
Ascan Lutteroth
Alejandra Mier y Teran
Mario Orso
Javier Plascencia
Ben Rohrbaugh
Roberto Romandía
Pedro Romero
Jerry Sanders
Elsa Saxod
Lynn Schenk
Larry Smarr
Deborah Szekely
Hugo Torres
Enrique Valle
Hector Vanegas
Mary Walshok
Yolanda Walther-Meade
Jason Wells
Steve Williams

Here's to a glorious future for the two cities, building upon what you already have accomplished.

FOREWORD

Although San Diego and Tijuana shared the same birthdate and family in the sixteenth century and stood just fifteen miles apart, these two great cities of the San Diego-Tijuana Coastal Plain experienced very different beginnings. Tijuana essentially grew as a result of an artificial boundary line, designated first by the Franciscan and Dominican Orders of the Catholic Church, and then by the Spanish government. That line was redrawn on a map, between Alta and Baja California, by an independent Mexican government, then finally marked on the ground as a border between the United States and Mexico, following the Mexican-American War, in 1848. For generations, Tijuana consisted of only a handful of privately owned ranches, with a tiny government presence at the border crossing, on a comparatively small strip of arable land, on the bank of a river that regularly flooded. Underscoring Tijuana's tenuous roots, the city's official church was Mission San Diego, north of today's border boundary.

By comparison, San Diego was created by the presence of that mission, founded by Father Junípero Serra, with its wide expanse of fertile land and proximity to San Diego Bay's all-season port. Designated part of Alta California, San Diego was tied to the rich lands and cities of the Spanish-Mexican empire in North America, while Tijuana was de facto lashed to a largely uninhabited, mostly desert terrain, on the impoverished peninsula of Baja California, and all but ignored by a distant government.

But most of all, by being north of that border, San Diego was destined to become part of the United States, with its unique location and bay making it a crucial US outpost on the Pacific Coast. After the Mexican-American War, San Diego was never again directly touched by war or serious political strife, but rather benefited from wartime investments in the military and nearly two centuries of peace and political continuity. South of the border, however, Tijuana experienced actual battles in its streets and decades of governmental neglect from Mexico City.

At the end of the eighteenth century, it was not yet clear which of the two countries would be paramount on the continent, let alone in the world. Mexico was more populated and much richer at the time, thanks to the gold and silver mines Spain had developed. By comparison, in the US a relatively small population of American colonists clung to the Atlantic Coast, far from the riches of the rest of the continent. Only at the time of the Mexican-American War did it become undeniably clear that the United States would triumph. This realization added further pain to the outcome of the war, when fully half of Mexican territory was surrendered by the Treaty of Guadalupe Hidalgo. Adding insult to injury, while most Mexicans have never forgotten this portion of their history, most Americans have never learned it, nor particularly cared.

Yet despite this contentious history, San Diego and Tijuana have had much in common, beyond geography and climate. Both, for example, exist at an extreme corner of their governing nations. Thus both have experienced the disadvantage of being largely ignored, as well as the benefits of that independence. Both cities have a long history of looking north to a larger, more powerful city—Tijuana to San Diego, San Diego to Los Angeles—with envy, anger, and a sense of inferiority. Both have chafed when those bigger cities exerted their power and prerogative.

Though Tijuana and San Diego have, on many occasions, defined themselves in contradistinction to the other, most of all, what these two cities have in common is their dependence upon one another. For many years, this dynamic was obvious to Tijuana, which seemed to exist solely in a dependent relationship with its northern neighbor.

Meanwhile, San Diego mostly dismissed the city across the border, except to treat it as a source of cheap labor and an outlet for the transgressive behavior of San Diegans. Not until the twenty-first century did San Diego fully come to realize that it, too, needed Tijuana for its youthful vitality, productivity, and competitiveness. Tijuana, a village of fewer than one thousand people in 1900, has grown today into a dynamic metropolis of nearly two million people, a population larger than San Diego's. Tijuana's transformation has been emblematic of similar developments taking place across Mexico.

Today the common destiny of the two cities, long denied, can no longer be ignored. Together, Tijuana and San Diego compose an economic powerhouse with billions and billions of dollars in cross-border trade and tens of thousands of their residents working in one of the cities while living in the other. They share the busiest land border crossing in the world and have pioneered and demonstrated how modern borders can be both smart and secure. Their example has been a model not only for the rest of the US-Mexico border but for other border cities around the world.

This book tells the story of how San Diego and Tijuana built one binational community across the border of their two countries. It is a modern tale of two cities, recounting the events and people who made it happen. It introduces the extraordinary individuals who made history along the way, including the latest pioneers, many of them still at work, who continue to find common cause between the cities and guide them on their shared trajectory into the future. Finally, it offers the shared story of these gemelos as an example for other transnational regions to consider, to follow, and to improve.

From their efforts emerged *El Tercer País,* the third country, to serve both as a bellwether for global borders and a leading indicator of the strategic bilateral relationship between Mexico and the United States, involving virtually every facet of their relations from free trade in North America, through countering transnational organized crime, to the COVID-19 pandemic. Tijuana and San Diego, in many ways, now point toward a future that could not have been predicted from their past. Therein may lie the enduring lesson they offer to a world in which, in the words of French poet Paul Valéry, "the challenge of our times is that the future is not what it used to be."

Janet Napolitano, US Secretary of Homeland Security, 2009–2013, and President of the University of California, 2013–2020

José Antonio Meade, Mexico Minister of Finance, 2011–2012, 2016–2017, and Minister of Foreign Affairs, 2012–2015

CHAPTER ONE

Bridge over an Imaginary Line

At the San Ysidro border crossing between Mexico and San Diego, if you were to stand on the roof of the new $741 million US Customs facility and look south, you would see Tijuana. This city, with its nearly two million residents, stretches from the shops and restaurants just a block away, to the high-rises (many of them currently under construction) just beyond, to a multitude of neighborhoods flowing like a tide over the southern hills. On the low hills sit the most impressive homes—gated villas—while the poorer *colonias* and districts spill toward the east and south.

If you looked in the opposite direction, you would see San Diego stretching twenty miles north. That city, home to almost as many people, begins a few feet away, at the vast shopping center, Las Americas Premium Outlets. Beyond the storefronts of Polo, North Face, Nordstrom, Nike, and Levi's, metallic spires mark the city's center. To the east, atop the nearby hills, lie entire suburbs of expensive homes. At the lower altitudes sit the poorer neighborhoods of San Diego.

From this vantage point, in the twenty-first century, it is easy to imagine this as one vast metropolitan region—twinned cities like Minneapolis and Saint Paul or Dallas and Fort Worth. Or these could be the developed districts of one great city, like New York or São Paulo, each with its own downtown and skyscrapers. In both directions you see the same fast-food franchises, the same automobiles, the same clothes, even the same billboards in the same languages.

Only a few clues indicate that you are looking at two countries. The first is right there above you: the giant flags presiding over an extraordinary number of customs inspection booths. You see it below you, too, in the lines of cars and pedestrians waiting for Customs and Border Protection's permission to continue north. But the most explicit reminder that San Diego and Tijuana are one of the fifteen sets of twinned cities, or *gemelos*, along the US-Mexico border is the fence: The Wall.

There has always been some kind of border barrier between San Diego and Tijuana, at least since the boundary was set by the Mexican-American War, about 170 years ago. Originally, it was merely a wide street. In 1909, the US Bureau of Animal Industry erected the first fence to stop the trans-border movement of cattle. That fence evolved with the two cities, not necessarily to stop passage back and forth, but to impede it long enough for inspection and law enforcement. The first true border fence between San Diego and Tijuana was ordered, to restrict the unlawful crossing of immigrants and drugs, by President Clinton in 1993. It consisted of a fourteen-mile barrier to pedestrians and vehicles. It was expanded by the Secure Fence Act of 2006 to seven hundred miles and completed in 2011.

Today, the barrier is a towering, fifty-foot-tall steel structure that—if its proposed two-thousand-mile length, from the Pacific Ocean to the Gulf of Mexico, is completed—will cost an estimated $48 billion.

Ironically, here on a stretch of the border where such an edifice was arguably least needed, the wall is essentially complete. From the Customs building's roof, you can see the wall stretch like a black scar cutting westward across the hillside to the Pacific Ocean, where it seems to march into the sea, submerge, and disappear. To the east it slices across the Otay Mesa, then into the seemingly endless Mojave and Sonoran Deserts. Directly below you, the wall tracks between factories, shops, and suburban sprawl, like an enduring geologic feature from a distant past.

Only from a satellite view does the impact of the border become clear. Though the structure is all but invisible from such heights, its effects are obvious: it is as if two cans of paint have been poured on the earth, their puddles spreading until—just before they merge—they hit some invisible barrier and expand bilaterally outward, never mixing. Mexicans call it *La Línea*, "The Line."

The wall was built first at this stretch of the border for many reasons, including politics, public relations, and the real migration problem that then existed. It became a flash point and a podium for protesters and politicians. But here on the ground, in the daily life of the two cities, its presence today is almost more symbolic than instrumental, more a nuisance than a benefit, a legacy of the past, rather than a celebration of the future. San Diego largely solved its illegal border-crossing problem years ago, in part because of unprecedented coordination between law enforcement agencies on both sides of the border but also because unprecedented prosperity and the rise of new industries in Tijuana have given migrants ever-greater reasons to stay in Mexico.

QUOTIDIAN REALITY

The reality of daily life at the border, and of the relations between these two great cities, bears little resemblance to the myths and the monochromatic opinions of most citizens of the United States or Mexico. Indeed, this reality differs from the opinions of most San Diegans and many Tijuanenses—especially, and surprisingly, those who can see across the border, but have never actually crossed it.

The image of hordes of migrants waiting on the border to sneak into El Norte may have some truth along wilder stretches of the US-Mexico border, but no longer here, where many Tijuanenses resent this behavior perhaps even more than their northern neighbors do. Equally untrue is the image of Tijuana as a dirty metropolis riven by crime and sin, where unwary tourists are set upon by petty criminals and con men. Those images belong to the past, when Tijuana, trapped in an endless cycle of catering to American desires, devoted itself to delivering services that, ironically, are now legal in the United States. Indeed, in the elegant districts of today's downtown Tijuana, a visitor is often safer than in many major American cities.

What is the real truth about the border two decades into the twenty-first century? It is seventy thousand vehicles (a number predicted to double over the next decade) heading north every morning through up to thirty-two lanes at the San Ysidro crossing. Today's truth is that these cars are filled with students and workers who have found quality schools and jobs in San Diego, but who consider Tijuana their home and Mexico their nation. Other commuters are heading to shop in the US, or to attend a Padres game, or to visit the San Diego Zoo. Today's truth is that these cars crossing into San Diego in the morning will be returning to Tijuana at night.

Conversely, on twenty-two highway lanes heading south at the border, through a newly constructed, glistening Mexican port of entry, the cars carry not only tourists, but US patients heading to appointments in Tijuana, where they can get superior medical attention at a fraction of the cost at home, not to mention the doctors who will treat them, commuting from their homes in Chula Vista. These southbound border crossers also include San Diego bankers, lawyers, and business professionals, retired US military officers with vacation homes near Rosarito Beach (Playas de Rosarito), and gourmands on pilgrimage to taste the offerings of Tijuana's world-famous Baja Cuisine or visit the Valle de Guadalupe to sample extraordinary New World wines.

In truth, San Diego and Tijuana in many ways have more similarities than differences. They share the same valley, the same landscape, the same water and air, the same weather. They watch each other's television shows, listen to each other's radio stations, attend each other's cultural events, and share many of each other's challenges.

Most of all, they increasingly share each other's destiny. In many ways, this has always been so—though until recently, both cities were loath to admit that central truth. San Diego, after all, was already a bustling city when Tijuana was still a cluster of *ranchos* on the other side of the river. In the early years of the twentieth century, when Tijuana was beset with civil war and crime, San Diego tried to keep its neighbor at arm's length—that is, except when San Diegans wanted to indulge their tastes in sin while presenting only rectitude to their neighbors back home.

But even then, the two cities couldn't help but be drawn to each other. The quintessential border town, Tijuana, at the extreme northwest corner of Mexico, has always felt forgotten—or at best, treated as second-class—by the capital in Mexico City, nearly fifteen hundred miles away. San Diego, at the extreme southwest corner of the United States, and isolated by mountains to the north and east, always has felt overshadowed by a bigger, more dominant Los Angeles (though San Diego was founded first), and also mostly ignored and forgotten by Washington, DC, more than twenty-two hundred miles away. It is not surprising, then—especially as Tijuana has grown in prosperity and surpassed San Diego in population—that the two cities have grown closer together in common cause.

The story of how they have come together—across the twists and turns, through the feuds and friendships, over nearly 250 years—is the subject of this book.

CROSSING

Twenty thousand pedestrians cross the border each day at the San Ysidro Port of Entry (POE) and perhaps half that many at the POE farther east, on the Otay Mesa. At the San Ysidro crossing, northbound pedestrians enter the US through one of two processing facilities: the 22,000-square-foot PedWest, or the recently opened 100,000-square-foot PedEast.

But first, they wait.

Along the sidewalk leading to PedEast, in thousands, they wait: parents shepherding their children, tourists pulling luggage, students shouldering backpacks loaded with books, tired seniors leaning against the railing to rest their feet, impatient businesspeople, *campesinos* in traditional clothes, bikers in their leathers, middle-aged daily travelers who have long since learned to bide their time.

They shuffle forward in fits and starts, parents hustling their kids along, those with heavy loads kicking their boxes and bags forward on the sidewalk. As they do, they slowly pass a line of shops reminiscent of another time in the Tijuana story—bars, curio shops, taco stands—all caked in soot kicked up by a seemingly endless line of cars idling at the auto crossing. Those travelers not obviously Mexican are approached by street vendors selling tiny Virgen de Guadalupe statues, stuffed animals, candy. There aren't many takers, and the line shuffles on.

Travelers who hold Secure Electronic Network for Travelers Rapid Inspection (SENTRI) or Global Entry cards get to bypass this ritual, but for the rest, the wait continues, often for an hour or more, until they near the gate of PedEast. There, US Customs and Border Protection (CBP) officers segment the line into groups, allowing only a few dozen at a time to enter the state-of-the-art building, where up to twenty-two pedestrian processing lanes greet them.

Once inside, the actual CBP clearance process—thanks to its recent upgrades and advanced technology—is remarkably efficient. The orderly lines move briskly, and the CBP officials are crisp and professional as they process border-crossing cards, passports, and visas.

The actual crossing of the Border—*La Frontera*—is itself an anticlimax; a brief glimpse out a window might reveal the wall below, but the rest of the experience is one of wide, sterile walkways, ramps, and escalators, until suddenly travelers step out of the facility, entering the US a few blocks from John Montgomery Highway, where Interstate 5 begins its nearly 1,400-mile journey north to the Canadian border.

It certainly doesn't look like the entrance to a great freeway. Here in San Ysidro, all is chaos. Crowds of mostly young people mill about, seemingly trying to determine where to go first, jamming the McDonald's a block away, hanging out on the filthy, gum-spotted sidewalks. The gutters are filled with trash, much of it advertising flyers continuously passed to new arrivals. Other travelers thread through these crowds: some to get to the buses or trolley that will take them to jobs and schools in San Diego, businesspeople walking several blocks to their awaiting Ubers and Lyfts, tourists looking about nervously for their promised rides. Within minutes, all will disperse down the streets of another country.

The border may be an invisible line that exists only by treaty and law or demarked by a giant steel fence and a narrow no-man's-land. But in the lives of those who cross it here in Tijuana and San Diego, it is a half-mile-wide strip of earth that has its own reality—its own culture, rules of behavior, history, and dreams for the future, and its own temporary citizenry.

BORDERLANDS

In San Diego, they call that strip The Borderland; in Mexico it is called *El Tercer País* (The Third Country)—a place of endless movement as thousands of people each day cross back and forth, or fidget in long lines, or search for their waiting rides. On the US side, they crowd around the Jack in the Box and McDonald's, catching a quick coffee and snack. Some wait for their rides or taxis or public transport. Others walk a little farther down the Camino de la Plaza to the Las Americas Premium Outlets, where they can browse, shop, eat, and move on. Though they may live in Tijuana or farther south, or in San Diego and farther north, for a few hours they are the de facto citizens of The Borderland, El Tercer País.

Las Americas premium outlets, with the border fence and Tijuana in the background.

Ingrid, 16 and a high school student, lives with her parents. Their San Diego home is close enough to the border that she simply walks when she wants to cross over to see the rest of her extended family, all of whom live in Tijuana. She also goes to church and does volunteer work there. She has been crossing regularly—with her parents—since she was five years old. She has long black hair parted in the middle, has paid exceptional attention to her lashes and brows, and she wears a black, zippered pullover with a corporate logo.

"Yeah," she says, "I feel quite comfortable on both sides, and I think I'm getting more so as I get older. But I've got to say the security at the border is way more than I have ever seen. I have to get here about 8:00 a.m. just to be sure to get across by 10:00. That's why I go for the weekend—and then get back on Monday for school."

Nevertheless, she says, "I'm going to try to cross more next year." One reason is that Ingrid, at the behest of an aunt who runs an educational program in Tijuana, tutors young children on the weekends. She likes the work.

Juan, 30, lives in Murrieta, commuting sixty-five miles south to work at a Marriott hotel in downtown San Diego. He is equally comfortable speaking in English and Spanish. He says that because of the long trip, he only crosses the border a couple of times each year to visit family in Tijuana. Having grown up in California, he is more comfortable on the US side, but he enjoys heading to Mexico for vacation. Being bilingual helps.

Despite the higher crime rate in Tijuana and Mexico, Juan says he doesn't worry when he is traveling alone, but when with his wife and two children, aged thirteen and seven, he admits to being more vigilant. Yet, he adds, there are so many things that are very attractive about life in Mexico—not least the lower cost of living and the possibility of a much shorter commute than the one he now endures.

"I think about that sometimes. My long commute is hard, you know. You've got to be dedicated and willing to sacrifice for your family to live in California. But you want to give them the best. It's a tough question.

"From what I hear from my relatives over there, it's a lot cheaper there—not so much in Tijuana anymore, but further into Mexico." He pauses. "I own a house, you know, so I know what it's like making those payments—how sometimes you just feel like you're drowning. Then I look at the Mexican side of my family. They own houses, too, but it just doesn't seem as stressful. Life just seems more relaxed over there."

In his job at the Marriott, Juan supervises a number of maintenance workers who live in Tijuana. "I work with people who cross every day, and it's tough on them. I can't really feel sorry for myself doing an hour commute when these people get up and get in line at three or four in the morning just to be at their jobs at seven or eight."

Jonathan lives in Rosarito Beach, a city of seventy thousand adjacent to Tijuana on the coast. He works in home construction—which he says is booming—and he is deeply involved in his local church. He is crossing today to visit his in-laws. "They live in Lemon Grove in San Diego County," he says in Spanish. Jonathan is Mexican; his wife is a US citizen. He crosses the border "one or two times a week," usually with his two young children, aged four and two, who were born in San Diego but also live in Rosarito. Crossing with two little kids is difficult even on good days, he says. "It is a lot harder where there's a lot of traffic, because they start getting bored and frustrated waiting, and then they start to cry. What do you call it when you have a bad dream? A nightmare. Yes, it's a nightmare."

Jonathan says that he and his wife are hoping to move to San Diego sometime in the next year, partly, he says, because of these border crossings with the children. But also because the crime in Mexico seems to be getting worse.

Cindy, 24, lives in Imperial Beach, not far from the border. She crosses the border into Tijuana every week or two, mostly to take advantage of the affordable medical care there. She is wearing a deep-blue San Diego hoodie.

"I don't have insurance here," she says, "so I have a form of cheaper insurance on the other side. It's called SIMNSA Health Plan. They're hooked up with [a] hospital in San Diego, which is doing a lot of upgrading and renovating its clinic in Tijuana, which is great. The only difficulty now is the crossing, which can be pretty hectic.

"I take my mother to the hospital there too. She's had three brain aneurisms. And again it's, it's the insurance thing—because it's hard to find someone to help us out with preexisting conditions. So we go to Mexico and try to get it cheaper. But it's a lot of process just to get there. My mom lives in [the city of] La Mesa, which is an hour from the border. So we go from there all the way here and then back.

"I was worried at first when we learned that our insurance wouldn't let her be treated up at [the hospital in] Chula Vista, but sent her to Tijuana. But when they took care of her there, they did everything: blood pressure, cholesterol, diabetes.

"My parents were both born in Mexico, and I have family there. Many of them suffer from the same medical problems—it's genetic— so that makes staying in Tijuana a lot easier. But I have to say that the border crossing is a miserable experience. It's not the actual process, but it's the fact that every time you cross you just don't know what is going to happen. Even if you have the papers, it's a hassle. You're never sure if, this time, you're not going to get to the clinic or see your relatives. It just seems so arbitrary: your movement is controlled by the government. It is a very uncomfortable experience.

"I don't understand the border. I don't understand us being divided. For me, it's just like we are 'United' States for a reason, right?" Cindy says she isn't for a fully open border, but says, "Can't we make the experience more efficient for people like me, who cross often because we don't have a real choice?"

Sofia, 19, was born and raised in Tijuana. She has long black hair, hoop earrings, and glasses, and she wears a windbreaker over a knit shirt. Sofia lives with her mother and infant daughter. She has crossed to San Diego today to do some shopping. "I cross the border around three or four times a year," she says in Spanish. "Once at Christmas, once in January, and one or two times during summer. When I come, I shop at Las Americas, because it's close to the border. I don't have a car, and I have to cross the border walking.

"In all the stores they are very nice, and they make you feel welcome. They sometimes have people that speak Spanish or English, which is good because I can only speak English a little bit. Oftentimes I speak half Spanish and finish in English."

Other than her shopping trips, Sofia has little connection with life on the US side of the border, though she adds that she would if there were an easier way to cross. "I'd like to cross the border more as my little girl gets older. I've had a visa since I was her age, so that's not a problem. And I've always been a person that comes and goes. But coming here is work. So other than shopping, I really only have crossed to visit Six Flags or Disneyland, and once for a high school graduation event."

Do politics impact her decision of whether or not to cross the border? "No," she says, shaking her head. "It's my own decision. It's personal."

José, 21, is a bearded young man in a hurry, and not anxious to talk. José is wearing jeans and an Aéropostale T-shirt and ball cap, and he has bags slung over his shoulder. He lives in Tijuana and crosses to San Diego a couple of times each year. Why not more often? "Because Tijuana is more free," he says cryptically, then adds, "I can drink there." He walks on, not looking back.

Joanna, 30, wears black yoga pants and an olive-green T-shirt. She has two Victoria's Secret bags slung over her arm. Asked about what she's purchased, she replies excitedly, "Two-dollar-and-ninety-nine-cent shirts! They're normally thirty-five dollars. I got heather gray, burgundy, black, white, and turquoise. They're all the same style, because I'm going to sell them online." Is she going to keep any for herself? "No."

She points at some other items. "See these bottles? Ninety-nine cents. And at North Face I got a forty-dollar rain jacket that's usually ninety dollars." Is she going to resell it all? "Most of it. That's what people come here for. You'll see people come with empty luggage and they'll fill them up and sell it all in TJ at triple the original price, especially American name brands. Victoria's Secret is one of the most popular."

Joanna says she makes this shopping trip several times per month, and sometimes much more often. In fact, this is her second shopping trip this week. She's been doing this for two years, she says, driving over from her home in Chula Vista in San Diego County, where she lives with her mother, three much younger sisters, and her six-year-old daughter. "So I have to get deals," she says, "for the family."

Joanna, who describes herself as Mexican-American, grew up in the San Francisco Bay area, in Sunnyvale. When she first moved south, she originally lived in Mexico. "I actually lived in TJ," she says. It was not a happy experience. "People would always try to overcharge me. They would talk about me and expect me not to know. And they would call me names like *pocha*—which is someone who has Mexican parents, but doesn't speak the language. Actually, I speak Spanish, but it is with an accent. Luckily, it's slowly going away."

Joanna used to work as a trainer at a manufacturing plant, but she quit to help her mother recover from brain surgery. These days, her mother often comes along—as she has this day—"just for fun." Joanna got the idea for her current work from an earlier job, working at online reseller Ebuys.

How much does she make on these shopping expeditions? "Well, this thirty-four-dollar shirt I got for $2.99, I'll sell online for about twenty dollars and then give them a deal, because the shipping is like six bucks. So I'll make six to eight dollars on each shirt." When buying clothes, she says, she'll buy multiple sizes, then list them all together. That way she only pays for a single listing.

Joanna often sells her items to customers in Tijuana. Does she ever buy any goods there? "Oh no," she replies. "Everything's too expensive down there. I only go to visit family."

FACTORY AS FAMILY

The Borderland doesn't just exist at the crossings. Several miles east, in an industrial park just beyond the Abelardo Rodríguez Tijuana International Airport, one of the best factory managers in Mexico steps out of his office and heads toward the assembly floor of the Tijuana division of the venerable headset maker, Poly (known as Plantronics until a merger with Polycom Corp. in early 2019). He is a short, stocky man with a bristling gray mustache, a jaunty walk, and a perpetual smile.

Alejandro Bustamante is a Tijuana native, a member of one of the city's most distinguished families—indeed, his cousin Carlos was mayor of the city. He is also a product of Mexico's educational system, earning his bachelor's in business administration at La Salle University in Mexico City. Only in graduate school (an MBA from Pepperdine) and executive training (UCLA and Harvard) has he matriculated outside of his native country. It is a testament to the quality of that Mexican education, and to Bustamante's leadership skills, that in the trophy case he passes as he heads down the hall, his factory is consistently named one of the best places to work in Mexico. Poly has won national awards for product quality, technology, exports, and workplace quality.

The Poly/Plamex facility, one of 750 large maquiladoras in Tijuana.

Yet, for all this, Bustamante is equally at home in the United States. Poly is headquartered in the Northern California beach town of Santa Cruz. As president of Plamex, Poly's Tijuana-based manufacturing division, Bustamante spends a lot of time there, and over the hill in Silicon Valley. Needless to say, his English is impeccable, and he can casually recount the best meals he has enjoyed in Palo Alto and San Francisco. He is also a huge baseball fan. He collects autographed baseballs from the San Diego Padres, with the characteristic personal touch that the signatures are all from Mexican-born players. "I'm especially proud of them," he says.

As he walks down the hall, with its mirror-shiny linoleum, Bustamante smiles and greets every passing lab-coat-clad employee, most of them young women and men from villages throughout Mexico. They are accustomed to this. They smile back without breaking stride and say a quick "good morning." None seem intimidated by the most powerful man in the building.

Bustamante bounces on, gesturing toward doors as he passes, each of them housing state-of-the-art audio research equipment. Inside, technicians look up and wave as he passes by, then he pivots on his heel and pushes through a set of dust-proof double doors.

"Here we are," he announces and holds his arms wide.

Before him is a giant hall: more than 120,000 square feet of assembly area, with another 145,000 square feet of service and inventory storage beyond. The assembly area is all open workstations, exposed pipes and power cables, flashing and glowing electronic lights, and natural light from windows high above. Nearly five thousand workers sit at their stations, assembling motherboards and soldering leads, installing the casings, testing, and packing the finished goods. They are working assiduously, though no one seems rushed. The only people rushing are those walking swiftly down the aisles delivering and transferring components and tools. A deep, oceanic thrumming sound of humanity and electronics fills the cavernous building.

So engaged in their work does everyone seem that when Bustamante approaches a random employee, she seems momentarily surprised—nobody noticed the boss walking by. She politely answers his questions but seems more interested in getting back to work.

The Poly plant is one of the most celebrated factories of the *maquiladora* movement that inaugurated the rise of the "new" Tijuana in the 1990s. The movement had its roots in the 1965 Border Industrialization Program between Mexico and the United States. But this was not the first program to promote cross-border collaboration. Earlier, the Bracero Program, dating from the 1940s, permitted Mexican "guest workers" into the United States, mostly for jobs in agriculture. As the Bracero Program ended, the Border Industrialization Program aimed to create jobs in Mexico. It reduced restrictions and duties on machinery, raw materials, and equipment crossing the border, and it encouraged improving the infrastructure—roads, electricity, water, factories, and such—in the borderlands on both sides. Most importantly, to increase investment, Mexico allowed American and other foreign firms to import raw materials at a reduced cost, while the US permitted the export of finished goods into the United States without the payment of taxes, tariffs, or other duties.

Tijuana, desperate for an alternative native industry besides the volatile tourism industry, especially after the devastating Mexican debt crisis a few years prior, jumped on this new opportunity. It was helped by a new "Decree for Development and Operation of the Maquiladora Industry" from the federal government, which further lowered barriers to foreign investment. Soon the first foreign-funded factories were popping up in the city proper and in its barren eastern stretches along the border.

One of the first companies to establish a maquiladora was Plantronics (now Poly), which set up its Plamex operations in 1985 with a $30 million investment. Coincidentally, that was the year that maquiladoras surpassed tourism as Mexico's largest source of foreign exchange. The movement went into overdrive with the passage of the North American Free Trade Agreement (NAFTA) in 1994, and within two years, maquiladoras represented Mexico's second-largest industry, after petroleum. Further, they became a key contributor to the country's growing trade with the US.

Plantronics was already a highly developed US technology corporation before it landed in Tijuana. It had been founded in 1961 by two commercial airline pilots who had developed a lighter, more functional design for the communication headsets pilots wore. Within five years, Plantronics's headsets were chosen by the Federal Aviation Agency as the sole supplier of headsets to air traffic controllers. Airlines standardized them, as did the Bell Telephone Company for its operators.

When NASA adopted the Plantronics MS-50 headset for the astronauts and mission control of the Mercury program, the company's headsets entered into the public eye and the history of the era. Neil Armstrong announced his first step on the moon through a Plantronics headset. NASA astronauts use the company's headsets to this day.

Poly still builds the MS-50, as well as its most popular headset, the StarSet, with its characteristic plastic tube microphone. But in the intervening years, the company's product line has extended to wireless, mobile, and Bluetooth headsets; specialty headsets for computer games, stereo speakers, and audio software; and, with the purchase of Polycom in 2018, speakerphones and video-conferencing systems. Most of these products are, or will soon be, manufactured at the Plamex Tijuana facility.

The facility is ready for them. From the outside, this huge, sleek steel structure manages to be both simple and imposing at once. Its white walls are delineated by a carbon-black slab adorned with vertical silver bars that seem like a commentary on the border wall that runs along the hilltop a few blocks away. Anywhere else, the factory would be a showpiece. But here, in a two-square-mile industrial park, it is just one of dozens of equally giant factories bearing names such as Samsung, Honeywell, and Coca-Cola. What distinguishes Plamex is its roof covered with solar panels, which power many of its operations.

Bustamante has been with Plamex Tijuana since 1994, when he joined from a management position at an aviation company headquartered at the international airport a couple of miles away. He had assisted the government in negotiating NAFTA and had helped write Mexico's National Development Plan 1995–2000. Working on both—and seeing the competitive advantage Mexico would have in manufacturing—convinced Alejandro to find employment at a maquiladora.

With his leadership skills, Bustamante quickly rose through Plamex until he was named president of the Tijuana facility. About the time the new plant opened in 2013, he was also named vice president of Global Operations for Poly, the parent company. As a result, his life in recent years has been increasingly binational. "These days," he says, "it seems like I spend nearly as much time in Northern California as I do here."

Even as he has leapt into the global economy, Alejandro has taken enormous pains to help his employees enter into the modern world. While some of his workers are contemporary urban dwellers from Tijuana and other Mexican cities (and a few deported Mexican citizens raised in the US), a majority of Plamex Tijuana employees come from small towns and villages in Central Mexico, marked by poverty and limited education. This job is their first taste of a much bigger world.

Toward that end, Bustamante has turned the factory not only into a high-production workplace but also a surrogate home and school for his employees. During the week, workers often stay for the evening to take part in different social groups, work on charitable activities, or advance their education. They take classes on-site to earn their high school, bachelor's, and master's degrees. They are served ten free meals per week, and they can receive medical care at an on-site clinic. On weekends, it is not uncommon to see the social halls at the factory booked for weddings of employees. The company even brings in the local symphony and opera for performances. For employees who have left their families and the security of their villages, these added services, which might seem extravagant, even intrusive, on the other side of the wall, are a comfort to many here.

There are good reasons why Plamex Tijuana has won so many Best Places to Work awards. But Bustamante doesn't stop there. The factory also supports ten orphanages throughout the region.

For Alejandro Bustamante, it is all part of his job. As much as he is dedicated to the success of his employees, he is equally committed to the success of the city he loves. In his lifetime, Tijuana has seen everything from the humiliation of being known as a sin city to drug wars in its streets to its current prosperity. He is dedicated to ensuring that Tijuana triumphs, and to do that, he must bring his fellow citizens up with it.

"Sure, our primary responsibility always is to build the best Plantronics products we can," he says. "But I also consider helping our employees to build successful lives one of our responsibilities too. In the long run, they are our most important products." He smiles and waves to a few more workers and then walks briskly on down the aisle to his next meeting.

***

For nearly 250 years, Tijuana and San Diego have shared the Tijuana Valley. They have grown up apart, but together. With distinctly different births, the two cities spent their first two centuries developing in tense contrast to each other. But in the last fifty years, they have begun to accept their common destiny and work together in a manner that is not only unique, but remarkable, given their past. These twin cities offer a model for border cooperation for the rest of the world.

This is the story of Tijuana and San Diego's histories, the transformation of their relationship, and the hard work to finally find common ground.

From the beginning, San Diego developed with great advantages: a Catholic mission, a port, and perhaps most important of all, citizenship in the wealthiest and most powerful country in history. Tijuana had none of these advantages. When San Diego became a metropolis with thousands of citizens, trolley cars, tall buildings, and a global presence, Tijuana remained little more than a few stores, ranches, and government buildings, most operating at the mercy of their neighbor to the north.

As the twentieth century dawned, while San Diego enjoyed one of the most elegant and cultured settings anywhere on the continent, just a few miles away Tijuana was wracked by revolution and civil war. Worse, it had gained a reputation as a crime-ridden den of illicit activities, the dark counterpart to a shiny northern city so close that Tijuanenses could see its towers sparkling on the horizon.

Back then, San Diegans who visited Tijuana did so seeking a taste of the exotic and the strange. Tijuana provided those activities that, by law or the disapproval of your neighbors, you were not allowed to do at home: gambling, drinking, buying drugs, soliciting women, getting an abortion or a quickie divorce. Aside from that, most San Diegans largely ignored Tijuana.

By comparison, it was impossible for Tijuanenses to ignore San Diego, the source of Tijuana's wealth, investment capital, infrastructure construction, medical care, and charity. San Diego provided sanctuary during dangerous times and education for the children of wealthy Tijuanenses. Hard times in San Diego triggered terrible times in Tijuana, while good times in the north propelled prosperity across the border. When Mexico City seemed to forget Tijuana, at least San Diego—or more accurately, some of its citizens—could be trusted to care.

Not surprisingly, this unequal relationship led to arrogant contempt of Tijuana by San Diego and overweening, hurt pride by Tijuana. As the decades passed and these attitudes became ossified in received truths and conventional wisdom, it became increasingly difficult for these two cities to see each other clearly. The reality, hidden behind these opinions and the prejudice they embodied, was that both cities were changing radically, especially Tijuana.

By the final decade of the twentieth century, Tijuana had begun to transform itself. Though many of the old social problems remained, a new Tijuana was emerging: world-class cuisine and wine, distinguished universities, celebrated cultural institutions, vast new industries, and a reputation for superior service. Tijuana still depended upon San Diego, but now San Diegans drove south because many things Tijuana offered were better than at home. Conversely, now Tijuana's citizens crossed the border to do what San Diegans had done for two centuries: raid what was best in the other city and bring it home. Tijuana, growing twice as fast as the aging population of San Diego, was quietly becoming equal in size to its northern neighbor but also equal in many other ways.

It took a long time, until the end of the 1990s, for San Diego to appreciate what was happening south of the border. Tijuana, for its part, seemed to be in disbelief that its perpetually subordinate and dependent position vis-à-vis San Diego had changed.

Ultimately, it took a small, forward-looking group of leading San Diego citizens to challenge the status quo and promote what Tijuana had always known: the two cities are inextricably linked. They asked difficult questions, broke through the clichés, and did the fieldwork to uncover empirical truths. Most of all, they began a dialogue—first among themselves, and then with their counterparts, the civic leaders of Tijuana, men and women as extraordinary as themselves.

The result first was a conversation between leaders in the two cities and then an unprecedented coordination of action on both sides and at the border, which continues to this day. In the process, over the course of three decades, this binational group of trailblazers and those who followed them have forged perhaps the strongest and most successful cross-border partnership found anywhere.

In El Tercer País, between San Diego and Tijuana, the once-sharp demarcation between the two nations has blurred. Hundreds of thousands of citizens of both cities now live as if La Línea didn't exist, and binational institutions are being created that have never existed anywhere before.

Most remarkably, at a time when tensions have escalated between their two nations, these two cities have found their separate peace. At a time when accusations about illegal immigration fly between the two national capitals, San Diego and Tijuana, once the synecdoche of the border crisis, had already found a workable solution, together, a decade before. The same is true in terms of law enforcement, customs, transportation, pollution, communication, manufacturing, and trade.

San Diego and Tijuana have found solutions because a small number of dedicated and open-minded people on both sides of the border have dispelled myths, dismantled prejudices, taken risks, and led the way.

CHAPTER TWO

Tijuana—So Far from Mexico City, So Near to San Diego

Few cities contradict their reputations as decisively as Tijuana.

Tijuana is seen as an old city, set as it is in one of the hemisphere's oldest countries, but in fact Tijuana is one of the youngest major cities in North America. Though ruled by Mexico, Tijuana devotes most of its livelihood to the United States. The city has long been perceived as subservient in its relationship to the US, yet today, a not inconsiderable fraction of the US economy depends on Tijuana's labor and productivity. In important ways, San Diego now needs Tijuana as much as Tijuana needs San Diego.

Tijuana has a long-held reputation for fulfilling Yankee desire for sin and vice, yet most of its famous illicit institutions were designed, owned, and even run by US citizens. Further, Tijuana's image is that of a debased antipode to San Diego's shiny perfection when, in fact, historically Tijuana has helped maintain San Diego's pure facade by bearing and concealing many of its northern neighbor's sins.

In a thousand other ways, Tijuana contradicts its image. Currently Tijuana is seen as a primary entry point for undocumented migrants from the interior of Mexico and, even more so, from Central America to enter the United States. However, rather than opening the door to the US, Tijuana's business community prefers to encourage migrants to remain in town to be trained to work in the burgeoning high-tech factories. In truth, many business leaders attribute the city's entrepreneurial energy in part to its multicultural migrant population from within Mexico as well as from abroad.

But here is perhaps the most important contradiction, at least in the twentieth century: while in Washington, DC, and Mexico City, government leaders see the border as a seemingly endless, intractable problem, Tijuana and San Diego's civic, business, cultural, and academic leaders work together, today better than ever before, to make the border operate effectively for both sides.

In short, where the rest of the world sees a confrontation, San Diego and Tijuana see an opportunity.

For many Americans, even San Diegans who never cross the border, their image of Tijuana—dirty, violent, dangerous—is more than a decade obsolete, replaced by a city of shiny high-rises, Yankee fast-food franchises, and elegant restaurants. Today's Tijuana features immaculate, affluent neighborhoods and vast business parks. Yet on the outskirts of the city, poverty reigns, gangs rule, and the homicide rate soars as high as ever.

This is nothing new. Tijuana, perpetually pulled between the demands of Mexico City and the desires of San Diego and Southern California, has exhibited these contradictions from its founding—forever blessed and punished by the dictates of geography and politics. To paraphrase President Porfirio Díaz's rueful words about Mexico, still repeated after 130 years: "Poor Tijuana, so far from God, so close to the United States of America."

A SENSE OF PLACE

To understand the source of San Diego's and Tijuana's commonalities—and differences—you must begin with geography.

Tijuana and San Diego share a large valley, largely of rock and scrub, created by the river alluvia of mountains, some three thousand feet tall, to the south and east, and a marine terrace extending to the Pacific Ocean. Of the two cities, San Diego enjoys the gentler topography, with large, low mesas, wide beaches, and its magnificent bay. Tijuana lies on much rougher, rocky ground, with limited arable land, mostly along the Tijuana River, which bisects the Valley, and the larger Otay Mesa (Mesa de Otay). Together Tijuana's usable land encompasses a little more than twenty thousand acres.

Crucial to the geography of the area are the Ice Age–created rivers, notably the Tijuana River but also the Alamar and Las Palmas, not just because their sediment created the valley and cut through the landscape, but because the wetlands along their banks, expanding beyond as they approach the ocean, attracted the flora and wildlife that made the valley uniquely hospitable. Indeed, the valley is one of the most remarkable ecological sites on the planet for its numbers of plant and animal species. The rivers, especially the Tijuana, are also crucial to the story of the region's human habitation, because of their tendency to flood during especially rainy winters.

Unlike many international borders around the world, there is no natural geographic border between the United States and Mexico west of the Rio Grande/Rio Bravo del Norte River, which divides the two countries farther east. On the contrary, the valley itself, from the climate, to water usage, to accessibility, seems designed to force Tijuana and San Diego closer together in a common destiny.

The first known inhabitants of the Tijuana River Valley, the Kumeyaay Indians who are believed to have inhabited the area for more than one hundred thousand years, certainly had no conception of natural, much less political, borders. They seasonally migrated across a large, diverse region that ranged north to modern San Diego, east to the Imperial and Mexicali Valleys, west and south to modern Ensenada on the coast, and from desert to mountains to chaparral to the coast, in perpetual movement, hunting, fishing, and gathering. What villages the Kumeyaay created were either temporary or only inhabited for a few months each year.

The Kumeyaay, like indigenous people everywhere, lived a comparatively simple, hunter-gatherer existence and produced unique articles of dress, weapons, pottery, and crafts, but little else has survived aside from their words, still alive in the region as place names. Few native Kumeyaay have lived into the twenty-first century, though enough have that the US has designated them as eighteen distinct, recognized Native American bands. They live in San Diego County, which has more Indian reservations (although very small) than any other county in the United States. North of the border, many though not all descendants of the Kumeyaay have prospered, thanks to truck stops and federal- and state-mandated casino compacts with several of the tribes. Indeed, San Diego County has the largest concentrations of indigenous peoples' casinos and luxury hotels in the United States. By comparison, in Mexico, their tribal counterparts, mostly clustered in villages near Ensenada, now largely live in extreme poverty. The Baja Kumeyaay, however, have retained much of their culture and language, while the United States Kumeyaay have not done so. The post-9/11 restrictions on the cross-border movement of people have severely limited the intratribal connections between these native communities.

A NEW LAND

The story of Northern Mexico—and of California—begins with the Spanish explorers. As might be expected given the nature of the land-scape, the first of these explorers, Juan Rodríguez Cabrillo in 1542 and Sebastián Vizcaíno in 1602, sailed up the coast and entered what is now San Diego Bay. Though they left extensive descriptions of the bay, the nearby islands, and even the "well-armed" Kumeyaay who traded mussels with them, they did not travel inland, nor cross the Tijuana River to look at the southern valley.

It is important to note the dates of these voyages. By the time of Cabrillo's voyage, more than seven decades before the Pilgrims would arrive at Plymouth Rock, the colony of Mexico was already being populated by Europeans. Mexico City had been founded in 1521, on the site of the Aztec capital Tenochtitlan, which was a century older. By the time Vizcaíno arrived, the capital, conquered by Hernán Cortés in the name of King Ferdinand and Queen Isabella, had been ruled by Spain for more than eighty years. Construction of Mexico City's great cathedral had already been underway for two decades. In other words, even to the Spanish colonizers of Mexico, the Tijuana Valley was as inaccessible and forbidding as the moon.

A FUTURE SAINT ARRIVES

Shortly before the American Revolution started across the continent, two Spanish expeditions set out with the intention of leaving a permanent presence in the Tijuana Valley. Both of these expeditions crossed the Sea of Cortez from Mexico's mainland, then sailed along or marched north up the Baja Peninsula. The first of these, in May 1769, was led by Captain Fernando de Rivera y Moncada. He was accompanied by a friar, Juan Crespí, to serve as a missionary to any local natives they encountered. They set a precedent for exploration of the Tijuana Valley, but it was the second expedition, led by Gaspar de Portolá two months later, that would ring down through history, in part because of the many place names along the Pacific Coast that survive to this day, but more so because of the monk who marched beside him, Junípero Serra.

The Portolá party of ten soldiers, two servants, and forty-four natives reached San Diego Bay, and met Captain Rivera, on July 1, 1769. On the last leg of that journey, they crossed the Tijuana River at what are now the coastal suburbs of modern Tijuana. Tellingly, they didn't linger but marched farther north, to the inviting bay and its gentler, more inviting landscape. There, Father Serra celebrated Mass and founded Mission San Diego de Alcalá, on the morning of July 16, 1769.

Like all the missions established by Father Serra throughout the Mexican territory of Alta California, Mission San Diego served as a powerful magnet for native tribes, as well as pioneering farmers and entrepreneurs, to gather and trade. Alongside these missions, the military would often build a fort, not only to protect the growing local population but also to use the roads and trails that were established for hundreds of miles between the missions, most famously the El Camino Real, the Royal Road.

As the settlements around these missions grew, the Spanish government in Mexico recognized the need to organize the region politically, from a single enormous territory stretching from what is now the entire US Southwest to southern Oregon, into smaller governed provinces. On the Pacific Coast, Mexico City, on April 24, 1772, officially divided "California" into two parts: upper (alta) and lower (baja). The southern territory was designated "Baja California," a name that endures today. It encompassed the peninsula off the coast of the main-land, with a northern terminus at the southwestern end of Tijuana Valley. (Today, the Baja Peninsula is divided into two states: Baja California, with its capital in Mexicali, and Baja California Sur, with its capital in La Paz.) Everything north of that—that is, to Mission Solano beyond the San Francisco Bay—was named "Alta California."

Postcard of Mission Basilica San Diego de Alcalá.

Under this scheme, the site of modern Tijuana was part of a diocese controlled by Mission San Diego and the Franciscans, which contin-ued more than one hundred miles south, beyond the valley. However, in 1778 a Dominican monk established his own mission in El Rosario, 215 miles to the south. He claimed considerable territory to his north, violating a Church Concordat signed in 1772. Seeking peace between two competing orders, the Church agreed to the new borders that same year. This new agreement had a far-reaching impact, because on March 26, 1804, the viceroy of New Spain, Antonio Bucareli y Ursúa, accepted the Church's boundary as the civil one as well. Henceforth, the northern boundary of Baja California would be set much farther south.

In practice, this meant that, even before it was born, Tijuana was considered part of the future California. Its political, economic, and spiritual orientation was directed not to the distant capital of Mexico

City, but to the nearby hamlet of San Diego, its mission, and beyond, to the provincial capital of Alta California in Monterey. Equally important, the border itself, running in a straight, east-to-west line, was almost wholly artificial, untethered from any feature in the landscape. Even the dominant Tijuana River was bisected. As a result, this borderline on a map demarcating where one jurisdiction ends and another begins has always seemed imposed rather than inevitable.

BY THE SEA

Though the name *Tijuana* may sound like a quintessential Mexican name, its origins are not only obscure, but most likely not Spanish at all. Here are the two most popular theories:

1. One, proposed by the late historian W. Michael Mathes in the twentieth century, was that Tijuana's name derived from the Southern Baja Yuman tribal word *Tiwan*, meaning "close to the sea," which indeed Tijuana is. Though increasingly accepted, this theory remains disputed.
2. Another once-popular claim, now largely dismissed, is that the town was named after an inhabitant of a local ranch named Tia Juana, "Aunt Jane."

What is known is that early documents related to the settlement exhibit the fluid spelling of the era and call the town a range of variants: La Tia Juana, Tiguana, Tiuana, Teguana, Tiwana, Tijuan, Ticuan, and finally, the spelling that stuck: Tijuana.

English speakers in the US and elsewhere tend to pronounce the city "Tee-ah Wa-na," which makes Tijuana residents grind their teeth. But Anglos can be somewhat forgiven. For one thing, the internal rhyme of Tia-Juana rolls better off the English-speaking tongue. But there is also a historical justification: right across the border from Tijuana is the San Diego district of San Ysidro, which began its existence more than a century ago as the city of Tia Juana—Aunt Jane. Further confusing matters, this may have been a bowdlerization of an original wording of the Tijuana name. In the era of more accessible borders, San Diegans traveling south usually used the two destination names interchangeably, and that pronunciation entered into the common parlance north of the border.

FAMILY RANCH

In the nineteenth century, politics became as important as geography to Tijuana's destiny. With the official political border many miles to the south, there was little need for a settlement in Tijuana's modern location. After all, part of the land in the region was rocky or ravined, and the good, cultivatable bottomland of the Tijuana River Valley regularly suffered extensive flooding. By comparison, Ensenada had a coastal port, and San Diego had both considerable arable land and a world-class seaport. Not surprisingly, both those cities grew quickly. Meanwhile, for decades Tijuana remained the home of a handful of large, and largely hardscrabble, ranches owned by a few families.

In the early years, the most notable of these families were the Arguellos. Their story would track with the rise of the Mexican state, following its independence from Spain in 1821. Two of the sons of Captain José Dario and Maria Ignacia Moraga were among the earliest beneficiaries of this fundamental political change. One of the sons, Captain Luis Arguello, stationed with the garrison in San Diego, was appointed political chief of the Californias, a position of immense power and influence in the region, in November 1823.

During this same period, and perhaps not by coincidence, his brother Santiago, a lieutenant at the San Diego Presidio, became the first owner of the territory of today's Tijuana. Santiago's appearance in the story may be directly connected to another important milestone in Mexico's history. In 1824, the young government of Mexico passed the Law of General Colonization. It was designed to promote the development of considerable untouched regions of the nation, especially in Alta and Baja California.

Before this law, especially under Spanish rule, Mexico had been quite stingy with its unused tracts of land. About the only exceptions were for soldiers stationed at the various presidios. As gratitude for their service, and with their commitment to become farmers upon leaving the military, they were awarded land to work. But this was a rare event. It is estimated that over the decades only two dozen soldiers took advantage of the offer.

By comparison, in a move predating but similar to the Homestead Act signed into law by President Lincoln during the Civil War, Mexico now set out to create a land rush in the territories, geared to attract as many Europeans as it could to settle those lands. Under the Law of Colonization, if a colonist took Mexican citizenship, professed to be of the Catholic faith, and agreed to work the land, he could apply for eleven square leagues (thirty-three square miles, or approximately twenty-one thousand acres). This land grant was many times larger than the 640 acres the Homestead Act would make available later to homesteaders in the United States.

In this moment of opportunity, the promotion of Luis Arguello to political prominence in the region, and the (Mexican) Homestead Act, Santiago Arguello obtained his forty-one-square-mile ranch (including six property extensions for cattle). Within months, this door of opportunity closed, when brother Luis was replaced as governor of the Californias.

Remarkably, rather than ending Santiago's good fortune, Luis's retirement and his replacement by Lieutenant Colonel José María de Echeandía extended it. Governor Echeandía had never liked the cold, foggy weather up the coast in Alta California's capital, Monterey. So as soon as he had the chance, he left that city (though keeping territorial governance there) and moved down to San Diego. Having the de facto capital in residence nearby only increased the value of Tijuana Valley land, drawing more colonists than before. As part of his new administration, and to attract even more settlers, Governor Echeandía conducted a full survey of the valley, in the process granting permanent title of the "Ti Juana Ranch" to Santiago Arguello, on March 24, 1829.

Whatever the source of his new empire, Santiago proved to be a capable and hardworking rancher. He not only managed Ti Juana well by all accounts, but he and his wife, Pilar, were particularly fecund: they produced fifteen children, eight boys and seven girls. All survived, and the last dozen were all married at the San Diego Mission. The result in the short term was an instant dynasty: the many marriages to other families in the region over the next couple of generations all but guaranteed that the ranch and its environs would soon be populated with numerous farms and a growing, cohesive population. In the long term, however, these interrelated stakeholders were doomed to clash over their share of the family inheritance.

MANIFEST DESTINY

The next two decades of the Ti Juana Ranch were relatively peaceful and prosperous. The Arguellos raised their children, their cattle, and their crops. The only important event during this interregnum occurred in 1833, when the Mexican government ordered the secularization of the Catholic missions. This was important because, until then, the Franciscans (and to a lesser degree the Dominicans) had enjoyed holdings of thousands of square miles of superior farm and grazing land around their missions, especially in Alta California. As settlements had grown up around many of these missions (such as San Diego, Los Angeles, San Jose, Santa Clara, and San Francisco), the Church had also become a powerful landlord. Too powerful, apparently, because Mexico officially stripped it of these holdings and made them available to the public.

While this secularization had a profound effect on the rest of the territory, for the Ti Juana Ranch, and the growing number of smaller, adjacent ranches on the other side of the river from their mission, the impact was largely secondary: instead of two masters, they now served just one.

Otherwise, these years were among the most peaceful in the history of the Tijuana Valley. All that changed in 1846, when the United States declared war on Mexico.

Trouble had been brewing between an expansionist US and a politically divided Mexico for a number of years. It began in 1836 when Texas, a region Mexico/Spain had ruled for centuries, declared its independence. Immense grazing lands and relative lawlessness, combined with Mexico's Law of General Colonization, had proven a powerful draw for American pioneers, including Stephen Austin. They had moved to Texas but had never lost their allegiance to the United States.

They dubbed themselves "Texicans" and Texas territory an independent nation.

Mexico at the time was ruled by the dictator Antonio López de Santa Anna. In the course of his disastrous eleven separate presidencies between 1833 and 1855, López de Santa Anna would manage to lose first Texas, then much of the current American West to the United States. His brutal suppression of the Texicans at Goliad and the Alamo inflamed US public opinion, while his total defeat at San Jacinto in 1836 by Sam Houston guaranteed not only that Mexico lost ownership of Texas, but that thereafter the United States would look upon itself as the liberator of other Mexican territories, an attitude that neatly coincided with the younger country's own desires for national expansion.

In the end, the only reason the US did not quickly grant statehood to Texas in the 1830s was the fear that it would enter as a slave state and disrupt the delicate political balance achieved by the Missouri Compromise of 1820. Instead, the United States bided its time for the right opportunity—and a willing leader—to seize more Mexican land with less political baggage.

That opportunity came ten years later with the election of President James Knox Polk. Polk was an unabashed expansionist and staunch believer in the Manifest Destiny of the United States to become territorially extended, unfettered, from the Atlantic to the Pacific. Having arranged statehood for Texas in 1845 and settled with Great Britain a long-standing territorial dispute regarding the Oregon Territory on the border with Canada, Polk offered Mexico $30 million to buy its northern territories. Rebuffed, he stationed troops along the Rio Grande River on land disputed by the two nations. The official reason—not entirely pretextual—was that the Mexican government, fearing American ambitions and still laying claim to Texas, had been supporting systematic border raids on its northern neighbor.

Polk provoked the reaction he sought when, on April 25, 1846, a Mexican cavalry contingent attacked a scouting party of US soldiers commanded by America's then top general, Zachary Taylor. A dozen US soldiers were killed; the rest retreated to a US Army post nearby, to which the Mexicans laid siege. General Taylor called in reinforcements and defeated the Mexicans in the two battles of Palo Alto and Resaca de la Palma, on prairie fields near present-day Brownsville on the Gulf of Mexico. President Polk responded to the news by quickly asking the US Congress for a declaration of war. He got it two days later, on May 13. For its part, the Mexican government, realizing it was now about to face the might of the US Army, and suffering through the political chaos of multiple presidents all serving brief terms, chose not to declare war in response.

It didn't matter. The United States was intent on fighting its first war in a foreign land. In the end, the Mexican American War lasted two years, much of it spent transporting American troops across land and sea to lay siege to Mexico City. The Mexican Army fought valiantly, including the young cadets who would become the Hero Cadets of Chapultepec, but it was hopelessly outmanned, outgunned, and most of all outcommanded by the likes of Ulysses S. Grant and Robert E. Lee in their first combat roles.

As expected, the war, still called by some Mexicans "the War of the North American Invasion," was an almost completely one-sided victory. Morally, it was more complicated. Some people in the US, including Daniel Webster and a young Abraham Lincoln, expressed deep reservations about the casus belli of the war, seeing it as little more than a land grab, while some Mexicans welcomed being absorbed by such a dynamic, wealthy nation. One of the biggest cheerleaders of the war was, oddly, Karl Marx of all people: "Is it a misfortune that magnificent California was seized from the lazy Mexicans who did not know what to do with it?"

In the end, Mexico was defeated not only militarily, but politically. President Mariano Paredes resigned. In his absence, the country scrambled to assemble a new government. It was this essentially provisional government, under US occupation, that negotiated the still-controversial (especially among Mexicans) Treaty of Guadalupe Hidalgo.

This treaty, which was signed on February 2, 1848, surrendered one half of Mexico's claimed territory—in particular, the land north of the Rio Grande that now encompasses much of California, New Mexico, Arizona, Utah, and Nevada, as well as parts of Colorado and Wyoming—to the United States. The US paid $15 million for more than 525,000 square miles of annexed territory. Guadalupe Hidalgo, along with the subsequent purchase in 1854 of more Southwest territory from Mexico (the Gadsden Purchase in Arizona), permanently and legally established the southwest border of the United States and the northern border of Mexico. Culturally, however, the permanence of that border has never been quite clear.

The Treaty of Guadalupe Hidalgo was a transformative event in the founding story of Tijuana. This political borderline, which exists only on maps—and is barely reinforced by the landscape—is the reason Tijuana exists, and why it has grown to such prominence. Without that invisible line, Tijuana might still be mostly Ti Juana Ranch, or more likely a distant suburb of San Diego. Perhaps a different city, with a different name, would have formed elsewhere.

In fact, that almost happened. Reportedly, during the negotiations for the Treaty of Guadalupe Hidalgo, the victorious US demanded the new border be established approximately fifty miles farther south, near Ensenada. But in this case, the Mexican government fought back, for a reason that had little to do with the California-Baja California border (after all, there was nothing to gain from the annexation of a Tijuana that wasn't there). Rather, the problem was farther east. Below today's Arizona, the current Mexican land passage between the Baja California peninsula and mainland Mexico is just sixty miles wide. Had the US government gotten their way, that narrow corridor would have been less than ten miles across. The Mexican negotiators shrewdly recognized this, realizing that it would be a simple matter for the United States to block that passage and annex Baja California, leaving Mexico surrounded on two sides by the Americans. Instead, a rare moment of resistance by the Mexican negotiators cemented the creation of Tijuana where it is today.

BORDER TOWN

In their excellent book, *Tijuana in History*, historians David Piñera and Gabriel Rivera have described the years following the creation of the international border as a historic turning point in the story of the region. During these years, "the Tijuana Valley, in general, acquired different characteristics from San Diego. These were first religious and then political because the Valley became part of Baja California. From that time on, it acquired a border character, which [resulted in] a fundamental change in its future historical development."

Since the eighteenth century, the entire region had largely evolved in concert with one identity. All the residents owed their allegiance to the Catholic Church, embodied as Mission San Diego. The future site of Tijuana was as much a part of Alta California as San Diego. Residents of the region moved about without restriction. That was true under the colonial rule of the Spanish and also true for two decades under the governance of Mexico City.

But all that changed after the Mexican-American War. Now, north of the border, the new settlers—largely Protestant, products of Northern European cultures and adhering to English common law and the US Constitution—set out to create their city as a semitropical mirror image of the great cities of the East. By comparison, the handful of family ranches south of the new border found themselves without many of the institutions—the church, local government, commerce, and trade—on which they had built their lives. While those institutions were still just fifteen miles away, in reality they were now in a different country. Furthermore, as San Diego began to lose its Wild West character and settle down into a comparatively safe community, the residents of Tijuana found themselves saddled with an indifferent, volatile, and increasingly corrupt national government in Mexico City, not to mention growing crime in the form of bandit gangs such as the one led by the notorious Juan Mendoza.

After the war, San Diego continued to grow rapidly, not least because of the discovery of gold in California just days after the signing of Guadalupe Hidalgo, as well as the presence of the US Army to fight off the bandit raids. Meanwhile, Tijuana, all but abandoned by Mexico City, left vulnerable to bandits, actually lost population. Many Tijuanenses decamped across the border to San Diego, a pattern of response to turbulence in their home country that has repeated itself, regularly, up to this day.

A series of letters survives between a San Diego businessman named Abel Stearns, who was married to an Arguello relation, and another member of the Arguello family, Guadalupe Estudillo, still hunkered down on the Ti Juana Ranch:

You know how sad and disastrous disturbances in the border are and how everyone is withdrawing all their interests . . . Mendoza has herded everything he could to the river, and it is said he will be back with more men. (November 13, 1860)

With this level of lawlessness, cattle rustling, and violence, Tijuana would have no chance to grow, nor for its pioneers to return, for years. Meanwhile, despite the advent of the US Civil War—which put a halt to emigration from the East for five years—San Diego remained relatively peaceful and untouched by domestic conflict or cross-border banditry. For now, its primary relationship with Tijuana would remain one of sanctuary.

LEGACY FIGHT

In 1862, the patriarch of Ti Juana, Santiago Arguello, died at the ranch. Tellingly, he was buried at Mission San Diego.

Santiago died intestate. The lack of a written will would haunt the Arguello family and ultimately set the stage for the next era of Tijuana. Initially, the question of Santiago's legacy didn't present a problem, as his widow, Pilar Ortega de Arguello, automatically inherited the entire estate. But then, in the face of either new Mexican real estate regulations (the Juarez Law) or pressure from one of her descendants, Pilar decided to divide the ranch in two and sell thirteen thousand acres to her son, Ignacio.

As might be expected, this arrangement didn't sit well with the rest of the huge family. The resulting disputes and legal battles consumed the next decade. The most far-reaching act took place in 1870, when another of Santiago's and Pilar's sons, Francisco, and his wife, Tomasa, sold another section of the land holdings—described in the paperwork as the "Tia Juana" or "Rancho Tijuan"—to a US investor, Caesar A. Luckhardt, for $2,000 US. Interestingly, not only was the contract written in English and filed in far-away San Francisco, but Francisco and Tomasa listed their place of residence as "Los Angeles."

Clearly the monolithic Arguello family, with its control of their giant ranch, was beginning to break apart.

The door was now opening for investors and entrepreneurs from outside the family to begin to buy and develop properties and businesses on the Mexican side of the Tijuana River. The stage was now set for the next era of Tijuana's story.

On August 6, 1874, Mexican president Sebastián Lerdo de Tejada signed a decree that ordered the construction of a customs house to, in its words, "be set in a place called Tijuana, located at the intersection of the international border with the United States and Baja California. It will monitor traffic and the collection of the respective taxes."

There were a number of reasons for the Mexican government to place the customs house at that location. For one thing, as far back as 1857, the California Stage Company, a Northern California operation, had inaugurated a stage line to carry mail and passengers from San Antonio, Texas, to San Diego. The route of this "Jackass Line," by geographical necessity, followed the Colorado River, which, in its sinuous path, passed at various points into Mexico. This operation was replaced by Butterfield Overland Mail, which was even more important to San Diego because it carried goods back and forth all the way to the Mississippi River, where goods could be transferred to or from steamboats.

Just as important, Butterfield established horse-changing posts roughly every fifteen miles. That mattered because, while many of these stations were in the US, where they typically served as delivery depots to military camps, there were also many located in Mexico, serving villages and other communities. Travelers on this line would use these posts to rest, eat, and purchase local items, thus bringing money to local economies across the Southwest.

Importantly, rather than rolling directly into San Diego, the Butterfield line instead entered the Tijuana Valley from the south. So, although the route was closed by the Civil War, it reopened soon after the war and was used by a new, overland mail line. This one, owned by American John Capron, chose to open another horse-changing station on the Mexican side of the river, in Tijuana—perhaps the first official cross-border collaboration. Moreover, the coach company decided— probably to appease the regional government—to hire Mexicans to manage the site. A wooden building with a dining room, rest area, and a stable was quickly constructed. Soon, not only were long-distance travelers regularly passing through the Tijuana station but also curious San Diegans were taking the first leg of the coach's journey to visit this exotic, yet nearby, locale and to purchase local craft items.

The government in Mexico City, always looking for a new revenue source, heard about these growing numbers of visitors, not to mention the goods being transported, albeit temporarily, into Mexican territory. They quickly moved to regulate and, of course, tax both. The customs house resulted, presaging the decisive role customs and border management would play throughout the future development of Tijuana.

Construction of the customs house began on September 1, 1874, and immediately ran into legal difficulty. In particular, there was no land anywhere in the area that wasn't in private hands. This was resolved by the subprefect of the district, who found a landowner willing, for a sizable payment, not only to provide the land but also to build a solid and secure facility.

Tijuana Customs House, 1887.

As one can imagine, the people of Tijuana and the surrounding countryside, most of them struggling to maintain even a subsistence living and accustomed to decades of moving unmolested back and forth from San Diego (particularly to a store just across the border) to obtain the necessities of life, were not keen on the arrival of the customs house. Now they had to pay duties every time they crossed the border to conduct a transaction, under pain of fine or arrest.

The immediate impact of the customs house was to crush the already tiny Tijuana economy, as it retarded the number of visitors from the north. Unsurprisingly, the citizens of Tijuana rebelled, filing a petition signed by most of Tijuana's leaders to the subprefect, Emilio Legaspy. He, in turn, appealed to the political leader of the district, Braulio Caballar, who concurred and ordered the customs house shut down, to the rejoicing of the Tijuanenses.

Though officially shut down (and with a replacement customs house under construction in Ensenada), the Tijuana custom house apparently continued to operate in a reduced capacity, which angered the Tijuanenses. They filed another petition, this one saying, "The office has only served to create scandal in San Diego and to greatly increase the price of goods we consume . . ."

That petition, delivered in 1880, was the culmination of more than a year during which the customs house suffered various indignities, including an armed robbery by the local Badillo gang, who wounded a guard and took money, gold, silver, and valuables. Then, less than a month later, while a manager and two guards slept inside, the customs house was set afire. A few months after that, rebel troops under General Manuel Márquez de León swept through, their presence keeping the customs house from operating.

Yet, ultimately, over time the customs house proved to be a positive force in Tijuana. For one thing, operating it required the presence of a number of employees, all paid (usually late) by the federal government. That money found its way into the local economy. So, too, the presence of a government facility enhanced the image of safety to San Diegans and helped to increase steadily the number of cross-border visitors (and their money) from the north. It also served as an inducement for American businessmen to set up businesses on the other side of the border, but near the customs house, to cater to the growing number of well-heeled visitors to Tijuana.

The first of these ventures involved the hot springs (*agua caliente*) that had existed from time immemorial on Arguello land, serendipitously near the customs house and on the river bottom just two miles from the border. The nineteenth century was an early zenith of the spa health craze in both Europe and North America, and the Arguello springs were sulfurous, which at the time was deemed the most healthful for the human body. With so many visitors now coming to the region, it wasn't long before some US entrepreneurs heard of the springs and leased their use from the Arguello family.

The spa they developed, which opened in August 1880, was called Tia Juana Hot Springs. Soon it was being promoted to potential customers through articles and advertisements in the *San Diego Union* and other Southern California print media.

So successful did Tia Juana Hot Springs prove to be—indeed, it still exists today—that within months other entrepreneurs had created carriage services that picked up tourists in the morning in downtown San Diego and delivered them by horse-drawn cars to the springs for the day, returning at sundown. When a growing number of visitors expressed a desire to stay in Tijuana for more than one day to tour and shop, the Hot Springs built a hotel. It, too, proved hugely successful. To cater to these populations of prosperous San Diegans, in the geographic nexus between the customs house and the Tia Juana Hot Springs a number of shops appeared, drawing even more visitors from the north, in a virtuous cycle.

AN ESTABLISHED CITY

Sixty years after its founding, by the 1880s Tijuana at last was becoming a real town.

But it was real with some severe structural problems. The biggest was topographic. Had Tijuana been founded to conform to the landscape, it would have been built on its plateau. But it was built to cater to visitors from the United States, that is, as close as possible to the border. A border that, unfortunately, stretched across the marshy banks of the Tijuana River.

What might have been foreseen happened in March 1884, when the region experienced exceptionally heavy rains. The Tijuana River quickly rose, then jumped its banks. Snaking along the base of a mountain range and finishing its journey to the ocean across a flat alluvial plain, the Tijuana River had flooded regularly for hundreds, possibly thousands, of years. The early indigenous tribes knew this, and since they were relatively nomadic, they knew when to move their camps to higher ground. The Arguellos and their neighbors knew from experience about the flooding, so they had built their farmhouses at the other side of their land holdings, on higher ground.

But now, fixed structures, including the customs house, the Hot Springs hotel, and numerous shops snubbed up to the river border, sat right in the flood path. The flooding was devastating. Even the hot springs themselves were quenched by cold, muddy water. Tijuana survived, but it was still repairing itself two years later, when a second flood hit. Despite a massive civic-works project to contain the Tijuana River, flooding continues as a perennial problem to this day.

Flooding aside, the two decades at the end of the nineteenth century were golden years in Tijuana's history. Largely because of the growing number of Spanish-speaking children across the border in Tia Juana, California, Tijuana gained its first school. Roads, some a century old, were finally repaired after severe damage from the recent rains. A new telegraph line, aimed at Ensenada, passed through Tijuana and became a harbinger of massive infrastructure improvements across the border in San Diego.

In 1885, the transcontinental railroad finally came to San Diego, and a year later the city was electrified. In 1888, the first major dam was built to supply water to the city. As San Diego's population (and real estate prices) rose, new arrivals began to fill a growing number of new suburbs to the south of the city. One of these suburban cities was Tia Juana, Tijuana's American twin (the San Ysidro district of San Diego today). In many ways it enjoyed the economic benefits of the customs house even more than Tijuana itself. A number of Mexican ranchers, farmers, and businessmen chose to live on the US side, especially as Mexico's political turmoil stirred once again.

In 1887, American merchant Joseph Messenger bought sixty-five acres of land in Tia Juana, abutting the border. He then sold the land to a real estate developer who subdivided it into home plots. The new sites sold quickly, not just because the developer offered easy terms, but because it embarked on a massive, and effective, regional promotional campaign. Here is a taste of it:

> Tia Juana City! THE EL PASO OF CALIFORNIA.
> Situated on the American Line, Fifteen Miles South of
> San Diego, in The Rich and Fertile Tia Juana Valley!
> The Only Commercial Point of Importance! In San
> Diego County Outside of the City of San Diego. It has
> Three Stores Doing a Large and Prosperous Business
> with Lower California. It Has a Large Hotel Which
> Will Soon be Opened! . . . Tia Juana Will Soon be a
> City of Several Thousand Souls . . . THE FAMOUS
> HOT SPRINGS Only Two and a Half Miles Distant is
> Another Attraction Offered to Health Seekers.

Tijuana, as always, benefited from this growth and development to the north. The city continued to gain population, largely arrivals from the rest of Baja California drawn to Tijuana's wealth and increasing political dominance in the region. But in good weather, especially on weekends and holidays, the population of the city temporarily multiplied with the arrival of tourists, including (and belying the city's later image) fashionable groups of Victorian ladies from San Diego, down for day-long excursions of lunching and shopping. Now, with Tia Juana emerging as a well-developed community, Tijuanenses could merely walk a few blocks to buy American-made goods at nearby stores.

Also benefiting Tijuana during that era was the continuity represented by the Porfiriato, the term used to describe the three-decade presidency of Porfirio Díaz, who headed the Liberal Party. He was Mexico's long-serving president, his leadership lasting—with a few breaks—from December 1876 to May 1911. Whatever his flaws, Díaz, at least in his early years as president, was a reformer bent on driving Mexico's economic development. He surrounded himself with technocrats and welcomed foreign investors on most favorable terms. In the process, he turned a largely backward and impoverished Mexico into the beginnings of a modern nation. By the sheer durability of his tenure, Díaz also brought to places like Tijuana relief from years of seemingly arbitrary changes in laws and regulations, enabling local leaders and businesspeople to plan for the long term.

By the turn of the century, the aging Díaz administration had sunken into corruption, sclerosis, and decadence. The wealthy were rewarded and the campesinos were abandoned to fall into even greater poverty. Díaz himself began to behave like an emperor, treating the elected presidency as his alone, an attitude that would lead not only to his forced resignation during his eighth term, but to the revolution that would soon throw Mexico into chaos. But by then, Tijuana, having benefited from decades of Mexico City's benign neglect, had modeled itself into a thriving city. To do so, it had tied itself irrevocably—for both good and evil—to the sparkling city to the north.

CHAPTER THREE

San Diego—Splendid Isolation

San Diego also was founded at dawn, during Mass, on July 1, 1769—and officially established on July 26—by Father Junípero Serra, the sickly, lame Franciscan monk with a will of iron. As part of a Spanish expeditionary force marching north through Spain's territorial claims on the Pacific Coast, Serra's task was to establish missions to bring Christianity to the region and to convert the native population. Serra, born Miguel José on the Spanish island of Mallorca in 1713, would be canonized by the Church in 2015, for the benevolent work he was to carry on in the Americas.

ADOPTING A NAME

Mission San Diego became the first mission Serra established, and for that reason, San Diego is often called the first city in California. The city had gained its name in 1602, when an expedition led by Sebastián Vizcaíno became the first to sail into the future San Diego Bay. Vizcaíno recorded in his diary:

> On the twelfth of said month, which was the day of the
> glorious San Diego [de Alcala], almost everyone went
> ashore. They built a hut, said Mass, and celebrated the
> feast of San Diego.

Diego himself was a Franciscan monk in the fifteenth century, who had performed his work in Madrid. At the urging of Spain's Philip II, he was canonized in 1588, a point of pride for Spaniards everywhere. Diego's sainthood was still fresh when the Vizcaíno party arrived in the bay that day, so it stood to reason that he would give the saint's name to this beautiful location.

STAKING OUT A SITE

One hundred sixty years later, another expedition, in three cohorts, arrived in the bay after a cruel journey. One ship had been lost at sea with all aboard. On the remaining ships, sixty crewmen were ill with scurvy and other diseases. All would die in a makeshift hospital set up on the beach at what is now known, appropriately, as Dead Man's Point. The last, and mostly unscathed cohort, led by Gaspar de Portolá, arrived a month late. This final group made their way north to join the others at the future site of the mission.

The spiritual leader of Portolá's group, Father Serra had already made a name for himself twice, first as a professor of theology in Mallorca, then, after he abandoned his position to serve the natives of the New World, among the natives of eastern mainland Mexico. Now in Alta California, Father Serra chose to give San Diego's name to the new mission. (In doing so, unknowingly he put himself in the rare position of a future saint christening a mission in the name of another saint.) Within days of the mission's founding, Father Serra and most of his party were gone, marching north to establish more missions along the way.

Before they left, though, the Portolá party, including its four Franciscan fathers, had constructed a crude chapel made of brush on what would be known as Chapel Hill, to serve as the first Mission San Diego. This simple structure was left in the hands of two monks,

Father Luis Jayme and Father Vicente Fuster, who were joined by additional members of the Order in 1772, when the Dominicans assumed religious control over Baja California.

Somehow this handful of monks, living in the most primitive conditions imaginable, managed to baptize one hundred Kumeyaay, ninety-seven of whom chose to live at the mission.

By 1774, it had become apparent that the mission, lacking water and built on poor soil for cultivation, was incapable of providing for the future needs of the growing population. So the mission was moved six miles inland, nearer to the San Diego River and the Kumeyaay village of Nipaguay.

Here the mission became a resting place for travelers and explorers, a gathering location for the Kumeyaay, and a crossroads for trade in the Tijuana Valley. Spain, anxious to consolidate its territorial gains, sent soldiers to fortify its missions in Alta and Baja California. Mission San Diego itself was garrisoned in the same year as Lexington and Concord sparked the American Revolution, with nearly thirty troops under the command of Lt. Francesco de Ortega. As was the standard procedure, the first order of business was to construct a fort—the San Diego Presidio—adjacent to the mission.

Despite the move inland, life at Mission San Diego remained difficult. As historian Iris Engstrand describes it:

> Presidio rations were scarce. Married women obtained extra food for their families by making tortillas and preparing meals for bachelor soldiers in exchange for additional corn and beans. New crops were planted at the mission in hopes of more abundant provisions.

Neither the expansion nor these activities went over well with a majority of Kumeyaay in nearby Nipaguay, especially among those tribal members who had resisted conversion to Christianity. Secretly, even as their fellow tribespeople were taking Mass at the Mission, they made plans to remove the interlopers.

THE KUMEYAAY UPRISING

San Diego's shining future would not have been apparent in 1775. The settlement established by Father Serra and de Portolá consisted of little more than a primitive church, a rudimentary fort, and a handful of huts and outbuildings. The residents, mostly soldiers and a few priests, perpetually lived at the brink of starvation. Worse, the natives in their nearby encampment were beginning to seethe about the Spaniards, who, treating the Kumeyaay like savages, were systematically trying to convince them to abandon both their keenly spiritual religion and seminomadic lives.

The Kumeyaay in the coastal region had been friendly, even welcoming, when these first Europeans had arrived. They had even helped the people at the mission survive the first few difficult months. But when the invaders decided to reestablish the mission close by, resulting both in an increased rate of baptismal conversions as well as rape of native women by Spanish soldiers, the Kumeyaays' feelings toward the newcomers changed. Now, seven years on, their resentment was ready to boil over.

There was no obvious spark to the conflagration. What is known is that on November 5, 1775, four hundred Kumeyaay warriors, led by shamans and religious leaders, attacked the mission without warning. They murdered Father Jayme and two others and burned the mission to the ground. The survivors ran to find sanctuary in the fort. The warriors turned on the presidio, but lacking the weapons or equipment to take on the armed, European-style structure, eventually they were beaten off, and they retreated.

After the attack came the regret. Back in their village, the Kumeyaay realized they had taken on too strong a foe, and now that foe, with their weapons, surely would counterattack ruthlessly, in revenge. The Kumeyaay decided to preempt that attack. Over the next few days, while the sanctuary was still smoldering, groups of Kumeyaay returned to the mission and begged to be forgiven and converted to the faith. Father Serra prevailed on Spanish Crown authorities in the north to forgo revenge and retribution.

A month after the attack, with the arrival of two more Franciscans to join the sole survivor, Father Fuster, the mission (and its new converts) shrewdly moved up to Presidio Hill. Closer to the fort, what would be called "Mission Valley" would prove to be Mission San Diego's permanent home.

In July 1776, as colonists a continent away were signing their Declaration of Independence from the British Empire, Father Serra supervised soldiers and natives in the construction of a real mission church building. They made their own adobe bricks, cut timber for framing and beams, and dug trenches. The resulting structure was among the first of its kind in Alta California.

In a 1783 report to Father Serra, the new mission was described as eighty-four feet long and fifteen feet wide, "with walls two adobes thick, its large beams of pine with corbels of oak, and over that eleven unpolished beams of alder and poplar." Constructed with fire-resistant mud and tile, "the entire aspect, especially the interior of the church and sacristy, is attractive, clean, and pleasing, because of the excellent ensemble achieved by the skill of the workers in using the resources of the mission. Thanks be to God."

As with Serra's other missions, Mission San Diego de Alcalá became a locus of activity for the region's residents, not least the California native tribes. In reality, many of these tribes were little more than collections of extended family groups without larger cohesion, and often they were mutually antagonistic. Missions provided a safe ground where these families could gather to celebrate Mass, trade among themselves, even set up a permanent domicile, and in the process realize that they were part of a distinct people. The mission's bells, rung for each service throughout the day, also put the natives on a clock for the first time, structuring their days and ultimately changing their culture as much as the new religion had.

SPIRITUAL HOME

The magnetic pull of the mission had a remarkable effect. By 1783, the church had performed nearly one thousand baptisms, and by 1797, Mission San Diego boasted the largest native population in Alta California, with more than 1,400 native neophytes living in and around the compound. This explosion in growth was even more remarkable given the high mortality rate of the natives from epidemics of communicable diseases brought by the Europeans.

By the turn of the eighteenth century, Mission San Diego boasted as impressive a community as any in Alta California. The populations of the mission and presidio alone grew to nearly 150 residents, with hundreds more natives living nearby or regularly visiting to trade. Indeed, the local population had grown so much that San Diego could send troops north to guard the new pueblo of Los Angeles (El Pueblo de Nuestra Señora Reina de los Angeles—"Lady Queen of the Angels"). Retired soldiers and ranchers also moved to the Los Angeles Basin and, with land grants from Spain, set up the first great ranchos there. In other words, San Diego can be credited with creating Los Angeles, something many future San Diegans would regard with more than a little irony.

A NEW AGE

Outside the Tijuana Valley, the world was changing. The Age of Empires was ending. Some, like France, collapsed internally; Great Britain lost its greatest colony; and the Hapsburg monarchy in Spain began a slow decline into decrepitude and corruption. Isolated though it was, San Diego was far from immune. In the last quarter of the eighteenth century, two of history's greatest sailor-explorers would pass by or visit Alta California: Captain James Cook, on his ill-fated third voyage, in 1778, and George Vancouver, on the return leg of his voyage to the Pacific Northwest, in 1793. Vancouver actually sailed into San Diego Bay and visited the mission. He would later report to London that the harbor was not only a great location for trade with China but also lightly defended, so a British fleet could take it easily. The Spanish military at the San Diego Presidio noticed Vancouver's interest and hurriedly constructed Fort San Joaquin (now Ballast Point) at the entrance to the harbor.

While San Diego and Tijuana would share largely the same history until war (between a future Mexico and the United States) established an international boundary between them in 1846, one major geographic feature differentiated them: San Diego Bay attracted out-siders coming by sea.

Work on the new harbor defenses was completed just in time. In 1800, the first US ship to enter San Diego Bay, the brig *Betsy*, stopped to take on wood and water. Other American ships stopped by in the next few years. All noticed—and spread the word back east—that the region was heavily populated with sea otter and that China was paying premium prices for their skins.

Before long, the coast was regularly visited by ships on the hunt for the creatures. Seeing a loss of revenues on a prime local product, Spanish authorities set out to stop the trade. In 1803 they prevented the ship *Alexander* from leaving port with five hundred smuggled otter skins. That same year, when another ship, the *Lelia Byrd*, seem-ingly on another hunting expedition, entered the bay at San Diego, it was ordered to halt, drop anchor, and be inspected. When it refused, the new fort's battery fired on the ship. The *Lelia Byrd* responded with a broadside of its own. No damage was done by either side. This little skirmish, recorded as "The Battle of San Diego," remains the only time the port's defenses have been fired on, or fired, in anger.

Meanwhile, sea otter harvesting by Americans undeterred by the ineffectual Spanish government continued to grow all along the Alta California coast, helping to establish the first real US presence in the region.

In the first two decades of the nineteenth century, Mission San Diego began to expand its reach across the valley, establishing sat-ellite missions at San Luis Rey de Francia and San Antonia de Pala. Infrastructure continued apace as well, including the construction of a dam in the Mission Gorge as a guaranteed water source. When a major earthquake in 1812 damaged the newly constructed fourth church at Mission San Diego (the previous church had been destroyed by an earthquake in 1801), its walls were reinforced to make it less vulner-able to future seismic events. This time it worked; the fourth Mission church still stands today.

By 1820, Mission San Diego and its installations throughout the north Tijuana Valley served a booming local population of more than five hundred Spaniards, some of whom were building permanent structures on Presidio Hill beyond the walls of the fort, and several thousand converted local natives. Just as it seemed that everything was in place for an extended age of peaceful and perpetual growth, everything turned upside down.

INDEPENDENCE

The Mexican War of Independence, proclaimed in 1810 and lasting until 1821, produced no great battles in the Tijuana Valley. But it did revamp the political and social institutions of the region. No longer was the land controlled by a Spanish monarchy six thousand miles away, giving away vast tracts to courtiers and self-promoters. Now land was available to any pioneer willing to farm it. Not surprisingly, former soldiers from the San Diego Presidio began to make plans to settle down and build farms on plots near the mission. Of particular interest were the properties at the base of Presidio Hill. Taking their cue from the burgeoning community they had helped create in Los Angeles, these former soldiers set about planning an independent town of their own, what is now Old Town San Diego.

Leading the way was Captain Francisco María Ruiz, the last Spanish commander of the San Diego Presidio. Ruiz was soon joined by, among others, the Pico family, whose second son, Pio, eventually would become the last Mexican governor of California.

Remember, San Diego had become a seat of political power when Governor José María de Echeandía decamped south to escape Monterey's foggy climate. Here Echeandía governed a state in transition. Foreign ships now regularly appeared in San Diego Bay and elsewhere along the Pacific Coast, often evading customs, smuggling, and poaching, not to mention their crews raising hell in the still-small towns while on shore leave. Echeandía also managed the secularization of the missions and the resulting need for the state to provide services to, and protection of, the native population, previously handled by the priests (and, it turns out, to be handled badly by government bureaucrats). In all, Echeandía spent his time in office dealing with fundamental structural changes for which he had no real solution.

One of those changes, which was rightly seen as a minor threat at the time—but would prove to be bigger than anyone could imagine—was the arrival in California of a party of mountain men, led by the legendary Jedediah Smith. Echeandía threw them out of the territory, but they were the first trickle of what would soon be a flood of Americans—first trappers like Smith, then miners, and soon illegal settlers.

The 1830s saw enormous changes in Alta California. A victim of political unrest in Mexico, Governor Echeandía was removed from office. In short order, the new government changed the rules on immigrants, allowing Americans and others to enter California, as they had done in Texas, to become citizens if they took an oath to join the Catholic Church and swore fealty to Mexico. Once they did, they were also eligible to apply for a land grant. Given the return on just a sworn statement of loyalty and conversion to another Christian faith—even Papism—this proved an easy choice for hundreds of émigrés from the East.

During this decade, San Diego entered into another time of gains and losses. On the one hand, Echeandía's replacement, Brig. General José Figueroa, in one of his first acts as a Mexican governor in 1833, moved the capital back to Monterey in Northern California—a decided loss of power for San Diego. On the other hand, that same year, the village, now numbering 435 souls, applied to and received permission from Monterey to become an official town. Now a pueblo, San Diego could elect a local government, choosing Juan María Osuna as the first mayor. Interestingly, the city's first attorney appears to have been a new American arrival, Henry Fitch.

Until now, San Diego had largely remained outside of the consciousness of most Americans. It was too far away, too Mexican (that is, it had a fort and soldiers to enforce the law), and most of all, too hard to reach. Most American travelers emerged from months-long trips farther up the coast, too weary to continue south, especially when they were met with so much good, farmable land up north. Understandably, few attempted to cross the Mojave Desert on the southern route.

But in 1835, that changed, thanks to the publication in the United States of one of the bestselling books of the era, Richard Henry Dana Jr.'s *Two Years Before the Mast*. As part of the crew of the brig *Pilgrim*, Dana, a Yankee from Massachusetts, visited all the major towns and forts of California, from San Diego to San Francisco. Of them all, Dana declared San Diego, with its small, landlocked harbor (perfect for loading hides), its impeccable weather, and its friendly locals, to be best. He stayed for a period in San Diego and thoroughly enjoyed his visit. Though a proper Bostonian, he reveled in the huge feasts and abundant wine, the music, and the local citizenry, describing the men as "thriftless, proud, and extravagant, and very much given to gaming" and the women as having "little education and a great deal of beauty" (which must have caught the attention of other sailors back home). From that moment on, San Diego held a place in the American imagination.

LAND GRAB

As a consequence of the new laws, in the first half of the 1840s San Diego was characterized by a kind of land rush, in which rancho grants, typically in increments of tens of thousands of acres, were awarded across the valley to established families and newcomers. In 1845, Pio Pico was elected governor, a role he had been preparing for most of his life. (He had served as an interim governor a few years earlier.) Almost from the moment of his election, Governor Pico accelerated the awarding of land grants, many of them to his friends and business acquaintances.

In a terrible twist of fate, Pico would enjoy his new title for just eighteen months, and many of his land grantees would enjoy their bonanza not much longer than that. The reason: Mexico's war with the United States. Impending conflict was in the air when Pico took the oath of office, but its arrival came earlier than almost anyone imagined.

Already, in 1842, three American ships, including the frigate *United States*, under the command of Thomas Jones, commodore of America's Pacific Fleet, had sailed into Monterey Bay. Under the mistaken impression that war had been declared, Jones captured the city. Learning his mistake, he then surrendered it. After this incident, Mexico, now on notice, bolstered its defenses at all its Pacific ports.

Four years later, those warnings became real. Newly elected US president Polk, as we have seen, was an unrepentant empire builder who saw as his destiny making the United States a continental nation at its southern, northern, and western borders. He just needed a pretext, which came first on the Texas border. The US declared war on Mexico.

The last Mexican governor of Alta California, Pio Pico, and his family.

At the time of the declaration, the only US military unit near California was a military survey party under the command of the celebrated explorer John C. Frémont and led by one of the towering figures in the history of the West, the scout Kit Carson. Notified that war was imminent, Frémont immediately marched toward and camped near Monterey, under the guise of conducting yet another topographic survey.

Recognizing the threat, the Mexican captain of Monterey's presidio ordered Frémont and his troops to leave. With war not yet declared, Frémont led his men north, almost to the Canadian border, then turned around and marched south in June 1846, to Sutter's Fort near Sacramento. Now, with war declared, the citizens of Sacramento had raised a Bear Flag (the future California state flag) and declared the region an independent republic. Frémont's men, bolstered by new arrivals, including the future founders of some of the cities of the San Francisco Bay, set out to defeat any Mexican army they met and thereby capture the state.

On July 29, 1846, the warship USS *Cyan* sailed into San Diego Bay carrying Frémont, Carson, and a contingent of California volunteers. Upon landing, the soldiers rushed to the town and raised the Stars and Stripes in the plaza. Expecting resistance, they were stunned to be met by many open arms, not just from American ex-pats but Mexican nationals as well. This underscored the growing resentment among Californians against the high-handed treatment and corruption of the territory by Mexico City. As any resistance went underground, the pueblo held a multiday party. Even the town's wealthiest matriarchs were seen dancing among the revelers.

Understandably, Frémont was entranced by the region and would later write in his memoirs:

> Among the arid, brush-covered hills south of San Diego we found little valleys converted by a single spring into crowded gardens, where pears, peaches, quinces, pomegranate, grapes, olives, and other fruits grew luxuriantly together, the little stream acting upon them like a principle of life. This southern frontier of Upper California seems eminently adapted to the cultivation of the vine and the olive. A single vine has been known to yield a barrel of wine, and the olive trees are burdened with the weight of fruit.

Ten days later, Frémont, believing San Diego fully pacified, led his troops north to capture Los Angeles. Almost from the instant his army disappeared from sight, the hidden resistance—the "Tory" members of the San Diego community—reemerged and attempted to recapture the now-unprotected town. They tore down the American flag and restored the Mexican flag in its place. It didn't last long: a local sailmaker, Albert Smith, took down that flag, then climbed the pole and permanently nailed his own banner of the Stars and Stripes in its place.

This time the flag remained. In November, dominion over San Diego by the United States of America was underscored when the sixty-gun frigate, the *US Congress*, commanded by Commodore Robert Stockton, sailed into the bay. He brought numerous sailors and marines ashore who built and manned a defensive position atop Presidio Hill near the crumbling old presidio. He named it Fort Stockton.

Meanwhile, a contingent of 110 US Army soldiers and officers, under the command of General Stephen Kearny, was marching from Santa Fe, New Mexico, as part of a thousand-mile journey to support the Bear Flag revolt. Riding out alone to meet Kearny was Kit Carson, dispatched by Frémont to find and guide the arriving army. Once Carson located Kearny and his troops, he led them into California to an encampment at Warner's Ranch, near present-day Escondido, thirty miles northeast of San Diego.

Informed of this new threat, Mexico immediately sent a troop of two hundred lancers, commanded by Governor Pico's brother Andres, to intercept the American army. Kearny decided to attack first. His early morning attack on December 6, 1846, was poorly planned and led. The lancers inflicted thirty-one casualties on the Americans, including eighteen dead, while suffering only a single casualty of their own. The Battle of San Pascual, as it would be called, was a clear victory for the Mexicans.

SECRET WEAPON

Kearny, realizing that he was outnumbered two-to-one, retreated to the top of a nearby hill, later called Mule Hill because the starving American soldiers soon had to slaughter their mules to survive. There they established a defensive perimeter, but the lancers thought they merely had to wait out the trapped Americans in a siege that wouldn't last long.

They did not know, however, that Kearny had a secret weapon in the unprepossessing presence of Kit Carson. He ordered Carson, accompanied by a young lieutenant and a native scout, to sneak down the hill, break through the Mexican lines, and get help from the military contingent in San Diego. Carson stealthily picked his way downhill, under the cover of darkness. In the midst of the enemy, they removed their boots, walking silently over sharp rocks and cactus. Then, barefoot, their feet in shreds, Carson, the scout, and the lieutenant rushed over the two dozen remaining miles to Fort Stockton. According to Carson, the lieutenant who accompanied him on this journey "became deranged from fatigue . . . and did not entirely recover for two years."

Within hours of his arrival in San Diego, Carson was on horseback, guiding a relief party—two hundred soldiers—back to San Pascual. The Mexican lancers, recognizing it was their turn to be outnumbered, wisely beat a hasty retreat, only to be crushed in battle later by Frémont's army, ending the Mexican War in California. Meanwhile, Kearny's contingent, escorted by its rescuers, limped into San Diego under a heavy rain and spent Christmas in miserable hovels in the mud.

As for Kit Carson, having just added one of the best-known chapters to his growing legend, he proceeded to acquire another. In San Diego, General Kearny handed Carson a message describing the decisive victories in California and ordered him to deliver it to the president of the United States in Washington, DC. Carson did just that, riding alone on a mule across brutal deserts and empty prairie, ultimately across the entire United States. He returned months later, reporting to now-Governor Kearny of the US Territory of California. (The ever-vainglorious Frémont, craving the title of California's first territorial governor, had negotiated the surrender of Pio Pico. A furious Kearny intervened, awarded himself the governorship, and then had Frémont arrested.)

As noted in the Tijuana chapter, Mexico suffered the misfortune of signing the Treaty of Guadalupe Hidalgo just days before gold was discovered at Sutter's Fort, thus delivering one of history's great gold rushes to its northern neighbor. Other than Sutter himself, who would soon lose everything in the ensuing free-for-all, perhaps the only other person in California who wasn't excited by the news was Kit Carson. Just weeks after his return from the East, while he was still recovering from the journey's hardships, he was ordered by Kearny to repeat the journey, this time bringing the news of the gold strike to the president (and by extension, the rest of the US and the world). Regarding the seemingly impossible task of crossing a largely trackless continent, on a mule, four times in two years, an awed historian, David Roberts, would write at the dawn of the twenty-first century, "He accomplished these marathon treks as if they were mere errands."

A CONTINENTAL NATION

The Treaty of Guadalupe Hidalgo, signed in February 1848, and news a month later of the discovery of gold in California, comprised one of the greatest one-two punches in US history. Not only was a vast and beautiful territory newly opened to American settlement, but it offered settlers a chance of getting rich staking a claim. They came by the thousands in a gold rush from all over the United States and many other places in the world.

Because the gold country of the Sierra Nevada was best reached by traveling upriver from San Francisco to Sacramento and beyond into the foothills, those two cities enjoyed precipitous growth, the former becoming notorious for its lawlessness and instant tycoons. But even San Diego, as a necessary port of call for prospectors and entrepreneurs from the East sailing up the Pacific Coast, enjoyed its own boom.

For these visitors, San Diego put its best face forward. A battalion of soldiers, composed mostly of Mormons, had arrived in San Diego too late to fight in the war. So, with nothing else to do, they hired themselves out to the local citizens. Before they were done, they had whitewashed many of the local homes, made thousands of adobe bricks for construction, built a bakery, dug wells, and generally upgraded the town's infrastructure. They also left another mark on San Diego: while the contingent was there, a Mexican woman married to a Mormon captain gave birth to a boy, named Diego after the town, arguably the first birth of an American child recorded in San Diego.

Most of the Mormon soldiers eventually returned to Salt Lake City, but seventy-eight stayed behind at Fort Stockton. Joined by other newly arrived soldiers, they made the former mission their headquarters and barracks. They also conducted the first census of the city: according to San Diego historian Iris Engstrand, this census found 248 white residents, "483 converted Indians, 1,550 wild Indians, three Negroes and three Sandwich Islanders [Hawaiians]." San Diego was now, in nineteenth-century terms, a real town. In recognition of that fact, on March 27, 1850, the City of San Diego was officially incorporated. Joshua H. Bean, a former soldier at the fort, was elected the first mayor. A district court was convened on May 6. The official city population was listed as 798 citizens, with a total property assessment of $375,000.

That same year, Hawaiian businessman William "Kanaka" Heath Davis, who had first fallen in love with San Diego when he visited seventeen years prior, returned with a plan for a thirty-two-block "New City" of San Diego, closer to the water's edge. He spent a small fortune building a wharf, laid out streets, put up a warehouse, and even built a home, but San Diegans weren't buying the new site, dubbing the place "Davis's Folly." So Davis donated some of the property to the US government to build what would be called the San Diego Barracks, which soon became the official Army supply depot for Southern California. Finally, a few businesses and private citizens began to build in New City.

Davis's dream had also incited his brother-in-law, José María Estudillo, to work with a group of investors to create a similar plot between Old Town and New Town, to be called Middletown. It suffered the same fate as New Town. It would take more than a decade for both to become a success.

But there was some good news in San Diego during that antebellum decade. The city gained several hotels, including the Franklin House, its first three-story building. A billiard parlor and bowling alley opened, and in 1851, its first newspaper, the weekly *San Diego Herald*, hit the stands. Celebrated (and despised) for its support of local natives' rights, the paper would survive until the end of the decade. Further, hoping to link San Diego to the East, several stagecoach lines were founded—but none would survive the outbreak of the Civil War in 1861. Meanwhile, San Diegans waited for the arrival of the promised transcontinental railroad in California. They would have to wait more than a decade, and even then it did not arrive in San Diego.

CIVIL WAR

The Battle of Fort Sumter, which kicked off the US Civil War on April 12, 1862, seemed to put San Diego into a state of suspended animation. Having achieved its statehood in 1850 as a Free State, California had few citizens who joined the Confederacy. The economic impact of the war, however, did reach the Pacific Coast. The previous decade's flow of gold-rush pioneers now slowed to a trickle. Trade also dried up because priority was given to the war. Most military contracts were awarded to East Coast or Midwestern businesses. The only real visitors to the Port of San Diego were military vessels sailing into the Pacific.

Meanwhile, the Tijuana Valley was having its own problems. A drought killed many of the area's cattle. As a result, the local ranchos, usually a major source of business for equipment and manufactured goods, had little money to spend. Iris Engstrand quotes local merchant Ephraim Morse:

> I'm still keeping store here but not making money. There is but little business here, the place not being so large as it was ten years ago . . . There are only two men in San Diego who don't occasionally get drunk, and they are James McCoy [a wealthy local resident], the sheriff, and myself.

Appomattox may have marked the end of the American Civil War in 1865, but it would still be several more years before San Diego again showed signs of life. One major event of the period seemed to announce that San Diego was coming back after nearly a decade of silence: the *San Diego Union*—destined to remain the city's largest newspaper right up to the present—published its first edition on October 10, 1868.

In May 1869, the city cheered the driving of the golden spike, completing the transcontinental railroad across the United States. But its western terminus in Sacramento was still hundreds of miles from San Diego. Nevertheless, the news imbued the city with a spirit of hope. It had long been appreciated that the final linchpin in making San Diego a major city was an efficient railroad to connect it to the outside world. In preparation for this eventuality, local investors even established a company, the San Diego & Gila, Southern Pacific & Atlantic Railroad, to meet any incoming railroad halfway. Unfortunately, the endeavor failed, never laying a single mile of rail.

For now, San Diego would need a different spark to restore its optimism about the future. That spark arrived on April 15, 1867, aboard the steamer *Pacific*. His name was Alonzo Horton, and he, along with

John Spreckels later, would prove as consequential to San Diego in the nineteenth century as Father Serra had been in the eighteenth.

In 1851, Horton had sold his business interests in Wisconsin for $5,000 and headed to California in search of a new adventure. He settled in San Francisco, opened a shop, made money off the gold rush, and like many California men of the era went back East and returned with a bride in 1860. By the end of the Civil War, Horton found himself desperately searching for one more new adventure. He found it one night in early 1867, when he attended a speech given by a real estate promoter. The promoter regaled the crowd about the wonders—and wonderful opportunities—to be found in a city six hundred miles to the south called San Diego. He declared the city one of the healthiest places on earth, blessed with one of the most beautiful harbors. Indeed, he said, it was the closest place to paradise on the planet.

Horton went home that night with his head swimming. He couldn't sleep. He knew where his destiny lay. He booked passage south on the *Pacific*.

Horton might have been disappointed by his first sight of San Diego, for a number of reasons. After all, the pier built by Davis had rotted and been abandoned, forcing the steamer to drop anchor and row its passengers ashore. Once on the beach, Horton discovered no city there; it lay miles inland. He could have become disenchanted by the reality of San Diego. Instead, he was thrilled. He thought he "must be in heaven on earth . . . the best spot for building [I] ever saw."

Such was his optimism that when at last Horton reached the plaza of Old Town, he looked around and saw only opportunity: "It doesn't lie right. Never in the world can you have a city here." He would not give five dollars to buy the entire city, but he would be willing to invest in creating a new one. Even when he learned of the failure of Davis in the creation of New Town, he remained upbeat—after all, that just meant less competition for his own plans.

In the course of his investigations, Horton met a kindred spirit in Ephraim Morse, and they became fast friends. Morse would prove to be Horton's guide through the politics of San Diego and to its most important citizens. Between Morse and a local priest, Horton learned of the availability of considerable acreage of the old Pueblo land. Organizing a board of investors, Horton quickly snatched up 960 acres

in the New Town area, at twenty-seven cents per acre, at an auction on
May 10, 1867.

The leaders of Old Town San Diego dismissed the newcomer. This
would be Horton's Folly, they said, just as it had been Davis's, and they
anticipated celebrating his comeuppance. But they underestimated
both Horton's gumption and San Diego's changing economy as it lit up
into the Gilded Age. Before long, homes and stores were popping up all
over "Horton's Addition."

Old Town didn't take this challenge lying down. One of its most
important businessmen, Alfred Seeley, owner of the largest local stable, responded to the threat by adding a story to one of Old Town's
most impressive homes and converting it to the Cosmopolitan Hotel.
He also built a stage depot, proclaiming, according to historian
Engstrand, "Old Town is the town, the real San Diego. Your mush-
room town [meaning Horton's Addition] will soon peter out, and all
the people who want to travel will have to come to Old Town to take
the stage." Even as Seeley announced this, many of his neighbors were
preparing to sell out and move to the new neighborhood.

By 1870, the *Union* was reporting, "One by one the leaves are fall-
ing from Old Town, and the old place looks desolate. Nothing will be
left in a short time but a few saloons and lawyers." In fact, the latter
would be gone as well: most attorneys moved to New Town early the
next year, when all the county records were officially relocated there.
A major fire the next year effectively ended the role of Old Town in the
life of the city. Ironically, the quick desertion of Old Town, rather than
its continuous destruction and rebuilding, did have one long-term
benefit: it saved many of the city's original buildings, and Old Town
San Diego stands today as a historic site and major tourist attraction.

Alonzo Horton was a man in a hurry. Upon his arrival in 1867, he
had learned that the city owned forty-seven thousand acres of the old
mission lands, and he had set about imagining what he might do with
it. Remembering the Boston Commons of his childhood, he realized
this might be San Diego's last chance to create its own signature park
before growth overran the area. Horton became the first treasurer of
the San Diego Chamber of Commerce when it was founded in 1870,
and through his lobbying efforts, before those lands were sold off, the
city set aside 1,400 acres for a park. Showing how forward-looking San

Diego had suddenly become, Balboa Park, ultimately 1,200 acres, was developed simultaneously with Central Park in New York City and Golden Gate Park in San Francisco.

Alonzo Horton.

But Horton wasn't done yet. On New Year's Day 1870, he opened the Horton House Hotel, one of the most magnificent hotels west of the Mississippi. It boasted one hundred beautiful rooms, with carpeting, running water, marble-topped tables, views of the bay, and well-appointed gardens. The region had never seen such grandeur.

This new hotel, the first world-class institution in the city, had an electrifying effect on the citizens of San Diego. The Chamber of Commerce now talked of building schools, a library, and churches of all faiths. The city gained its first bank and a post office in New Town. The construction of a new courthouse, with an accompanying jail, was underway. When completed, it would serve San Diego for ninety years.

It seemed everything was finally going the city's way. When gold was discovered at two locations outside of town, in an unincorporated village of ex-slaves from Georgia, it seemed just one more example of this good fortune. In the end, the gold mines quickly played out, but not before the residents of the newly founded Julian enjoyed a payday and produced some of the wealthiest African Americans in California. Leveraging their good fortune, one couple, Albert and Margaret Robinson, built the Robinson Hotel in 1887. Still open, it remains the oldest continuously operated hotel in Southern California.

Eighteen seventy would prove to be San Diego's annus mirabilis of the nineteenth century, much of it due to Alonzo Horton. The census that year disclosed that the city now consisted of three thousand people living in nearly one thousand houses and working in seventy commercial buildings, for a total real estate assessment of $2.28 million. It also now featured (in another glimpse of its future) a remarkable number of physicians (seventy) and dentists (ten). San Diego had entered 1870 as little more than a small town; it left that year with a new downtown, explosive growth (and a strategy for maintaining it), and talented civic leadership. It had become one of the most dynamic new cities in America.

This luck couldn't last. In 1873, San Diego's era of growth stalled in the face of the then-longest-running economic depression in America's history. The immediate cause was the shift by the US Treasury Department to an all-gold money standard. This resulted in a major money contraction in the US economy. Among the first impacted were the over-speculating financiers in the East, notably Jay Gould, the railroad tycoon. The implosion of his empire, along with those of other "robber-barons," not only crashed the national economy, it also ended San Diego's dream of a railroad for another decade. The Long Depression lasted until 1878, setting the stage for an even deeper (though shorter) depression in 1892, which ultimately bankrupted, in the US alone, eighteen thousand businesses, eighty-nine railroads, hundreds of banks, and ten states.

La Jolla Cove, circa 1889.

Interestingly, San Diego appears to have escaped the worst of the crash precisely because of its isolation from the larger American economy. Indeed, the city continued to grow throughout those years, albeit slowly.

It wasn't until 1880 that San Diego finally got its railroad, or so it seemed. The Atchison, Topeka and Santa Fe Railway Company announced that it was forming a syndicate to extend its track from Los Angeles through San Diego and on to join the Southern Pacific line in Barstow. Then, in February 1884, San Diego's dream was waylaid. The track had reached San Bernardino, one hundred miles short of San Diego, when Southern California again experienced its old nemesis: heavy winter rains. A twenty-inch downpour, in fact, which destroyed the newly laid tracks between San Luis Rey and Temecula. In the end, San Diego wouldn't get its train until the next year. Finally, on November 9, 1885, the first departing train left the city. The first train from the East Coast—an engine, two coaches, and a baggage car—would roll into San Diego six days later.

At last, San Diego was fully integrated into the United States. Four decades after the first American flag was raised there, the city was accessible to visitors from across the continent. Further, San Diego could send its endless array of agricultural products to the populous markets of the East. There the San Diego name began to appear on crates of fresh fruits, and it became synonymous with them.

With the arrival of the railroad, the city's business leaders predicted an economic boom, and they got it. Already, in anticipation of economic expansion, a gasworks had opened in town. So had a telephone company, with thirteen subscribers. The YMCA arrived, and the Consolidated Bank of San Diego was created. San Diego High School, the first in the region, opened. The first city park was established as well. But the signal event of the 1880s was the construction of what would be, and still remains, one of the world's most celebrated hotels: Hotel del Coronado.

San Diego gained several top-notch hotels during the decade, but the city had seen nothing like the edifice forming on a peninsula beside the bay. This enterprise had a most unlikely beginning. Two retired business executives, Elisha Babcock, a former railroad executive from Evansville, Indiana, and H. L. Story, a piano manufacturer from Chicago, liked to row across the bay to an isolated peninsula and shoot rabbits. Along the way, they would talk and scheme. Out of those conversations came a plan: to buy that peninsula and put up a hotel the likes of which the West had never seen, one "too gorgeous to be true." They bought the land in December 1885 for $110,000, and over the next three years, San Diegans watched in awe as the magnificent edifice rose across the water.

In support of the future hotel, Babcock and Story built a wharf on Coronado and organized the Coronado Ferry Company. They even created the San Diego Streetcar Company, to carry residents and visitors around the city and to the wharf. In September 1886, they bought a local electrical power plant, which, until then, had been operating the city's first streetlights, to power the new hotel's 2,500 light bulbs.

In case the lights failed—not uncommon for the era—the hotel also had the older gas lamps, to be powered by its own coke ovens.

The finished Hotel del Coronado, which opened on Valentine's Day 1888, featured 399 rooms, an unpillared circular dining room (the Crown Room) that was an act of engineering prodigy, a ballroom, and exquisitely tended gardens designed by the leading landscaper and horticulturalist of the era, thirty-one-year-old Kate Sessions.

Kate Sessions.

Sessions, a University of California, Berkeley, graduate and former schoolteacher, had moved to San Diego just five years before. Her design for Hotel del Coronado's grounds were so celebrated that she was quickly given a new assignment, one that would earn her the title, "the Mother of Balboa Park." First at the hotel, and later at the park, she would change the face of San Diego forever by introducing various Baja California flora, including palm trees and the jacaranda tree, now permanently associated with San Diego.

From the day it opened, the Hotel del Coronado changed the image of San Diego. Babcock and Story had indeed achieved their dream: the hotel deserved to be ranked with not only the best hotels in the New World but also with the most venerable of the Old World as well. Great cities always feature great accommodations, and San Diego had accomplished that with just fifteen thousand residents.

The Hotel del Coronado, opened in 1888, is the second largest wooden structure in the United States.

The Hotel del Coronado remains astonishing today, with an overnight stay there appearing on the wish lists of travelers from around the world. At the same time, it provides one of the most defining images of the fin de siècle: elegant ladies in white muslin and bonnets, men in blazers and straw boaters, promenading through Kate Sessions's gardens beneath the towers and verandas of the great hotel.

CHAPTER FOUR

Tijuana—The Homeland Starts Here/Aquí Empieza La Patria

As the twentieth century dawned, Tijuana's initial layout was about to take shape. Given the extraordinary growth the city would see by the end of the century, it is easy to forget just how tiny it was at the beginning. In 1900, the number of Tijuana residents totaled just 242 citizens (compared to 17,700 in San Diego). Ten years later, the number had increased to just 510 residents, with 223 more people living on surrounding ranches. Even in 1920, the city's population had reached only 1,228—compared to San Diego's 74,361 citizens that year—with perhaps three times that many in surrounding suburban communities. In other words, when nearby San Diego was becoming a metropolitan center with a distinct downtown featuring increasingly tall office buildings, Tijuana remained little more than a village.

Yet all the ingredients were coming into place for Tijuana's growth to explode.

One cause of the city's retarded growth was the seemingly endless lawsuits and counterlawsuits by Arguello descendants, which lasted through the 1880s. On January 30, 1889, the various family members decided to call an end to the dispute. Pilar Arguello's original transfer to her son—the three leagues of land that became the

site of Tijuana—was finally recognized. That property was immediately divided in two geographically unequal, but financially equivalent halves and awarded to the two disputing parties. The Arguellos
immediately hired an Ensenada engineer, Ricardo Orozco, to make an
official survey and map of the properties.

Orozco was not only a good engineer but also a superb city planner
and diplomat (it was he who proposed the unequal division in order to
include the hot springs in the less-valuable half). After completing the
survey, he laid out the plat of a proposed new city, to be located on the
southern half of the old rancho.

This proposed layout can still be found beneath the shiny new office
towers and shopping centers of modern Tijuana. That map, which still
survives, is essentially a square-shaped parcel of twenty mostly-square
blocks per side. Atop this grid, Orozco added a second, diagonal grid,
with a total of four central plazas where those angled streets met, and
a grand plaza at the central intersection.

His was a striking design, reminiscent of some of America's great
cities of the time, including Washington, DC, and Detroit, which max-
imizes population density and navigation. At the same time, it offers
those diagonals as quick shortcuts across the city, as well as traffic
circles at their intersections to speed passage. Orozco also had the
unique advantage of being able to create his design on mostly uninhabited grazing land, essentially a tabula rasa. The grand central plaza
design, already a part of Mexican culture, established a nexus for the
city's civic events, and, not surprisingly, it would become the site of the
cathedral and government offices.

Orozco's plan was a hit and was quickly adopted, in 1890—a good
thing, because in February 1891, the torrential rains returned. The
resulting flood was so powerful that it not only widened the channel
of the Tijuana River, but jumped its banks, racing across the north
bank, the site of the old city of Tijuana. Floodwaters either wrecked or
scoured away every building, including the old custom house. When
the water receded, the Tijuana of the nineteenth century was gone;
fortuitously the layout of the New Tijuana was in place, free from the
burden of legacy and able to start fresh.

Following the loss of Old Tijuana, the town didn't seem to miss a step.
Land speculation had already begun in New Tijuana, with investment

money flowing in from both sides of the border. Construction was already underway on homes and shops, especially in the grand plaza at the city's center. Indeed, the first filing to register the sale of a parcel in the new downtown took place in August 1889, just one month after the Arguello lawsuit settled. By 1890, speculators were already buying and flipping properties to make a quick profit, suggesting that land prices in Tijuana already were starting to climb.

View of Avenida Olvera (now Avenida Revolución), early twentieth century.

According to historians David Piñera and Gabriel Rivera, most of these early land purchases were made in the vicinity of Avenida Olvera (now Avenida Revolución), Avenida Cinco de Mayo, and Sixth and Seventh Streets. Why? Their proximity to the main road to the border, of course, but just as important, they were on comparatively high ground, and thus most likely to escape future floods. Over the rest of the decade a number of wooden buildings—hotel, taverns, and liquor and souvenir shops—would spring up on Avenida Olvera, all catering to American tourists. In the words of Piñera and Rivera, during this period the New Tijuana looked like "a Western town in the United States." That is, not a modern fin de siècle city like San Diego or San Francisco, but something more like Tombstone or Bodie.

BORDER TOWN

Something else, something darker, also changed in Tijuana during those years—and much of it was led by businessmen from north of the border.

American couples visiting Avenida Revolución, 1916.

Border towns are almost always characterized by the divergence in the laws and cultures of the two contiguous nations. Perhaps no city in North America was so defined by those differences as Tijuana. Though influenced by Catholicism, it was still a Wild West town, all but beyond the control of a national capital fifteen hundred miles away. By comparison, San Diego was becoming a civilized city, Protestant, and effectively enforcing its nation's laws (even though the US capital was even farther away).

Not surprisingly, in straitlaced, repressive San Diego, citizens (that is, men) looked at Tijuana just fifteen miles to the south and saw an easy outlet for their more atavistic desires. Tijuanenses, for their part, already imbued with a fairly permissive attitude toward gambling, vice, and other pursuits, saw these hungers in the gringo Norteamericanos and recognized a great opportunity to escape poverty and even grow wealthy by capitalizing on them.

The crucial missing factor was businesspeople—Mexican or American—with the knowledge, skill, and money to finance institutions dedicated to these darker pursuits.

The first clue of what was to come occurred in July 1894, when a group of distinguished Tijuanenses, led by Alejandro Savin, filed a proposal to the district's political director for permission to stage a bullfight, right at the border. They sweetened their request by saying it would help the community's generally impoverished economy. They even offered to donate 25 percent of their profits to local public education. But they were turned down, not least because the director felt the violence of bullfighting would reflect badly on Tijuana in the eyes of San Diegans.

Two years later, the same group tried again. This time they not only enlisted the support of Tijuana businesses but also offered to donate 20 percent of the bullfight's income to the "material improvement of the community." They also offered to invest 10,000 pesos to build the bullring, but in exchange, they wanted the right to use that bullring for ten years. Again, they were turned down.

But Alejandro Savin was not a man to give up easily. A recent arrival in Tijuana, he already had opened the popular Bazar Mexicano crafts and gift store. He had also, through a family connection to President Porfirio Díaz, managed to get himself named acting consul to San Diego. Now, with the support (and political advice) of his new contacts in the northern city, he cleverly changed his pitch: *No, no,* he told the regional government, *the proposed bullring was actually going to be used for boxing matches.*

For reasons lost to history, but perhaps greased by a *mordida* (a "little bite" of bribery), the powers that be accepted this new explanation and allowed construction to proceed. Needless to say, it wasn't long before bullfights joined the boxing matches on the arena's calendar.

Meanwhile, just down the avenue, the Tia Juana Hot Springs were suffering not only from intermittent floods but also from declining revenues. In an effort to survive, in 1897 owner Julio Arguello applied for a waiver on customs and transit fees for the springs' visitors. He was turned down. So he tried another tack: he built a hotel, Agua Caliente.

It was a small place—rooms and cottages for just one hundred guests—compared to what would come after, but it was an important beginning, and it succeeded against all odds. Arguello showed that a sizable percentage of typical day visitors were interested in staying and enjoying the local culture for several days, a harbinger of things to come.

THE FIRST ERA OF BORDER CROSSING

We think of cross-border cooperation and illegal immigration as late-twentieth-century phenomena at the US-Mexican border. In fact, they characterized the late nineteenth century as well.

American visitors posing next to an International Boundary Monument, circa 1908.

As the number of visitors from the US to Tijuana grew, combined with a still-porous border, inevitably, cross-border crime grew as well. Perpetrators on both sides used the border, imprecise extradition laws, and the lack of regular cross-border enforcement cooperation to escape arrest. At the same time, the United States was well along its trajectory to becoming the wealthiest country on earth. This magnet of opportunity was on full display, pulling people in not just to Ellis

Island in the east but also through empty desert landscapes in the US Southwest and Northern Mexico.

It wasn't long before law enforcement and immigration control at the border became a source of friction between San Diego and Tijuana. This erupted in September 1893, when the political leader of the territory accused the Tijuana justice of the peace, Francisco Arguello (in one of the last historic appearances of the venerable family surname) of conspiring with American police in the arrest of accused criminals in Mexican territory. For good measure, he added that Arguello was illiterate, apparently a slur at this point in the city's history. Arguello was fired.

Just seven months later, another transnational scandal erupted when Arguello's successor was accused of allowing US legal authorities to cross into Tijuana to arrest a group of Chinese nationals suspected of attempting to sneak into the United States.

The increasing activity at the border inevitably led to greater tensions between the two cities, further exacerbated by a growing number of cases of violent crime. For example, on October 22, 1908, a US Immigration officer was making his rounds when, according to the official report:

> [A]fter hearing someone approach[ing] him he said, "Who goes?" He received no response, despite asking in Spanish. Then the inspector lit a match to determine who the other guy was, and then saw that he was holding a large butcher knife, with which he tried to attack the officer. In response, Inspector Clark fired two shots into the air, but as the assailant continued his hostile demonstration, the inspector tried to wound him in the leg, but instead he missed, and shot him in the groin.

The assailant died. When it was discovered that he had no previous record of criminal behavior, doubts grew about what had really occurred that night. The Mexican government formally demanded an explanation, receiving only the official report as the US government's response. This was the forerunner of a problem—cross-border shootings with Mexican fatalities—that would bedevil the US-Mexico border periodically, continuing up to the present day.

In response to these and other events, the region's political leader, Rafael García Martínez, undertook a mission to make the government presence in Tijuana even stronger, by officially promoting the city into a municipality, explaining, "as this is the only way that this place will acquire more importance and [a] better class of people and authorities . . . it is urgent to put a stop to the bad influence that reigns in that place." This was in 1894; Mexico didn't act on that request until after the Second World War.

What gains Tijuana made in the 1890s—and there were many, including the modernization of the city's school and the development of Orozco's plat for the new city—were made against a headwind of growing turmoil in Mexico. Out at the farthest corner of the nation, Tijuana was partially insulated from this political turmoil, but it wasn't entirely immune and ended up writing its own chapter in the chaos to follow.

ANOTHER CIVIL WAR

In fact, one kind of revolutionary activity had periodically bedeviled the region ever since the Mexican-American War. These were the so-called *filibusteros*—non-Mexicans (mostly Americans) who looked to carve off, typically through a manufactured insurrection, portions of a weakened Mexico to create separate "sovereign nations" they could dominate. The Baja California peninsula, hanging off the bottom of California and all but detached from mainland Mexico, was a particularly attractive target. Most of these filibustero campaigns were small, uncoordinated efforts quickly suppressed. But at the end of the first decade of the 1900s, as the government of Porfirio Díaz began to collapse, these movements became more threatening.

The galvanizing event was the rise of an opposition party in Mexico. Throughout the first decade of the new century, Mexicans, especially those in the countryside, had begun to rebel against the authoritarian rule of the Díaz government through strikes, protests, and armed rebellion—all of which were crushed by the government, often bloodily.

This opposition remained ineffectual until 1905. That's when a wealthy landowner (and University of California, Berkeley, graduate), Francisco Madero, who had already been imprisoned by Díaz, organized the Anti-Reelection Party from Texas. This party recruited an army, and in late 1910 marched into Chihuahua, calling for armed revolution. Large portions of the population (known as Maderistas) throughout the nation rose up in solidarity and fought against the Porfiriato army in numerous skirmishes. The Mexican Revolution had begun. Díaz, seeing the writing on the wall, resigned and went into exile.

But revolutions take on a life of their own. Mexico would continue to experience civil war and strife, including pitched battles, presidential assassinations, the rise and death of Emiliano Zapata, and Pancho Villa's raids into the United States. The fighting wouldn't end for a decade, after 1920, leaving the country exhausted and deeply impoverished. More than a million people perished during Mexico's civil war, more than the US Civil War that preceded it or either the Russian or Chinese revolutions to follow.

Madero, who would be elected president of Mexico in May 1911 (and murdered two years later), was only the most visible of the early revolutionary leaders. Leading the rebellion in Baja California was Ricardo Flores Magón, a lawyer and journalist who began writing against Díaz as early as 1892. He, too, had been imprisoned, and he moved his operations to the United States, forming the Organizing Junta of the Liberal Party.

In the years that followed, there was regular talk of Flores Magón and Madero joining forces, but Flores Magón had plans of his own. In fact, he had converted to revolutionary anarchism, and from his base in Los Angeles began to gather support from other anarcho-syndicalist organizations, notably the International Workers of the World (IWW, or "Wobblies"), which had been trying to spark labor unrest in the northwestern United States. He even gained public support from San Francisco writer (and socialist) Jack London.

Seeing Madero's success in Chihuahua, Flores Magón knew he had to move quickly. So he embarked on a campaign to capture control of Baja California and use it as a recruiting base for an overall assault on Mexico. He chose Mexicali, a hundred and nine miles east of Tijuana, as the first target of the "Magonistas." With a total of twenty men, eight of them American, they took the town quickly, killing the local jailer to free some of their confederates.

Unfortunately for the Magonistas, the people of Baja California weren't that interested in rebellion. So Flores Magón recruited one hundred irregular soldiers from the ranks of the IWW, other American radicals, a few soldiers of fortune, and some local native scouts and marched on Tijuana. Learning of the impending attack, Baja California's governor, Colonel Celso Vega, with ninety soldiers, marched in the opposite direction from Ensenada, aiming to block them.

The advanced elements of the Magonista army clashed with Vega's troops in the Cocopah Mountains in a brief, bloody battle, were defeated, and retreated to Mexicali. Vega's troops followed in hopes of capturing the city, but they ran into entrenched Magonista forces just outside the city and suffered severe casualties, including Vega himself. Broken, the government troops beat a hasty retreat back to Ensenada.

With news of the victory, Flores Magón's army swelled with volunteers, mostly Americans (especially Spanish-American War veterans) but also Europeans, Australians, and South Africans. These recruits may have strengthened the Magonista army, but it was a propaganda boon for the Díaz government, which began to label the rebels as just the latest filibusteros, out to annex Mexico for the United States. Even the two San Diego newspapers, the *Union* and the *Tribune*, joined in the criticism. Magonista leaders didn't help by claiming their goal was to establish a "cooperative commonwealth."

At this point, one of the most bizarre characters in the Tijuana story entered the picture. Richard Wells Ferris was an actor and public-relations specialist, as well as a world-class huckster and self-promoter. Already he had nearly won election as lieutenant governor of California and had done a brilliant job promoting San Diego's upcoming Panama-California Exposition. Now he set his sights on his biggest publicity campaign ever: a takeover of Baja California.

In early 1911, at a press conference in San Francisco, Ferris announced his plan to purchase the Baja California peninsula from Mexico and convert it into a "sporting republic" complete with gambling casinos. He also hinted, unsubstantiated, that he had support for the project from the likes of J. P. Morgan. The new "nation" would initially be called the Republic of Díaz, and eventually he would sell it to the USA. Finally, modeling himself as General Ferris, he placed advertisements in numerous US publications, seeking a thousand volunteers for his new army.

It was, of course, all a sham. But the aging President Díaz took the bait and publicly denounced Ferris, thus crediting the con man with a diplomatic stature he didn't deserve.

On March 1911, with typical flamboyance, Ferris arranged from San Diego for a woman to ride across the border into Tijuana, plant a flag bearing the image of the scales of justice against the background of a rising sun, and read the following proclamation: "Lower California, I claim you in the name of equal suffrage and of model government, which I hereby christen as the future Republic of Díaz." (Ferris stayed behind in San Diego, just in case the announcement drew the wrong response.)

Meanwhile, in Mexicali, the Magonista army, other than a few small and inconclusive skirmishes, had missed its opportunity to chase the Mexican Army back to Ensenada, thus capturing all of Baja California. This failure to act was so frustrating to the foreigners in the insurrectionists' ranks that they staged a coup against their Mexican commanders, elected a new chief, a Scottish Boer War veteran named Caryl Ap Rhys Pryce, and marched on Tijuana with 220 men, fewer than 10 percent of them Mexicans. Waiting to confront them in Tijuana were approximately one hundred soldiers and civilian volunteers.

After the army's refusal to surrender, the Battle of Tijuana began, on the evening of May 8, 1911. The Magonistas surrounded the town, but they had a problem: they were short on ammunition, because President Taft had made good on a promise to President Díaz to send twenty thousand US troops to the border to stop weapon and ammunition smuggling. That agreement had arisen from a meeting in Ciudad Juarez between the two men, the first meeting between a US and a Mexican president. Local press at the time described it as the "Most Eventful Diplomatic Event in the History of the Two Nations."

For the Magonistas it was perhaps the most ill-timed event. Outgunned by their adversaries, they decided to wait until dawn to attack. But the Mexican Army took the initiative, conducting a midnight sortie that briefly overran the Magonista position and killed several insurrectionists. In the meantime, several Army snipers set up in a nearby church tower and began to pick off the rebels. In response, Pryce ordered the burning of the church and the nearby bullring.

The battle lasted much of the day. San Diegans, seeing the column of smoke and hearing the gunfire, crowded the hills overlooking the border to watch, joined by women and children of Tijuana fleeing the violence. What they saw: two armies skirmishing, then separating, with the Mexican Army retreating into breastworks. They watched a steady stream of wounded Mexican soldiers being evacuated to San Diego hospitals, while in the center of Tijuana, the insurrectionists assaulted the new customs house, captured it, and raised the Magonista flag, its red field bearing the anarchist motto, *Tierra y Libertad*, or "Land and Freedom" (a phrase later used in the Spanish Civil War).

Soon after, the fight was rejoined, and it continued until the next night. By then, most of the major structures of Tijuana were burning, the Mexican commander had been wounded, and the casualty rate was rising. The Mexican Army retreated (most of them across the border, where they were captured and interned by the US Army), leaving the city and the victory to the Magonistas. In the aftermath, twelve federal troops lay dead, with ten others wounded (bodies were discovered in the brush for weeks after the battle, so no precise fatality count was made). The Magonista casualties included twenty rebels dead and ten wounded. But they had won the Battle of Tijuana.

Even as the ruins of their largely destroyed city smoldered, Tijuanenses returned to recover what was left from their homes. Invited to stay in the city by the insurrectionists, reportedly not a single resident accepted the offer, and for good reason: Tijuana was soon overrun with looters who carted their stolen goods north into the United States. Meanwhile, ironically, the dead Mexican soldiers from the battle were buried in San Diego, while the dead American insurrectionists were buried beside Tijuana's now-scarred customs house.

Less than a week after the Magonistas' victory, and desperate for cash to pay his army, Pryce allowed gamblers into Tijuana to open poker and faro parlors, as long as they gave 25 percent of their take to the Magonistas. At the same time, Pryce ordered all the liquor in the city destroyed, mostly to keep his troops under control.

This would have been the propitious moment for Flores Magón to ride into Tijuana, take command of his troops, and capture all of Baja California. After all, he was barely one hundred miles away, in Los Angeles. But he never appeared; it seems he was a better journalist and promoter than warrior or leader. Meanwhile, Pryce talked about attacking Ensenada and carrying on the revolution. But his army was tired and the promised weapons from the north never appeared. So after a face-off with Flores Magón in LA, a frustrated Pryce rode away from the Mexican Revolution.

The Magonista revolt now turned into an open and visible farce.

By mid-May 1911, numerous American flags were flying over Tijuana, raised not just by the new American gambling-house owners but by everyone else trying to keep the looters at bay. The old filibustero dream of an independent Baja California state struck casual observers as more possible than ever. No one saw this illusion on the brink of reality with a greater sense of opportunity than the wily actor–con man, Dick Ferris, who reemerged on the scene.

Within a week of the battle, Ferris had already finagled an introduction to Pryce in Tijuana. By then, events were running wild. Volunteers, hired by wealthy Mexican-Americans, were flooding into the garrison in Ensenada. On May 25, President Díaz resigned, replaced by a transitional government. Five days later, Pryce had his showdown in Los Angeles with Flores Magón and quit. As the news of Pryce's resignation reached Tijuana, a number of insurrectionists abandoned their posts in response. Those who remained split into rival camps according to their nationality and political leanings. It was the beginning of June before the Magonista junta would at last send a commission to Tijuana to install new leadership. But by then it would be too late. Ferris, always ready to jump on an opportunity, had already made his move.

According to historian Bob Owens, Ferris returned to Tijuana and made a speech to the adventurers in the Liberal army:

> "You have got to haul down this red flag," he told them.
> "While that might be the symbol of the Liberal Party,
> so called in Mexico, it means anarchy in the US, and
> you have got to get that out of sight of every American

who passes this border. You have got to cut out your
socialism, your anarchism, and every other ism that
you have got into and form a new government if you
hope to do anything right."

Ferris also advised the soldiers that they had to appeal to the
American press and also to "the better class of Mexicans."

The soldiers obeyed, not least because of Ferris's violent new lieutenant, a Magonista veteran named Louis James, whom everybody
feared. It was James who also called a general meeting of the troops and
nominated Ferris to be the new governor of Baja California. Needless
to say, Ferris won the election. Of course, his first act as governor-elect
was not to visit his constituents in Mexico but to plan a celebration
party in Los Angeles. When James raced across the border to beg
Ferris to come south and talk to the Magonista army, Ferris replied
that he was too busy to come that day, but that he had designed a flag
for his new state, and that his tailor would have it ready for James the
next day. Then Ferris called another press conference to announce that
the new Madero government in Mexico City would have to accept the
new nation in Baja California, which he now renamed the Republic of
Madero, as if to assuage the Mexican president.

In Tijuana, the IWW members of the Magonista army were growing restive. Alarmed by news of Ferris's behavior, they elected a new
leader, Jack Mosby, an IWW member and Marine Corps deserter.
Mosby, in turn, released a statement: "Dick Ferris has absolutely nothing to do with the revolutionary movement, and his presence in Tijuana
is not desired." Mosby also reaffirmed the Wobblies' fight against capitalism. That last part didn't go down well among the halls of power
either in San Diego or Washington, DC.

As for Ferris, he now saw trouble coming for him on both sides of
the border. To hold those forces at bay, he wrote a letter of resignation
for the governorship and handed it to James in Los Angeles. James, still
a Ferris true believer, carried the letter to San Diego by train, rented a
chauffeured car, mounted the Republic of Madero banner to its hood,
and had himself driven to Tijuana.

It was not a smart move. The instant James reached Tijuana,
Magonista solders dragged him from the car, beat him, and set out to

execute him. He was saved by some old friends in the crowd, but as the flag was torn off the car and burned, James was physically thrown back across the border. Questioned about their behavior by the San Diego press, a Magonista explained, "Ferris seems to have been trying to make a joke out of the whole movement."

But the Magonistas had bigger matters to worry about. First, several dozen Mexican Magonistas, who had been off fighting with Madero's army, arrived in Tijuana and proceeded to tangle, to the point of gunfights, with the American Magonistas. They also apparently brought word that both the Maderista army in Ciudad Juarez and Vega's army in Ensenada were preparing to attack from the east and the south. Desperate to raise money for arms and distract his troops, Mosby decided to stage a Wild West show in the midst of it all. San Diegans wisely stayed away in droves.

On June 14, 1911, the US government arrested Ricardo Flores Magón and the rest of the Magonista leadership for violations of the neutrality law. Ferris knew he was next, so he reacted by doing what he did best: publicly promoting his case. He announced that he was ending what he described as a "live publicity stunt." Ever flamboyant, he closed by saying, "Tell the public that I have already denied any and all dealings with the *insurrectos*—past, present, and future—and if this is not enough, I will arrange a schedule for further denials three times a day, and at bedtime." The US government was not amused. Ferris was arrested the next day, even as he protested to the *San Diego Union* that his "little practical joke" had been taken far too seriously. For good measure, Pryce was also arrested on the much more serious charges of arson and murder during the Battle of Tijuana.

This whole absurd story might have ended here, but there was one more act to play. With the help of President Taft, the Maderista army in Juarez was allowed to travel by American rail to Tijuana to put down the border insurrection. Hearing this, Mosby wrote to the city leaders of San Diego, implying that if this happened, the Magonistas would blow up a stretch of the San Diego and Arizona railroad line. Alarmed, the most powerful businessman in the city, John Spreckels, used his influence in DC to get President Taft to bring back the American troops to guard the border.

Meanwhile, in Ensenada, General Vega ignored the terms of the armistice he had signed with the Magonistas and assembled a new army outfitted with the best new weapons. Now he marched on Tijuana. Learning the news, Mosby boarded a train with his 230 poorly armed men, the majority of them Americans and other foreigners, and set out to meet Vega south of town.

The battle lasted three hours, ending with a total victory for Vega and his forces. Thirty of the Magonistas were killed, some in the battle, but perhaps even more were murdered by Vega's soldiers as the insurrectionists lay wounded or in captivity. In their retreat, the surviving Magonistas split into two groups: the Mexicans ran to hide in the hills; the rest ran for the border.

A few hours later, San Diegans were treated to the memorable sight of 106 American and European Magonista soldiers marching double file into the city. At their head was Jack Mosby, sobbing, tears running down his face.

Rebels leaving Tijuana for United States, June 22, 1911.

Thus, on June 22, 1911, after nearly 140 years, the history of the original Tijuana came to an end. The retreating Magonistas had left behind a burned, largely abandoned city, now primarily inhabited by gamblers and criminals. Between floods and war, most of the institutions that had defined the city were now gone. The Mexican nation was immersed in revolution, civil war, assassination, and civil chaos. To the north, the United States, after more than a decade of unprecedented prosperity, was sliding into the First World War.

These larger forces would rule for the rest of the decade, and in light of everything, it was conceivable that Tijuana could have disappeared forever, replaced perhaps by a new border town. Instead, the 1920s would see Tijuana's extraordinary revival, partly because of the survivors' civic pride, partly because of the continuous and growing presence of a needy San Diego nearby, but likely most of all because of an unimaginable new opportunity—truly a deus ex machina—for the city: Prohibition.

THE ROARING TWENTIES

In the twentieth century, Tijuana grew and prospered because it turned its destiny over to its neighbor to the north. That it did so shrewdly and with such adaptability, retaining its own identity in spite of this gravitational pull, is a testament to the cultural pride and historical independence of the citizens of Tijuana.

But make no mistake, this symbiotic—some would say mutually parasitic—relationship to San Diego (and by extension the rest of the United States) was a two-edged sword: it came with considerable rewards but also devastating costs. Over the next forty years, Tijuana would explode in population and, eventually, in wealth. But its growing reputation as a den of sin for the wealthier Americans would give Tijuana a blackened reputation, not just in Mexico and the United States but around the world. From this it is still trying to escape.

The American hungers that Tijuana would satisfy for the next half century can be neatly characterized by the decade:

- The Twenties—Alcohol
- The Thirties—Nightclubs, casino gambling, bullfights, and jai alai
- The Forties—Brothels and cheap liquor for soldiers and sailors

- The Fifties—Abortions and divorces
- The Sixties—Duty-free shopping for foreign goods not available in San Diego.

The irony, of course, is that Tijuana's stigma was American-born. First of all, Tijuana's sullied reputation came from serving the changing needs and desires of Americans, who returned across the border cleansed by concealment of their sins. Second, most of the bars, bordellos, and gambling houses of mid-twentieth-century Tijuana were created, financed, and sometimes even operated by Americans, from mobsters to distinguished citizens. Tijuanenses were sometimes partners but for the most part were employees of these enterprises.

The story of the new Tijuana really begins in 1920, when, in a paroxysm of morality led by various religious temperance groups and progressives, the United States adopted the Eighteenth Amendment to the Constitution outlawing the manufacture, transportation, and sale of intoxicating liquors and the enabling Volstead Act, which gave the US government the authority to enforce its ban on alcoholic beverages.

This attempt to improve the morality of the American people quickly spawned an underground economy serving millions of citizens with illegal booze. It wasn't long before the Mob stepped in—indeed, Prohibition largely accelerated the growth of organized crime in the US—and took over the smuggling of liquor across the border from Canada and Mexico, bringing other forms of criminality in its train. Meanwhile, many of the best German-American brewers pulled up stakes and moved to Mexico, creating a Mexican beer industry that is still celebrated today.

On the US-Mexico border, and nowhere more than in Tijuana, Prohibition proved the greatest business opportunity the region had seen. After all, why should good American citizens, thirsty for a drink, have to deal with a speakeasy's questionable liquor, the threat of police raids, and the likes of Al Capone, when they could just drive across the border to a Tijuana saloon and drink legally, to their hearts' content?

Tijuana was ready for those secret scofflaws. Mostly destroyed and depopulated at the beginning of the 1920s, by decade's end the city had come back with a brand-new infrastructure, much of it funded by American entrepreneurs anticipating a new way to make a buck.

American tourists during Prohibition.

Unfortunately, as the years passed, Prohibition also would bring with it, as it had in the United States, organized crime. By the early 1930s, the Mafia—including such notorious figures as Bugsy Siegel, and reportedly at Agua Caliente, Al Capone—had begun to take control of Tijuana's gambling parlors. With the arrival of the Mob came the usual dip in petty crimes and a rise in corruption, extortion, and occasional bursts of violence.

TIJUANA RESTORED

The resurrection of Tijuana actually had begun in earnest just before Prohibition, with the 1916 appointment of Esteban Cantu as governor and military leader of the Northern District of Baja California. Cantu was hugely popular in the region, and he used that popularity, with his Mexico City connections, to gain support for a range of public-works projects, especially in Tijuana.

Already, before Cantu's arrival, a private company had been formed to improve the electrification of the city, along with adding a telephone network. Cantu added rebuilt military barracks near Our Lady of Guadalupe Cathedral, one of the city's few surviving edifices.

He also upgraded and renamed the city's primary school next door. Cantu oversaw the construction of the National Road—an extraordinary engineering effort to cut through the nearby Sierra Picachos Mountains—connecting Baja California to the Mexican mainland with a real road (called La Rumorosa) for the first time. Until then, the passage had to be made in part on American roads. (Interestingly, at the same time, the San Diego and Arizona railroad was completed, much of it passing through Mexican territory.) The Tijuana Valley was now properly connected to the outside world on both sides of the border that ran through it.

During this period, no doubt in response to the opportunity to attract visitors to the nearby San Diego International Exposition, Tijuana opened a "typical Mexican fair," commonly known as the Tijuana Fair. Marked by an entrance gate of two towers bearing Mexican flags, the fair brought together craft shops and multiple entertainments—including a casino, restaurant, nightclub, and bullring—into a single tourist destination just a few blocks from the border. It also housed cockfights and boxing matches (featuring, most famously, Jack Clark and Mexican Kid Carter). The fair was a microcosm, a template, for the Tijuana to come.

Thanks to the crowds of tourists from the rest of the US visiting San Diego for the Exposition, heavy advertising in the San Diego papers, and the opportunity to visit the best of Tijuana in one compact, safe spot with private parking, a taxi line from across the border, and a surrounding wall and fence, the Tijuana Fair proved a huge success. Investors and businessmen on both sides of the border studied the fair and started to imagine how to map its success across the whole city.

But probably the institution most important to Tijuana's rebirth was the opening, on January 1, 1916, of the rebuilt racetrack. This too was partly Governor Cantu's work: he had blessed the project, despite a lack of approval for the venture by Mexico's federal government, perhaps because the governor's friend was one of the Mexican investors. The financing of the track came mostly from north of the border, led by organized gambling veteran James Wood Coffroth, who represented a group of American and Mexican investors, including the sugar tycoon and the *San Diego Union* publisher, John Spreckels.

Historic Agua Caliente Racetrack.

Ten thousand people, including Governor Cantu, attended the opening day of the "Tijuana Race Track," temporarily boosting Tijuana's population more than sevenfold for the day. The racetrack was an immediate and enduring success, due in part to its location just four hundred yards from the border (today's Caliente racetrack is farther from the border). Even wary Americans could go to the track without passing through the rest of the city. More importantly, in a swoon of moralism that characterized the era, in 1911 Los Angeles had voted to ban saloons, gambling, and betting on horse racing. Five years later, Los Angelinos were desperately thirsty for all three, so for them the new racetrack in the revived Tijuana was like a gift from heaven.

What really made the racetrack was that back then, as today, Hollywood served as the national trendsetter, and Hollywood had the money to play the horses. Soon, top stars and celebrities of the era, from Charlie Chaplin to racecar driver Barney Oldfield, could be seen at the Tijuana racetrack. The chance to rub shoulders with the famous only added to the track's appeal.

However, the racetrack's start was anything but smooth, thanks to the city's old nemesis, the Tijuana River. Between the relentless rain and the great "Hatfield Rainmaker" flood in 1916, the racetrack closed just two weeks after it opened. Repaired, it reopened on April 15. Governor Cantu again attended, publicly giving his support to Coffroth, who, in turn, indulged in a bit of hyperbole, telling the crowd that the Tijuana racetrack would make the city "one of the most famous places in the world." As it turned out, he wasn't entirely wrong.

So great were the throngs attending the track during racing season that multiple enterprises sprang up nearby to cater to them and take their dollars. The most important of these was the Casino Monte Carlo, named to capture some of the luster of its namesake in Monaco, and built by the owner of the Tijuana Fair. To make the visit easier, Tijuana established both a tram service from San Diego and a wooden bridge over the borderline, dubbed "La Marimba" for the sound cars made on the wooden slats.

By 1917, Tijuana had everything in place. All that was needed now was a spark. Fortuitously, in came just three years later in the form of the Volstead Act. Prohibition turned Tijuana from an interesting new tourist destination into a full-blown land rush. By the time the Eighteenth Amendment was repealed thirteen years later, Tijuana would be transformed so completely that the aftershocks of the Prohibition era could still be felt almost a century later.

A BOTTOMLESS THIRST

San Diegans had always come to Tijuana for a drink, but it had mostly been for the price and the anonymity. In the late 1920s, they came, along with hundreds of thousands of other Americans, because Tijuana was the best place to get that drink legally.

Tijuana, famously, responded to Prohibition by opening bars and saloons on almost every corner of the city. Historians Piñera and Rivera offer an impressive (and one assumes incomplete) list of the most prominent of those watering holes:

> La Ballena (which advertised the longest bar in the world—229 feet), the Blue Fox, the Foreign Club, the Alhambra Café, the Turf Bar, the Tijuana Bar, the San Francisco Café, the Tivoli Bar, the California Café, Molino Rojo, the San Diego Bar, Café de Luxe, El Gato Negro, the Scandia Barrel House, Mi Lugar, El Caballito, El Faro, the Green Mill Bar, El Ancla Bar, El Palacio Royal, the Pullman Bar, the Vialla Bar, Ming Bar, Vernon Club Bar, the Garden Café, the Tunnel . . .

This list would be impressive for a major city. For Tijuana, at the time the size of an average San Diego neighborhood, it is both astounding and a measure of the impact Prohibition had on the city. Tijuana in the Roaring Twenties was new and fun, filled with Americans enjoying their post-war prosperity. Tijuana's streets were relatively safe, the saloonkeepers were relatively honest, and organized crime had yet to make major inroads on the city's commerce. But that wouldn't last.

Governor Cantu, who had done so much to prepare the city for the current boom, wasn't around to see much of it. In 1920, a new figure had appeared on the scene: Abelardo L. Rodríguez. He was part of the Sonoran group that had recently overthrown Mexican president Carranza. Now, as the head of a military force, he had been ordered to depose Governor Cantu, who had opposed the Sonorans. Cantu quickly surrendered his title, and Rodríguez assumed the title of military commander of the northern district of Baja California, then governor of the Territory. He would hold that title for more than a decade and have a major impact on the emerging Tijuana.

184:—INTERIOR OF CASINO AND FAMOUS GOLD BAR.

AGUA CALIENTE, TIJUANA HOT SPRINGS, MEXICO.

The famous Golden Room of Agua Caliente Casino, circa 1928.

Agua Caliente Hotel interior with Arabic design elements.

Much like his predecessors, Rodríguez ignored any conflict of interest and, in 1926, bought six hundred acres for himself at Agua Caliente springs. Then, leading a consortium of investors, he set about reviving the springs as a major tourist mecca, complete with a hotel, a casino, baths, horse and greyhound racetracks, a golf course, and an aircraft landing strip. All this was housed in stunning facilities combining Colonial California design, Spain's Alhambra, Art Deco, and early California Mission architecture. At its much-photographed entrance stood a multistory tower—the Minarete—reflecting all these styles, arching over Agua Caliente's driveway. The compound was as stunning as anything found in California, and it quickly became the place for celebrities to see and be seen.

Agua Caliente Tower.

With all these new tourist attractions, Tijuana became a twenty-four-hour city, with perpetual traffic jams at the border and on its downtown *avenidas*. Visitors now stayed multiple days at the city's elegant hotels, and millions of dollars passed hands in the city every week. Needless to say, the population of Tijuana jumped in the twenties, from 1,228 in 1920 to 11,271 in 1930, and predictably, the local infrastructure groaned as the city struggled to keep up. That didn't stop the city from promoting this gigantic growth rate. Publicity during this period claimed that the ratio of visitors to residents made Tijuana the most popular city on earth.

The real miracle of Tijuana in the 1920s, though, is that the good times lasted as long as they did. It seemed, as it did to Americans enjoying their own Roaring Twenties, this prosperity might endure forever. Of course, it all came crashing down in October 1929, leaving both countries struggling through the global Great Depression for the next decade. Tijuana's and Governor Rodríguez's last important civic act before the crash was to dedicate 8.5 million pesos to the construction of a dam to finally control the flooding of the Tijuana River. It would take a decade to complete.

FINANCIAL CRASH AND SIN CITY

The Great Depression and the 1930s created the most schizophrenic era in Tijuana's history.

On one hand, this decade marked the development of the first residential districts in the city, Castillo and Escobedo-Cacho. For the first time, the city became a true, multigenerational home for its citizens, people with a stake in Tijuana's future, not just this month's revenues earned from gringos.

On the other hand, the Great Depression dried up much of the flow of prosperous, free-spending tourists who had lifted up all those new bars, restaurants, and gambling houses. The competition for the remaining dollars became fiercer and the offerings more extreme—sex shows, brothels, and drugs. Meanwhile, the criminal element—fleece joints, con artists, purse snatchers, and muggers—grew apace.

Even today, Tijuanenses are hesitant to talk about the embarrassing two-decade era before World War II. Some dismiss it as capitalism run amok: the merchants of Tijuana simply did their usual job of giving Americans what they wanted, and what they wanted during this era was more desperate and extreme. Others engage in denial, arguing that the city's reputation is based on fantasy, attributing it to a period of sustained, biased, even fabricated reporting. But there remains too much documentation from this era to claim the reputation is false. Here is historian Oscar Jáquez Martínez:

> Practically overnight, Tijuana became the red-light district of San Diego, the favorite port of call for rowdy sailors. American investors in Tijuana promoted it as the place where "the drinks never stop," while the prohibitionists damned it as "the road to hell." Thus was born the "Black Legend of Tijuana," as Tijuanenses refer to their city's reputation as a sin capital. Meanwhile, San Diego began priding itself as a clean, all-American town.

As if the Depression wasn't hard enough on Tijuana's economy, in 1933 it was hit with a second challenge. Newly elected president Franklin Roosevelt, fulfilling a campaign promise, revoked the Volstead Act and successfully supported the repeal of the Eighteenth Amendment. Now able to buy a drink at the corner bar, why would Americans cross the border to get one, especially in a city reportedly growing meaner and more craven by the year?

Black Legend fantasies aside, in the end Tijuana had made a deal with the devil. It had chosen to pursue the Almighty Dollar wherever it led, and it had lost part of its soul in the process. Tijuana has borne that stigma ever since—even now, a sizable percentage of San Diegans never consider crossing the border. Modern Tijuanenses, as they travel the world, regularly encounter looks of concern, disgust, or pity when they utter the name of their hometown.

By the late thirties, Tijuana, still mired in economic distress, might well have retrenched and retracted, becoming less of a tourist destination and more of a Mexican city. But then, another extraordinary event intervened—another deus ex machina saving Tijuana from a seemingly hopeless situation, and placing the city on the path to its most booming decade yet. The trigger? World War II, particularly the portion of it fought in the Pacific.

A PACIFIC WAR

San Diego, always an important naval base, became a primary staging area for the United States during the Second World War. Beginning immediately after Pearl Harbor, in late 1941, hundreds of thousands of American sailors, marines, airmen, and soldiers would pass through the region to be trained at new bases such as Camp Pendleton and the San Diego Naval Air Station, before they shipped out to fight in the war's Pacific theater.

Like recruits awaiting combat throughout history, these legions of young men—away from home, with money in their pockets, and trying to fit in an entire life before their possible death—used their leave time to seek out booze, sex, and fun. Thanks to the movies and that sullied reputation, they knew where to go: Tijuana.

The city that awaited them was different from the relatively small town that had greeted their predecessors in the 1930s. In 1940, Tijuana was now a municipality of 16,500 residents, swelled not only by Mexicans arriving from other parts of the country but also by European refugees, especially Jews, fleeing Nazism but unable to enter the US. These refugees, bringing their cosmopolitan lifestyles, would soon make major contributions to the arts and commerce of the city.

Despite the enduring loss to its reputation, Tijuana had managed to survive both the end of Prohibition and the Great Depression. Most of its businesses and institutions were still intact. During this era, Tijuana's image was increasingly schizoid, part den of sin, part destination of sophistication and glamour, thanks to Hollywood and its stars (not least a teenage Tijuana dancer named Margarita Carmen Cansino, also known as Rita Hayworth). Alongside cruder institutions of the city developed sparkling new sites of elegance and international repute. The bullring had survived, as had Agua Caliente (but barely—thanks to a new Mexican law, its casino had closed, making the Depression even worse for Tijuana residents).

Tijuana even had a new unofficial patron saint, who arose under the most tragic and bizarre circumstances. In 1938, the eight-year-old daughter of a well-known local couple was found raped and murdered. The blame fell on a soldier named Juan Castillo Morales. The fact that he was a soldier made him the perfect propaganda target for two local labor organizations (the Confederación de Trabajadores de México, or CTM, and the Confederación Regional Obrera Mexicana, or CROM), which had been holding protests and sit-down strikes over the mass layoffs from the casino closing. They began organizing the outraged people in the neighborhoods, demanding that Castillo Morales be immediately "brought to justice"—lynched. An angry mob gathered at the military base and, whipped to a frenzy, burned down the nearby police station, then moved to do the same to the fort itself. Soldiers in the fort marched out to meet them and opened fire, killing one protester and wounding five others.

Frightened by the growing civic chaos, the local military leadership quickly convened a court-martial and tried Castillo Morales. Indicative of its desperation, the tribunal convicted Castillo Morales and executed him in the local cemetery that same day.

After the swift justice came the long regrets. Popular opinion slowly turned, not least because of its distrust of the military. Before long, Castillo Morales, the alleged rapist-murderer, had morphed into Juan Soldado (Juan the Soldier), innocent martyr to government corruption. A religious cult, outside of the official Catholic Church, developed around Juan Soldado. In time, this unlikely martyr became the patron saint of all those who try to enter the United States illegally. Miracles ascribed to Juan Soldado are regularly reported across Northern Mexico to this day.

American sailors in faux jail. Typical souvenir, circa 1943.

Children from San Diego and Tijuana at San Ysidro Kindergarten, 1931.

On a more positive note, Tijuana's residential neighborhoods were now filled, and newer ones were being built. The growing population demanded and got new schools, including a professional trade school, the Industrial Technical Institute of Agua Caliente. Most importantly for the city, its industry had branched out from entertainment and hospitality to new ventures in manufacturing. These pioneering manufacturers were primarily agricultural, especially foodstuffs such as pasta, bread, olive oil, and beer (the nearby Tecate Brewery was founded during this decade). By national decree, Tijuana also opened a trade zone—designed to make up for the economic losses from Prohibition's end and Mexican president Cárdenas's ban on gambling—to speed the transfer of foreign goods into Baja California. Interestingly, much of the electrical power that drove these new businesses came across the border from San Diego.

WARTIME BORDER

Mexico was, in fact, part of World War II. After Pearl Harbor, in solidarity with its northern neighbor, Mexico broke diplomatic ties with the Axis powers. (This break might have been propelled, at least in part, by the scandal of the Zimmerman telegram before World War I, in which the kaiser offered the US Southwest to Mexico, in exchange for a military alliance with Germany.) Five months later, when a German U-boat sank two Mexican tankers in the Caribbean, Mexico declared war.

Pearl Harbor and the loss of much of the US Pacific Fleet had exposed the vulnerability of the US Pacific Coast and sparked fears of an imminent Japanese invasion. One such fear was that the Japanese would land on the even less defended coast of Baja California, most likely in Ensenada, then march up through Tijuana to attack San Diego and its naval bases. To defend against this scenario, California called for the Department of War to dispatch the US Army across the border to guard those potential Mexican landing points. As a measure of the hysteria at the time—Japanese-Americans in California were being rounded up and interned in camps, and antiaircraft fire at phantom bombers was raining down shrapnel on Los Angeles—the military agreed.

On December 10, 1942, an American force moved to the border at Tijuana and prepared to enter the sovereign nation of Mexico, with or without permission. It was met by a Mexican force under the command of General Lázaro Cárdenas (who had just stepped down as a celebrated reformist president of Mexico) and composed of both soldiers and local civilian volunteers. They refused entry to the Americans, barricading themselves in nearby buildings in preparation for a fight. As described by an observer:

> Everyone was looking toward the border in an agonizing wait . . . The hours passed, and no one moved from their positions, until the time came when the American troops began to move from the border toward San Diego.

It could have been the lowest point in the relationship between the two cities and their respective countries in a century. Instead, and happily, the confrontation was used to establish a new wartime relationship. The two commanding officers, Cárdenas and General John L. Dewitt, held a series of meetings (two in Tijuana's closed Agua Caliente casino and one at Fort Rosecrans in San Diego's Point Loma). They reached a consensus agreement that kept American soldiers (at least armed soldiers) out of Mexico and provided for significant technical defense assistance from the United States. (This arrangement created a precedent for discreet cooperation that would come in very handy decades later, in the far different context of civilian law enforcement.)

Mexico's involvement in World War II did not end there. In fact, it reached France, where Mexico deployed an aviator squadron, Squadron 201, the only Mexican aviation unit to fight in the war. In honor of those aviators, Escuadrón 201 is now the name of the street that runs past many of Tijuana's top restaurants.

For the rest of the war, the two nations worked together harmoniously, even on nonmilitary matters, including a treaty dealing with the use of their shared rivers—not just the mighty Colorado and Rio Grande but also the Tijuana River. That treaty is still in effect today.

LIFE DURING WARTIME

As the two nations grappled with these larger issues, on the ground the two cities were dealing with changes brought by life during wartime. In Tijuana, the challenge was handling the battalions of marines and flotillas of sailors rolling into town on leave, pornographic "Tijuana Bible" comic books in their pockets, wandering Avenida Revolución drunk, in search of a good time. Tijuana was happy to oblige.

According to Piñera and Rivera, "This atmosphere was complemented with bold floorshows in nightclubs and the sale of marijuana and drugs in addition to the customary alcoholic beverages."

Not surprisingly, some servicemen were also spoiling for a fight. La Ballena, with its legendary long bar, was the site for several of these brawls, which typically began between US Marines and GIs or sailors, but often ended with the marines taking on the Tijuana constabulary. So common did these fights become that marines were barred by Tijuana from visiting the city, a serious decision given how much money they brought to the local economy.

Still, there was enough other business to bring a level of prosperity that Tijuana had never known, even during the twenties. Those end-less waves of American soldiers in uniform kept Tijuana's businesses humming both day and night. Meanwhile, tourists continued to visit, nearly all of them because of gas and rubber rationing at home. They came from Southern California to both enjoy a weekend and stock their larders when goods were available. In response, Tijuana saw an explosion of new businesses: restaurants, stores, even more saloons, car-repair garages, and the ever-present curio shops.

Less apparent at the time, but crucial for the future, was that much of this money was being invested in a wave of new manufacturing busi-nesses in the city, catering to the huge budget of the US war economy. These new industries, at the moment almost entirely small-scale oper-ations, would prove the basis for the next chapter of the Tijuana story.

ON A WAR FOOTING: THE BRACERO PROGRAM

Meanwhile, another historic change was at work. After Pearl Harbor, the United States economy quickly moved to a wartime footing. As a million American soldiers went off to war, even more Americans went to work in aircraft, munitions, and other military-supply fac-tories. The aircraft industry, in large part based in the Los Angeles area, grew from forty-nine thousand workers in 1939 to two million in 1943. The secondary effect of this massive labor shift was to empty American farms of their workers, not least in California's San Joaquin and Imperial Counties, together among the US's biggest food sources.

Desperate for replacement farm labor, the US government took an unprecedented step: it turned to Mexico for help. The result was the Bracero Program, an agreement between the two countries, signed in August 1942. The program, in theory, allowed Mexican *braceros* (laborers) to cross legally into California and temporarily work for US agricultural firms and individual farms, picking crops and performing other labor. Those firms, in turn, were to guarantee the workers' health, housing, and safety. In practice, the reality was much less enlightened. While many American farmers and other employers lived up to the agreement, others forced their laborers to endure racism, mistreatment, and unhealthy, unsafe conditions. For their part, many Mexican participants in the program, largely desperately poor campesinos from Central Mexico, anxious to get a piece of the wealthy country to the north, bypassed the formal entry process and entered the US illegally.

As for Tijuana, it suddenly found itself flooded not just with American sailors heading south for fun but with Mexican peasants heading north for months of paying work in California and the Pacific Northwest. Many of these southern migrants who waited to cross the border, legally or illegally, encamped in Tijuana. Some even decided to stay, making their new home a base for seasonal trips into California. The result was that the population of Tijuana not only jumped again—from sixteen thousand residents in 1940 to sixty-five thousand at the end of the decade—but in the process the city grew large enough to support neighborhoods, districts, even north and east commercial zones.

Ultimately, the Bracero Program would last two decades, profoundly impacting both Mexico and the United States. Though it would experience a number of scandals and strikes over work conditions, the program did, at its peak, employ a half million Mexican workers, a boon both to the Mexican and US economies. It also served as the beginning of new commercial and labor relationships between the two countries that would culminate ultimately first in the maquiladora movement, then the North American Free Trade Agreement (NAFTA) in 1994, and then its successor, the United States-Mexico-Canada Agreement (USMCA—T-MEC in Mexico) in July 2020.

A POST-WAR BOOM

Optimistic, expansive, filled with new enterprises and institutions, Tijuana emerged from the war years with tremendous momentum. The sailors, marines, and GIs on leave whose disposable income had generated most of this growth (as well as the accompanying crime) largely disappeared with demobilization. But after a brief post-war recession in the US, they were replaced by tourists. The war was over, and returning American servicemen quickly married and set off the greatest baby boom in history. Just as important, the car culture that had been percolating in the US for decades—previously thwarted by the unreliability of early automobiles, the Great Depression, and the war rationing of gasoline—now boiled over.

Americans, now increasingly new families, hit the road. It was the rise of the Great American Vacation. Those road trips weren't confined to the States but also encompassed visits to (if not stayovers in) border towns, most of all Tijuana. Many of those tourists were the same people who had frequented the city on shore leave just a few years before, who now wanted to show their families a bigger world.

Even more important, many American servicemen, having seen that bigger world during their tours of duty, found themselves no longer content in their hometowns. They moved, in a nationwide migration that lasted the next quarter century, south and west, in search of milder climates, better opportunities, and, most of all, new lives. No state was more affected by this migration than California, and soon expansive new suburbs popped up around Los Angeles, in the San Francisco Bay area and of course in San Diego.

Each of these factors multiplied the pool of potential visitors south of the border.

Tijuana in those years enjoyed its own demographic boom, thanks to new residents who had arrived in the previous five years. The city itself, so many years burdened with chronic poverty, now had the funds to embark on a major infrastructure upgrade. Roads and other services were improved. More than a dozen public elementary schools were opened in the city and its environs. Private schools for the wealthy also opened their doors. Churches—not just Roman Catholic but Protestant—sprang up everywhere. Social clubs emerged—not least the Masons, with three lodges. A baseball diamond. A library. Radio stations. And the capstone jewel, an impressive new jai alai facility in the center of town, the first on the West Coast.

The growing car culture in the States also impacted the face of Tijuana. Gas stations, garages, upholsterers, painting booths, and tire recappers popped up near the border, offering tourists deals they couldn't find at home. Before long, the city's main avenues experienced daily traffic jams, predictably worse on the weekends.

For the first time, Tijuana began to look, and behave, like a real city, not merely an amusement park for Americans. The downtown now featured hotels and four-star restaurants, retail stores, and, of course, endless craft and curio shops. Meanwhile, out in the neighborhoods, children filled the sidewalks on weekdays, going to and from school. On Sundays, families, in their finest, walked to Mass or to local parks.

Tijuana had always been a chameleon, able to transform itself on a moment's notice, to respond to the changing interests and desires of San Diego and the United States. But this transformation may have been the most impressive. Within two years, the city metamorphosed from a notorious magnet for drunken, lascivious American service-men to a colorful, family-friendly destination for young Yankee families. It never fully escaped the Black Legend, but it distanced itself enough that millions of tourists in the years to come willingly crossed the border, unafraid of encountering (too much) visible crime or vice (at least until the kids were tucked in). What Tijuana now offered was a hybrid: the frisson of adventure in an exotic and different culture that still bore a recognizable and comforting American touch.

As the forties ended, Tijuana, always the poor cousin of San Diego, began more and more to resemble its neighbor, as it became increasingly self-supportive. Several local newspapers opened. The city even gained its own airport, as well as its first homegrown airline, Aerovías Contreras, flying between Tijuana, Mexicali, and Ensenada. Tijuanenses could also listen to their own radio station, XEAZ, or better yet to XERB from nearby Rosarito Beach, whose 50,000-watt transmitter could be heard across Mexico and the Southwestern US (some nights even in Canada) and which, briefly, served as the home of legendary DJ, Wolfman Jack. Further, in 1953, the year after a presidential decree made the northern half of Baja California the twenty-ninth Mexican state (which enabled the city to elect its first local government), Tijuana's bilingual TV Channel 6 went live—the second such station after Mexico City's, and in the same year as San Diego's first television station.

THE MEXICAN MIRACLE

Alongside these developments, the late 1940s also saw the continuing influence of the political parties born from the revolution twenty-five years prior. In particular, PRI (Partido Revolucionario Institucional, or the Institutional Revolution Party) held a monopoly on power in the country from the 1920s until the end of the century, ruling as a de facto autocracy. PAN (Partido Acción Nacional, or the National Action Party), which became the key business-oriented opposition party in the 1930s, was always strong in Baja California and elected the first PAN governor, Ernesto Ruffo Appel, in 1989. It was not until the 2000 and 2006 elections that PAN finally won the presidency of Mexico, with the victories of Vicente Fox and Felipe Calderón.

From 1946 to 1952, the country's president was Miguel Alemán Valdés, the first civilian after a string of military presidents, and the first for the modern PRI. His tenure saw a burst of industrialization throughout the country—the so-called Mexican Miracle—but also considerable corruption. His successor, Adolfo Ruiz Cortines, whose administration covered much of the 1950s, extended the Miracle, while simultaneously countering corruption and implementing fiscal austerity. Cortines also gave women the right to vote.

Nowhere was the Mexican Miracle more visible, certainly in Northern Mexico, than in Tijuana. This era of stability and continuity—running in parallel to the United States' own prosperous and peaceful post-war decade—enabled both cities of the San Diego-Tijuana Coastal Plain to bloom. In Tijuana, arts and culture exploded as never before, producing important artists and writers and founding a celebrated symphony. By 1957, Tijuana had opened its first institution of higher learning, the Autonomous University of Baja California (UABC), the first in the state.

But not all the news was good. In 1951, a terrible fire at the El Coliseo building killed numerous people. In the now-crowded city, both crime and corruption were on the rise. One of its victims was crusading journalist Manuel Acosta Meza, who was murdered in 1956. That same year, attempting to deal with its crime problem, Tijuana opened a state penitentiary. Two years later, it opened a city jail.

Many of the new immigrants to the bright lights of Tijuana were poor farmers from Central Mexico. Finding the city teeming and real estate prices climbing, many chose to set up squatter camps in the dangerous (as we have seen), mostly dry riverbed on the Tijuana River, hoping eventually to earn deeds to their squats. When the city tried to extricate them, the squatters found the support of PAN, which saw potential new voters in its endless battle with the PRI. This all came to a head in the elections of 1959. Growing tensions surrounded life in Tijuana in the weeks before the election. PAN claimed a runaway victory, but after the PRI-dominated state police and Army seized the ballot boxes, the government claimed that the PRI had won a narrow victory. Violence by furious PAN voters threatened to spill out onto the streets of Tijuana in the worst riots in the city's history. To head off conflict, the state governor ordered the arrest of the local PAN leadership, who quickly escaped across the border. In Tijuana, a nervous peace returned.

A CITY TRANSFORMED

Still and all, Tijuanenses could look back on the 1950s as a time of relative peace, prosperity, and growth. In 1960, a year it celebrated a spectacular new bullring and a municipal auditorium, the city housed 165,000 citizens. Downtown, the first high-rises were beginning to appear, and in the surrounding hills, elegant new homes were under construction. At the border, the tourists still arrived in droves, feeding the local economy. But now Tijuana, with a growing manufacturing base, no longer depended entirely upon those tourists. In the intervening years, the city had developed an identity of its own, apart from its counterpart centered fifteen miles north.

Leaders in the city had a growing sense that it was time for Tijuana to transform once again. While the city still carried the stigma of the past, those memories were beginning to fade. Further, Tijuanenses were beginning to understand the fundamental hypocrisy of the Americans' attitudes toward Tijuana: Americans crossed their southern border because Tijuana endlessly adapted to provide much of what was not legally available in the States, but they would hold the city in contempt for doing so. Then, a generation later, Americans legal-ized many of those activities, feeling pure and innocent as they did so. Prohibition was quickly forgotten, the most extreme sex shows in Tijuana in the 1940s were available in movie theaters across the US by the 1960s, abortion became legal and divorce easier, and marijuana, sold illicitly on the backstreets of Tijuana, would be sold in shops across the States by the twenty-first century. Yet the stigma seemed to stick only to Tijuana.

Among the civic and business leaders of Tijuana—and soon, the leaders of San Diego—an understanding began to grow. It was time for the two cities, born together and fitfully sharing the same destiny, to recognize their common purpose: to evolve beyond a century of mutual exploitation toward something, despite the border between them, more like a partnership.

This change would begin in the 1960s, but slowly, and only after San Diego had undergone its own changes.

CHAPTER FIVE

San Diego—City in Motion

Looking back, the opening of the Hotel del Coronado in the 1880s, and the new class of people it attracted to San Diego, seemed to act as a catalyst for change across the entire city. A working port town until then, it began to look like a destination for the idle wealthy and the sophisticated. In quick order it gained the San Diego Yacht Club, the Cuyamaca Social Club, and the Excelsior Rowing and Swim Club. Ulysses S. Grant Jr. arrived in town, bought the Horton House Hotel, and moved into a mansion. Then the city built an elegant opera house.

More practically, San Diego finally overcame its biggest obstacle to growth: the lack of a reliable water supply. Thanks to the Southern California Mountain Water Company and its subsidiary, the San Diego Flume Company, water from the headwaters of the San Diego River was diverted into pipes and delivered to the heart of San Diego. The locals celebrated the arrival of the piped water by shooting it in fountains 125 feet into the air.

The man behind the water, John Spreckels, would become the most powerful figure in San Diego for the next forty years. Spreckels had made his name in sugar, added water to his portfolio, and now, as he moved from San Francisco to San Diego in 1889, decided to invest in real estate, commercial buildings, and other interests. His timing couldn't have been better.

The San Diego Flume, circa 1886.

The boom of the 1880s, which had fundamentally transformed the face of the city, was about to tip off the cliff into the Panic of 1893. Fortunately, Spreckels was not only a great businessman but a fiscally prudent one. With his big new sugar warehouse in the city, he weathered the economic storm, surviving even when the 1893 crash was followed by another in 1896, while his once-prosperous neighbors failed. Further, he used their bankruptcies as an opportunity to snap their businesses up for a song. As they failed one by one, he took over the city's streetcar lines and numerous established businesses.

By 1903, Spreckels had acquired most of Coronado, the Silver Strand, and North Island. Most famously, he bought the biggest jewel of them all, the Hotel del Coronado, as the crowning move in his strategy to incorporate separately the city of Coronado. Not many citizens complained, at least not publicly, because Spreckels also bought the *San Diego Union.*

Spreckels Organ Pavilion, 1915 Panama-California Exposition opening in Balboa Park.

Spreckels may have been a distant cousin of the robber barons back East, but he was also a dedicated booster of his adopted city. He met any criticism of San Diego—such as the suggestion by Los Angeles that visitors south should bring their own water because San Diego's was so unpalatable—by noisily fighting back on the pages of the paper. In the eyes of many, for good or evil (and it would prove to be both), John Spreckels began to personify San Diego.

Like the rest of the United States, San Diego spent much of the 1890s just trying to survive. The impact of the two panics might not have been as great there as other places in the United States (for example, unemployment in Michigan hit 43 percent), but the city hardly escaped unscathed. Besides all the businesses that Spreckels bought at discount, San Diego also saw five of its eight banks fail. In the final ignominy, the beautiful new Fisher Opera House went broke, was bought by Katherine Tingley of the Theosophical Society, and was used to perform her plays and promote theosophy.

CITY OF THE FUTURE

After the economic struggles of the 1890s, San Diego entered the twentieth century comparatively quietly. Now a city of seventeen thousand people, sizable for California in that era, San Diego was still relatively isolated, which had kept it from much of the explosive growth that other cities, notably Los Angeles, had experienced. If tiny Tijuana (population one thousand) looked north at its neighbor with envy and resentment, San Diego did the same to its bigger northern neighbor.

At the time of the Mexican War, the two California cities had been about the same size. San Diego may have had the advantage of its bay and superior moorage, but it was also in the most extreme corner of the United States and difficult to reach by land. Los Angeles, by comparison, had the advantage of location and superior overland accessibility, in addition to its seaports. The difference paid off quickly: LA got its Southern Pacific rail line in 1867 and the Santa Fe railroad in 1885, making it, aside from San Francisco, the most connected California city in the nineteenth century. By the end of that century, Los Angeles's population, at 102,000, was more than five times that of its little neighbor to the south.

As if that wasn't enough, Los Angeles also used its location—in particular, the fact that you basically had to pass through the Los Angeles Basin to get to the border—to choke off access to San Diego. With superior economic and political power in the state, Los Angeles used its weight to get what it wanted, often at the expense of San Diego. One of the biggest examples was water, always a valuable commodity in the arid Southwest. Already, by 1900, Los Angeles's need for water had become insatiable. Soon, with the help of engineer William Mulholland, its aqueducts were sucking much of the available water out of the region.

Adding insult to these injuries, Los Angeles also would soon have its own local source of revenue: oil, discovered in 1921. Then, in the city's defining twentieth-century event, the infant motion-picture industry, in search of four-season sunshine in which to film outdoors, began to move to Los Angeles in 1907, cloaking it with the mythical luster of Hollywood that continues to this day.

In the face of all of this, San Diegans could only look on from 120 miles to the south with what would become an obsession. The junior city began smugly to model itself as "not Los Angeles," with all the comforts of the ocean and the Southern California climate but none of the crowding, crime, and smog of its big brother. This positioning would continue for most of the twentieth century.

UTOPIA ON THE PACIFIC OCEAN

The first decade of the twentieth century was a legendary time for Main Street America, when the United States enjoyed both general prosperity and growing influence in the world. As both roads and railroads improved, more Americans began to move west in search of the palm trees, white beaches, and orange groves they saw in the first silent two-reelers. By decade's end they would triple San Diego's population.

New housing developments began to pop up around the city. The most unusual was Little Landings, conceived as a utopian community by historian William Smythe, newly moved to San Diego from Massachusetts. Caught up in the muckraking journalism of the era, Smythe declared San Diego corrupt and ruled by monopolies. His response was to purchase 550 acres south of the city in the Tia Juana district, divide the parcel into one-acre plots, and sell them for $250 to $550. Smythe's marketing hook for Little Landings: it would be a cooperative agricultural community of "a little land and a living." In theory, the working-class owners would be able to escape exploitation by the big trusts, by growing their own food and working as independent craftspeople. In reality, the area was filled largely by professionals who, after attempting to become farmers and share their profits, gave up and went back to their professions. Nevertheless, Little Landings retained its bohemian image for years.

During these years, John Spreckels expanded his already overwhelming influence in the city. He had finished his extraordinary 1890s by outbidding the competition for the rights to publish the county tax lists, installed a state-of-the-art linotype machine, and brought in the managing editor of the *San Francisco Call*, another paper he owned, quickly making the *San Diego Union* the dominant paper in the city and

Spreckels the dominant voice. He cemented his position in September 1901, by buying the *San Diego Tribune* from E. W. Scripps, making San Diego essentially a one-newspaper town. By 1907, he had moved both newspapers (published separately in morning and afternoon editions) into a landmark, six-story building.

A long-standing concern among San Diegans, beyond Spreckels's growing power, was his loyalty. He remained a two-city man, traveling back and forth between his interests in San Diego and San Francisco. That ended in 1906, with the great San Francisco earthquake and fire. Seeing years of economic distress and restoration ahead up north, Spreckels permanently decamped to San Diego. In the process, he became even more engaged with the city. Working with Scripps and retired sporting-goods magnate A. G. Spalding, he set about transforming the look of San Diego and its environs. They extended and graded for automobiles the many roads leading out of the city, thereby bringing young towns from Escondido to El Cajon into San Diego's orbit. At the end of one of those roads, at La Jolla, Scripps's sister, Ellen Browning, sponsored the creation of the Marine Biological Association (now the Scripps Institution of Oceanography), destined to become one of the world's greatest research institutions. Finally, the trio purchased the old city presidio and the hill—San Diego's own so-called Plymouth Rock—to preserve it for future generations.

Late 1905 through early 1906 was a period of natural catastrophes in California. Besides the near-destruction of San Francisco, in Southern California the Colorado River overran its banks in the Imperial Valley and created the Salton Sea. Suddenly, quiet, isolated San Diego looked even more appealing by comparison, spurring even greater growth.

By the end of the decade, San Diego was feeling so optimistic about its future that it decided to plan its own world's fair, to be called the Panama-California Exposition, timed with the opening of the Panama Canal in 1915. The city had reason to be optimistic: In just a few years, San Diego had gained a half dozen banks, a theater, a new water source on the San Luis Rey River, and a stunning new community at Ocean Beach. The huge new U. S. Grant Hotel construction was finally completed after years of being stalled by the fragile economy, and highrises were beginning to appear in the city's skyline.

The US Grant Hotel, circa 1910.

Now San Diego was ready to show itself off, and how better to do so than to invite the world to a fair? What better way to attract all those ships passing through the new canal to the first port they would encounter on the Pacific Coast of the United States? Preparations for the fair began in earnest. It was to be centered on the city's mammoth 1,200-acre park, now officially called Balboa Park to connect it to the Spanish explorer, Vasco Núñez de Balboa, who first crossed Panama and saw the Pacific. In violation of the city's long-standing plan for the park to remain pristine and natural, the new city leaders decided to construct a number of buildings in the ornate, Spanish Baroque style. Many survive today, reminders of the transformative fin de siècle years in San Diego, including the spectacular dome-and-tower California State Building (now the San Diego Museum of Us), Fine Arts Center (now the San Diego Museum of Art), and the Cabrillo Bridge. As much as the old mission, they would come to symbolize the city of San Diego and set the stage for the Panama-California Exposition in the next decade.

A final event of the city's first decade in the twentieth century—and one that would have a profound impact on the future of Tijuana—was the groundbreaking for the new San Diego & Arizona Eastern Railway. This, too, was a project of John Spreckels, who somehow found the time to pursue it amid all his other activities. Tijuana, though still little more than a village, had been in the consciousness of a small number of San Diegans, including Spreckels, as a place to invest, as a tourism and shopping destination, and as a gateway to trade with Mexico. Because of the topography of the Tijuana Valley, Spreckels had little choice but to track his new railroad south through Tijuana, then eastward along the Mexican side of the border to skirt around the rugged Laguna Mountains, then back north to cross the Imperial Valley. It proved an enormous, time-consuming effort that required twenty-one tunnels and cost $18 million (the equivalent of $500 million today).

This scenario proved fortuitous to Tijuana. From now on the border town wouldn't depend just upon the revenues of occasional day visitors but could benefit from a transportation link to far-flung markets. Entire trainloads of goods and travelers would stop at the customs house to pay their fees and, in the case of the passengers, tour the town. From its inception, the railway (operated as the Carrizo Gorge Railway for many years, and today as the Baja California Railroad), changed Tijuana. In an important way, Tijuana could now envision itself as a potential business partner of San Diego, even when the feeling was not quite yet mutual.

CITY ON DISPLAY

Three events dominated San Diego in the second decade of the century, in order: the Mexican Revolution, World War I, and the Panama-California Exposition. Between them, they would leave the city and its image around the world recast.

When the Mexican Revolution erupted in 1910, it interrupted what, for San Diego, had been a half century of relative peace and growth. Given its proximity to Mexico and the battles that took place in and around Tijuana in 1911, of course the conflict boiled over into San Diego, as told in the previous chapter.

World War I naval formation in Balboa Park, 1917.

Indeed, San Diego became its own battleground, this one mostly of ideology, as the revolution moved into Baja California. The Magonistas were essentially anarchist in their philosophy and as such, received heavy support from America's homegrown anarchist party, the IWW. As the Magonistas began to enjoy victories in Mexico, IWW members from across the West, but especially from Los Angeles, poured into San Diego to influence local politics and recruit new soldiers for the Magonistas. Even the IWW's famous spiritual mentor, Emma Goldman, publicly called on San Diego and Washington, DC, to remove all federal troops from the border.

They quickly confronted local shopkeepers, made speeches on city corners, and called for the overthrow of capitalism in the city. San Diego responded by passing an ordinance against these activities, and when that didn't work, police arrested forty-one of the ringleaders. That, in turn, led to a protest by a mob of five thousand locals and outside instigators, demanding their release. The mob was broken up with fire hoses. Next a citizen vigilante committee formed to drive the IWW out of town, which largely succeeded. When socialist Joseph

Mikolasek arrived in town to organize, he managed to get himself shot, leading to another riot. This was barely quelled when Emma Goldman herself arrived in San Diego, only to be bundled onto the next train and unceremoniously run out of town.

WORLD'S FAIR

The Panama-California Exposition opened in Balboa Park on January 1, 1915. The First World War had already been underway in Europe for five months. While it did impact the Southern California economy later (mostly in a positive way, thanks to military contracts), it had little effect on the celebrations of the day. As the crowd cheered, President Wilson, in the White House, pressed a button that turned on a light—from across the continent—hanging from a balloon floating over the exposition. Guns at Fort Rosecrans and on ships in the harbor roared. A fireworks show at the Spreckels Organ Pavilion lit up to show a replica of the Panama Canal being traversed by a ship with "1915" on its prow. The governor of California was there, as was a representative of King Alfonso XII of Spain, and, representing the US government was Vice President Thomas Marshall, former president Theodore Roosevelt, perennial presidential candidate William Jennings Bryan, and Secretary of the Navy (and future president) Franklin Roosevelt. To highlight and promote automobiles at the exposition, four travelers drove a motorcar from the exposition to Washington, DC. The trip took twenty-three and a half days.

Visitors marveled at the rococo buildings, the bridge, exhibits, and perhaps most of all, the brand-new San Diego Zoo, whose resident animals had been assembled for the exposition. The zoo quickly became a treasured jewel of the city and a source of considerable community pride. That boost led to its continuous growth and ever-greater municipal support, in time making it one of the finest zoos in the world.

The Panama-California Exposition formally closed on December 31, 1916, to the playing of taps, the singing of "Auld Lang Syne," and a fireworks display reading "World Peace 1917"—ironic, as that would be the year the United States entered WWI. But the impact of the exhibition would extend for years in the pride of the citizens, the image of the city around the world, and the improved infrastructure and stunning new structures and institutions that survive to the present.

THE PARTY NEXT DOOR

For San Diego, the 1920s began in horror, defined by the first global pandemic, the Spanish Flu, which killed tens of millions of people. San Diego wasn't spared—an estimated 202 citizens died from the disease, mostly young and middle-aged adults. Simultaneously, the United States passed the Eighteenth Amendment and the Volstead Act, bringing either the triumph or the frustration (depending upon your point of view) of Prohibition. In response to the flu, the city could only nurse the sick, bury the dead, and mourn. Regarding Prohibition, though, thirsty San Diegans could head south, to that thousand-person town across the border, with its still-legal saloons.

Before that moment, few San Diegans knew anything about Tijuana. Even fewer had ever visited the place. But now, with cheap liquor just fifteen miles away, they began to make regular visits. As they did, they also took advantage of the growing number of gambling places and bordellos, the racetracks and bullring. They also saw opportunities for investment, and as they invested in their own edifices, such as the Agua Caliente hotel, casino, and resort, San Diegan visitors lingered even longer.

San Diego spent those heady years solving many of its water concerns, building dams, and asserting its regional watershed rights. However, it opted out of the nascent Boulder Dam project on the Colorado River, while Los Angeles shrewdly built an aqueduct and took care of its water needs for generations. San Diego's own efforts were given additional impetus when both the San Diego and Tijuana Rivers again flooded. In the process, the Tijuana River destroyed the artist village of Little Landings.

In 1926, the two defining builders of modern San Diego, Spreckels and Scripps, died. They had already been replaced by a new generation of city leaders and real estate promoters. One of this generation's signal achievements was the creation of the planned suburb of Rancho Santa Fe, in a location so appealing that the king and queen of silent film, Douglas Fairbanks and Mary Pickford, established a ranch there, setting a trend that would last beyond the Second World War—Hollywood stars building ranches and vacation homes in San Diego. Meanwhile, throughout the county of San Diego, the smaller towns—Encinitas, La Mesa, Chula Vista, National City, Escondido—grew rapidly in the economic penumbra of San Diego. The city held up its end by building roads and other infrastructure, movie theaters, a museum atop Presidio Hill, and its first radio stations.

San Diego's shining moment came in the mid-twenties, when a local airplane manufacturing company, Ryan Airlines, received the contract to build an experimental monoplane, designated the Ryan NYP, for $10,580. As the company built the plane, it was regularly visited by its future pilot, a young man named Charles Lindbergh, who was going to attempt to win the $25,000 Orteig Prize for flying solo, nonstop across the Atlantic. Lindbergh named the plane the *Spirit of Saint Louis* after his hometown, but it might just as well have been the *Spirit of San Diego* for that city's contribution. On May 20, 1927, Lindbergh lifted off from a field in Garden City, New York, and flew into history. By the time he landed near Paris, the world knew of San Diego's contribution to aeronautics, a reputation that would change the city's future.

CRASH

The cost of becoming a major player in the modern world was that you also had to share in its economic crashes. The Great Depression hit San Diego just as hard as anywhere else in the United States. In the grim words of historian Engstrand, "[t]he mild climate in San Diego made standing in breadlines at least more comfortable."

As might be expected, the Depression mostly paralyzed the growth of San Diego, now a city of 150,000, as it did Tijuana, which also suffered from the end of Prohibition. Still, there were some positive developments. For example, the city started its first professional (minor-league) baseball team, the Padres. At the end of the decade, San Diego cheered local boy Ted Williams as he reached the majors and became one of the greatest hitters in baseball history.

Perhaps the most important event of the decade in the city was the construction of the new San Diego State College campus, born from the forty-year-old San Diego Normal School. It was, controversially, located ten miles east of downtown, and it was dedicated on May 1, 1931. The Mission Revival–style buildings of the college were designed to house two thousand students. Ninety years later, it has a student body of thirty-five thousand and an alumni base of nearly three-hundred thousand graduates.

But overall, the 1930s were a mean, angry decade. San Diegans watched helplessly as Los Angeles hosted the 1932 Olympics to global acclaim. Meanwhile, at home, the city suffered racist incidents against Mexican children from Tijuana commuting to study in San Diego public schools.

One ongoing development that only gained momentum during the Depression years was the growing presence of the military. San Diego had enjoyed a military presence since its founding, but just prior to World War I, the US military had become a major force in the daily life of the city. In 1904, President Theodore Roosevelt's Great White Fleet stopped in the city for four days on its voyage—a demonstration of US naval power—around the world. Aviation pioneer Glenn Curtiss's flight tests in San Diego, notably the first-ever seaplane flight, transformed aviation. The US Army Signal Corps training school moved to North Island in 1911, and the site became Rockwell Field a year later. The year after that, the US Army established Camp Kearny in Mission Valley (the Navy would later take over the site and rename it Camp Elliott). By 1925, the Navy had established the Eleventh Naval District Headquarters in San Diego, a military hospital, and ten naval and marine bases. That year, to inaugurate San Diego's new importance as a military port, 125 US Navy warships, including battleships, sailed into San Diego Bay.

Now, as the 1930s came to an end, and war clouds once again loomed, San Diego military operations took on a vital importance. Already a city of two-hundred thousand, after Pearl Harbor it saw its population multiply as vast numbers of sailors and marines converged on the port to be shipped out to combat in the Pacific. Meanwhile, the demand for war-industry work drew another fifty thousand civilians to the city. The result: during the war years, San Diego looked like an immense, crowded dormitory, with young men on leave hitting the blacked-out town or going south to Tijuana; women rushing to work in factories each morning; military and civilian hospitals swollen with wounded; and a bay swarming with the most powerful warships ever seen.

During this period, the city's infrastructure was pushed to the limit and regularly threatened to collapse. Linda Vista, a 1,500-acre housing development funded by the federal government, was built to relieve some of the pressure. Incredibly, it saw the construction of three thousand houses in two hundred days. A year later, another 1,900 homes and four schools were built.

Linda Vista housing project, World War II.

Meanwhile, the Marines purchased 125,000 acres of Rancho Santa Margarita and built Camp Pendleton, the world's largest military base, and the Navy established a naval aviation base at Miramar.

CARS AND THE CORPS

By the end of World War II, the US military's presence in San Diego was so embedded that, though it diminished, it never really left. Most of the bases survived. Their new role was to protect the West Coast of the United States in the Cold War, and to project America's interests in what increasingly was being described as the emerging "Pacific Century." Young sailors and marines who had passed through the city on their way to war, now, in the post-war boom, looked back fondly on their time under the sun and beneath the palms in San Diego. They decided to get married, have children, and settle down there, even overlooking several of the coldest winters on record.

Those who left the military and entered private careers fed the area's growing technology industries. Those who stayed in the military would eventually turn San Diego into one of the nation's biggest retirement communities. Young sailors still arrived every year to join the fleet, which dominated the bay, and new Marine recruits arrived to endure boot camp at the Marine Corps Recruit Depot and then deployment to Camp Pendleton.

But beyond its growing image as a military town, another important cultural force was at work in the 1950s, redefining the future of San Diego: the American car culture. Cars were now better built and more reliable, gas was no longer rationed, and soon, the new interstate highway system would make every part of the USA—even the southwest corner of the country—reachable in a matter of days. A defining image of the era was the American nuclear family jumping into the station wagon and racing to exotic vacation locations that even twenty years before would have been unreachable in the limited time available. The grand opening of Disneyland in Anaheim in 1956 made Southern California one of the world's most popular destinations.

Even more than that, the choke point that Los Angeles had always represented to frustrated San Diegans became a portal by virtue of the automobile. The armies of tourists heading to LA could take a day trip to San Diego and discover its own wonders, such as the city's legendary zoo. Tijuana, too, benefited, especially in those years of comparatively open borders, because those same San Diego visitors could take a vacation within a vacation, all in a couple of days, and experience life in another country. These new visitors—family-oriented, culturally curious, and bearing disposable income—quickly transformed the tourist, entertainment, and hospitality offerings of both cities. They could even try out a brand-new, San Diego–based fast-food restaurant named Jack in the Box.

By 1950, San Diego was a city of 330,000 citizens—the previous decade of growth exploding the city's physical development in every direction, even across Mission Bay. In the process, downtown became less important, at least in retail services, as stand-alone shopping malls popped up in residential areas. In an effort to retain government control over these new regions, San Diego embarked on a twenty-year program of annexing newly developing neighborhoods and suburban cities until, by 1970, it would grow from ninety-nine to 307 square miles. Between its geographic growth and its new arrivals, San Diego would more than double in size to seven hundred thousand residents by the end of the 1960s.

Interestingly, and perhaps because a sizable portion of the population (particularly the voting public) were now retirees on fixed incomes, despite all this growth San Diego's attempts during these years to improve its physical infrastructure ran into one obstacle after another. Some projects, such as a public auditorium (San Diego was the largest city without one) and a new sewer system to prevent raw sewage from flowing into San Diego Bay, failed because voters didn't support a bond issue. Others that did succeed, such as the development of Mission Valley and Mission Bay, and the construction of a freeway through Balboa Park, typically met with considerable local resistance.

The one area where San Diego saw the most success during the immediate post-war period was in education. The University of California had been eyeing the city as the next home for one of its campuses. John Jay Hopkins, chairman of the two biggest local aerospace firms, Convair and General Dynamics Corporation, desperately wanted the presence of a scientific research university nearby. So he decided to kick-start the process by offering a one-million-dollar grant to help the UC system begin construction. He further sweetened the deal by offering to build his own ten-million-dollar research center nearby.

It worked. On July 10, 1956, Hopkins was invited to dedicate the site of the new University of California, San Diego, on the mesa at Torrey Pines, fourteen miles north of downtown San Diego, in La Jolla. There the university would build a close relationship with an adjacent research center, the Scripps Institution of Oceanography.

Perhaps not surprisingly, UC San Diego would become one of the world's leading research universities, especially in the biological sciences, not to mention the wellspring for a number of independent medical and genetic research foundations and laboratories that would make La Jolla one of the most important basic and applied research communities on the planet.

BUILDING CONNECTIONS

Thanks to its rapid growth and growing reputation, a fundamental shift in San Diego's perspective occurred toward the end of the 1950s and the beginning of the 1960s. Though its old envy of the giant metropolis to the north remained, the city now felt surer of itself. Increasingly, it saw itself on its own terms, not in relation to Los Angeles. As this feeling of civic pride grew, the city found itself looking in a different direction: south, to that little town, now exploding to a population of nearly eighty thousand residents. Tijuana, forever tantalizing but treated as invisible, could no longer be ignored.

Tijuana was ever mindful that it shared the fate of its northern neighbor, San Diego, in good times and bad. Now San Diego began to understand the same about its southern neighbor. Every year, the connections between the cities grew stronger, as did their sense of common destiny.

Already in the 1930s, children of wealthier Tijuanenses families crossed the border each weekday to attend school. At first, these students met entrenched, institutional racism. But as the years passed and San Diegans became accustomed to Mexican students in their schools, as their kids played after-school sports and made friends with their Mexican classmates, the first social ties between San Diego and Tijuana began—ties that would strengthen as these schoolchildren grew into adults and community leaders on both sides of the border.

Meanwhile, a growing number of residents from Tijuana were crossing the border into Chula Vista and San Diego to work with landscapers, in restaurants, and as domestic helpers, and to shop for goods they couldn't buy at home. Though on a given day the sum total of these Mexican citizens in San Diego and its environs amounted to a scant percentage of the total population, those numbers would soon grow.

As they did, civic connections linked up as well, beginning with a collaboration between the San Diego and Tijuana sewage systems to deal with emergency overflows that threatened to release raw sewage into the Tijuana River. An unusual point of connection, perhaps, but this was the start of the two cities coming together to solve common problems. By the end of the decade, the Bracero Program was in full swing, with thousands of Mexican farmworkers crossing the border, heading east to the Imperial Valley and north to San Joaquin Valley, with thousands more waiting south of the border for permission to do the same.

At the dawn of the 1960s, San Diego was on the brink of the greatest period of growth in its history, much of it propelled by the Vietnam War, the space program, and the Electronics Age. During that decade, once again these game-changing developments would alter San Diego's relationship with Tijuana as both cities started to recognize not just their shared history but also their common destiny, one filled with great potential.

CHAPTER SIX

The Fifty-Year Conversation

In retrospect, the 1960s saw the first glimmerings of a new, richer relationship between Tijuana and San Diego. It happened almost invisibly, largely through personal connections between individual citizens of the two cities. Clearly, there were a growing number of reasons—commercial, environmental, political, and social—for these cities to bind more closely together. But there were also a number of other sources of friction—historical and cultural—keeping them apart.

At the beginning of the decade, the gravitational forces dominated. Tijuana happily welcomed tourists and investors from San Diego and certainly enjoyed taking their money. As a boy in Tijuana, José ("Pepe") Galicot, who would become one of the city's most important retailers, learned that Mexican money (which he tried not to take) "was called 'silver' (plata), while American money was called 'gold' (oro)," a measure of the currencies' perceived worth.

But behind Tijuana's welcoming smile there was considerable contempt for the Americans. After all, Mexico had been one of the six cradles of civilization, the Aztecs the most powerful empire in North America for a thousand years. The North American portion of the Spanish colony of New Spain was already one hundred years old when the Pilgrims arrived at Plymouth Rock, and when the British colonists in America were still clinging to small patches of ground on the Atlantic Coast, Mexico City was already a thriving metropolis, boasting one of the world's most magnificent cathedrals. In 1802, before Jefferson's Louisiana Purchase from Napoleon, it was New Spain, not the United States, that appeared more clearly headed for world domination by the end of the nineteenth century. But now, these upstart hypocrites were strutting through Tijuana, flashing their dollars, looking down on Mexicans as uneducated peasants, and moralizing about their sinful behavior while indulging in it? How many times—Aaron Burr, defeated Confederates, filibusteros, con men like Dick Ferris—had Americans tried to conquer Baja California or mainland Mexico?

In the United States, the Mexican War was little more than a footnote in school history books, best known as the training ground for the important generals of the American Civil War. But in Mexico, and certainly not least in Tijuana, 120 years later, that war loomed large, a wound that would not heal. In the aftermath of Guadalupe Hidalgo, Mexico lost half of its size, some of its finest territory, and—including the California gold rush that exploded just days after the treaty—much of its wealth. It did not help that even one of the American heroes of that war, Ulysses Grant, later admitted to Mexican president Díaz that he had always thought the war was unjust. In his memoirs, Grant would call the war "one of the most unjust ever waged by a stronger nation against a weaker nation," even admitting he thought the American Civil War was, in part, God's punishment for attacking Mexico.

Nor did it help that Americans seemed to know nothing about this history. American tourists may have seen wide smiles on the faces of the Tijuanenses they encountered, but if they had looked into their eyes, they would likely have seen something far less welcoming.

If proud resentment was the mortal flaw in Tijuana's attitude toward its neighbor to the north, on San Diego's part, the greatest impediment to an authentic relationship was disdainful and dismissive prejudice. Sure, San Diegans were happy to purchase produce and merchandise from Tijuana farmers and craftsmen and to buy their services cheaply. But aside from Mexico's handcrafted furniture, San Diegans saw manufactured and finished goods from south of the border as little more than junk. Ignorantly, that attitude extended to most of the citizens of Tijuana and Mexico.

Tourist postcards sold in Tijuana display this attitude, typically featuring a cartoon rather than an image of the city. Historian Oscar Jáquez Martínez:

> The single most widespread image is probably of a campesino reclining against a saguaro [cactus] with his knees drawn up to his chest and his sombrero tilted over his face while he takes a siesta. When a woman is portrayed, she typically has a high lady-of-Spain hairstyle and is wearing a frilly, low-cut, off-shoulder dress. Her head is thrown back gaily, and yes, she has dark "flashing" eyes and a rose in her mouth.

Lazy Mexican men and loose Mexican women, donkeys painted with zebra stripes, cactus, and adobe walls—this is what the average American citizen imagined when he or she thought about Tijuana. They also thought—and not without reason—of vice, crime, drugs, corruption, and banditry. Of the first, historically Tijuana had been a den of vice (not to mention a place to procure quickie divorces and abortions), but what Americans failed to remember and refused to admit was that its own citizens were the primary financiers and consumers of those services. Not to mention that Tijuana had since morphed into a very different place. Of the rest of the black marks, in the previous one hundred years Mexico certainly had its share of corruption, assassinations, and violence, but other than the events surrounding the 1911 revolution, Tijuana had not seen much more organized violence than had San Diego. Still, the bandit raids, the Battle of Tijuana, Richard Ferris, and the incursions by Pancho Villa into Columbus, New Mexico— nearly all of it in the twentieth century—was not easily forgotten by the northern neighbor.

Both cities now had a lot to forgive—or more importantly, forget. That process—leaving the past to seek a new, common path into the future—began with a series of personal relationships and individual accomplishments that depended upon help from people across the border. For fifty years, San Diego and Tijuana would engage in a dance, two steps forward, one back, before their partnership would emerge on the public stage.

The story of today's relationship between Tijuana and San Diego is considered by many to begin, of all places, at a ranch forty miles outside Tijuana, in the tiny village of Tecate, in 1939.

RANCHO LA PUERTA

I didn't choose to be there. My husband had to leave the United States because he was an illegal alien. A Hungarian. His Hungarian papers were not renewed because he didn't go to fight on the side of Hitler. There were hundreds whose papers did not get renewed who had to leave the United States. This was a tremendous brain drain from the US, sending out all the university professors as enemy aliens. Mexico got the energy of all these Europeans, mostly Jewish, who were kicked out of the States. Nobody stayed on the border. They went to Mexico City. I insisted on living on the border because my parents were moving to San Diego. We looked at Mexicali, and we looked at Tijuana, and oh, Tecate! We had no choice.

Deborah Szekely is ninety-eight years old. She has seen the entire story of Tijuana and San Diego as they evolved from the Wild West ("It wasn't really the Wild West, but that's how we considered it"), through the Depression and the explosive growth of both cities during the Second World War to today's twin metropolises. But most of all, she was there at the start—indeed, her Tecate ranch, Rancho La Puerta, and ever more, her exclusive resort, the Golden Door, near Escondido— are considered by many observers to be the sparks for much that has followed.

It didn't start out that way. Because her husband, Edmond, carried no valid documents, he was considered illegal on both sides of the border. Concluding that he had a better chance of escaping deportation in Mexico, the couple made their way to a plot of land they named Rancho La Puerta. The property sat outside of Tecate, at the time little more than a collection of small houses and a population of just four hundred. For the next nine years, Professor Szekely would hide out at that ranch, rarely visiting Tecate, much less Tijuana itself. It was only after the war, when he was no longer considered an enemy combatant—and by which time, he was friends with local police—that he dared to venture far. So it fell upon Deborah Szekely to find a way to keep them alive in their sanctuary.

Luckily, Deborah Szekely's already-extraordinary life experience had prepared her well for the task. She had been born in Brooklyn in 1922, to health-obsessed parents. The family was fruitarian—that is, they only ate raw fruits, vegetables, and nuts—and her mother was vice president of the New York Vegetarian Society. Deborah spent her childhood attending health lectures on weekdays and hiking to health camps on weekends.

After the 1929 crash, as fresh vegetables and fruits became scarce and expensive in Manhattan, her parents decided to decamp the family, including seven-year-old Deborah and her brother, to a place where both were in abundance: Tahiti.

There the family met Hungarian scholar Edmond Bordeaux Szekely, a relatively ineffectual, but charismatic, student of early civilizations—in particular, how the natural living of those cultures could be applied to the unnatural world of modern life. So taken was the family by his teachings that even after returning to the United States, they regularly attended Szekely's health camps in California and Mexico. By the time she was sixteen years old, Deborah was Dr. Szekely's secretary. "The professor was totally helpless about day-to-day practical details," she would recall. By age seventeen she had married him.

A year later, Deborah found herself living in a tiny adobe house with a dirt floor, married to a man without a country, in a village with fewer residents than a typical Manhattan apartment building. But her years in Tahiti had prepared her for this: "When we settled the ranch, I didn't have to learn from scratch. We had nothing, but I could make do. If I'd been just a little girl from Brooklyn, it wouldn't work. But I was the girl from Tahiti."

Dr. Szekely could not risk going into Tijuana or San Diego—at least not until the war was over—because he might be arrested and sent back to Hungary, where his life would be imperiled. There wasn't much demand for lectures on ancient history and nutrition among the mostly illiterate residents of Tecate, subsistence farmers who spent their days working the land.

But Edmond had a loyal following, and Deborah had business savvy, organizational skills, marketing acumen, and a will of iron. During their first summer in Tecate, the couple invited visitors to pitch a tent at Rancho La Puerta, where, for the price of $17.50 and two and a half hours of labor a week, they slept under the stars, bathed in the nearby river, and listened to Professor Szekely's lectures by kerosene lantern. His talks must have seemed radical at the time, but the subject matter is familiar today. Deborah: "We read and discussed and tried every health discipline and diet theory . . . bean sprouts and acidophilus milk, total fasting and interval fasting, the grape cure, the mucus-free diet, morning walks, and mud baths."

Just as World War II had forced the Szekelys' move to Tecate, indirectly the war provided the seed money that Rancho La Puerta needed to expand its operations. When the fighting reached Java, the British rubber company Balfour, Guthrie & Co. evacuated the spouses of their British employees. "Their husbands were gone," Szekely explains. "[They] all became prisoners of war." The women had nothing—no papers to travel back to England, no tickets home. While the company worked out the details in San Francisco, the women "were dumped on us. But Balfour Guthrie paid their room and board, so it was very helpful."

Under Deborah Szekely's guiding hand, Rancho La Puerta grew from a place to pitch a tent in the summer to a year-round retreat with accommodations in decommissioned military storage structures, to a world-class resort, one of the very first such institutions in Northern Mexico.

It wasn't long before word got out about this unusual retreat just across the border. Thanks to Tijuana's venerable Agua Caliente resort and its thermal waters, Southern Californians already were accustomed to Mexico offering a superior health spa. Rancho La Puerta, with its more spartan regimen of fish and vegetarian food alternating with fasting, appealed to the growing numbers of health fanatics. Among those passionate Americans were Hollywood movie stars. Some came on the recommendation of their peers; others were drawn south of the border to indulge in lesser passions.

Deborah shrugs:

> In those days we didn't have a regular mayor. But we
> had the local officials. Anything we needed, anything,
> they smoothed it over. Sometimes, a movie star would
> get drunk and find himself on a bench at the police
> station. They were never put in jail, or even booked.
> They never even asked the person his name. We'd just
> get a call saying, "You have a guest." And that was that.

That warm relationship with law enforcement had other benefits.
Before long, Professor Szekely was able to travel around the region
undisturbed. Everyone recognized the important contribution the
Szekelys were making to the local reputation and economy.

Partly because of their initial circumstances, as well as Deborah's
personal philosophy, Rancho La Puerta hired almost exclusively local
Mexicans for its staff. At first, nearly all were illiterate.

Deborah:

> They couldn't even sign their names. They were so
> embarrassed. If they were given a check, they would
> have to put their fingerprints on it [for validation].
> They didn't want people to know. So I'd be sitting in
> my office doing something, and I'd hear, "So-and-so is
> in the other room. Could she have a moment?" All that
> poor woman wanted was to leave her fingerprint and
> get her check where no one could see. So the first thing
> I ever taught anyone was to sign their name.

Before long, Deborah had started a school. The first school for
adults in Tecate, it offered a one-year program that taught her growing
number of employees how to read and write. Two generations later,
the grandchildren and great-grandchildren of those first students are
nearly all college graduates.

A source of pride for the region, "the Ranch," as Deborah calls it,
continued to serve as a mecca for Hollywood celebrities, for many their

first real contact with everyday, hardworking Mexicans. The result was a transformation in many individuals' attitudes north of the border.

Deborah knew how to customize the experiences of these VIPs by making their visits unforgettable. For example, for Burt Lancaster, a regular, she installed a trapeze so he could exercise his lifelong craft. She didn't go quite so far for others, but everyone, whether celebrities or tourists, came away with an experience all but unmatched in the States. It wasn't long before the Szekelys were able to buy the Ranch—which, because of Mexico's rules against foreign ownership of property within sixty-two miles of the border (the so-called Forbidden Zone), they did by putting the deed in the name of one of their loyal Mexican employees. (Mexicans who assumed that role were called "Storm Men.")

Szekely's tenacity impacted more than her business dealings. In fact, it was her penchant for finding opportunity in unexpected places that enabled Deborah's husband to become a Mexican citizen after nine years:

> My mother had been ill, and I used to spend the night with her [in San Diego], and then early, early I would go to the ranch. One morning, very early, we're talking about like 6:30 or 7:00 in the morning, I drove by Rancho Florida, the house where the president [Alemán] stayed, and there were all the soldiers. Usually we knew in advance when he was going to be there. He had the house for parties; people came from Hollywood. Alemán liked the good life. Anyhow, when he was there, everybody knew about it. But we hadn't heard anything [this time], and there he was.
>
> So I drove to the ranch, and I told my husband, "Get dressed. Tie and jacket. The president's there." He grumbled, grumbled the whole way going, but I insisted, "Nobody knows he's there."
>
> [The soldiers] saw our car drive in. Nobody stopped us. They assumed at that time in the morning—like 7:15 or 7:00—we knew what we were doing. We just drove into the porte cochere, which is just opposite the

breakfast room. We walked in, and there he was, having coffee all by himself.

So my husband had [written] two books on Mexico, which he presented, and we talked and explained our situation. There was a young man in the pantry, and [Alemán] sent for him. He said, "Take the names and dates and everything." The young man took the information and the president shook our hands and we went home, and my husband grumbled, grumbled the whole way back. You know, because he had to get dressed in a suit and tie in the morning.

About two weeks later, the mayor's office called. They needed [Edmond's] fingerprints. He was a Mexican citizen. Then the land could be ours. The first thing he did was get a green card so we could cross the border.

Though Deborah refers to the event as a "happy accident," she seems to have an innate ability to make such accidents happen.

By the 1950s, Deborah and Edmond had grown apart. He had continued with his research and lectures, while she had become one of the first important businesswomen on either side of the border and, increasingly, a major force in numerous business development and nonprofit initiatives in both Tijuana and San Diego. Rancho La Puerta was no longer big enough for Deborah. She had trained new management to lead the place, and she set her sights on a bigger dream: opening the world's first elegant fitness resort. In 1958, she set out to make that dream real.

The resulting resort, located just north of San Diego in Escondido, was called the Golden Door after its beautiful entrance portal. Initially, it was essentially a large ranch house with accommodations for just twelve guests (all men or all women) per week. It pioneered many of the experiences that are now copied throughout the world—yoga classes, exercise instructors trained in modern dance, "fitness days," and more. Old clients and new, not least those from Hollywood such as Robert Cummings, Kim Novak, and Zsa Zsa Gabor—and, of course, Burt Lancaster—switched their allegiance to this new resort.

Rancho La Puerta has been named one of the world's best destination spas.

This time, there was no long ramp-up period as there had been at Rancho La Puerta. The Golden Door was an immediate hit—and so successful that Deborah was able to rebuild everything behind those now-famous doors into her original dream of a Japanese retreat. Tellingly, even though the Golden Door was fifty miles north of the border, she filled its staff with Mexican citizens, saying that during her years in Tecate she had come to admire the hard work, dedication, and entrepreneurial spirit of the Mexican people.

These days, as she approaches her one hundredth year, Deborah Szekely is still busy at work. She sold the Golden Door in 1998 to an investment group, and she turned over control of Rancho La Puerta in 2011 to her daughter, Sarah Livia Brightwood. (Two days after Brightwood was born in San Diego, Deborah registered her birth in Mexico. Still a Mexican citizen, Sarah now serves as her mother's official Mexican partner.) Deborah continues to visit both sites regularly, offering lectures to guests.

For her work, Szekely has earned numerous honors on both sides of the border. She was the first woman in California (and the fifth in the US) to receive the Small Business Administration Award. For a quarter century (during the Nixon, Ford, and Reagan administrations) she served on the President's Council for Physical Fitness. She still sits on numerous boards, including the Save the Children Federation for Mexico, the Claremont Graduate University, and the National Council of La Raza, as well as numerous other community organizations. The San Diego Rotary has named her Mrs. San Diego.

Both the Golden Door and Rancho La Puerta remain thriving, celebrated operations. Indeed, in 2019, sixty years after its founding, the Golden Door was named the number-one spa in the world by Condé Nast Traveler.

But more than the spas and the awards, the future is likely to celebrate Deborah Szekely's greatest achievement as showing the proud people on both sides of the border that they could work together, building on each of their strengths to create something virtually unparalleled on earth. From World War II to the Internet Age, Rancho La Puerta and the Golden Door have stood as shining examples of what can be accomplished when old grievances and superior attitudes are laid to rest in service of a vision that benefits the whole region.

BIRTH OF A MOVEMENT

It was wonderful. It still is. I thought everyone had the
opportunities that I did, where you get to experience

the wonderful things that Mexico had to offer and then the wonderful things that California had to offer. I commuted two years to school in San Diego, to a private school, for first and second grade. I remember not knowing English when I started school there. But when you're young, you just learn, I guess. It's just easier. I also remember going to restaurants, too, when I was young. And Disneyland. And the San Diego Zoo.

Alejandra Mier y Teran was born in Tijuana in 1971. After two years of school in San Diego, she entered the school system in her hometown, eventually graduating from the Instituto Tecnológico Autónomo de México (ITAM), located in Mexico City. Today, she is executive director of the Otay Mesa Chamber of Commerce, a position she has held for twenty years. Otay Mesa is one of the southernmost districts of San Diego, right up against the border. Mier y Teran also lives today in San Diego where her son, Simon, attends Saint Augustine, a prestigious Catholic high school. He is emblematic of the next-gen, thoroughly binational Norteamericanos who are emerging in the region.

For her entire life, Mier y Teran has lived a cross-border life, traversing the invisible line as easily as the political circumstances of the moment would allow. Throughout her childhood, Tijuana was the neighborhood where she and her siblings would explore the nearby streets and walk the two miles to buy ice cream cones, never feeling less than safe. San Diego, by comparison, was her playground. While Tijuana in those days had few parks (even today it still does), San Diego seemed to have more than its share—even for an American city. And a zoo. And shops that sold beautiful items. It was a child's fantasy, especially for the daughter of an increasingly prominent Tijuana citizen.

Mier y Teran remembers her father, Enrique Mier y Teran, as a cheerful man, thoroughly humane, open-minded, and ebullient— Saint Nicholas-like—who played with his children whenever he got the chance. He was also an important figure in the history of Tijuana. In the late 1950s, at just fourteen years old, he came to Tijuana from Mexico City. A natural entrepreneur, within a couple of years he had established a small manufacturing company, making contracted goods for local companies. Then came the turning point in his young life.

Despite being underage, he was sitting in a bar in San Diego and struck up a conversation with another man, an American:

> My dad apparently asked, Well, what do you do for liv-
> ing? And the other man, whose name was Ron Kalin,
> replied, Well, I manufacture this and that, including
> hairpins.
> So my father started asking, How much does it
> cost for you to do such and such?
> Kalin told him his production costs, and my dad
> was like, Really? I could do that for you for a lot less.
> That's how it all started, in a bar.

Remarkably, what came out of that meeting, a contract manu-facturing agreement between a company in San Diego and a supplier factory in Tijuana, almost had no historic precedent anywhere along the US-Mexico border. This innovative relationship even got its own name: maquiladora (from the Mexican-Spanish word meaning "to assemble"). A maquiladora is an assembly plant in Mexico, near the United States border, where parts are shipped and assembled, then the finished product is shipped back across the border.

At this point, Enrique had been in town for just two years. He was so young that historians have often credited the maquiladora move-ment to his father, whom Enrique would bring into his business. But the truth was that eighteen-year-old Enrique Mier y Teran had just discovered Tijuana's future.

THE BENEVOLENT GODFATHER

José Galicot has lived the changes in Tijuana and San Diego—and has been part and parcel of the cities' developing relationship—for over seventy years.

He arrived in Tijuana as a young boy with his family, in 1946. Galicot recalls seeing remnants of World War II: camouflage nets hung over the roads in both cities to hide them from potential air attacks, and signs demarked the evacuation routes from San Diego south through Tijuana into Mexico. He also remembers his first impression of his new hometown: chokingly dusty from the infrastructure neglect of the war years. At that time, the population of Tijuana had swollen to twenty thousand, and the town was struggling to catch up.

The border of Galicot's childhood was so porous his family would often pass between the countries to purchase staples or even as a lark. "My father told me: 'Don't simply go there. Take advantage of the two worlds.'" Even currency exchange was relatively nonexistent: "We had our [wartime ration] cards that we could use everywhere to buy oil, butter, shoes . . . If I wanted to buy something, I'd just go over there, as if it was my own downtown. The relationship with the people of San Diego was comfortable."

Galicot's father was a small businessman selling supplies such as thread and silk linings to Tijuana's (and Mexicali's) outsized population of tailors catering to American customers. He operated his business out of his car, bringing ten-year-old José along on sales and delivery runs, to teach him the trade. The currency of exchange was always American dollars—the "gold."

Despite José's value as a helper, Galicot's father insisted he attend school. It was not a pleasant experience for the boy: "They were very tough schools. And they had no equipment or supplies. You even needed to buy your own desk and bring it to class." The classrooms were crowded as well, with as many as sixty students to a room. But most of all, the educational system itself was incomplete: primary school finished at age nine. For secondary school, a child had to leave the family and go to school in Mexico City, where José stayed through college, earning a degree in civil engineering. (One of his friends from those years was Carlos Slim, who would one day become the richest man in the world.) It was only in 1957 that Tijuana finally had its own university, where Galicot earned yet another degree, this time in economics. In between, Galicot served as president for a Jewish youth organization for Latin America, speaking at the world's first Young Jewish Congress.

José Galicot came home to Tijuana at age twenty-three to become a businessman. It was the 1960s, and life was good for Galicot. His first job had been working for his uncle in a small store, making $18 per week. José's wife, Ana Raquel Levine Galicot, was a teacher in the city's much-improved schools, making $50 per week. Friends joked that he had married her for her money. Meanwhile, the Galicots were assiduously saving their money until, in 1964, José was finally able to scrape together $1,000 and open a business for himself. He worked all day in his shop, then at night cut fabric to patterns, which would be sewn and sold as finished attire, such as jackets.

Galicot specialized in buying perfumes and fashion goods in Europe—some unavailable in the US, other items cheaper than in the States—and selling them in his shop, primarily to San Diegans. By picking the right merchandise, turning it over as fast as possible, and giving Americans the bargains they were looking for, Galicot quickly grew that $1,000 to $10,000. He wasn't alone in pursuing this business model, just among the most successful. Before long, Galicot opened his own clothing factory.

Factories were starting to open everywhere—and paying very low salaries. The Americans began to appreciate that it was worthwhile to start manufacturing their merchandise here. Pretty soon, almost everywhere you looked in the United States, people were using items made in Mexico. Galicot:

> I realized that something important was going on here. Factory buildings were going up everywhere in Tijuana. But they were all closed to outsiders, guarded from entry. The people who worked in them weren't talking much, but I could sense it was something big—and I just had to know more.

It took months, but Galicot was eventually able to get a sense of the magnitude of this new world of manufacturing in Tijuana, much of it contract work from American companies. He set out to join this maquiladora movement. But he was a small-time manufacturer, and he knew next to nothing about building a large-scale factory. So, instead, he played to his strength: sales.

Galicot opened a department store, selling many of the products made in those factories, as well as other items from around the world. Though it targeted Americans by offering bargain prices on European goods, especially perfumes, the store also drew a growing number of Tijuanenses who were becoming prosperous owning or working at those new local factories. This had two effects: Americans learned that they could visit Tijuana not just for cheap crafts and bullfights but now for the most luxurious items available anywhere. Tijuanenses also had a new source of pride—they no longer had to travel to San Diego to acquire the best; they could now enjoy their new lifestyle with items bought in their hometown.

The department stores were a huge success. By the late 1960s, José Galicot was one of the wealthiest men in Tijuana.

"And then in 1976 came another devaluation," Galicot recalls ruefully.

Employment and prosperity on both sides of the border—but especially in Mexico—had long been dependent upon the relative value of the two countries' currencies, which typically varied with their respective rates of inflation. When the peso became too expensive versus the dollar, Americans stopped buying south of the border, the economies of border cities such as Tijuana collapsed, and unemployment skyrocketed. The same was true in reverse, but the impact more muted, except for business right along the border. In 1976, more than two decades after the previous adjustment, the Mexican government, believing the peso too inflated, devalued the currency by 45 percent. According to historians Louis Harrell and Dale Fischer:

> The unexpected magnitude of the 1976 devaluation caused immediate and severe shocks to border economies. Goods and services in the United States became prohibitively expensive for Mexican consumers. Mexican out-shopper activity was drastically reduced. Some United States counties along the border were hit so severely that they qualified for federal economic disaster aid.

No retailer along the border felt the impact of this crash more severely than José Galicot. The US was already in recession, reducing the numbers of his valued American customers; now the Mexican economic collapse tightened Tijuanenses belts as well. Still, instituting austerity measures, Galicot resolved to carry on. Then, in 1982, the government devalued the peso once again, this time by 30 percent.

According to Harrell and Fischer, "The equivalent peso price of goods and services in the United States increased by 70 percent, causing a painful shock to border economies."

It was the last straw for José Galicot and his department stores. "I lost every penny that I had made. I had to begin again. But where?"

He found the answer in telecommunications. Tijuana was becoming a global community, and its businesses (and citizens) needed a connection to the international communications grid. With his longtime connections to industry in Europe, Galicot set out to find a carrier that could serve his city. He found it in the Swiss company, BBG Global AG, and Galicot accomplished the seemingly impossible: he founded a second empire, this time not just in Tijuana, but in San Diego as well. By the end of the 2010s, BBG Telecommunications was handling hundreds of millions of phone calls and data transfers each month.

Eventually, leaving the business to his two entrepreneurial sons, Rafael and Gregorio, who expanded and diversified the enterprise, José Galicot decided, as we shall see, to devote the rest of his life to good works and further strengthening the bond between Tijuana and San Diego.

THE BICENTENNIAL

While cross-border business relationships were starting to grow, another chapter of the San Diego-Tijuana story was being written, interestingly enough, during the preparations for the two-hundredth-anniversary celebration of the founding of the United States.

Dr. Mary Walshok, who was at the time a professor of sociology at UC San Diego, would play a central role in initiating the cross-border era. Walshok:

> It started with a group of the San Diego elite. This is the seventies, so, it was kind of "The Establishment, Inc." These were the people who helped raise money for the symphony, the people who served on library commissions. It was the small elite in a Republican military town. But there was this consciousness,

both of the border but also of history. Membership included Bill Rick, whose company, Rick Engineering, had designed and built Mission Bay Park; Mickey Fredman, who was a real estate attorney and had many clients from both sides of the border; Marine general Victor Krulak, who was commander of the San Diego Marine Corps Recruit Depot (and whose son, Charles, would hold the same position and go on to become the thirty-first commandant of the Marine Corps in the 1990s); Deborah Szekely; *San Diego Union-Tribune* editor Jerry Warren, and the leading local newspaper columnist, Neil Morgan.

Many of these people lived or worked near the border, and most of them knew Jack Killea, who had been the US consul general in Tijuana. Through him they knew Lucy Killea, who had been in the foreign service and who came back to UC San Diego (UCSD) to earn a PhD in Latin American history. She was often at Francis Parker [School], where her children went to school. My kids went there, too, as did [philanthropist] Yolanda Walther-Meade's children.

So there were a number of social bonds already in place.

All of these details are important, because in 1975 they all came together: all of us connected to Francis Parker School, Lucy coming to UCSD, and city leaders of San Diego searching for a way to celebrate the Bicentennial, not to mention the newspaper editors wanting to write more news and thus sell more advertising in the cross-border region.

Now, add to all of this an understanding by everyone involved that you couldn't celebrate the history of the region without including Tijuana in the story. This group wasn't just visionary but also opportunistic—they wanted more business across the border.

The result was *Fronteras de las Californias*—Frontiers of the Californias. They had in the person of

Lucy Killea someone who was intellectually grounded, not to mention well connected. She approached my then-boss, the dean of the extension program, about developing the content of the Bicentennial program. He assigned me to work with her. That's how it began.

Ultimately, Killea and Walshok—joined by Elsa Saxod, a long-time civic leader of binational relations—organized a year-long series of public musical and cultural events to celebrate the Bicentennial in 1976. The events drew large audiences from both sides of the border.

It also had a long-term impact. Says Walshok: "There was a broader consciousness about San Diego's historical roots in Mexico."

Elsa Saxod:

> The *Fronteras de Californias* program was slated to shut down at the end of the year. But [San Diego mayor] Pete Wilson instead set up an office to keep it going. It wasn't part of the city structure, but it got money from the city. Wilson said, "Our future is tied to Tijuana, to Baja California, and the rest of Mexico, and not to Los Angeles." He was the first politician who said, "This is where we have to be looking: south." From what I heard from Lucy, he then went to the city council and said, "This is important. It'll be a growth for our economy. We need to keep it, and we need to fund it."

Looking back, Mary Walshok says, "I think this process was what differentiates us profoundly from the places like El Paso and the other border cities. In those places the relationships and the border environment were primarily transactional and business-anchored. Here, it was a cultural, social, and historical sense of a shared history. It was *personal*. And that enabled us to develop a deeper level of trust."

Fronteras de las Californias would, within a few years, lead to the founding of the San Diego Dialogue. That organization would set the foundational agenda for San Diego's relationship with the border and Tijuana, an agenda that would last right up to the present. Says Walshok, "Who were the founding members of the San Diego

Dialogue in the late 1980s? The same people who were with the forum from Fronteras de las Californias in 1975, 1976, and 1977."

CRISIS, CORRUPTION, AND CRASH

The late 1980s were a painful time of transition for San Diego. The city was beset with scandals in the government that sent a number of leading citizens to jail. Even more devastating were the multiple banking scandals of the era—the Charles Keating Savings and Loan crisis, US Financial scam, the Dominelli fraud, the Pioneer Savings and Loan Ponzi scheme—which together cost depositors and taxpayers across the US hundreds of millions of dollars.

Based in Irvine, one of Keating's banks, Lincoln Savings, did considerable business in San Diego. Because it was in a rapid growth phase, the city was especially hard hit, resulting in a collapse of home sales and new construction. All this revealed a weakness that would culminate years later when San Diego was caught up in a municipal pension fund scam that nearly bankrupted the city and saddled San Diego with nicknames such as Enron by the Sea and the Fraud Capital of America. Further besmirching the city's name was a judicial scandal that resulted in the felony RICO (Racketeer Influenced and Corrupt Organizations Act) conviction of three of its superior court judges— the only such cases in California history.

Notoriously arrogant except when dealing with Los Angeles, the city found these experiences humbling. Among the positive results of confronting serial fraud in its own midst was a change in attitude: San Diego opinion leaders became more understanding and tolerant of the "defects" in Tijuana they had always so readily identified and condemned.

Then, beginning in 1989, with the fall of the Soviet Union, the US defense industry underwent a massive reduction, cutting the size of the military, redirecting funds ("the peace bonus"), and eliminating many government contracts. San Diego, where defense was nearly 50 percent of the economy, suffered a major blow: in fifteen months, the city lost sixty thousand jobs, sending it plummeting into a recession.

Unemployment jumped to 10.5 percent. General Dynamics, a long-time mainstay of the local economy, closed.

Walshok:

> The old local economy is imploding and then everybody says, "Oh my God, what are we going to do now?" Then they notice that there is this incredible growth still happening on the Otay Mesa and around the border, and there is simultaneous growth of the manufacturing infrastructure in Tijuana.
>
> Suddenly, people were saying, "Oh my God. Our future is tech. Our future is the border. It's not only defense contracting."

On the heels of all this, to help contribute to the city's recovery, UCSD convened a group of citizens and educators to talk about the leadership crisis in San Diego. In the process, Mary Walshok discovered that she had a gift for bringing people together to discuss issues and plan action. She decided to put those skills to work.

WATER MATTERS

In retrospect, the moment it became apparent that the two great cities of the Tijuana Valley could work together practically and, over time, effectively, centered on concerns they had always shared: water and the environment.

For two hundred years, floods, droughts, and pollution largely had been dealt with by each city alone. It seems hard to ignore these facts: Tijuana and San Diego share the same landscape, climate, and weather; and the Tijuana River, as it passes through the valley, meanders across both sides of the border. Yet for two centuries, that's exactly what both cities did.

However, as the valley became populated by hundreds of thousands of Mexican and American citizens, and as the outer edges of the two metropolitan regions grew closer, it became increasingly impossible to ignore the impact they were having upon each other. It was recognition of the environmental unity of San Diego and Tijuana that, beginning in the 1980s, broke new ground for the cross-border community.

A key figure in this pioneering effort was Paul Ganster, who had grown up in San Diego and had joined the faculty of San Diego State in 1984 as director of its Institute for Regional Studies of the Californias, a think tank focused on the San Diego-Tijuana border. In the years that followed, Ganster authored several dozen papers about the US-Mexico border area, became recognized as one of the leading scholars on border policy, and served as coeditor of the *Journal of Borderlands Studies*. In the process, he raised more than $15 million for science and policy research in the US-Mexico border region.

Beyond his unmatched knowledge of the subject, Ganster brought a singular contribution to the discussion of Tijuana-San Diego border policy: his interest in the flora and fauna of the region. In time it would lead him to chair the Good Neighbor Environmental Board, which advises the president and Congress on border environmental issues—concerns that he was instrumental in establishing.

In the early 1980s, worries about the Tijuana Valley and its environment were anecdotal, mostly complaints by San Diego beachgoers about the garbage and toxic waste flowing down the Tijuana River, polluting local beaches. These complaints were largely shrugged off, until June 1988, when Ganster held a conference at San Diego State, entitled "Water Quality Issues of the California-Baja California Border Region."

The conference was, in part, the result of desperation. The two cities could no longer ignore the water situation. The level of raw sewage in the Tijuana River, created when Tijuana's aging sewage treatment system was overwhelmed, was reaching dangerous levels. The talks presented were a breakthrough in themselves: *Roles and Responsibilities of Agencies Regarding Border Water Quality Issues, Wastewater Treatment and Reclamation, the Tijuana Estuarine Reserve, Wastewater Reclamation and Groundwater Issues, Oceanographic Factors and Marine Pollution.* Moreover, remarkable for the era, Ganster invited scientists and government officials from both sides of the border to make presentations.

The conference proved a wake-up call for the public and its officials. Government on both sides of the border had known little about what the other side was doing. The Mexican attendees were uninformed about the initiatives taking place on the American side, the tools available to help, or even the depth of American concern about the deteriorating environment. The US attendees were amazed that Tijuana, which it assumed was indifferent to the problem, was actually deeply concerned about the situation and already at work, though perpetually constrained by politics and funding challenges.

By the late 1980s, Ganster and his institute were working closely with Mexican public- and private-sector individuals and organizations, as Ganster says, "to look at the Tijuana River watershed as a unified ecosystem, which it is."

> It's just divided by an international border and very different social administrative systems. For years, we've advocated dealing with the issues of the watershed, which are most manifested by pollution in the lower end of the valley, and pollution in the near shore marine environment, which results in beach closures in the city of Imperial Beach, or the city of Coronado.

That last is important, Ganster says, because "when the contaminated waters move north to Coronado, that's when the effluent meets the affluent. And people from Coronado are never happy [when pollution] causes beach closures."

The timing of the 1988 conference was propitious. Within a year, the water situation had become so dire that the US Congress authorized the creation of the International Wastewater Treatment Plant (IWTP) on a seventy-five-acre site west of San Ysidro. The $250 million facility was officially a joint effort of the two countries, but the US government agreed to pay for the majority of the construction. The signing of the agreement took place in July 1990, and there is no question that the work of Ganster's Institute for Regional Studies of the Californias, with its conferences, papers, and meetings, played a critical role in smoothing what could have been contentious negotiations.

The plant came online in May 1997 and is owned by the US portion of the International Boundary and Water Commission.

With the IWTP, the stopgap had been built. But the challenge of extending this success by working together to solve future environmental challenges continued. So for much of the next decade, Ganster and his team captured geographic data from both sides of the border—not an easy process when even the measurements were in different units: feet and meters.

> By the early 2000s, we undertook work along with the Regional Water Quality Control Board and the County of San Diego to conduct a study and an applied research project to develop a conceptual vision for management of the binational Tijuana River watershed. We did basic scientific research, pulling together what data and information we could, and then community engagement by having hearings at different areas within the watershed.

Many of those hearings were held on the Mexican side. One, in Tecate, was especially interesting, Ganster recalls, "because we had representatives of the indigenous groups in Baja California, sand miners, ranchers, environmental activists"—individuals very different, and with very different interests, from the suburban homeowners in San Diego.

The result of all this research and these meetings was a visioning document. Its conclusion? The only way to escape future emergencies was to create some sort of permanent mechanism to facilitate binational watershed management. Because there was nothing to serve that role at the time, this, in turn, led to the rewriting of the 1944 water treaty between the two cities to enhance the authority of the International Boundary and Water Commission, established in 1889. The commissioners were even given diplomatic status so that they could talk to each other directly, thus circumventing the usual bureaucracies on both sides.

Next came the politics. Ganster and his team worked with their Mexican counterparts to receive formal acceptance of the new regulation. Meanwhile, California state senator (and former state assemblywoman) Denise Ducheny, who represented San Diego at the border and much of Imperial Valley, took it upon herself to successfully work the regulation through Sacramento.

Other early environmental pioneers were Gastón Luken Aguilar, whose family would play multiple roles over the years in the unfolding cross-border story. Luken Aguilar recalls: "About 20 years ago, I ran into friends in Mexico in the capital who were associates in business of mine, and they introduced me to the concept of the environment." At the time, Luken Aguilar was president of GE Capital Bank México, a subsidiary of General Electric, but his interest in the environment was piqued:

> I decided that I was going to phase out of business completely, except sitting on boards, and I was going to try to focus on something that I was totally ignorant of, which is the environment in which I lived. My friends told me, "You know? You live in a unique area of the world. It's called the Sea of Cortez, which Jacques Cousteau mentioned is the aquarium of the world." I mean, this thing is on the world screen. Well, you know, I lived here all my life, and I didn't know. I fished, I hunted, but I wasn't aware of what was there, except trying to catch something. This intrigued me, and then I was able to meet through them people on the scientific side, on the academic side, and I began to become gradually involved.

In his efforts to raise awareness about environmental issues in the border region, Luken Aguilar joined efforts with another environmental trailblazer, Enrique Hambleton, one of the founding members of Pronatura Noroeste, a path-breaking conservancy organization that mobilized action in the wake of the Ganster team's revelatory studies.

Luken Aguilar laments, "You know, we are terrible sons of Mother Nature. She gives us the water and we take it all, and we starve her. But you know something that's ironic? We will die first."

Also key to regional efforts was Mick Hager, then newly installed as president of the San Diego Natural History Museum. Hager thoroughly—and not without controversy—reoriented the mission of that venerable institution to take account of Tijuana and Baja California as intrinsically and eternally connected to San Diego and Southern California. In fact, many of the individuals from the US who would figure greatly in the developments to come would have their very first glimpse of Tijuana and its environs on the celebrated Baja Tours sponsored by Hager's museum and Hambleton's Pronatura.

What Ganster learned from his experience would become the hallmark insight of future cooperation between the two cities: "We need to find answers that really reflect the region's interests, not just the narrow interests of individual communities. That is, we need win-win solutions for both sides of the border, with a sense of mutual benefit and equity among all the participants."

He adds, like a true academic, "The border is a fabulous research opportunity."

THE DINNER

If there was a single event that brought together leaders from Tijuana and San Diego to meet as equals on common ground, it was, of all things, a dinner at a home in Tijuana, hosted by philanthropist and community catalyst Yolanda Walther-Meade. At the time, it seemed like a casual, one-time event, but in the years that followed, the guests would look back at "the Dinner" and realize that something profound had occurred that evening, the first step along a new path for the two cities.

Walther-Meade's husband, Jorge, was a businessman whose work regularly took him not only across the border between Tijuana and San Diego but also to Mexico City. With five children, and considerable wealth, the couple decided to maintain residences in all three locations. Further, because of the top-flight private schools north of the border, beginning in 1982 they enrolled their children in Francis Parker School, a K-12 college preparatory school that had been a San

Diego mainstay for children from privileged families on both sides of the border since 1912.

The Walther-Meades kept a home in La Jolla for many reasons, not the least of which was the challenge of getting their kids across the border each day to school. Indeed, at that time, because of the growing delays, the border was becoming known as the Turtle Crossing. Yolanda and her kids used to get up in the dark hours of the morning to make sure they got to school on time. Some mornings the passage took a matter of minutes, other times hours. Over time, Yolanda developed various stratagems to speed the passage:

> We used to get all the way to nearly the front of the line—and then try to cut in. Sometimes a driver would see all of us and let us in. Other times I'd get out and give a driver some money to let us in. Other times, the border guards (US Immigration in white shirts or US Customs in blue shirts) would open a lane and wave through anyone who managed to get hold of a government pass. Those were the best commutes.

Often arriving early, and with many of her five kids in after-school programs, Yolanda spent considerable time at Francis Parker. A naturally friendly and talkative person, she soon got to know the other parents there, in particular, the mother of a classmate of one of her sons, Mary Walshok.

It was a serendipitous connection. The two struck up a friendship, talking about their children but also about their respective lives. Yolanda enrolled her older kids in a summer program hosted by the UCSD Extension, a program now being run by Mary. Yolanda began to cherish her friendships, as well as her part-time life in San Diego.

Through Mary, Yolanda heard about the Junior League of San Diego. At the time, this particular chapter of the women's leadership organization was quite active and offered classes on local civic leadership. Yolanda asked Mary if she might nominate her, and Mary readily agreed. Both remain members today.

Because of her already-deep involvement in both communities, Yolanda was soon asked to take on ever-greater responsibilities in the Junior League, teaching the leadership seminar. It was out of this work—and in her conversations with Mary Walshok—that she realized that something needed to be done to link leading San Diegans with their counterparts in Yolanda's other world, Tijuana.

Around the same time, on April 1, 1988, Yolanda suffered a horrible shock: her husband died suddenly. Her children were eight, eleven, fifteen, seventeen, and nineteen years old. "I prayed the rosary every single day for thirteen years, to my husband, you know, and I used to feel, 'You are not here, but you have to help me.'"

It seems he did. The connections Yolanda Walther-Meade had made throughout Jorge's career helped lay the groundwork for her future civic engagement. While raising their five children on her own, she ramped up her efforts to promote her cross-border community.

The Dinner, for all its later impact, was just another event in a whirlwind of philanthropic work and networking activities Yolanda engaged in during those years.

> Mary knew it was easy for me to go back and forth between the two countries and belong to all sorts of different organizations. So one day she asked, "How can we get together businesspeople and other people from both sides of the border?"
>
> This was another level than what I was used to— not just friends, but influential people who had never met each other. I said, "Well, we can have a dinner in my home." So Mary invited people from San Diego, and I invited people from Tijuana to have dinner and meet their counterparts from across the border.
>
> My husband had been a businessman his whole life, especially in Tijuana and all of Baja, so I had met many people—in government, but especially in business—through the years. Everybody knew me because I was his wife. So I knew who to invite and how to contact them.
>
> I started making phone calls. Everybody liked the idea. The same thing happened on Mary's side. We set up the dinner outside my house because the weather

was nice. I can put about a hundred people in the area between my house and my pool, so that was a perfect, casual location where people could have dinner and talk and be comfortable.

Recalls Gastón Luken Aguilar:

It was a fine event. It was an exciting gathering of people from two cities that in many ways throughout the years have been back-to-back neighbors but that wanted to find ways of being hand-in-hand partners. This does not imply a generalization, nor that other efforts had not been made with this in mind. It was just acknowledging that it simply makes sense to partner, to be better informed, to have deeper understanding, to avoid stereotypes, to live with a broad sense of community, to build a more competitive region, to build win-win relationships, to strengthen bonds in order to weather the storms (like the one we have now), that naturally come and go. In short, to be good neighbors.

There was no agenda at the Dinner, nor did a strategy come out of it. Rather, it was simply a gathering of successful men and women from two different worlds who came together and saw themselves in each other: serious professionals building their enterprises in the face of political, cultural, and economic challenges. They may have needed translators to talk to each other, but they used the same words.

As the guests left Yolanda Walther-Meade's house late that night, they shook hands, exchanged *abrazos* (hugs), and traded business cards. No one knew what would come out of this first encounter, but they knew something had changed.

THE CONSCIENCE OF SAN DIEGO

In the twentieth century, great American daily newspapers invariably had one columnist who served as the voice, and often the conscience, of their city. In California, there was Herb Caen at the *San Francisco Chronicle*, Leigh Weimers at the *San Jose Mercury News*, Jack Smith at the *Los Angeles Times*, and Neil Morgan at the *San Diego Tribune*. Unlike his mostly quick-item, "three dot" gossip peers, Morgan was much more of a prose stylist, often writing about his day in a personal, limpid style. As he wrote in his 1963 book about San Diego, he loved his adopted city:

> San Diego ranks as the Western city most transformed by its waves of settlers.
>
> In quite suddenly becoming a metropolitan area, San Diego has accepted the missile, the atom, the laboratory, the campus, and even a casual California sophistication, which World War II visitors thought foreign to its nature.
>
> Her incomparable zoo, her bays and sea, and Mexico are as alluring as ever. Everywhere there is freshness, leisure, an air of gentleness, a benign dignity that seems to say: we put living first.

Note the presence of Mexico in this paean to Morgan's beloved city. As a survey of his columns shows, Mexico—and Tijuana in partic-ular—was always in the back of Morgan's mind. Beginning in the late 1990s he would use his column (initially entitled "Crosstown" but in time, recognizing his stature, bearing only his name) to pioneer a new way of looking at San Diego's cross-border neighbors not as an alien society but as part of the larger common culture of a single region.

Morgan was born in North Carolina and first saw San Diego, like so many other young men of the era, as a sailor during the Second World War—and like many of his generation who'd been shipped out to the Pacific, when he returned he decided to stay. He took a job at the *San Diego Daily Journal* in 1946. The newspaper spotted his prose gifts and made him its city columnist in 1946. When the paper was absorbed into the *San Diego Evening Tribune* two years later, he was invited to move his column to the bigger venue.

Before long, Neil Morgan was the most influential voice in the city. Not all of his columns were benign and upbeat about events in the daily life of San Diego. He could be controversial, even crusading—as when in 1952 he went after a local mobster's attempts to get a liquor license. As the newspaper wrote in his obituary, "He was an elegant writer who had the discerning eye of a watchdog."

Another of those controversial columns came in 1981 when Morgan proposed that Tijuana be incorporated into all future planning for the San Diego region. "He was criticized for being heretical; now that notion is commonly accepted," Karin Winner, former editor of the paper, would recall.

Morgan followed his own advice. By 1989, he was regularly including a section in his column, "Border City," describing Tijuana news. Just as important, what he wrote there treated that city not as a distant, exotic location, but as something closer to a suburb of San Diego, with many of the same, quotidian problems. Here are observations Morgan noted in 1989:

> Some real estate prices in central Tijuana are now higher than in downtown Phoenix and approaching the San Diego market level. Garage parking certainly is. A morning's parking in a twin-tower garage in Tijuana now costs more than $5 . . .
>
> From the nineteenth-floor offices in one of the twin towers that have become landmarks of the cosmopolitan new Tijuana, Atty. Gonzalo Gomez-Mont represents 20 of 23 Japanese companies that have built factories along the border. He gazes out at his adopted city and muses: "You San Diego people look north, obsessed with Los Angeles, forgetting that a small giant has been born at your back. You cherish Camp Pendleton as a wall against Los Angeles, and you think of the border as a leaky wall at your back. But San Diego businessmen come here now every day, anxious to share in Tijuana's future. They believe as I do that the future of San Diego is linked not with Los Angeles, but Tijuana."

This was not the writing of a San Diegan looking at the climbing office towers to the south through a telescope, but someone on the ground in Tijuana, seeing its changes, recognizing the common future of the two cities, and trying to carry that message home to his neighbors.

That year, 1989, Morgan was given his greatest platform to make his case about the two cities when *National Geographic* assigned him to write an essay for its special cover story on San Diego. *Nat Geo* had given similar coverage to San Diego twenty years before and devoted just two paragraphs to Tijuana. Now, the heart of the thirty-six-page cover story was an exploration of the often rocky and "growing symbiotic relationship"—notably the maquiladoras and assembly plants—between the two cities.

In his essay, Morgan celebrated Tijuana's achievements and its recent boom. But he was also unflinching—as he was in his column—about the region's challenge, much of it centered around the increasingly contentious border. He told the story of a campfire along the border and the migrants—including a young Mexican child with "brown saucer eyes" named Carlito—waiting to cross, and a sobbing woman in a red dress who had just been arrested with a truck full of marijuana, and "crack hookers" plying their trade on the north side of the border. *National Geographic* had feared that "Mr. San Diego" would be too much of a booster for his city—instead it got the unflinching eye of a reporter who celebrated the glories of the two cities but refused to avert his eyes from their dark sides.

By the 1990s, and with the merger of the *Tribune* with the *Union*, Neil Morgan's presence in the new paper expanded. Now his column became more of a single-topic feature with entire stories dedicated to cross-border relations. One of the earliest dealt with the first students in MEXUS, which, as its name suggests, was an international college exchange program between the two countries, in which graduates would earn degrees both from San Diego State and a Mexican university. In the essay, Morgan made a bold prediction:

> What . . . the MEXUS staff envisions is to graduate
> a cadre of potential local leaders on both sides of the
> border. They will be bonded by the shared experiences

of going not only to school and [the] library but also cafés, to the beach, and entertainment together, and to each other's homes.

There will be culture shock on both sides . . . but because of it MEXUS graduates will be better able to bridge cultural chasms when negotiating trans-border affairs.

Not surprisingly, Morgan was a career-long advocate of a rational border migration policy. He found a kindred soul in President Clinton's fiery new border czar, Alan Bersin, and devoted a column to him. Noting approvingly that, concerning the Mariel boatlift of Cuban refugees, Bersin had faxed a friend in Attorney General Reno's office, saying, "Let's not exaggerate the crisis in Cuba. That would be just two weeks' work for us here on the Mexican border." Morgan went on to note that:

Bersin believes that if Americans are serious about enforcing law along our southern border, we must go high tech, we must find trade-offs to encourage Mexican government cooperation, and above all we must reach some national consensus on what we intend our border policies to accomplish.

In another column about Bersin, Morgan noted that he had recently spent the night on horseback with the Border Patrol:

Border Patrol people come to work each night knowing they will lose. Unless a migrant heaves a rock their way or makes a flagrant bid to elude them, they are gentle with their prey.

They know that this border is a unique collision of the economies of the first world and the third, and the immigrants, usually docile and obedient when caught, rarely give them trouble.

After all, most Americans are descended from immigrants of another generation, and there is no

American will to shoot them. Short of that, so far, government has found no successful technique for stopping them.

Bersin spends many early mornings at the San Ysidro [P]ort of [E]ntry, with its long northbound lanes, mainly of those working in San Diego . . .

"We are going to make this a predictable port so people can plan their lives . . . We are making progress with more effective policing of the border."

In the future, Bersin hopes, Mexicans will move toward discussion of a binational authority to serve as [a] clearinghouse for border affairs. That would mean more than all the border fences.

In the early 2000s, Morgan was among the first to note that the booming economy of Tijuana—especially the maquiladora factories—was also enriching San Diego:

> The latest count of Tijuana maquiladora factories is 560. *Forbes* estimates Tijuana's population at 1.5 million and projects 3 million by 2008. Free trade "has transformed a once ramshackle place into a city that may grow as large as Chicago is today." As Mayor Golding and others argue, often with citizens who are too angry about the border to listen, San Diego profits by the billions each year from Tijuana trade, intensified by this boom.

Neil Morgan would continue to write his column until 2004, still the biggest booster of San Diego, still a thorn in the side of the city's leadership, and still writing about life at, and beyond, the border. He accumulated numerous honors for his writing, from the title "Mr. San Diego 1999" to an Ernie Pyle award. When he died in February 2014 at the age of 89, he was recognized as the individual who did more than anyone in the second half of the twentieth century to teach San Diegans who they were, to establish the city's identity, and to show it the real meaning of its relationship with its neighbors to the south.

Perhaps Neil Morgan's most important statement of his feelings about the shared destiny of San Diego and Tijuana can be found in an August 1994 column, where he describes the border between them, "swirling with treacherous cultural tides":

> Here, two metropolises touch uneasily, as unlike as cities can be, tossed against each other by history and geography.
>
> We are fenced apart but increasingly aware of our interdependence. On both sides rabble-rousers prate on, obsessed with their own myopic motives, exploiting human prejudices to breed hostility and postpone the grace of understanding. But on both sides thousands of people of good will try harder than ever to meet and hear each other out.

THE GREAT CONVERSATION

The many threads—individual, institutional, political—that had been tying San Diego to Tijuana, finally, inevitably, pulled together in 1991, with the San Diego Dialogue, a collaboration described by UC Berkeley urban and regional development historians Karen Christensen and Jane Rongerude as "a unique collaboration which brought together the University of California, San Diego; the San Diego region's emerging high technology business leaders; and business leaders from downtown San Diego's established banking, real estate, and tourism sectors."

The Dialogue's charter was ambitious at a time when the border was still at best largely ignored by most San Diegans, and at worst seen as a potential threat from crime, corruption, and growing numbers of illegal immigrants. The Dialogue's avowed goal was to "promote a renewal of civic discussion, thoughtful research, and consensus building on the future of the San Diego region . . . and to engage the public at large and elected officials in a program of regional initiatives." Telling for the time, and a measure of the historically limited interaction between the two cities, nobody from the Mexican side was invited to the conversation at its outset—a fact underscored by the program's name.

UC San Diego proved to be the key to opening a sustained cross-border conversation. Yet, focused on its own development as a world-class university, UCSD in those years had very little connection to the city of San Diego. Indeed, there was no transport link between the university and its namesake city, nor even an extension of the campus downtown, until well into the twenty-first century.

Still, the launch of the Dialogue was a historic moment. Never before, anywhere on the border of the United States, had the influential members of a major city come together to address the present and future challenges not only of that city and its metropolitan area but of an entire region, including a city in another nation. Indeed, the San Diego Dialogue would become best known for its cross-border initiatives, especially for identifying the true nature of the San Diego-Tijuana border crossing, and then developing the first practical response. In the process, by treating the Tijuana Valley as a region and not just two different nations, the Dialogue transformed the thinking of leaders on both sides.

Once again, a critical figure in the creation of the San Diego Dialogue—she had been at Yolanda Walther-Meade's dinner two decades before—was Mary Walshok, the sociologist and director of UCSD's extension program. As one Dialogue participant would later say, "Mary Walshok had a decisive and creative role. I think that in the area of substantive community outreach, she is the most imaginative, effective leader I have seen around universities."

For Walshok, the San Diego Dialogue was the culmination of years of building an unequalled network of San Diego community leaders, through both her work establishing UC San Diego and its outreach programs in the community, as well as her personal contacts with the leading families of Tijuana. Moreover, Walshok's training in sociology—notably the model of Swedish learning communities—had taught her the power of getting important figures out of their professional niches to engage in true conversations, to address common problems, and to use their singular talents to bring about a solution. Walshok may have been the only person in San Diego to combine all these talents, and given her role at the beginning of the Dialogue, it might never have begun without her.

The seeds of the San Diego Dialogue were planted in 1984, when San Diego found itself mired in the national recession. Real estate prices had collapsed, and banks were in financial trouble. It appeared that the region's traditional industries—tourism, defense, and agriculture—were in trouble as well, threatening the economic life of the city. The only hope seemed to lie with the area's new economy—high tech and biotech—but they were still in their adolescence. Worse, the area's new and traditional economies seemed to have no contact with each other. Thus, there was little chance of old and new working together in common cause.

In the face of this crisis, Walshok approached Dick Atkinson, then-chancellor of UCSD, with an idea: Why not create a new organization to engage the leading representatives of both economies to work together on solutions? Given the green light on the plan, Walshok brought together, according to Christensen and Rongerude:

> [A] number of downtown stakeholders and a handful of
> scientists and engineers who were starting small com-
> panies near the university to talk about jobs, develop-
> ment, and economic growth. Their goal was to create a
> new network of leaders and voices in San Diego.

The result was UCSD CONNECT. It not only brought together the diverse leaders of San Diego but as the years passed, it created a cohort of powerful individuals dedicated to a successful future for the city and its environs. By the beginning of the 1990s, some of these members believed they had identified a new and pressing need—leadership—that involved not just the city of San Diego but the entire region, including Tijuana. They approached Mary Walshok, who remembers them saying, "You have done such a good job of organizing the interest groups that can affect the direction of the regional economy. Why don't you start focusing on some of the leadership and public challenges we face in the region?"

Walshok's answer was the San Diego Dialogue. The way the Dialogue was constructed has been a model for other cities, and will likely continue to be for years to come. In particular, according to Christensen and Rongerude, writing at the time, the organizational structure of the Dialogue "emphasizes relationships over hierarchy and flexibility over continuity."

> Members are hand picked, and the exclusive membership list signifies how the organization places itself in the region and how it goes about doing its work. A flexible structure allows the organization to change as circumstances require and to pick up issues and put them aside as opportunities present themselves.

Walshok was unashamedly elitist when she recruited for the Dialogue what came to be called "the List." Said the man who would become the Dialogue's acknowledged leader and the driving force of its success, Dr. Charles E. ("Chuck") Nathanson:

> When you look at the membership list, people say, "That's a wonderful list, that's a terrific group of people." These are the people who built San Diego or built Baja California or built the maquiladora industry. They have a civic reputation.

Importantly, the List was composed of powerful, successful people who had shown a deep commitment to the health and success of the region and who were accomplished leaders with a track record of working together, accepting compromise, and building consensus. What the List didn't exhibit was any prejudice regarding race, gender, or even political views. Indeed, if there was any complaint about the composition of the Dialogue, it was its bias toward age. The recruiting, it seemed, had emphasized experience and wisdom, such as that found in men and women who had spent years in the region and experienced its changes, but who also were old enough and successful enough not to care about asserting their egos or seeking personal celebrity from the Dialogue. Indeed, the San Diego Dialogue, for all its impact, operated almost invisibly for many years.

The original invitation-only membership of the San Diego Dialogue in 1991 was just sixty individuals. The single most important participant—so important that he is considered, with Mary Walshok, as a cofounder—was fellow sociologist Chuck Nathanson, who became the Dialogue's personification. As Steve Erie, director of the Urban Studies and Planning Program at UCSD, would describe him:

> Chuck was the very model of a civic entrepreneur, promoting critically needed dialogue among a host of regional stakeholders about important policy issues in San Diego and across the border. He made UCSD both a forum and partner in these extraordinary conversations. He was a regional treasure.

Nathanson was born in Detroit, earned his bachelor's degree from Harvard and his PhD from Brandeis, and then spent much of his career as an academic at Brandeis and the New England Conservatory of Music, as a journalist in Washington, DC, and as assistant city editor at the *Detroit Free Press*, before settling in San Diego as a professor of sociology at UCSD. Deeply committed to community service, Nathanson was soon sitting on numerous boards around the city, from the San Diego Convention & Visitors Bureau to the Museum of New Americans, and the Port of San Diego. His enormous erudition—Walshok called him "a true public intellectual"—and extensive, ever-growing network of connections, as well as his engaging, inclusive personality, quickly made him the acknowledged leader of the burgeoning cross-border enterprise.

Remembered Robert Dynes, chancellor of UCSD: "He set the gold standard for straight talk, civic pride, and farsighted planning." His words were echoed by his counterpart, Augustine P. Gallego, chancellor of the San Diego Community College District and chair of the San Diego Dialogue: "Chuck was deeply respected by colleagues on both sides of the border. He saw a pressing need to bring people together, and he did it so well."

Among the tasks Nathanson reserved for himself was selecting who to recruit to the Dialogue. Many of the names he recruited are those who would figure prominently in the story recounted by this book, including José Galicot, Malin Burnham, Enrique Mier y Teran, Salomón Cohen, Deborah Szekely, Raymundo Arnaiz, Alan Bersin, José Fimbres Moreno, Hector Lutteroth, José Larroque, and Gastón Luken Aguilar. For many of these distinguished citizens living across the border from one another, it was the first time they had met each other—and for many, it was the first time they had ever considered regional policy.

The charter of the San Diego Dialogue was as follows:

1. The purpose of the Dialogue is to promote a renewal of civic discussion, thoughtful research, and consensus-building on the future of the San Diego region.
2. Every effort will be made to recruit distinguished participants from diverse backgrounds with special competence in the issues under discussion and a reputation for broad views and service to the community.
3. To encourage in-depth discussion of new ideas and a full exchange of views, the initial meetings will be private, the size of the group limited, and publicity avoided.
4. Ultimately, however, the Dialogue will seek to engage the public-at-large and elected officials in a program of regional initiatives.
5. UCSD Extension will serve in the role of convener of the Dialogue.

In practice, there were other rules. One was that elected officials were not allowed to be members, in order to keep politics out of the process. Further, as an unwritten rule, newcomers to the community, neighborhood activists and leaders, and representatives of government agencies ordinarily were not invited to join. Moreover, the Dialogue was designed to be pragmatic—that is, it was not only organized to accumulate information about the workings of the region but also to use that knowledge to catalyze change. As Nathanson explained at the time, "Our criteria are for people who can transcend their special interests and think about the region as an interest and think about the common good. Also, people who have a reputation for fairness." He might have mentioned that those recruited also offered a special expertise or skill, unique connections, or fulfill a diversity need. In pursuit of those goals, Nathanson interviewed every single nominee.

Also, despite its cordial and private image, in operation the Dialogue was anything but democratic. Frankly, it was downright secretive. Nathanson was a politically adept, congenial leader, but after hearing everyone out, he ruled with a firm hand. Christensen and Rongerude, writing at the time:

> Nathanson's role as facilitator of the organization is critical. His behind-the-scenes work and one-on-one conversations create a fluid decision-making process and an atmosphere of collegiality where internal consensus can seem almost effortless. It is his political savvy that leverages this network of relationships into an opportunity for regional change.

In truth, Nathanson organized the San Diego Dialogue for decision-making and action, not merely as a debating society or an academic forum. It was structured essentially as three concentric rings. In the outer ring was the general public, who could help support the organization with their donations—$200 per year—and in return receive a monthly report and invitations to the Dialogue's monthly plenary sessions.

In the middle ring were those members who had been invited to join the Dialogue and participated in all discussions and research, but who ultimately were only allowed limited influence on any decision-making regarding new initiatives. Christensen and Rongerude:

> These members reported being unaware of how decisions were made because they were excluded from decisions. The only meetings they were invited to attend were the quarterly plenary sessions. They were not included in individual consultations with Nathanson. They were not asked to help develop new projects or to serve on the oversight committees of existing projects.

Finally, there was the inner ring, the (Bill) "McGill Circle," named after the founding chair of the San Diego Dialogue. Never numbering more than a dozen individuals, Circle members were already among the most powerful figures in the region. They also were required to donate at least $5,000 per year for three years. In return, Circle members were given a special status: they not only sat on multiple Dialogue committees but they participated in regular forums that connected them to high-level regional decision-makers, and most of all, they worked closely with Nathanson to choose the Dialogue's official positions and any new initiatives the organization would pursue.

Being in the McGill Circle had many other benefits as well, including deep personal relationships—friendships that would ultimately play a major role in the future of the city. As one member said, "People know each other now. They go to each other's weddings and bar mitzvahs. It has never been this good." Not surprisingly, membership in the Dialogue not only became a goal for every important San Diego (and Tijuana) figure but the Dialogue's events in time became a very hot ticket for insiders and aspiring leaders in the region.

Perhaps the youngest member of the McGill Circle in later years was José Larroque, a real estate professional destined to become a partner of Baker-McKenzie, the first genuinely global law firm to open an office in Tijuana. Larroque not only brought his role as one of the new generation of Mexican leadership to the Dialogue but also a unique history: his great-grandfather, at the time the mayor of Tijuana, had been killed in the Battle of Tijuana during the Mexican Revolution.

> At first, the others would look at me, like: "This is the *San Diego* Dialogue. What are you here for?" But very quickly, the border became a top issue for the group, and that's where I found my role.

In the years that followed, Larroque became good friends with such important San Diegans as Neil Morgan and Malin Burnham, who proved important to his subsequent career. In time, José himself became one of the leading figures in cross-border development, joint ventures, and investments. He also became a major figure in the Dialogue's successor, the Smart Border Coalition, for which he is the Tijuana co-chair (beside Steve Williams as the San Diego chair). Indeed, most of the living San Diego Dialogue leaders are now part of the Smart Border Coalition's board of directors.

One of Nathanson's most important recruits from across the border was Tijuana department-store magnate Salomón Cohen.

Cohen:

> I don't remember how I met Chuck Nathanson, but I do remember he told me that he was thinking of getting a group from Tijuana to be part of the San Diego Dialogue to see how we could help both governments to understand the border. Then he asked me if I could help—if I could put together the most prominent people in Tijuana so they could become members of the San Diego Dialogue.
>
> At that time, I figured the only way I could do that was to hold a dinner in my home. I invited all the people from the San Diego Dialogue from San Diego to join us in Tijuana. Then I invited the most prominent people I knew in Tijuana to meet Chuck Nathanson and his colleagues. It was an unforgettable night. We thought their plans were excellent. And that time was the beginning of our being part of the San Diego Dialogue. It was a great start to the two cities working together on common projects—particularly the border crossing, which we thought was very important.

The "Dialogue" was at last living up to its name.

THE REPORT

One might imagine that the Dialogue's hierarchical organization would lead to both friction and resentment, especially among those members who were denied participation in the decision-making of the inner circle. Yet beyond occasional grumbling that their particular interests had not been adequately addressed, that seems not to have been the case. There are probably several reasons for this. One is that the members were all busy, highly successful people who were thrilled just to be members without taking on the time commitment associated with decision-making.

But perhaps even more important was the leadership of Chuck Nathanson, whom they trusted completely. He may have been a strong-minded and passionate advocate, but he was an enlightened one. Courteous and affable, he treated all members, including those with general, public subscriptions, with dignity and respect. It was also apparent that he was deeply committed to the success of the region and was willing to sublimate his own ego (thus the ban on publicity) to that end.

Finally, there was the obvious fact that the San Diego Dialogue got things done. It had a real impact, both in its core mission and peripherally (as with the growing friendships between the region's leaders) in less tangible ways. It is a testimony to Nathanson's leadership and tenacity that he managed from the beginning to bridge the (then still-wide) distance between UC San Diego and the city of San Diego, so that they almost always spoke as one.

The San Diego Dialogue may have operated more like a business than a faculty lounge or a nonprofit group, but that likely spared it from devolving into endless meetings, feuds, and internal politics that would have resulted in nothing being accomplished.

In the spirit of getting things done, Chuck Nathanson hired Alejandra Mier y Teran. Her father, Enrique, had been at Yolanda Walther-Meade's dinner years before, was a founding member of the Dialogue, and had gone from running cross-border companies to building the maquiladora industrial parks that now housed them in Tijuana. So when the call came from Nathanson, Alejandra, who had just returned from Mexico City, already knew much about the Dialogue and its purpose.

Nathanson brought Mier y Teran on board in connection with a specific Dialogue project dealing with the border: profiling the individuals who were crossing—something that, remarkably, had never been done before. Alejandra's task was to follow up and analyze interviews conducted with people at the crossing itself—"what kind of educational level they had, why they were crossing, that sort of thing."

Initially the subjects were people who had been caught at the San Ysidro crossing using fraudulent papers. But the data collected was so unexpected that the Dialogue soon expanded its polling to everyone crossing the border. The study was called *Who Crosses the Border?* and not only would it prove to be the most famous and influential work of the Dialogue but it would change Tijuana-San Diego relations—and the region—permanently and irrevocably.

Like many instances of genius, the insight revealed was simple and straightforward. The most important discovery of *Who Crosses the Border?*: contrary to the popular view, the majority of the border cross- ers—both ways—were not one-off visitors or migrating workers but commuters, people who crossed almost every day of the week. Further, the border-crossing experience, which could take hours each time, was not only a huge impediment to their daily work lives but also deeply damaging to the productivity of both companies and communities in San Diego and Tijuana.

How great an impact did the border-crossing experience have? Serendipitously, a newly published economic atlas offered a timely answer. It declared the San Diego-Tijuana nexus the world's largest binational metropolitan area and economic zone. Now everyone knew the stakes. And the rest of the world was equally interested in the news: the Chamber of Commerce found itself flooded with orders for the atlas from companies, governments, and international consulting firms such as Deloitte.

Meanwhile, the Dialogue had hired an economist, Dr. Millicent Cox, who was now running the quarterly *San Diego/Tijuana Economic Review*, a San Diego Dialogue publication that delved even deeper into the econometrics of the region and specifically of the border. It added further ammunition to the argument that the relationship between the two cities was deeper and much more complicated than anyone had ever known. Alejandra Mier y Teran:

> I really think the San Diego Dialogue was the first entity to make a real connection between the business communities on both sides. And with *Who Crosses the Border?* and all the research the Dialogue did after- wards, it finally gave both cities real data that they

could act upon—and just as important, see how much
they depended upon each other for their success.

One of the most immediate and enduring effects of *Who Crosses the Border?* was a new and focused emphasis on the border and its crossing. Mier y Teran believes it was Nathanson himself who first came up with a potential solution—the creation of a separate commuter lane for regular border crossers. It would prove the first step in a transformation of the border experience that continues to this day.

Over the course of the twentieth century, individuals on both sides of the border—refugees, small-business owners, professionals—had privately found their way to a deeper understanding of the true nature of the San Diego-Tijuana relationship and the border that divided them. Now, at last, an organization (composed of many of those individuals) not only had made that wisdom public but had backed it up with empirical evidence—and with the support of many of the community's most powerful individuals.

The San Diego Dialogue would do other important work under Chuck Nathanson's leadership, but nothing would be as important as its first initiative. *Who Crosses the Border?* landed like a bombshell. No more could San Diegans and Tijuanenses look upon the border through the lens of myth and prejudice. No more could they ignore each other or argue they had little need for each other. The truth was right before them, in the columns of figures and the personal testimonies.

Anyone who participated in the San Diego Dialogue will tell you it was not the same after Nathanson's untimely death from a rare form of cancer in 2003. Lacking the support of UCSD (due to budget constraints), the organization soon faded away. Says Salomón Cohen, "When Nathanson passed away, San Diego lost his presence. Luckily the Smart Border Coalition, supported by Malin Burnham and other Dialogue stalwarts, (eventually) picked up the pieces." It was joined in this effort by the San Diego Regional Chamber of Commerce's Mexico Business Center.

But the Dialogue's contribution to the region's understanding of the border was enough for it to be celebrated today. The organization—and Chuck Nathanson—taught San Diego and Tijuana that they shared not only the border but the responsibility and the capacity to change it.

The challenge now was for the two cities to take this new understanding and develop a strategy to make the border work for everyone.

CHAPTER SEVEN

Lines and Flows— Securing the Border and Making It Work

On August 18, 1971, First Lady Pat Nixon traveled to the San Diego-Tijuana border to inaugurate Friendship Park, where the extreme southwest corner of the United States abuts the farthest northwest point of Mexico.

A half-acre parcel that straddles the border where it meets the Pacific, Friendship Park, known before as Border Field State Park, incorporates a picnic area on the San Diego side and a section of Playas de Tijuana on the other. It is the site of Monument No. 258, a stone marker placed in 1851 in accordance with the Treaty of Guadalupe Hidalgo, that defines the boundary between Mexico and the United States, from El Paso-Ciudad Juarez to San Diego-Tijuana.

As a symbol of international amity between the two countries, the park featured only a simple barbed-wire border fence in 1971—the idea being that the people of the two nations could meet and reach across to shake hands, all under the benevolent eye of the US Border Patrol. In the early years, Friendship Park seemed to fulfill its purpose. Numerous social and cultural events—church services, weddings, dances, baptisms, even yoga classes—took place there. Mrs. Nixon even symbolically had her security team cut down a segment of the fence so she could cross over and meet Tijuana citizens standing on the other side.

Then in 1994, stirred by American fears about runaway illegal immigration from Mexico, the US Border Patrol began installing a fourteen-mile-long border fence from the Pacific Ocean inland— starting, ironically enough, with a section through Friendship Park. Outside the park, the wall was constructed by standing up and welding together corrugated metal slabs, military surplus that had served as helicopter landing pads during the Vietnam War. Inside the park, the barrier was chain link through which visitors from both sides could still see each other, touch fingers, and even pass small objects. Seven years later, after the 9/11 attacks, the barrier fence was strengthened to prevent any physical contact or exchange.

In 2009, the US Department of Homeland Security closed Friendship Park. It also installed a second, parallel fence that included barbed wire, sensors, and surveillance cameras; and it built a twenty-foot-wide Border Patrol access road and added a third, twenty-foot wall of steel bollards.

In 2012, under public pressure from the local community, Homeland Security reopened the park. But before it did so, it added an outer perimeter fence blocking public access to the park except when permitted by the Border Patrol. The new fence consisted of a dense steel mesh that filled in the gaps between the steel posts.

Today, visitors to Friendship Park, if they peer closely, can see their counterparts on the other side and try to touch their fingertips. No more than ten visitors at a time are allowed into the space between the parallel fences.

THE PIVOTAL YEAR

In the long, tumultuous history of the San Diego-Tijuana relationship, 1994 may be viewed as the most consequential year.

That year the decades of private, personal connections between the two cities finally burst to the surface. At the same time, larger forces in both the United States and Mexico, some positive and others deeply distressing, demanded the cities put aside their historic animosities, jealousies, and prejudices and search for a separate peace and shared future.

The two cities—and the two nations that hold sovereignty over them—still live in the aftermath of that year, in the form of a new relationship and some painful scars.

The work of the San Diego Dialogue had opened the eyes of citizens on both sides of the border to the mutual dependency of the Mexican and US economies, as well as the need to develop a more pragmatic, efficient solution to the movement of people and goods across that border.

This need was further highlighted by the growing maquiladora movement. Now dozens of American and foreign enterprises were contracting work, especially component manufacturing and finished-goods assembly, to scores of Mexican companies. However, a multitude of regulations and border-crossing obstacles on both sides remained, costing those companies countless millions of dollars (and pesos) in lost revenue and profits.

Serendipitously, the United States had already addressed similar issues affecting commerce on its northern border, with Canada. In 1988, the two nations signed the Canada-United States Free Trade Agreement (CFTA). This agreement gradually phased out a number of burdensome trade restrictions instituted over the course of the previous two centuries. It also reduced paperwork, liberalized cross-border investment, enforced fair competition, and established border dispute resolution organizations.

The impact of this agreement was both impressive and immediate: cross-border trade between the US and Canada jumped substantially, to the significant benefit of both countries. It wasn't long before both countries looked south, eyeing a possible similar agreement with Mexico that would encompass all of the continent in a single trade zone: the North American Free Trade Agreement (NAFTA). In 1977, law professor Bayless Manning coined a term that would describe the result: "Our relationships with Canada and Mexico are not international . . . nor are they domestic . . . Our relationship is 'intermestic.'"

Creating this Free Trade Zone took three US presidential administrations. The Canadian agreement was embarked upon by President Ronald Reagan, who had made its creation part of his 1980 presidential platform ("Let's stop referring to Mexicans and Canadians as foreigners; they're neighbors"). Negotiations with Mexican President Carlos Salinas de Gortari took place with President George H. W. Bush and Canadian Prime Minister Brian Mulroney. Finally, a deal was completed and signed, in 1993—to go into effect on January 1, 1994—by President Bill Clinton.

One reason the agreement—the first free trade accord between two developed economies and a largely undeveloped one—took so long was that it was controversial in all three countries, for very different reasons. President Salinas initially approached President Bush to help his country get out from under the Latin American debt crisis and to intensify the trade liberalization program he had instituted in Mexico. Salinas hoped that a substantial increase in trade with the far wealthier nations to his north would be a centerpiece of Mexico's recovery and further progress. But his country's major industries, long protected by tariffs, worried they would be overrun by their American counterparts.

In the United States, politicians and small businesses feared they were gaining a low-cost competitor right at the time the nation was mired in its own recession. Presidential candidate H. Ross Perot characterized the deal as creating a "giant sucking sound" of jobs pulled out of the US across the southern border. In Canada, Prime Minister Mulroney worried that NAFTA would erase all the gains he had made in negotiating CFTA separately with the United States.

Thus, the ultimate signing of NAFTA (in Mexico: Tratado del Libre Comercio, or TLC) was an extraordinary feat of diplomacy by all three nations. Its results would be dramatic, more prodigious and far-ranging than even the Canada-United States Agreement.

NAFTA, in fact, was a true game changer. In the years to come, all three nations would recognize gains from the agreement. A 2012 study found that as a result of the reduced trade tariffs instituted by NAFTA, trade between Mexico and the United States jumped 118 percent (from Mexico to the US) and 41 percent (from the US to Mexico) in the intervening eighteen years. As for Canada, its agricultural trade with the US tripled.

In many ways, Mexico was the biggest beneficiary of NAFTA, as the maquiladora community expanded to accommodate the shift of manufacturing and assembly operations south by US companies seeking lower production costs. As a result, the maquiladoras, until then an interesting sideshow in Tijuana and other border cities, moved to the center of the Mexican economy to become a principal engine of its growth, as hundreds of thousands of Mexicans from poorer parts of the country moved north to find work.

All told, because of the agreement, Mexico's trade leapt from 8.6 percent of the country's GDP in 1993 to 37 percent in 2013. Mexico's debt crisis essentially evaporated. Moreover, billions of investment dollars flowed into Mexico, enabling the country to better compete on the world stage. Mexico's success with NAFTA might have been even greater—and more widespread—had it invested more in roads and other infrastructure during the agreement's early years.

As it was, however, the agreement proved to be a two-edged sword for Mexico. While incomes went up and poverty levels dropped in the more developed, northern regions of the country, these benefits were not evenly distributed. Many agricultural regions, particularly in the south, became even poorer, as the free trade regulations enabled subsidized American farmers to flood Mexican markets with cheaper products. Mexican campesinos were uprooted from the countryside where their families had lived and worked for centuries. This result, a classic consequence of increased industrialization, hit agricultural communities in Mexico particularly hard—and quickly.

One immediate impact in Mexico of NAFTA was the Zapatista Uprising in Chiapas, the country's southernmost and poorest state. As part of the agreement, Mexico had to modify Article 27, which had been the heart of Emiliano Zapata's campaign in the Mexican Revolution seventy years before. Under Article 27, indigenous communal lands (*ejidos*) were protected from privatization or sale—a law beloved by poor campesinos but counter to the spirit and reality of free trade. The result was the rise of the Zapatista Army of National Liberation, largely composed of native Mayan farmers, that pronounced NAFTA a "death sentence" to indigenous peoples. The Zapatista Army declared war on Mexico on January 1, 1994, the day NAFTA went into effect. The tension engendered by this conflict, always a more symbolic than actual threat to the government, continues to reverberate to this day.

Despite this rear-guard action, elsewhere, where prosperity reigned, Mexican shoppers developed a greater taste for foods and a wide array of other consumer goods produced north of the border and now available to them. This generated an affinity for NAFTA but also a vulnerability to it. Mexico, especially the northern cities, such as Tijuana, had always suffered from economic downturns in the US, but this greater dependence on American commodities and goods linked Mexico even more to US business cycles.

Ultimately, most economic research has found that NAFTA delivered a significant net benefit to Mexico. One survey found that 80 percent of the nation's trade was now with the United States. If Mexico suffered from the US's occasional recessions—getting sick when the colossus to its north sneezed—it also managed to link itself inextricably to the most powerful economy on earth. One result, seen every day in the shopping centers on the San Diego side of the border, has been the rise of a Mexican middle class, a stabilizing political force in a nation too often wracked by the violence and corruption attendant to vast income inequality. Indeed, as we will see, much of the new wealth has been spent on education: Mexico now graduates more engineers each year than either Germany or the United States, the latter a country with almost three times its population.

One of the most interesting cultural phenomena is how NAFTA changed the orientation of Mexico's professional class. For centuries, Mexicans had always looked south, identifying themselves with Latin America. But now, beginning in the mid-80s, these same individuals began to see themselves as North Americans, a shift that continues to this day. Jorge Castaneda, a former foreign minister, has remarked: "As Mexicans . . . our hearts remain decidedly Latino, but our wallets have become purely Norte Americano." This, in turn, according to Tufts University political scientist Daniel W. Drezner, enabled Mexico not only to work in greater cooperation with the United States but ultimately to begin the process of transforming itself into a genuine democracy.

Meanwhile in the US, the consensus view among economists is that NAFTA has been a net boon to the nation's economy, at least in general. On the downside, as many as 850,000 workers—700,000 of them in manufacturing—lost their jobs to either Canada or, more often, Mexico. Exacerbated by other global trends, this contributed to creating the Rust Belt in hollowed-out parts of the American Midwest. On top of that, the United States' trade deficit with Mexico and Canada jumped from $17 billion in 1993 to $177 billion by 2013, comprising 27 percent of the total US trade deficit.

That said, the Congressional Research Service in 2017 credited NAFTA with adding a total of $80 billion (or .5 percent in GDP) to the US economy since its signing. The US Chamber of Commerce estimated that US trade in goods and services with Canada and Mexico had jumped from $337 billion in 1993 to $1.2 trillion in 2011. Also, by 2009, the US private sector had already invested $328 billion in Mexico and Canada, improving economic vitality in both countries.

Less obvious, but in many ways more important, was the way NAFTA, by enabling the US to reduce labor costs, helped the States continue to compete in the world economy. According to UC San Diego economist Gordon Hanson, while NAFTA may have cost the US jobs over the long term, by improving the United States' ability to compete with a rising China, ultimately it may have saved more net jobs that would have been lost. He cites the example of the US automobile industry:

> What NAFTA did was allow the US to partner with Mexico, to expand what you could think of as the North American auto complex, and that enabled the partnership to face competition from China and the rest of Asia much more robustly. China hasn't developed a world-class automobile sector, and the fact that [the] US, Canada, and Mexico have worked so closely together is partly a reason for that.

NAFTA would continue to define US-Mexico relations—and deeply influence life in Tijuana and San Diego—through five US presidential administrations, over a span of more than three decades, including the presidency of Donald Trump, who would make renegotiating NAFTA, which he considered to be detrimental to the United States, a key part of his administration's policy platform. Yet even then, and though it bore a different name (the United States-Mexico-Canada Agreement—USMCA), the basic principle of NAFTA was maintained: recognizing the value and streamlining the process of free trade among the three core nations of North America (each of which gave a different name to the revised pact).

Ironically, despite NAFTA being a nation-to-nation relationship, it quickly became sharply focused at that infinitely narrow, juridical boundary line between the United States and Mexico: the Border, La Línea.

There were two reasons for this. First, it quickly became apparent that truly "free" trade between the two nations, if successful, would ultimately multiply the magnitude and intensity of cross-border trade (and the same was true, albeit to a lesser degree, at the Canadian border). It followed that the actual movement and transfer of cargo and goods, in either direction, would have to become more efficient, or the entire process could jam up at any paralyzing bottlenecks. It was obvious that the primary checkpoints, border crossings on the south at Tijuana-San Diego and Juarez-El Paso, and on the north at Detroit-Windsor, for example, were already under strain. As the situation grew worse, if these border crossings weren't made more efficient—and quickly—the potential benefits of NAFTA would be slowed down and could be lost.

The second reason for a new focus on the border was cultural, with significant political undercurrents and implications. In Tijuana, the maquiladora movement had already made some citizens nervous, as it fed into the century-long fear of a northern invasion, only this time it wouldn't be military but economic. What would keep the rich Yankees from coming down, as they always had, but this time in force, buying up everything south of the border, and keeping locals poor by underpaying them, and (ironically, given the past) swamping Mexico with underpriced goods?

North of the border, San Diegans looked at the growing number of Mexicans who were now sneaking across the border illegally, staying, taking jobs from Americans, refusing to assimilate, and (it was believed) raising the crime rate. Moreover, San Diegans (and the rest of the US) fearfully watched the news stories about mounting violence in Mexico, especially near the border, by vicious and growing drug cartels. Did they really want to open their borders to that level of crime and social chaos, just for the sake of better trade? While the United States increasingly was concerned about border security, it didn't help matters that in Mexico security seemed far less important. What concern Mexico did have about a porous border involved firearms and cash smuggled south into the country from the US, further empowering the drug cartels.

For the most forward-looking thinkers on both sides of the border, including the folks at the San Diego Dialogue, the long-term solution was apparent, even as NAFTA was being signed. The Dialogue's seminal *Who Crosses the Border?* report underscored this belief: the best path to successful future relations between the two countries—and the two cities—was to make the border more difficult to cross going north for undocumented persons and illicit goods, while at the same time making it ever-easier for lawful trade and travel to pass through a "smarter," more efficient border at the official ports of entry.

In theory, this sounded easy. But in practice, it would take a quarter century to make notable progress—with a lot of human misery and billions of dollars in funds expended—and, even as this book is being written, much work remains to be done.

The first and most pressing obstacle to a partnership between Tijuana and San Diego was that, despite the fact that they shared the same geography and much of the same history, and even though thousands of their residents crossed back and forth between the two cities as de facto binational citizens, there was almost no official established relationship between the two. On the ground the shared lives of many of their citizens may have been comfortable and respectful, but in their respective city halls there was no shortage of ignorance and distrust. Any formal rapprochement between the two cities was going to have to begin with baby steps. Moreover, since border security, legally, was a matter of exclusive federal jurisdiction under the constitutions of both their countries, Tijuana and San Diego would require the support, political and financial, of Mexico City and Washington, DC. In the past, except in times of acute crisis and conflict, the border had been mostly ignored by both capitals. It remained an unclaimed stepchild of the two nations.

As described by future US border czar Alan Bersin:

> Known during the nineteenth century as the "Badlands," the [border was] characterized by defiant lawlessness and violence. [It] remained a province and playground for outlaws and the workplace of bandits and smugglers. Citizens from both Mexico and the United States were at their mercy as goods and people moved across the border in both directions, largely without regulation. While the contraband changed over the decades—from bootleg liquor to cigarettes, then to drugs and firearms—the culture of lawlessness and license remained constant. Border problems were deemed intractable and too far removed from the center of power in either country to be of concern except during isolated occasions of crisis.

In retrospect, the important year, inaugurating change in this historical status quo, again and not coincidentally, was 1994. In that year, according to policy historians Guadalupe Correa-Cabrera of George Mason University and Evan McCormick of the University of Texas at Austin:

> [T]he US and Mexican governments began to view border security as a shared responsibility. The emergence of this cooperative framework was made possible by two broad transformations in approaches to the border. The first was a shift [gradually over time] in the way borders were viewed by both sides: away from the [traditional] notion of lines demarcating sovereignties and towards a conception of [borders as including] flows of goods and people between economies and labor markets. The second was the erosion of the long-held belief that securing the border and facilitating transport across it were exclusive motivations,

> replaced by a paradigm in which security and [expedit-
> ing lawful] trade were seen as complementary dimen-
> sions of border management.

These new conceptions were not easy to grasp by many opinion leaders, much less by the larger publics in the interior of the two countries. San Diegans and Tijuanenses alike would learn the painful lesson that the farther their fellow citizens were from the border, the more they would and could be confused about it. In fact, the lives and experiences of the people daily crossing the border at San Diego-Tijuana were profoundly different from what the rest of the world imagined. The challenge of developing a common approach to security and migration problems at the border, in the face of larger resistance from the respective countries, was exceedingly difficult to overcome. Reliable metrics measuring border security remained thoroughly elusive, and anecdotes—almost always depicting extremely negative events—became the bane of border politics and would occasion many setbacks along the way.

As of 1994, the chances of law enforcement cooperation at the border between the two nations seemed more remote than ever. Worse, in 1985, Drug Enforcement Agency agent Enrique "Kiki" Camarena, while on assignment in Mexico, had been brutally tortured and murdered by the Guadalajara drug cartel. US Customs Commissioner William von Raab responded to the American public's resulting outcry by ordering a complete shutdown of the border. One reason for such a draconian move was the alleged connivance of the Mexican government in Camarena's murder. The absence of any constructive official communications about the matter made finding a resolution difficult.

Von Raab's order, however, was quickly rescinded by the Reagan administration—not least because American business interests reminded Washington just how much the US economy—even before NAFTA—depended on trade with Mexico.

This debacle telegraphed a clear message to American and Mexican government officials, not least in Tijuana and San Diego: before they could learn to work together, they would first have to know how to speak to one another. Tijuanenses and San Diegan parents might talk every day on the sports fields or in the parking lots of San Diego's schools, and San Diegan businesspeople could meet weekly in Tijuana office towers with their Mexican partners, but in the halls of political power on both sides of the border, it might as well have been the end of the nineteenth century, rather than the twentieth.

Within the next decade, thanks to the work of a number of dedicated officials in both countries—some working independently, others in concert—all that began to change.

None of this change occurred in a vacuum. NAFTA was not the only major bilateral news event of the era. Mexico, in particular, was undergoing an enormous period of upheaval. The PRI, which had held a lock on the Mexican government for seven decades, found itself facing the first real challenge to its dominance, and it lashed back, often ruthlessly, to maintain its power. Between 1993 and 1995, not only was massive and widespread corruption exposed in the party but during the 1994 presidential campaign a series of assassinations—including that of PRI presidential candidate Luis Donaldo Colosio in the Lomas Taurinas neighborhood of Tijuana—raised fears the country might slide into anarchy. Exacerbating this fear among citizens was the rise in the violence between the growing drug cartels—one shootout between rival gangs in Guadalajara had killed Cardinal Juan Jesús Posadas Ocampo, who was caught inadvertently in the crossfire.

As if that wasn't enough, just weeks after the new Zedillo administration took office in 1994, the Mexican peso collapsed, due in part to a growing lack of confidence in Mexico's future by banks, which failed to grasp the promise NAFTA/TLC held for the Mexican economy. The result was a run on those banks, and a burst of inflation that substantially wiped out the value of people's savings in the country.

So concerned was Washington, DC, about the unfolding chaos on the southern border that, unlike its heavy-handed interventions in the past, the Clinton administration wisely offered the Zedillo government a $20 billion bailout, believing this was a bargain compared to the potential cost of a Mexican collapse spilling over the border. The offer was controversial both in the United States—*Why send billions to prop up a failing state?*—and in Mexico—*Why are we, a proud nation, taking charity from the gringos?*

In the end, the bailout did have a measurably positive impact in stabilizing the peso and, therefore, the Mexican economy. But it also had a number of secondary effects. For one thing, according to Correa-Cabrera and McCormick, it "had the effect of binding the Clinton administration tightly to the economic fortunes of Zedillo's Mexico." Likewise, among Mexicans there was a growing appreciation of the value of the United States to the country's economic future. This, in turn, finally oriented the government in Mexico City toward its northern border and cities such as Tijuana. For the first time, Mexican border cities were viewed with appreciation for their cross-border relationships with twin cities on the US side, for the maquiladoras with their rapid growth and attraction of American and other foreign investment, and for the border region's relative stability compared to other parts of the country.

But if a city like Tijuana was to become a shining example of a healthy Mexico and the nation's face welcoming ever-more business and capital to the country, the border would need to be cleaned up—made more safe, efficient, and productive. Better security would be the linchpin of further progress.

Meanwhile, Washington, DC, realizing that it now had a direct stake in Mexico's future, feeling pressure from the business sector to rationalize the cross-border process, and facing pushback from voters fearful of hordes of "illegal aliens" rushing the border, now began to pay unprecedented attention to the southern border as well.

Out of this mix of confusion, competing interests, and desperation, there emerged on both sides a new notion called by Mexicans "El Tercer País"—The Third Country. This was the land immediately adjoining the border, historically treated (except within the border cities) as a no-man's-land. From now on, it would be perceived, in Alan Bersin's words, as "a thermostat for bilateral relations." The two-thousand-mile stretch of territory would become the focus of both the free trade opportunity of NAFTA and law enforcement and public concern over the growing levels of undocumented migration, drug trafficking, and other crimes. The border between Mexico and the United States—where the so-called first world met the third world—was about to change forever. Many of these changes would be "Made in San Diego-Tijuana" before being exported elsewhere.

THE GREAT MIGRATION AND THE BACKLASH

NAFTA already had begun to bring prosperity and attention to Northern Mexico. Suddenly, Tijuana offered jobs and prosperity, and beyond, in the United States, lay streets perceived by impoverished Mexicans to be paved with gold. Not surprisingly, for millions of Mexican campesinos, after a century of revolution, assassination, corruption, and the growing income inequality catalyzed by NAFTA/TLC, migrating north—despite its risks and privations—had enormous appeal. Early evidence of this mounting wave of migrants was what the San Diego Dialogue's Alejandra Mier y Teran saw firsthand as a young woman growing up in Tijuana in the late 1980s, in the wake of the Immigration Reform and Control Act of 1986:

> There was a road that ran to the beach along the [US] border. You would see people—hundreds of them—lining up on that road at sunset, getting ready to cross the border illegally. This happened every day. There were a few small shops on the American side, but not much else. I suppose there was a fence, but it couldn't have been much.
>
> The US Border Patrol would be there as well, waiting. When there were enough people gathered on the Tijuana side, they'd all charge at once. The idea was that the Border Patrol couldn't catch them all. Usually they caught only a [tiny fraction] of the illegal crossers. The rest would make it across.

Mark Reed, Immigration and Naturalization Service senior executive and port director of San Diego during the 1990s, explains:

> Between 1986 and 1994, there were few credible efforts to secure the border or bar unauthorized workers from jobs. With passage of [various] legislation, lights, cameras, and some personnel were thrown at the border. [That was] enough for the optics, but not enough to stop the illegal flow of migrants. Initially, there was a

lull, but soon the number of illegals multiplied expo-
nentially. At the same time, interior enforcement operations were gutted to support the "amnesty" program,
and too few of the agents left over were assigned to
educate US employers about their new obligations to
establish identity and eligibility to work legally in the
country. Worksite enforcement disappeared and the
Form I-9 process became a joke.

By the 1990s, the migrant flow turned into a flood. Some migrants
stayed in Tijuana and found work. But the city, still growing and adding maquiladoras and building infrastructure, could not offer housing
or employment to more than a fraction of this onslaught of migrants.
The rest loitered around town or camped in the riverbed for a few days
and plotted their entry into the United States, often with smugglers
known as "coyotes." NAFTA, still in its infancy, reinforced this behavior. Correa-Cabrera and McCormick:

> The economic model established under NAFTA,
> which allowed for the free mobility of goods, but not
> of labor, [was designed] to concentrate development in
> the maquila industries along Mexico's northern bor-
> der, allowing US transnational companies to access
> cheaper labor while keeping jobs in Mexico.

In other words, having come this far and not finding their dream,
there was every reason for the migrants to keep going, even if it meant
running a gauntlet of criminals and crooked coyotes, then border
agents and the threat of detention and deportation.

Mark Reed described the scene:

> The border was wide open, and thousands of people
> would challenge the border daily. We used to take
> numerous congressional delegations to a vantage point
> near [the] San Ysidro [Port of Entry] overlooking the
> field where literally thousands of people gathered in
> plain sight during the day in preparation for rushing

the border at night. We called it "the soccer field" because, to pass time during the day, many would play soccer. When dusk arrived, hordes of people rushed the border. It happened night after night. The sheer mass overwhelmed our resources.

Alan Bersin, recently appointed US Attorney in San Diego, also saw the result firsthand—indeed, it ultimately became his problem—as the mobs of migrants swarmed the border every night:

> There were so few Border Patrol agents on duty [in 1993 and 1994] in the usual crossing places—such as "the soccer field"—that when migrants rushed the border en masse they would simply overrun the officers. All the Border Patrol agents could do was grab one migrant in each hand. By morning, the agents processed the few hundred they could catch and arrange for their voluntary return to Mexico. The rest were gone. This started happening on every shift.
>
> At that time, illegal crossings were primarily accomplished by adult males traveling with other men from their villages in Mexico where they left their families. They knew if they were arrested, they would be returned to Mexico and be back at the soccer field within a day or two to try again—until they were successful.

Meanwhile at San Ysidro, hundreds of migrants were massing at the port of entry there and spilling in "banzai rushes" onto the freeway at Interstate 5.

In the early 1990s, a new road sign appeared in San Diego whose imagery was so compelling—and moving—that it quickly came to symbolize for an entire generation of Americans the tragic dilemma of illegal immigration across the border. Just ten of these signs were quietly installed near the San Ysidro Point of Entry and fifty miles north at the San Clemente Border Patrol checkpoint at Camp Pendleton, but the news of their presence quickly swept around the world.

The rectangular signs were yellow with the capitalized word *CAUTION* across the top. In that respect, they were similar to the signs that had preceded them, but those signs bore only words: "Caution/ Watch For/People/Crossing/Road."

On these new signs, below the solitary word of warning was the image of three people, in silhouette: a man, a woman, and a little girl. The trio, presumably a family, was running to the left, father in front, seemingly ducking his head, mother next, reaching back to hold the wrist of the daughter, who was nearly being pulled off her feet, pigtails flying behind her. Somehow, this simple image, in the postures of the runners, captured their focus, their goal, and their terror. Even for commuters racing past in their cars, the message was powerful and unmistakable.

The highway department had erected the signs with a different sense of desperation. Over three years, at these two sites, more than one hundred immigrant pedestrians, often in families, had been killed in traffic collisions, and the numbers were climbing each year.

There was no doubt as to the cause of this carnage, but there was also no ready solution. Smugglers, having successfully crossed the border with their human cargo, still faced discovery at the checkpoint further north on Interstate 5. To circumvent these obstacles, the smugglers would stop on the freeway shoulder and dump off their migrants, then wait for them just beyond the checkpoint. It was up to the migrants to make their way on foot past the border guards to rejoin their rides.

The problem was that checkpoints presented severe obstacles to foot travelers. At Camp Pendleton, the checkpoint straddled the freeway's northbound lanes, forcing the migrants to cross the freeway to the southbound shoulder to escape capture—a total of as much as ten lanes of busy traffic. Away from the checkpoint was even worse—rocky terrain and regular Marine patrols made the foot passage even more perilous.

The Border Patrol, Caltrans, and even the Marine Corps felt helpless to deal with the problem and still enforce the law—which is why they resorted to posting the warning signs on the freeway, with little hope that it would make much of a difference.

The sign was designed for Caltrans by a graphic artist named John Hood. He proved to be the perfect choice. A Navajo and a Vietnam War

veteran, Hood drew on his experiences of both—desperate refugees in
the war, and his tribal stories of the Navajo Long March in 1864. He
would later say that he modeled the profile of the father after labor
activist Cesar Chavez and that he chose a girl for the image because of
paternal feeling of fathers to their daughters:

> It was troublesome that there was a mass exodus, espe-
> cially families. And when you talk about families, you
> talk about children. They were getting slaughtered in
> the freeways. The children don't know what's happen-
> ing and why they are there. [And] why their parents
> are doing it. They just know this is not their home. The
> sign conveys that they are away from home. And the
> children are asking, "What are we running for?" Today,
> even when I watch parents walking in malls with their
> kids, it's like they are dragging them. That was the idea:
> clutching something that is dear to our heart.

In the years that followed, Hood's sign-turned-meme would be
adopted and adapted for an endless number of political cartoons,
T-shirts, and other cultural products. But none would capture the
shock of that original appearance of the image on highway signs.
There is no evidence that they had any substantial effect in diminish-
ing traffic deaths near the two checkpoints. But the signs did have one
significant result: the unforgettable image of the vulnerable, terrified
migrant family has never really left the mind of anyone who saw the
sign. The reactions varied between sympathy and fear, often in the
same individual. One by one, the signs eventually disappeared, some
officially removed, a few taken by collectors. (Today, just one of John
Hood's iconic signs remains in place, protected as a historic site, a lone
surviving reminder of a darker time in the Tijuana-San Diego border's
history.) Ultimately, what finally did reduce migrant traffic deaths was
the success of border-security efforts, notably Operation Gatekeeper.
But that was yet to come. This was 1994, and there remained only fear
on both sides of the border.

In the US, especially in the border states, voters' growing fears of
an invasion of migrants from Mexico, over a border virtually out of

control, forced a shift in regional politics. Americans saw the rise of politicians who made ending illegal—and even reducing legal—immigration the heart of their campaigns. Their positions ranged from playing upon nativist fear of the Other, to requiring English as the official language (including in schools among new immigrants), to punishing US employers who hired "illegals," to stronger enforcement of deportation laws, to building stronger border barriers (to the point, still considered more polemical than practical, of building a two-thousand-mile wall at the US-Mexican border).

No event better exemplified this growing backlash against migrants than the 1994 reelection of incumbent Republican governor Pete Wilson. Wilson had been a California state assemblyman and had most recently been the twelve-year mayor of San Diego. His success at redeveloping the city's downtown, keeping the San Diego Padres baseball team in the city, and restructuring the city council had made Wilson hugely popular in San Diego. This enabled him to win the elections for his three terms by two-to-one margins or greater. Wilson parlayed this popularity into his election as a US senator from California, an office he held for eight years, until 1991, when he stepped down to run for governor.

Including his eight-year tenure as governor (1991–1999), Wilson would ultimately spend more than three decades at the center of San Diego and, ultimately, California political life. Wilson governed as a social liberal and fiscal conservative, and his two terms are generally considered a success. He dealt with the cultural changes taking place in the state, while still keeping the budget under control and leading the state out of its greatest economic downturn since the Great Depression. But another key to Pete Wilson's enduring popularity was that all his years in state politics had given him a deep understanding of the shifting attitudes of the average California voter. One of those shifts, driven by the changes created by the presence of hundreds of thousands of new Mexican migrants in the state, was a growing animus against immigration, especially illegal immigration from across the southern border.

For that reason, in 1994, as part of his campaign for a second term, Wilson made support of Proposition 187 a centerpiece of his platform. Prop 187, also known as Save Our State (SOS), created by citizen petition and on the ballot that year, established a state-run citizenship screening program that, when implemented, would prohibit illegal immigrants from using California's healthcare, public education, and other social services.

Indeed, it was the very idea of Proposition 187 and growing media coverage of the increasingly out-of-control border—combined with the prospect of Wilson as an up-and-coming Republican governor announcing his presidential candidacy at the 1996 Republican convention in San Diego—that propelled the Clinton administration to rush implementation of its border-security program, Operation Gatekeeper. President Clinton didn't want the border-control crisis to be weaponized against his reelection.

GUARDING THE GATE

On September 17, 1994, the Clinton administration announced Operation Gatekeeper, with its avowed goal, in the words of Attorney General Janet Reno, "to restore integrity and safety to the nation's busiest border." The program was highly controversial, with particular pushback by American migrant and human rights activists, who saw the strategy as repressive. One of the most vocal critics was academic and activist Noam Chomsky, who declared Gatekeeper to be a "militarization of the US-Mexican border" designed to deal with the increased illegal immigration driven by the implementation of NAFTA nine months earlier and the monetary collapse of the peso that accompanied it.

Operation Gatekeeper represented the first serious effort to deal with US-Mexico border security in the new era of binational cooperation. It also represented a recognition that illegal immigration, drug smuggling, human and drug trafficking, and cartel violence represented a serious new threat to the health of both countries. Over the next few years, under the regime of Operation Gatekeeper, the budget for border security would increase to $800 million. Under Gatekeeper, the number of Border Patrol agents doubled; miles of fences and barriers were installed, and the lighted roads built would more than double;

and the number of underground sensors to detect border crossers nearly tripled.

Gatekeeper was implemented by Attorney General Janet Reno and Doris Meissner, commissioner of the Immigration and Naturalization Service (INS), then in the Department of Justice. Both Reno and Meissner traveled frequently to San Diego in those early years, to highlight the administration's border-control efforts. Back in Washington, DC, they mobilized the resources and shepherded political support for the effort. But the local faces of Gatekeeper's leadership in San Diego were Gustavo "Gus" De La Viña, chief of the Border Patrol sector in San Diego, and Alan Bersin.

Bersin, a native Brooklynite, Harvard football player, and Yale-trained corporate lawyer in Los Angeles before entering public service, was there as the US Attorney in San Diego, and as the attorney general's new southwest border representative, the so-called border czar. His job was to coordinate federal border law enforcement on the US side, from California to Texas, and, as Janet Reno's point person on the ground, to foster cooperation between federal law enforcement and local city and county officials, among themselves and with Mexico. As a newcomer to San Diego-Tijuana, Bersin was able to start with a clean slate on Mexico-US border relations, without the baggage of previous involvement, but he still would have to deal with the weight of two centuries of friction and animosity.

De La Viña was the brains and driving force behind Operation Gatekeeper. Born and raised in Edinburg, on the border in Texas's Rio Grande Valley, Gus was a brilliant strategist who would go on to lead the Border Patrol nationally. As Doris Meissner described him: "Gus grew up on the southwest border and understood its special character and terrain like the back of his hand. Traveling the border with him meant meeting not only with Border Patrol agents and leaders but with local officials, community groups, and Mexican counterparts. He recognized that border enforcement is a central feature in the life of border regions and needs to be accountable to many different actors and crosscurrents. His was a steady hand on the tiller, bringing a sense of balance and calm amid sometimes chaotic situations at our borders."

At five feet six in his Lucchese cowboy boots, with a cigarette in his mouth, De La Viña was a genuine Marlboro Man. Bersin was a corporate lawyer and Rhodes scholar. The two men could not have come from farther corners of the American experience. But they developed an abiding respect and deep friendship that ended up—with Reno and Meissner's unflinching encouragement and support—serving the border well.

The objective behind Operation Gatekeeper was based on a policy of prevention through deterrence, which sought to limit irregular migration through the deployment of agents, fences and other physical barriers, and technology. Correa-Cabrera and McCormick describe the strategy through the words of David Aguilar—a protégé of both De La Viña and Silvestre Reyes, the remarkable Border Patrol leader who headed up the El Paso sector at the time (Aguilar would succeed De La Viña as national chief of the US Border Patrol during the Bush administration):

> [T]his was the start of a deterrence-type strategy that would later become the prevailing strategy across the entire southern border. [It was] the "gain, maintain, and expand" effort: provide sufficient resources to *gain* control of an area; continue providing resources to support and *maintain*; and then *expand* operations linearly across the border. Rather than dedicating resources to apprehend [every individual] crossing the border, transport them to the station, process and feed them, and then return them across the border (all while drawing personnel and resources from the border), it was much more efficient and effective to prevent them from entering in the first place by having a visible and prominent presence at key border areas.

Setting the strategy, however, was only the beginning of the problem. Implementing it effectively was the real challenge. This would require the forging of relationships, over years, between law enforcement agencies operationally on the ground. Such relationships did not exist in 1994. Indeed, they had never really existed systematically—neither among the federal agencies nor between them and local law enforcement. Bersin recounts those days of Border Patrol agents snagging one or two people as the multitude rushed by amid migrant "banzai rushes" across the border:

> Even when the agents took the handful of people they'd caught to the station for processing, there was no biometric equipment available to identify those individuals or any automated system even to record their arrest. Agents were keeping their own handwritten three-by-five file cards, but that was a poor solution. When you asked a migrant for his or her name, you obviously weren't getting an honest answer. The only way you could identify someone would be to make notes about gang tattoos or some other distinguishing feature. It was an utter mess, and everyone on all sides knew it.

There was little coordination between the different US law enforcement agencies. So Bersin brought William Esposito, the special agent in charge for the FBI in San Diego (who would go on to become Louis Freeh's FBI deputy director nationally), down to the border to meet Chief De La Viña. They had never before met. Bersin:

> It demonstrated how far apart and isolated border enforcement was from the rest of law enforcement. The gap began to close that day. One immediate result was that Bill [Esposito] made an early, technologically primitive fingerprint machine available to Gus so that serious criminal offenders among the migrants could be fingerprinted and identified for the first time (it took eight hours) and then prosecuted rather than released.
>
> The federal caseload was transformed from one dominated by misdemeanor prosecutions against "economic migrants" to thousands of [Section 1326] felony prosecutions, and the largest criminal caseload in the nation, directed against dangerous criminals, all of whom had been previously convicted and deported and who were trying to reenter the United States.

The stand-alone, computer-based biometric data collection of sus-
pect individual border crossers would evolve over the ensuing years into
the IDENT protocol, a web-based system that created a massive data-
base of all migrants crossing the border. It could make nearly instant
identification of thousands of people per hour. Today, IDENT, in turn,
has evolved again, this time to the use of the faster and more predictive
power of big data and machine learning. It can identify potential criminality based upon millions of records of past migrant behavior. The
new system is so powerful and pervasive that it has raised important
civil liberty and privacy questions that remain to be resolved.

Meanwhile, in San Diego and elsewhere along the border, other
crises were erupting that threatened the growing relationship between
the two countries. On more than one occasion, migrants on one side
of the fence would throw rocks at US Border Patrol agents, injuring
them, sometimes seriously. In some situations, agents, fearing deadly
threat—several border agents struck by rocks had lost their sight—
drew their weapons and returned fire, not infrequently with fatal
results in Mexico.

These threats from across the border, combined with the perceived
use of inappropriate force by the Border Patrol, inevitably became the
source of bitter recriminations and heated disputes on both sides.
Exacerbating the situation was the fact that there was no cooperation
at all between the different law enforcement agencies in the US and
their counterparts in Mexico.

It didn't help, either, that both sides simply lacked confidence in
each other. Bersin:

> You really can't imagine how much antipathy there
> was in those days between American law enforcement
> and Mexican law enforcement. Officers from the two
> countries did not deal professionally with one another
> because they did not trust and, for the most part, like
> one another. Nothing symbolized this tense relation-
> ship more than the Enrique Camarena murder, which
> had made US authorities more suspicious of and hos-
> tile toward Mexican law enforcement than ever. On the
> Mexican side, officials saw the gringos' arrogance and

how so many of them treated Mexicans and Mexico with condescension and disdain, and it made them even less willing to help.

As for narcotics, the situation was worse. American law enforcement saw their Mexican counterparts as either indifferent to the matter—after all, the Mexicans would argue with disgust that it was the Yankees who were creating the enormous demand for those drugs—or taking bribes to look the other way. Even worse, more than a few Mexican policemen, and often their higher-ups, were closely working with the cartels.

This situation would have to change if basic law and order were to be brought to a lawless, chaotic border. Operation Gatekeeper, and everything else thoughtful citizens wanted for their region, depended on it.

A FATEFUL MEETING

The breakthrough came in mid-1995 at the most unlikely of places: a firehouse near the tiny border town of Campo, thirty miles east of San Diego, in southeastern San Diego County. It was a historic moment: the first time a Mexican consul general, Luis Herrera-Lasso, officially met with American law enforcement officials in a public event to discuss border security. Significantly, he had been authorized by the federal government in Mexico City to do so. The import of this meeting was not lost on the media: camera crews mobbed the barnlike building, with its long central table and high ceiling fan.

Bersin, who would play a decisive role in the evolution of border crossing over the next two decades—and in the increasing cooperation between the two great cities and their respective countries—was the chief American representative at the meeting. He had come with one agenda: to get the Mexican representatives to acknowledge the growing crisis at the border and to understand how it might sabotage the newly signed NAFTA agreement.

The choice of the little town of Campo (so small the town would eventually be sold as a single parcel) was not a coincidence. That portion of San Diego County had been riven in recent years by cross-border violence that eventually spilled out to the boundary of the city of San Diego itself.

Among the American representatives with Bersin at the meeting was Johnny Williams, a veteran Border Patrol chief who would succeed De La Viña in San Diego and brilliantly manage much of the operational implementation of Gatekeeper. Also notably present was Bill Kolender, then the San Diego County sheriff, following a long stint as San Diego City's chief of police. Kolender was there not only because of his position but because he was more experienced than anyone in dealing with border crime and because he was close to Jerry Sanders, his successor and San Diego's then-current police chief. Sanders, although his jurisdiction did not extend to Campo in the southeastern part of the county, would be crucial to any sustained cross-border law enforcement cooperation with Mexico. For Sanders, as for Kolender, the border remained an open wound that had refused to heal.

Today, Otay Mesa, a flat plateau that extends across the border, is covered with thousands of homes, but in the late 1980s and early 1990s, it was largely barren, its level surface scarred by shallow canyons. Migrants crossing the border would often choose this path because of its proximity both to Tijuana (for a quick return to Mexico if necessary) and San Diego (to quickly escape into the city and disappear). Bandits, mostly Mexican, but from both sides of the border, knew this too, and they would hide in the canyons to ambush the migrants (and drug mules) to rob, rape, and occasionally kill them. The mayhem was so dangerous and violent that crime writer Joseph Wambaugh would pen a bestselling book, *Lines and Shadows*, depicting it. As the number of victims began to mount, Chief Kolender concluded the only answer was to establish a squad of seasoned police officers specially trained to engage the bandits and protect the migrants—even if a close proximity of American law enforcement activity, including the frequent use of force, made Mexican authorities nervous.

When he succeeded Kolender, Jerry Sanders not only continued this program but expanded it to include all his department's law enforcement operations on the border. These operations were conducted in close coordination with federal authorities, who had primary jurisdiction over border security. In the process, individual San Diego police officers began to interact and cooperate not only with their federal colleagues but also with their Tijuana counterparts more and more.

Across the table from Kolender and Bersin that day was Consul General Luis Herrera-Lasso, a highly distinguished, well-respected, and connected civil servant in Mexico, who had been sent by his government to calm the waters in preparation for the new era of binational amity signaled by NAFTA. He and Bersin met weekly at a coffeehouse in San Diego's Little Italy, across the street from the Mexican Consulate, to hammer out a common approach. Herrera-Lasso well understood that cross-border relations were never going to get better as long as the US accused Mexico of laxity regarding undocumented Mexican migrants and drug smugglers sneaking across the border. As he later observed:

> [I]llegality, lack of control, and lack of effective border management to regulate immigration and assure safety then severely affected border communities, border people, as well as the safety and human rights of migrants. [Therefore], something effective needed to be done to gain control of the border, and bilateral cooperation was a key element to achieving this task.

Consul General Herrera-Lasso's attitude and public statements differed greatly from anything ever heard before by the American public, which mostly had involved stories about the Mexican government's support for the movement, legal and illegal, of its citizens north of the border.

Now, the ice had been broken. It was a start. The growing professional—and personal—relationships in law enforcement on both sides of the border would prove particularly important. These deepened after that meeting in the firehouse at Campo. Bersin:

> Just to have Luis [Herrera-Lasso] present and the fact that we were addressing a shared problem together was unbelievably productive in terms of finally being

able to say: it's okay to cooperate. Here were Mexican officials we could work with. We even ended up creating joint working groups to address a whole variety of public safety and cross-border issues. We started to build the bonds of personal knowledge and then trust and confidence between law enforcement officials so that we could begin to close the gap between us and start sealing the dangerous seam the border represented as a safe harbor and haven for serious criminals.

Much of the credit for the success of the meeting can be given to Consul General Herrera-Lasso and his Mexican colleagues. The consul general worked tirelessly to bridge the cultural and political divide in a way that enabled both countries to see that it was in their best interests to find areas of mutual concern and work together to address them. For the Americans, the challenge was dealing with the flood of undocumented Mexican immigrants. But for the Mexicans, they were dealing with a country possibly slipping into a mortal crisis. Not only was the country facing dire economic challenges but the drug cartels—and the violence they brought to the nation—were on the rise.

At this time of national vulnerability, the local and national Mexican governments could have retreated to a defensive posture—a reasonable reaction given past aggressive US responses to such periods at the border. Stunningly, just the opposite occurred: Tijuana-based officials began regularly contacting their San Diego counterparts for help in monitoring the border. Meanwhile, Mexican foreign minister José Angel Gurría and US Attorney General Janet Reno remained in close contact as subsequent events unfolded. Mexican president Ernesto Zedillo, elected in 1994, engaged in regular talks with American president Bill Clinton about border-security cooperation as well as NAFTA/TLC.

AN ERA OF GOOD FEELING—WITH GOOD RESULTS

The good news in all this improved communication was that, on the ground in places such as Otay Mesa, interdiction and migrant security were showing positive results. Federal US and Mexican border offi-cials, and San Diego and Tijuana police, were working together—and in the process learning to view each other with increasing respect. It was a work in progress to be sure, but it would prove to be a platform for the big changes to come.

Without minimizing their differences, or the ongoing corruption on the Mexican side, law enforcement officials learned to look beyond those past impediments to focus on aspects of regional and mutual public safety. The collaboration was based not on sentiment but on hardheaded calculations of self-interest from both sides of the border. It resulted from the understanding, borne of experience, that Mexico and the United States were equal at the border—at least in the law enforcement context—as nowhere else in the otherwise asymmetric relationship between the two countries.

From these joint activities came important steps forward in the collaboration, including a counterdrug alliance, coordinated public efforts to warn migrants away from dangerous areas on the border, the blocking of the banzai rushes through ports of entry out onto the free-way, the exchange of information to identify and dismantle migrant smuggling rings, and close consultation regarding reports of civil rights violations.

In May and June 1996, a spate of cross-border shootings from inside Tijuana, aimed at US Border Patrol agents positioned in the Imperial Beach area of San Diego, presented a case in point. These vio-lent attacks represented a dramatic departure. Most past incidents of border violence were caused by border banditry or "transactional" con-frontations between Border Patrol agents and smugglers of migrants or drugs. In those cases, the violence was contained, directed against either a specific victim or the perpetrator.

The Imperial Beach shootings—triggered first by a cross-bor-der sniper and then by drive-by gunmen firing from vehicles on the Tijuana roadway parallel to the border fence—were different. These attacks randomly targeted US officers, who returned fire back across the border in self-defense. The episode had a terrorist quality to it and seemed calculated to challenge and disrupt the binational collabora-tive activity that was occurring at the Tijuana-San Diego border.

Alan Bersin:

In the past, a cross-border shooting of this type would have provoked an international crisis with recriminations from both sides and a media frenzy. Instead border authorities from both countries conferred promptly in the aftermath of the shootings to formulate a coordinated plan of action. The officials jointly viewed the crime scene from the US side in Imperial Beach where the agent was shot, then together traveled to Tijuana to the spot on the highway from which the weapons were fired at the US agent. The FBI and Mexican police investigated in tandem, sharing access to witnesses, evidence, and locations in San Diego and Tijuana.

Public officials from the two countries also communicated. They even held a joint press conference, attended by Mexican and US press and media representatives, to express their mutual concern over the threat to regional public safety. The "Camarena syndrome," in short, was over. The game had changed, and the message was sent.

These developments might never have occurred if Herrera-Lasso, Bersin, De La Viña, Williams, Kolender, Sanders, Esposito, and their colleagues (including Paul Pfingst, San Diego's district attorney, and Richard Emerson, the police chief in neighboring Chula Vista) hadn't first set the foundation for cooperation between law enforcement operations at the border. As Bersin would later say of these local leaders:

They were instrumental in supporting the Federal buildup, which, over the course of four or five years went from 300 Border Patrol agents in San Diego to more than 3,500. And there was real coordination and cooperation with Mexico between state and local police and federal authorities that was unprecedented. Jerry Sanders and Rick Emerson were not only completely supportive of federal enforcement efforts but also entirely willing to deploy more of their own police

officers down at the border, at places where they had
jurisdiction. DA Pfingst's office prosecuted in state
court hundreds of "drug mules" caught smuggling
marijuana at ports of entry, thereby permitting federal
authorities to concentrate their resources on investi-
gating and prosecuting cartels trafficking in heroin,
cocaine, and methamphetamines.

This spirit of cooperation between government employees and
officials in the two cities extended to other agencies as well. In 1997,
during the season of strong Santa Ana winds, a major wildfire broke
out in the outskirts of Tecate and quickly raced north toward the border in San Diego's east county. Local officials in Tijuana and Tecate
asked for help. In response, the San Diego and Tijuana fire departments decided to ignore the protocols for cross-border interactions
and coordinate their efforts—even if it meant crossing back and forth
across the border.

Bersin describes what would have happened had the two fire
departments decided to go through official channels:

The protocols at that time, in terms of international law
and relations between Mexico and the United States,
were that formal authorization from both Washington,
DC, and Mexico City was required for American officers to enter Mexico. So while the fire was raging,
there would have to be a call back to Mexico City to
explain the situation, which would take many layers of
discussion within the Mexican government.

Meanwhile, we'd have to call the Justice
Department headquarters in Washington, DC, which,
in turn, would then have to work with the State
Department there. After exhausting their processes,
they would telephone us in San Diego saying, "Fine, it's
okay to do that."

Faced with a dire emergency, we all just decided—
local Mexican and American officials alike on the
ground—to ignore all of that. That is, not to ask for

permission, but to work together, and ask for forgiveness when the fire was finally put out.

A further example of the mutual effort between law enforcement on both sides of the border arose from a growing number of complaints by Mexico about the abuse of migrants by US Border Patrol agents. This led to the creation of a joint task force between the two countries, based at Luis Herrera-Lasso's Mexican consulate in San Diego. The result was the first modern-day prosecution of an American border agent for the violation of a migrant's civil rights brought by Assistant US Attorney (now Judge) Amalia Meza.

Ultimately, despite its birth in political expediency, Operation Gatekeeper, and the binational cooperation it engendered, gained the support of both American political parties, and it proved to be a genuine start in enhancing border security. Gatekeeper has continued through four administrations, under presidents Clinton, Bush, Obama, and Trump, operating for years on a steady $18 billion annual budget.

Operation Gatekeeper survived because it worked, and it worked because it was built atop the solid foundation created by officials on both sides of the San Diego-Tijuana border, in particular, the protocols and precedents for working smoothly together.

THE POLITICAL AFTERMATH

Politically, Operation Gatekeeper's success did defuse much of the debate over undocumented immigration during the 1996 presidential campaign season. The Clinton administration's concern that a surging Governor Pete Wilson would ride to a nomination at the 1996 Republican presidential convention in San Diego was never realized. Not only did the improved security at the border largely take the issue off the table (temporarily) but Wilson's throat surgery and weeks of recovery derailed the governor's campaign. Instead, during Clinton's debate at the University of San Diego with the actual GOP nominee, Kansas senator Bob Dole, in October of that year, remarkably there was not a single question raised about immigration or border security.

As for Proposition 187, it proved a singularly destructive experience for everyone concerned. The proposition was passed decisively (by nearly 60 percent, a 1.5 million vote plurality) by California voters in a referendum on November 8, 1994. The next day, it was challenged in a lawsuit, and just four days after that a federal district court found it unconstitutional. Five years later, California's new governor, Gray Davis, halted all state appeals of the ruling.

The repercussions of Proposition 187 are still felt to this day. In the aftermath, California voters who had supported the measure felt betrayed. They had believed that, as with 1978's controversial property tax, Proposition 13 (and every other state proposition to that date), a successful proposition automatically became law.

Meanwhile, among much of California's Hispanic population, the sense of betrayal was far greater. They weren't alone. In the ramp-up to the election, the PRI Mexican president Carlos Salinas de Gortari, and even some prominent Republicans (including former Housing and Urban Development Secretary Jack Kemp), decried the proposition. Three weeks before the vote, more than seventy thousand people marched in protest in Los Angeles.

This sense of betrayal reached across all people of color and their allies, but its largest impact was on the Latino community, which was becoming the state's largest voting bloc. The passage of the proposition is credited with mobilizing unprecedented numbers of California's Hispanics to political activism. In fact, some credit Proposition 187 with the shifting of California from a nominally Republican state to a reliably Democratic one—the reason why, with the exception of Arnold Schwarzenegger, California has not again elected a Republican governor.

Certainly, Proposition 187 brought into sharp relief the growing distrust between peoples, which didn't help what had been a half decade of growing amity and cooperation between the cross-border "trailblazers" in San Diego and Tijuana. Fortunately, those bonds were too strong to break. Through the rest of 1990s, law enforcement in the two cities would continue to work together to an ever-greater degree and across a wider scope of activities, particularly with respect to the narcotics-trafficking cartels that had taken root in Tijuana.

AFO

Crime and cartel gang violence, contrary to myth, didn't just flow north from Central Mexico into the US. In the 1990s, a notorious drug cartel, the Arellano-Félix Organization, described by the *Arizona Daily Star* as "one of the biggest and most violent criminal groups in Mexico," arose in Tijuana. Ironically, it came to power because the Colombian Cali and Medellín drug cartels were being driven out of their traditional Florida maritime access corridor by US drug enforcement agents and other law enforcement agencies there, and they were looking for new partners elsewhere to penetrate the United States. The Colombians found willing partners in Ramon and Benjamin Arellano Félix, who had gotten their start with cocaine in the Tijuana drug plaza through Miguel Ángel Félix Gallardo, the head of the Guadalajara Cartel and the godfather of narcotics trafficking in Mexico.

As it grew in wealth and power, eventually controlling all of Northwest Mexico, the Arellano-Félix Organization (AFO), also known as the Tijuana Cartel or Tijuana Gang (names Tijuanenses hate because they reflect badly on their city, though the gang leaders came from elsewhere), now began to recruit on both sides of the border. In Tijuana, the increasingly arrogant and flashy gang members began to hang out in the nightclubs and other playgrounds of the wealthy, attracting and recruiting the city's young aristocrats. These sons of the rich eventually formed their own faction in the AFO, the so-called Narco Juniors, and used their superior cross-border access to move into heroin distribution in addition to the staples of cocaine and marijuana.

The Narco Juniors also used their growing celebrity to make contact with gangs on the American side of the border, notably the Logan Heights Gang, a Latino street gang based in southeast San Diego County. Soon the Arellano-Félix Organization was recruiting Logan Heights Gang members as sicarios (assassins and bodyguards) to conduct its most violent work.

It wasn't long before the Arellano-Félix brothers unleashed these sicarios on their enemies—not only rival gangs but civic leaders and officials in both cities. One such target was Gonzalo Curiel, an Assistant US Attorney in San Diego, who was forced to leave the city and relocate to a safer location for more than a year. (Curiel would go on to become a federal judge in San Diego and later become enmeshed in a notorious episode regarding Trump University during the presidential campaign of 2016.)

In Mexico, the AFO's primary target was the Sinaloa Cartel, led by Héctor Luis Palma Salazar and Joaquín Archivaldo Guzmán Loera ("El Chapo"). In revenge for Salazar deploying his soldiers to assassinate the two brothers (their attempt failed, but eight AFO members were killed nevertheless), Benjamin and Ramon ordered a hit on the Sinaloa leaders and assigned the Logan Heights Gang the job. The botched attack, held at the Guadalajara airport, resulted in the death of six civilians, including Cardinal Posadas Ocampo.

The AFO had other Mexican targets as well. A major source of embarrassment to the gang was the heroic, crusading *Zeta* magazine. Founded in 1980, the magazine devoted many of its pages to exposés of local organized crime, drug trafficking, and government corruption. One of its founders, Héctor Félix Miranda, had already been murdered in 1988, by the bodyguards of a local politician. Now, another founder and editor, Jesús Blancornelas, was targeted by the AFO and nearly assassinated by Logan Heights leader David Barron, who himself died in the shoot-out.

With the narco-violence situation spinning out of control, law enforcement agencies of both countries knew they needed to collaborate, but it would be a risky move. The respective agencies feared resistance and potential backlash in both countries. Bersin: "Everyone was so nervous about the danger and creating a brouhaha, that the whole operation was kept quiet and unpublicized."

The resulting joint task force—spearheaded by Chuck La Bella, Bersin's first Assistant in the US Attorney's office, and Samuel Gonzalez, a crusading Mexican prosecutor—created some strange bedfellows. Not only were American and Mexican federal agencies working together but on the US side, the Drug Enforcement Agency and the FBI (despite their historic rivalry in the US Department of Justice) teamed up. The various agencies in the joint task force shared information, people, and resources. Mexican task-force members crossed back and forth across the border in coordinated surveillance and raids. The results were spectacular.

With the eventual deaths of the most violent gang members and a stunning series of highly publicized convictions obtained by prosecutors Cindy Millsaps, Laura Birkmeyer, Cindy Bashant, and Laura Duffy from the US Attorney's office, the binational task force broke the back of the AFO. (Birkmeyer and Duffy are now superior court judges for San Diego County, and Bashant is a US district judge.) Mexico, for the first time, even extradited a Tijuanenses cartel leader, setting the stage decades later for a similar fate for the notorious "El Chapo" Guzmán. According to political scientists Emily Edmonds-Poli and David Shirk:

> US and Mexican officials were able to gradually build working relationships based on mutual respect and cooperation. For example, Mexico demonstrated its good will and desire to work with the United States to combat drug trafficking in 1997 when [the Mexican government] approved the US's request to detain and extradite Everardo Arturo "Kitty" Páez, a top lieutenant in the Arellano-Félix Organization, arguably Mexico's most powerful drug cartel at the time. Mexican authorities arrested Páez in Tijuana, but his extradition was blocked by legal challenges questioning the constitutionality of extraditing Mexican nationals. The Mexican Supreme Court's decision in January 2001 upholding the constitutionality of extraditing Mexican citizens paved the way for Páez's transfer to the United States just four months later.

The AFO and its muscle, the Logan Heights Gang, would return a decade later with new leadership and new ambitions. But they would face a very different law enforcement reality—cross-border cooperation and mutual support—and they would never be as powerful again.

DANGER AND OPPORTUNITY

Operation Gatekeeper proved an enduring success, quickly reducing—if not quite eliminating—illegal migrant crossings at the Tijuana-San Diego border. There, at least, the "border crisis" was solved.

But every success has its good results and its bad (mostly unanticipated) consequences. If Operation Gatekeeper rendered those "Migrant Crossing" signs in San Diego a curious anachronism, it also moved much of that horror elsewhere. As migrants found urban crossing in Tijuana increasingly difficult, they moved to less-populated stretches of the border to the east: to the dangerous and inhospitable Sonoran Desert. This, in turn, forced a fundamental change in their strategy. Mark Reed:

> The framework for Gatekeeper and modern border tactics [was] forged in that time at the San Diego-Tijuana border. Enforcement was effective in targeted areas. But the migrants kept coming. They walked, hiked, climbed, and crawled into the country . . . Except now, passage was not safe and the terrain threatening. Now migrants needed to pay a smuggler to gain passage and a forged-document vendor for false documents for access to the workplace. Organized cottage industries of smugglers and forgers appeared.
>
> Gatekeeper changed the nature of illegal immigration across the border. Hefty fees paid increased the cost of passage to the point where migrants could not afford to go home. So the migrants opted for one big-time expense and sent for their families . . . And the increased security that came with Gatekeeper made it much more difficult to cross back and forth than it had been in the "soccer field" days. So they stayed. They didn't go back.

Border security would remain a perennial and polarizing issue in American politics. Now, the American public would be shocked with endless stories of migrants abandoned by "coyotes" and dying of exposure and thirst, gang members making their way north to disappear in cities as far away as New England, and the threat of international terrorists sneaking in through the US's back door.

In San Diego-Tijuana, however, the issue had been joined, and successfully. So the leaders in these two cities, now closer than ever, could focus their attention and energy on the other side of the border-management coin: making the border efficient for lawful trade and travel.

CHAPTER EIGHT

The Heart of the Matter—
Moving People and Cargo
Efficiently Across the Border

With Operation Gatekeeper, San Diego finally began to gain control over runaway undocumented migrant flows.

But paradoxically, even as authorities were slowing one type of border crossing, they were trying to speed up another: legal crossings, often several times each day, by the residents of San Diego and Tijuana; visits by tourists and businesspeople from outside the region; and commercial traffic crossing the border constantly in both directions.

The San Diego Dialogue study had been a revelation. What had been for decades considered a minor, anecdotal matter—border wait times—suddenly was understood as monumentally costly, deeply inimical to both cities. The individual productivity lost each day, from hours wasted waiting to cross the border, had to be addressed. So did the adverse economic impact of these losses on Tijuana and San Diego, and on their two national economies.

Alan Bersin:

It became obvious to us that unless people and goods could move efficiently and more rapidly across the border, the enterprise value of the Tijuana-San Diego partnership, and the larger link between their two countries, would be severely compromised. The "Turtle Crossing," as Yolanda Walther-Meade had described it, if left intact, would doom trade, business, social visitation, and shopping, and harm commuters, tourists, and school children alike.

But what was to be done? Washington, DC, was fully focused on border protection, and spending billions of dollars in the process. While Mexico City was interested in improving legal crossing at the border, the endeavor was, as with most matters involving Tijuana, still low priority. In the 1990s, as we have seen, Mexico was dealing with much larger problems. So if any governmental entities were going to address the border in terms of efficiency, it would have to be the city and county of San Diego working with the federal government in Washington, DC. In addition, private-sector leaders from both cities would have to inspire, pressure, encourage, and support public-sector leaders from all levels of government to pay attention. It wouldn't just happen on its own. Without momentum to move in a different direction, inertia would take over and the status quo would remain firmly in place.

Over the course of twenty-five years, the San Diego-Tijuana border transformed from an acknowledged embarrassment to an international model of binational cooperation and efficiency. How? The process involved multiple institutional and individual players on both sides of the border, as well as innovations that are now being studied by contiguous border cities around the world. This is a story worthy of deeper investigation.

After the pioneering efforts of the San Diego Dialogue, no organization was more important to this work—and remains more important—than the San Diego Association of Governments (SANDAG). Created to deal with common issues and interests among the cities of San Diego County, SANDAG took on the question of the congested border crossing almost by default, and it ended up, for its members'

economic health, taking the lead on the evolving economic relationship between its cities and those of the Tijuana metropolitan area.
Thus, while the organization still keeps its US-centric name, like the
San Diego Dialogue, its interests now extend across the binational
breadth of the San Diego-Tijuana Coastal Plain. SANDAG takes the
border into account but, unlike the past, it does not permit La Línea
to cut short the discussion. It is now embedded in the organization's
DNA that San Diego and Tijuana constitute one region, a single metropolitan area in two countries.

SANDAG was founded in 1966 as the Comprehensive Planning
Organization (CPO), a small department within the San Diego County
government under a California State–authorized joint powers agreement. Its charter was to conduct long-range planning for the county.
By the end of the decade, its duties were expanded by Governor Jerry
Brown during his first tenure in office, to include planning coordinated efforts among all the cities in the region and acting as a technical and informational resource for all local governments. Those duties
were further expanded to include managing all regional transportation planning and airport land use and acting as the clearinghouse for
federal and state grants.

By 1975, CPO had become a major force in the county, the key
government agency when it came to regional planning and growth. It
flexed its new muscle by embarking on a major project: the first-ever
comprehensive Regional Transportation Plan. What emerged from
researching that plan forced San Diego County to face the truth that the
roads approaching the border from the US side were utterly inadequate
for the daily traffic there. It would be another fifteen years before the
San Diego Dialogue's *Who Crosses the Border?* report finally provided
precise numbers about and characterizations of the border-crossing
experience. But CPO's transportation plan offered a glimpse of what
was to come.

In 1980, CPO renamed itself the San Diego Association of
Governments. Over the next decade, the Association devoted itself
to developing a financial structure to do more than write reports, but
actually to create real structural change in the county. Thus, in 1987, it
gave broad support to Proposition A, a local .5 percent transportation
sales tax measure. That same year it founded TransNet, a twenty-year,

$3.3 billion program to support local highways, transit, local roads, and bicycle lanes and paths. These efforts, inevitably, brought SANDAG to programs at the border and in contact with Tijuana. So did California's 1990 designation of SANDAG as the Integrated Waste Management Task Force. Its first major challenge: dealing with sewage and toxic waste emanating from Tijuana and passing down the Tijuana River to flow through south San Diego County and onto its southernmost beaches. This work resulted, in 1999, in the construction of the quarter-billion-dollar South Bay International Wastewater Treatment Plant near the San Ysidro Port of Entry. For the first time, facilities financed and built in the United States were geared to solving a regional problem that started with a cause in Tijuana and ended with an effect in San Diego.

Thus, while SANDAG's efforts in these years, driven by the deep insight and broad vision of its gifted director, Gary Gallegos, were targeted at improving the quality of life, especially in transportation throughout the county—from highway construction projects to restoring eroded beaches to light rail—it couldn't help but constantly encounter problems San Diego shared with Tijuana and the state of Baja California. In 1990, following research and interviews on both sides of the border, a seminal report on the San Diego-Tijuana water supply was produced that would play a central role in the two cities working together to preserve a safe common water supply (and ultimately the South Bay treatment plant). Finally, in 1998, the organization acknowledged the inevitable and established the Committee on Binational Regional Opportunities (COBRO), its charter to "provide public forums for cross-border planning in the area of transportation, environmental management, education, water supply, and economic development."

In 2003, SANDAG adopted a new $42 billion, thirty-year Regional Transportation Plan, focusing on a mass transit system. This time connection to Tijuana and its environs was explicitly a critical part of the plan. So, too, was Tijuana's place in the Association's Regional Comprehensive Plan, completed in 2004. This plan dealt with the challenge of reducing urban sprawl and traffic congestion, increasing affordable housing, saving habitat, and bolstering the local economy, all with a nod to the city's interaction with its rapidly growing neighbor. The plan also focused attention on the consequences of long waits to cross the border.

Bersin:

> The SANDAG study did for cargo and trade what the Dialogue had achieved for passengers and people. It demonstrated that cross-border delays were hitting us hard in the pocketbook—to the tune of more than $7 billion annually. Ultimately, these two studies created the political will, through an economic impetus, to make change. The civic and business coalition in San Diego-Tijuana is what persuaded governmental authorities at the federal, state, and local levels on both sides of the shared border that significant change was essential and that its absence would be unacceptably costly.

By 2007, the now decade-long relationship between SANDAG and the city of Tijuana's Municipal Planning Institute had grown stronger, such that the Association and the city approved a joint project to create an Otay Mesa-Mesa de Otay Binational Corridor Strategic Plan for that common geographical region that was growing rapidly, especially on the San Diego side. What made this project unprecedented was that it wasn't simply Americans interviewing Mexicans but a true binational planning project that solicited input from stakeholders on both sides. For the first time the plan also needed to be approved by the Tijuana City Council.

The Otay Mesa joint plan ultimately produced a call for international cooperation that was greater than ever before seen along the Mexican-American border. Among its many initiatives, it included coordination between US Customs and Border Protection (CBP) and Mexican Customs to fund short-term capital and operational improvements at the Otay Mesa-Mesa de Otay Commercial and Passenger Points of Entry.

Keystone of the San Diego-Tijuana economy: cargo entering the US at Otay Mesa.

Beyond the creation of these long-term engagement plans, the immediate result, in 2008, was a presidential permit granting the right to build a second US-Mexico border-crossing facility in Otay, two miles from the existing point of entry. This facility, to be named Otay II, would join Otay I and San Ysidro, the world's busiest, to create three crossing points in San Diego County. This effort, conceived and led by then–California state senator Denise Ducheny and Gary Gallegos, featured a revolutionary financing technique: for the first time anywhere, state tolls, rather than federal funding, would be used to build the new port of entry.

Gallegos recalls:

> The city of San Diego, the county of San Diego, Caltrans, [and] the city of Tijuana had signed [a memorandum of understanding] trying to pursue another border crossing. So it's already on the radar screen that we needed a new border crossing. With [the SANDAG] economic study in hand, we also then did a feasibility study. Would a new border crossing be feasible? In this case we were working very closely with

my good friend, Senator Denise Ducheny. When we
started working with her, she hated toll roads.

Ducheny:

Gary Gallegos comes to me and says we need a new
border crossing. We're heading into the 2008 recession at this point. We're not seeing the money coming from the feds. We're going to be fighting just to
get the money for San Ysidro that they've technically
already committed. We're still building 905 [the freeway connecting Otay I to the interstate] with both federal and state funds. We need to start thinking about
the new border crossing, and we don't see that money
coming down the pipe. So we're trying to be creative.
They want to do tolls. I was always very resistant to the
notion of tolls at the border. I remember going to lunch
with [former California State Treasurer] Kathleen
Brown and Gary at one point. [They] tried to sell me
on this whole toll business. We went back and forth for
a while, and I finally came around. I understood that
[the crossing] couldn't get built fast enough if we didn't
find some creative way to do it. So I came around to
seeing it the way you see the Bay bridges. We could
borrow the money to build the crossing, and the toll
would pay off the bond. In theory, we weren't tolling
the crossing; we were tolling the freeway that gets you
to the crossing.

This would be the first time, anywhere across the US borders, that
state tolls would be used to build a federal port of entry.

Ducheny's support was essential, but Gallegos had more work to do:

The challenge for border crossings is that elected officials, for good or bad, they really try to reflect what
their constituents are telling them. They've got to go
ask for people to vote for them every two or four years.

The goods and services that come across the border, most of them don't vote. There are no votes to be had from a bunch of trucks. Now if we can tie in the jobs in Carlsbad [a city far from the border], then maybe that's a whole different argument. But it's also another level of complexity.

So by looking at the economic opportunities that were being foregone in the region and by using the fact that this road could pay for itself by tolling—it wouldn't necessarily become a competitor with any individual project in any city—we were able to get the SANDAG board unanimously behind the project. We had the Chamber of Commerce pushing for it, Denise carried the bill.

In true San Diego-Tijuana style, the master plan was a binational effort, featuring, according to Ducheny, "something like seventeen agencies on each side of the table."

But the cross-border effort did not stop there. "Quite frankly," says Gallegos, "I've found that many, many times, the easiest way to Washington is through Mexico City, or the easiest way to Sacramento is through the state of Baja (California)."

Gallegos:

> We got a good sense that once the bill passed the legislature, Governor [Schwarzenegger] was contemplating redoing the bill, because some of his advisers were telling him, "This is really not as good as it sounds." Arnold at that time was pretty involved in the Binational Governors Conference, where all the [Mexican and US border state] governors met together. The governor of Baja California at the time was Eugenio Elorduy Walther. We leveraged our relationship with the governor of Baja to get to Governor Schwarzenegger, to convince [Schwarzenegger] he needed to sign this bill.

For now, the new crossing remains on the drawing board, though the state of California has already paid San Diego $45 million to buy the real estate at the proposed site.

Meanwhile, Ducheny credits SANDAG for providing the data she and politicians on both sides of the border needed to bring to their federal capitals, to lobby for the needs of the border region. She says, "The lesson—and it goes to the watershed, it goes to transportation—is: if we come together and decide as a region what we want, then we're in a position to go with strength to the federal governments when we need their assistance."

SANDAG also was deeply involved in the construction of South Bay Rapid, a twenty-six-mile transit route starting at the Otay Mesa border crossing and designed to carry passengers between the border crossing and Chula Vista, as well as downtown San Diego. Through these years, even as it was improving the transportation infrastructure throughout the county, SANDAG continued to work on the roads approaching the border points of entry, making massive improvements at the approaches on Interstate 5 / State Route 805 and State Routes 125 and 905.

Not all this work at the border was commercially oriented, though. With time—and the influence of the San Diego Dialogue's research and follow-up studies sparked by Cindy Gompper-Graves leading the South County Economic Development Council—the importance of the trans-border area to everyday citizens was slowly recognized as well. Finally, in 2016, SANDAG began planning a new 8.5-mile Border to Bayshore Bikeway to enable cyclists to ride from Imperial Beach to San Ysidro and on to the border point of entry. Construction is scheduled for completion in 2021.

Clearly, approaching and crossing the border was now acknowledged as integral to the present and future of San Diego. This new reality—a binational relationship between SANDAG and Mexico's federal government—was formally acknowledged in 2018 with the first visit by a Mexican diplomat, Secretary of Foreign Affairs Luis Videgaray, to attend a SANDAG Board of Directors meeting. The occasion was a celebration of the partnership SANDAG (with the California Department of Transportation) has formed with its counterpart organizations in Mexico, on the Otay Mesa East Point of Entry Project. This marked a decisive turning point, not only with SANDAG but also significantly in the Mexican government's recognition of Tijuana's critical importance to the US-Mexico relationship and its pivotal, regional role with San Diego.

INTEGRATING TRAVEL AND TRADE
FACILITATION WITH SECURITY

From the outset, we never saw security and the expediting of lawful trade and travel as being mutually exclusive and irrevocably in conflict. Right from the beginning, our idea was that for the border to work properly, we required both elements. We needed security and we needed to move traffic—lawful traffic, passengers and cargo—in an expedited way.

What grew out of that as a result of experience in San Diego-Tijuana over time, was the concept that expediting lawful trade and travel necessarily is part of the security regime. That's because, if you arrange for trusted, low-risk travelers whom you have previously vetted to move through the border quickly, you can focus your remaining resources on other kinds of traffic. This includes border crossers about whom you have derogatory information showing that they are high risk, or those people and cargo about which you lack sufficient information to make a judgment about the degree of risk they pose. In either of those cases, you want your officers to take a closer look and they are better able to do that if they are not devoting their scarce time to people and goods that we know do not pose a threat.

As US Attorney for San Diego and Imperial counties, and the attorney general's southwest border representative from 1995 to 1998, Alan Bersin had played a critical role in coordinating law enforcement on the border between the US and Mexico. He had been among the first US officials to develop a relationship with his counterparts across the border to coordinate in dealing with trans-border criminal activity during Operation Gatekeeper and in battling the Arellano-Félix drug cartel. Moreover, he had established a tight working friendship with San Diego Police Chief Jerry Sanders, and other local law enforcement officials, that set the foundation for a much-improved federal-city-county relationship. These bonds enhanced border enforcement immensely with beneficial results for regional public safety overall. San Diego's crime rate dropped 40 percent during these years, in significant part because of Operation Gatekeeper and Sanders's "community policing" initiatives, for which he earned national attention.

Now, a decade later, both men had moved on. Sanders had left the police department in 1999 to become president and CEO of the United Way. Then, in 2005, in a special run-off election, he was elected mayor of San Diego, a position he would hold for the next seven years. After valiantly rescuing the city from its self-inflicted municipal pension woes, Sanders would then become the president of the San Diego Regional Chamber of Commerce. Thus, the border, which had been a law enforcement concern for Sanders as police chief, became his economic, political, and cultural challenge as mayor and later in heading up the Chamber.

As for Alan Bersin, after his five-year term as US Attorney, he was appointed as superintendent of public education in the San Diego City schools, the eighth-largest urban school district in the United States—a job that included dealing with thousands of migrant children (primarily from Mexico) as well as the estimated hundreds of Tijuanenses children studying in San Diego's classrooms. After seven tumultuous reform-minded years on the job, Bersin was called to Sacramento by Governor Schwarzenegger, who appointed him as California's education secretary and a member of the state board of education.

But Bersin missed San Diego—and just as much Tijuana, a city with which he had fallen in love. He returned from Sacramento in 2006 and was appointed by Mayor Jerry Sanders as board chair of the San Diego International Airport Authority. Rumors circulated that he was contemplating a run for San Diego City Attorney. Instead, in April 2009, Homeland Security Secretary Janet Napolitano appointed Bersin as Assistant Secretary for International Affairs and special representative for Border Affairs in the Department of Homeland Security in Washington. Said Napolitano:

> Alan brings years of vital experience with local, state, and international partners to help us meet the challenges we face at our borders. He will lead the effort to make our borders safe while working to promote commerce and trade.

Bersin was then nominated by President Barack Obama as commissioner of US Customs and Border Protection. But it was a recess appointment, only effective until the end of the next session of Congress, unless he was formally confirmed by the US Senate. The Republican-led Senate, in dispute with a Democratic president, stalled the confirmation, and in December 2011, Bersin was forced to step down as CBP commissioner. However, Secretary Napolitano immediately installed him as Assistant Secretary of International Affairs and also named him chief diplomatic officer for the Department of Homeland Security. Napolitano's successor as secretary, Jeh Johnson, kept Bersin in these positions but also made him the head of the department's Office of Policy. Bersin remained at DHS through the end of the Obama administration in January 2017.

His sequence of positions placed Alan Bersin directly in the policy space between the federal governments of Mexico and the United States. This tenure gave him almost eight years to bring all his experience in border relations—law enforcement, national security, education, and politics—to bear and to build a team that could bring about real change by knitting together local vision and federal power. At the heart of his efforts would be the philosophy—born many years before, from the San Diego Dialogue report—that the situation at the border presented not just an issue of crime and security but also involved a massive logistics puzzle with enormous economic and social implications. The supreme challenge was to rationalize border crossing, taking all these factors into account. This would unlock and capitalize on the values that a more efficient border could bring for everyone from ordinary people to global businesses. This would be accomplished by increasing crossing efficiency for the vast majority of people on both sides of the border, who had a legitimate purpose and need to move back and forth between Tijuana and San Diego.

Bersin knew he had to work fast.

The US-Mexico border in 2011 was a considerably different place from the one Bersin, as US Attorney, had left a decade before. The good news: one initiative that had been successful at improving border efficiency, which had been introduced in San Diego-Tijuana in the 1990s, had now been implemented widely along the entire border. The Secure Electronic Network for Travelers Rapid Inspection, or SENTRI, had been expanded border-wide by a joint team composed of members of the INS, US Customs Service, and various other agencies before they were merged into the Department of Homeland Security in 2003 in the aftermath of 9/11.

The innovation created a separate commuter lane at Mexico-US border crossings that would allow preapproved, low-risk travelers to drive across the border and avoid the usual time-consuming customs and immigration inspections in the US (Mexico's border-crossing inspections are random and very infrequent). To earn SENTRI approval, a commuter had to undergo a rigorous background check (against criminal, customs, terrorist, and law enforcement databases), a biometric check through fingerprinting, and an in-person interview with a Customs and Border Protection officer. The commuter also had to register his or her car and pay a membership fee. Participants would hold SENTRI status for a five-year period, unless revoked because of a violation, before having to renew it. It cost $125 (or more depending upon the number of family members) for the five years, but that was a pittance given the benefits—worth their weight in gold—SENTRI conveyed: reducing the time to cross the border, usually to fifteen minutes.

The first SENTRI system had been deployed in 1997 at the Otay Mesa POE. That this site was chosen was a measure of how Washington, DC, viewed the border with Mexico at San Diego-Tijuana as the role model for the rest of the southern border and the crossings there as the pilot project sites for new procedures and technologies that would eventually be applied elsewhere.

There was no shortage of SENTRI skeptics, concerned that the system would break down, that it would be abused, that criminals would find a way around its protections, or even that it would be so popular that it would be quickly overwhelmed. Nonetheless, under the skilled (and courageous) leadership of Mark Reed and Rudy Camacho, who headed up federal immigration and customs functions, respectively, in San Diego at the time, the innovation was introduced and gained traction immediately.

Bersin:

> The tense security situation at the time regarding irregular migration and drug trafficking was the context in which this remarkable civic achievement unfolded. It was a tribute to Rudy and Mark and their staffs, and their superiors at Justice and Treasury in Washington, that the program got off the drawing board and into operation. The local community's advocacy and support in San Diego was essential. The border governance strategic doctrine was crucial. We had to persuade, and then demonstrate, that security and the facilitation of lawful trade and travel were not in conflict as had always been assumed.

In fact, other than its swift, enormous popularity, none of the fears about compromising border security were realized. On the contrary, SENTRI proved so popular and effective in reducing wait times that the other border ports of entry along the entire Mexican border clamored for the chance to deploy the system. Meanwhile, at Otay Mesa, Customs and Border Protection used the new portal as a beta site, testing various technologies—some of which, such as facial recognition and in-vehicle biometrics, would eventually be incorporated into the program as it rolled out.

A year later, in 1998, the SENTRI system was inaugurated in El Paso, Texas. It, too, was successful, though the initial plan dedicating a special lane proved impossible because of the traffic on the International Bridge, the main artery, and instead had to operate on another bridge nearby. This required adjustment didn't bode well for planned implementation at the next port of entry, the ultimate test, San Ysidro, the busiest border crossing on earth.

The challenge presented by the San Ysidro crossing was not just the sheer volume of the daily traffic across the border but the relatively cramped nature of its location. In the end, in another milestone event in the story of San Diego-Tijuana relations, numerous private organizations and government agencies on both sides of the border worked together to find the real estate, change zoning regulations, and create space for the new SENTRI lane. It worked, and in 2000, SENTRI opened in San Ysidro to nearly universal acclaim. At last, after decades of confrontation, debate, and neglect, the regular commuters between two cities could treat the border as any other toll crossing: a minor delay in their daily drive to and from work and school. The border, for the first time in more than a century, became readily crossable for people who qualified for SENTRI.

From 2003 to this day, SENTRI continues under the auspices of the Department of Homeland Security's Customs and Border Protection agency. SENTRI cardholders represent 40 percent of border crossers daily.

A WORLD TURNED UPSIDE DOWN

On September 11, 2001, the attack on the Pentagon and the World Trade Center put the United States on a perpetual war footing, anxiously awaiting the next terrorist attack.

In the days that followed, every point of entry into the United States was choked down, as massive security and inspection efforts were initiated and kept in place until a more systematic security apparatus was established to protect a fearful nation.

At the border, the impact of this shutdown was catastrophic. Traffic jams extended each direction from the border crossings and stretched as far as twenty miles—that is, past the municipal boundaries of both San Diego and Tijuana. As a result, commerce between the two nations, which had been growing steadily for nearly two decades, all but ground to a halt.

After the initial panic, over the following weeks and months it became obvious to leaders on both sides of the border that a new operating philosophy had to be put into place, one that recognized, paradoxically, both the new reality of a perpetually high level of alert and the need to make the border crossings ever-more efficient. Solving this would be the biggest challenge Alan Bersin would face during his second tour of duty at the border.

Bersin:

> We finally figured out that the key to resolving this dilemma lay in understanding not only that security and expediting trade and traveler cross-border movement were not mutually exclusive variables but also, in fact, were two sides of the same coin. They did not need to be "balanced" against one another as we had thought before, in the early days of SENTRI, but rather needed to be implemented together simultaneously as a single process. By dramatically increasing the amount of lawful trade and travel whose crossing could be expedited—that is, not expending scarce enforcement resources on low-risk subjects—we would be able to devote substantially greater resources to known high-risk crossings and to those crossings about which we lacked sufficient information in advance to make a reliable judgment concerning the degree of risk they presented. We showed that increasing security did not mean we had to slow down traffic to inspect each passenger and every cargo shipment; nor did trade and travel facilitation mean that we had to compromise, let alone sacrifice, security.

But how was that to be explained in a hyper-security-conscious environment? SENTRI was now under the command of Homeland Security, a massive bureaucracy that had not existed when Bersin was US Attorney. Now Bersin's team—including Chappell Lawson, a national expert on targeting and professor on leave from the Massachusetts Institute of Technology (MIT), his colleagues Nate Bruggeman and Ben Rohrbaugh, and subsequently Seth Stodder—would build upon groundbreaking work that DHS had accomplished during the Bush administration. They came up with four different scenarios and laid out the potential solutions each implied. They used the analogy of finding a needle (the bad guys) in a haystack (all border crossers). How do you find that needle?

1. *You burn down the haystack.* In other words, you shut down the border. This solution was quickly dismissed as self-defeating and unworkable.

2. *You look at every piece of straw individually.* That is, you go back to the immediate post-9/11 solution of carefully inspecting each passenger and opening up the trunk of every single car. Back to the twenty-mile traffic jams? Not good. This solution would set cross-border commerce back decades.

3. *You target the needle search.* In this scenario, Customs and Border Protection would obtain specific intelligence that would enable its officers to reach into the haystack and pull out the offending needle. Says Bersin, "This would have been the ideal solution, but we didn't routinely have access to such [granular] and actionable information."

4. *You invert the process and make the haystack smaller.* In this scenario, you do not focus exclusively on targeting the criminals, but instead devote equal attention to identifying the legitimate travelers. Then the remaining, smaller population of potentially risky border crossers undergoes intensive inspection and attention.

Bersin:

> It was this last option in which we found our salvation. By identifying and expediting lawful trade and travel, we discovered that we could have our cake and eat it too. The more we could identify and move legitimate traffic quickly across the borderline, the higher the security profile we could achieve at any level of enforcement resource allocation. In effect, expediting

lawful trade and travel became, in practice, another
security policy.

Implementing this fourth policy option would have an extraordinary number of long-term implications that continue to this day. What
began with SENTRI and its success soon after the turn of the century has grown into a panoply of "global entry" programs that now
not only encompass a range of different private and commercial activities but also extend beyond Mexico (and Canada) to other nations.
The Trusted Traveler programs within DHS include SENTRI, NEXUS
(Canada), and FAST (trucks), as well as Global Entry (international)
and TSA PreCheck (domestic).

None of these transformative programs would have occurred without strong advocates in Washington, DC, particularly at the beginning,
for the adoption and implementation of SENTRI. San Diego found
those legislative advocates at a crucial time in an unlikely duo of congressional representatives and their staff: Democratic representative
Lynn Schenk and her assistant, Rochelle Bold, and Republican representative Brian Bilbray and his staff. "Unlikely" because these members
of Congress not only belonged to different political parties but also
otherwise expressed utterly antithetical political philosophies, running against each other in the same San Diego congressional district.

Democratic congresswoman Schenk was a Bronx-born daughter
of Holocaust survivors and a centrist liberal known for breaking the
gender barrier at the all-male Grant Grill at the US Grant Hotel in
downtown San Diego. She had already run for Congress once but lost
in a questionable election. She ran again in 1992, in a redistricted San
Diego 49th district, and won the seat previously held by a six-term
GOP congressman. She would only serve in Congress for one term
before signing on as California Governor Gray Davis's "suffer no fools"
chief of staff for five years.

Schenk was defeated in the 1994 election by Brian Bilbray, a
staunchly conservative Republican. Bilbray was a local boy, born in
Coronado. He grew up surfing, an activity he compared to politics.
Serving as mayor of Imperial Beach from 1978 to 1985, he was best
known for his failed attempt to build a yacht marina in the Tijuana

Estuary and a breakwater off Imperial Beach—both efforts stopped by local environmentalists.

In contrast to Schenk, Bilbray was strongly and vocally anti–illegal immigration. But he was also a deep advocate for free trade. Somehow at this nexus of competing political worldviews, Schenk and Bilbray found a common cause in the support of improving the efficiency of the San Diego-Tijuana border. Civic leaders in both cities credit them with taking the case to Washington, ramming through funding, and making possible the SENTRI program. Absent their efforts—principally those of Lynn Schenk, without whom the original legislation never would have passed—it is likely that the various components of the Trusted Traveler programs might have taken years, even decades, more.

As SENTRI, and the programs that grew out of it, proved increasingly successful—and influential—it began to have ancillary effects.

One was the general acceptance of the fourth strategy—now officially called the Critical Border Governance (Strategic) Doctrine—that held that security/trade and traveler facilitation were two sides of the same coin. A commitment to one, done properly, should result in great efficiency in the other.

The implementation team for SENTRI, despite it being an American project, included representatives from the civic communities on both sides of the San Ysidro crossing. This would have important long-term implications because, once SENTRI (which, interestingly, has no Spanish translation) was officially inaugurated, Mexican citizens subsequently were offered membership in the international Global Entry program—the first time they were allowed to sign up for a US government–based certification of this type.

Bersin, who was US Attorney when SENTRI was implemented and Customs and Border commissioner during the subsequent rollout of Global Entry to Mexico and other countries, looks back upon this as among the most important work he and his colleagues have achieved at the border:

> SENTRI led directly to Global Entry, which today has more than six million members, and is growing daily. The border between Tijuana and San Diego was the

breakthrough. It showed that the calculus of shrinking the haystack applied everywhere in the world and
that you don't have to be an American to be considered
low-risk. Risk management is absolutely color-blind,
and nationality and ethnicity are completely irrelevant
when sufficient advance information is available about
individuals.

It's not a coincidence that SENTRI started at the Tijuana-San
Diego crossing. After all, it was the most active binational border, one
with more than a century of individuals and goods moving across
the international boundary between the two cities. Those millions of
crossings had deeply affected each city more than either was willing to
admit. Not even 9/11 could stop for long the growth taking place in the
border-policy petri dish that San Diego-Tijuana had created.

FREEING TRADE

The expanded array of Trusted Traveler programs, oriented to people and originating with SENTRI in the 1990s, took their place alongside the Customs Trade Partnership Against Terrorism (CTPAT),
which had its roots in 9/11. This Trusted Trader program—designed
to streamline the process for importers to move goods across the border—is the embodiment, and was a genesis, of the risk-management
strategy now in place across the federal government. According to federal policy:

> The Trusted Trader program [strengthens] security,
> identif[ies] low-risk trade entities, and increase[s]
> overall efficiency of trade, by segmenting risk and
> processing by account . . . [T]he Trusted Trader pro-
> gram aims to move toward a whole [new] government
> approach to supply chain security and trade compli-
> ance by strengthening government [and private sec-
> tor] collaboration.

What began for trusted traders through the FAST program evolved into CTPAT after 9/11—proving that even an event of that magnitude could not slow for long the vast expansion of North American trading relationships generated by NAFTA. Indeed, 9/11 and the crisis it produced impelled the implementation of a comprehensive commercial risk-management program at the border. That CTPAT was instigated by a telephone call from the CEO of General Motors, G. Richard Wagoner Jr., to US president George W. Bush speaks volumes about how critical trans-border trade between the United States and Mexico (and Canada) had become.

What Wagoner told President Bush was that the emergency slowdown at the border in the immediate aftermath of the Al-Qaeda attack had so disrupted GM's internal supply chain that the company would have to shut down manufacturing plants and lay off workers. It was a reminder of Charles Erwin Wilson's famous phrase from seventy years before: "What's good for General Motors is good for the country."

Bush's Customs commissioner, Robert Bonner, oversaw the development of CTPAT. Needless to say, the Trusted Trader program was not designed with traditional Mexican craft exporters in mind but rather the powerful enterprises and US corporate clients moving billions of dollars of high-end components, systems, and finished goods across the border not only from Mexico (and Canada) but from US trading partners across the globe. The goal was, in the official words of the *Federal Register*, "to safeguard the world's vibrant trade industry from terrorists, maintaining the economic health of the United States and its neighbors. The partnership develops and adopts measures that add security but [do] not have a chilling effect on trade."

Once again, over the years that followed, the Tijuana-San Diego border crossings became the chief pioneer and test bed for innovative new processes and procedures, this time regarding the international passage of cargo. The San Diego business and Tijuana maquiladora communities were crucial to this development, motivated in part by SANDAG's influential study of the economic impact of border wait times. Regarding trucking, the report had found that delays at Otay Mesa and San Ysidro were costing the regional economy sixty thousand jobs and more than $7 billion per year. The opportunity to capture some of those lost revenues and jobs would help propel every transportation and cargo initiative that followed.

Among these initiatives was the Cargo Pre-Inspection Program, first tested at the Otay Commercial Crossing (and reciprocally by Mexican Customs at the Laredo airport in Texas). In a stunning example of cross-border law enforcement cooperation, US Customs and Border Protection officers were stationed in the Mexican commercial port of entry at Otay to conduct the preinspection of goods while they were still on the Mexican side of the border, permitting them to bypass inspection on the US side. But because CBP would not permit its officers to be stationed anywhere, let alone in Mexico, without carrying their firearms for self-defense and protection, Mexico would need to grant American law enforcement permission to cross the border with weapons.

This was an incredibly sensitive matter, with contentious historical roots as far back as the Mexican-American War.

Not surprisingly, getting the law changed in Mexico proved to be a monumental task, with the lion's share of the credit going to Mexican Tax and Customs chief Alfredo Gutiérrez Ortiz Mena (who, in time, became a justice on Mexico's Supreme Court) and Gastón Luken Garza, a congressman from Tijuana and influential *fronterizo* (whose father, Gastón Luken Aguilar, was one of the Tijuana-San Diego trailblazers in the 1970s and a mainstay influence ever since). These two men shepherded the measure through the Mexican Congress. But it could not have happened in 2015 without a final push and the unwavering support of Foreign Minister Jose Antonio Meade who had been Ortiz Mena's boss at the Treasury Ministry when the proposal was first hatched in 2012. Bersin:

> Those of us working through this issue on both sides were referred to, not so jokingly, as "Don Quixotes" because, as in *Man of La Mancha*, we were "dreaming the impossible dream." But in our case, the dream came true—and it did so first in Tijuana-San Diego—tracing profiles in political courage in Mexico at both the national and local levels. Congressman Luken Garza was tasked with getting the legislation passed:

> The purpose of the change in legislation was to improve the degree of cooperation at the border checkpoints on both sides, in order to improve the flow while improving security. It allows for US Customs inspectors to work jointly with Mexican Customs inspectors in the Mexican Customs facilities located on the south side of the border. The US officers are limited to the Mexican Customs facilities but can't go beyond those facilities while armed or on official duty. It logically wasn't easy to pass this legislation, because no country wants to have armed agents from another country in their territory. The idea obviously generated a lot of tension. But I think we were lucky in being able to explain the context and the reason behind this . . . It prevents duplicities, saves money and time. This translates into a better flow of goods with a higher level of security.

Among the later manifestations of cargo preinspection was the Unified Cargo Processing Program, now in place across most of the US-Mexico border. In this effort, begun in San Diego-Tijuana, Mexican Customs officials cross over into the US and work side-by-side with US Customs and Border Protection (CBP) officers inspecting the same cargo, at the same time and in unison.

Pete Flores, born and raised on the border, in Imperial County, has been stationed with CBP in San Diego since 2006 and has headed up the field office there since 2012, making him the chief of Passenger and Cargo Operations at the busiest crossing in the world. In fiscal year 2019, he oversaw the import from Mexico of $53 billion in merchandise and the processing of 1.4 million trucks (not to mention forty-five million people). He describes how his agency's work with Mexico has paid off:

> We've been able to work on joint inspections with Mexican Customs for truck and even for rail

[traffic] across the land border here. Instead of Mexican Customs doing an independent inspection, and then us doing a [separate] inspection of that same truck, we've consolidated those inspections here in California. We're doing those inspections jointly to prevent the shipments being inspected twice by the two governments in order to create facilitation and efficiencies for our trade stakeholders.

Anytime you create new partnerships, there's always a little bit of nervousness [about] how people are going to act together and how that will work out. I can tell you that so far, the partnership has been great. The interaction between employees has been great as well, in sharing information and working together on joint inspections. It's really created a lot more ability to have real-time conversations about issues or concerns about a shipment, an inspection of a shipment, and the real-time results of the inspection, negative or positive. More immediate interaction improves our communication and improves our ability to do our job. This absolutely has a [positive] impact on [both] security and efficiency.

In the twenty-first century, the cargo and transport innovations incubated at the Tijuana-San Diego border have stretched well beyond the region, not just on the US-Mexico border, but around the world. In retrospect, without the long-standing relationships between leaders in Tijuana and San Diego—within and outside government agencies— these milestone achievements may never have happened at all.

SHARING THE SKIES

San Diego's spectacular growth, beginning in the sixties and climbing to 1.5 million citizens by 2018, exposed a fundamental weakness in the city's transportation system: its airport.

The city and county had assiduously updated its highway system to match the needs of its growing population. The rail system, with its topographic necessity of a cross-border route, remained problematic. Meanwhile the expansion of the highways allowed trucking to answer some of the need for volume delivery to the city. And of course, San Diego's seaport was one of the best in the world (although its use was reserved mostly for maritime military purposes rather than commercial ones).

But it was air travel—that defining form of travel at the end of the twentieth century—that bedeviled San Diego. This was particularly ironic because of the city's historic relationship with the development of the airplane. Some locals still called San Diego International Airport by its original name: Lindbergh Field. Indeed, the original name might have been more appropriate, given that the airport, even with regular upgrades, still resembled that of some midsize metropolis in the Midwest, rather than the airport of the eighth-largest city in the US (and second-largest in California).

The problem, as had often been the case in the region, was not a lack of ambition but of real estate. Simply put, there is not enough room for a world-class facility at San Diego International Airport. In 1928, when it was the soon-to-be-named Lindbergh Field, there had been enough room—nearly seven hundred acres surrounded by farm fields three miles north of downtown—to handle the couple dozen biplane departures and arrivals each day. But by the turn of the century, the airport was handling as many as fifty thousand passengers per day on five hundred scheduled flights—on a single runway. Indeed, San Diego International has the dubious distinction of being the busiest single-runway airport in the US, and the third-busiest after London's Gatwick and Mumbai.

This future choke point was not lost on San Diego's leaders in the years after WWII. Indeed, it led to a fifty-year debate: Should the airport be expanded? Moved? But where?

Bersin:

> Before joining the Obama administration, I was appointed by Mayor Jerry Sanders as board chair of the Airport Authority tasked with devising and

gaining approval for an expansion plan following the voters' 2004 rejection—in an election held during the Iraq War—of a proposed move to the Navy's air base at Miramar. We then came up, under the leadership of the mayor and San Diego International Airport CEO Thella Bowens, with plan B: a $2 billion renovation and expansion plan on-site, along with a reignition of studies regarding a potential relationship with Abelardo Rodríguez [Tijuana International] Airport.

As is often the case, it wasn't the politicians but desperate citizens who found the solution first. Because traveling to cities in Mexico was much easier to do by flying inside the country, an estimated 45 percent of all people going to Mexico from Southern California would simply drive down to Tijuana International Airport and catch a flight south. That trip usually went smoothly. It was going home that was the nightmare—the delay getting back across the border at San Ysidro or Otay often took longer than the previous flight across Mexico.

Meanwhile, as San Diego had now grown, surrounding the airport with shopping centers, office buildings, and housing developments, the prospects for expanding San Diego International were essentially zero. As a result, though the airport did offer the major airlines (Southwest, American, United, Delta, and Alaska) and some international destinations (including Japan, Germany, and the United Kingdom), the operation had long since become compromised. Just as bad, given San Diego's long history in Los Angeles's shadow, the city was faced with a growing number of its visitors—and its own citizens—choosing to take quick hops to and from a real international airport, Los Angeles International (LAX), to catch long flights to their distant destinations.

If that wasn't enough, as the downtown had grown into a forest of skyscrapers, the final approach path of flights into San Diego International gave nervous fliers the disconcerting impression that they were landing between office towers. Veteran fliers would wave out the window and joke with their seatmates that they had spotted one of their friends in a nearby office just beyond the wingtip.

The truth was much more threatening, as was driven home tragically on September 25, 1978, when a PSA passenger jet collided with a Cessna 172 light aircraft over the city, killing all 144 aboard.

San Diego International did undergo a major expansion in 2013. That project added a second terminal, access roads, ten more passenger gates, and more parking—all at a cost of nearly $1 billion—to make the facility more appealing and efficient. This alone took the combined efforts of Jerry Sanders and Thella Bowens holding a year's worth of 7:00 a.m. meetings with representatives from forty different jurisdictions to get ratification. In the end, while it made San Diego International more friendly and efficient, the single-runway limitation could not—and likely never will—be overcome.

By comparison, Tijuana didn't have such a real estate problem with its airport. For a city that had always been forced to compromise due to geographical limitations—and that was founded almost a century later than its northern neighbor—this was one time when Tijuana enjoyed a geographical advantage and when being late to the party turned out to be a big plus.

Tijuana had enjoyed its own small airport, located on Agua Caliente Boulevard, on the edge of town, since the 1930s. But the city's first "real" airport, the Aeropuerto Federal de Tijuana, was opened on May 1, 1951. It was officially named after General Abelardo L. Rodríguez, Baja California's governor from 1923–1929 (and for a portion of 1932).

Initially, Tijuana's Rodríguez Airport was also a single runway (6,500 feet) with one terminal, which during the 1950s mostly handled flights between Tijuana and Mexico City. But as Tijuana grew in the 1960s and demand for flights to multiple locations grew, the airport took two important steps: it reoriented the existing runway to eliminate the need to encroach on US airspace over San Ysidro (and fly over a two-thousand-foot mountain, which, because of the steep approach, made instrument landing impossible) and to add a second, nine-thousand-foot runaway. These were critical steps, because now not only did Tijuana International Airport have two runways, one long enough to handle the biggest aircraft, but it could now operate even in foul weather.

Credit for these historically important changes belongs to Gilberto Valenzuela Ezquerro, Mexico's minister of Public Works. In 1965 he was ordered by Mexico's then-president Gustavo Díaz Ordaz to modernize all of Mexico's airports and transportation systems. As he considered the situation in Tijuana, Valenzuela Ezquerro hit upon an innovative solution: Why not propose to San Diego the creation of the world's first binational airport to be built on the cross-border Otay Mesa shared by the two cities in the Tijuana Valley? He approached San Diego's mayor, Frank Curran, with the proposal, but he was rebuffed. Mayor Curran believed the proposed site was just too far away from his city. (It goes without saying that, today, a half century later, the American side of the Otay Mesa is a well-populated neighborhood of San Diego.)

Undeterred, Valenzuela Ezquerro turned his attention to rebuilding Tijuana Airport alone. Luckily for San Diego's future, the airport, which was already located on the Mesa, wasn't moved. Further, in addition to adding a second runway and modernizing the facilities, Valenzuela expanded the site, from just 316 acres to 1,107 acres. In doing so, the forward-looking minister set the stage for a potential solution to San Diego's biggest future transportation headache.

For the next twenty years, the two airports in the two cities developed along their own separate paths. During that time, the cross-border airport concept lay largely dormant but not forgotten. Then, in 1987, San Diegan Dennis Conner's America's Cup sailing victory promised to bring tens of thousands of visitors to San Diego to watch the next Cup challenge. British no-frills airline entrepreneur Sir Frederick (Freddie) Alfred Laker saw a business opportunity for his Laker Airways. He approached Mexican charter airline tycoon Rodolfo Ramos Ortiz and proposed to build a cross-border joint venture. Unfortunately, the deal fell through.

But the idea continued to intrigue entrepreneurs in both the United States and Mexico. In 1990, one of the participants in the Freddie Laker negotiations, Mexican-American real estate developer Ralph Nieders of San Diego, approached the Mexico City aeronautics firm Mexicana de Aviación, SA with a similar proposal. This time the proposal actually was accepted and progressed through a letter of intent.

Nieders's scenario this time was to purchase the Martinez Ranch in Otay and use it as the site of the new airport. He also approached SANDAG with his plans. SANDAG was still nursing the failure of its own binational airport plan, which had been foiled by the city of San

Diego the previous November when it lifted its ban on building on the Mesa, setting off a residential-home land rush. SANDAG signed on to Nieders's plan.

The Nieders-Mexicana de Aviación plan was ambitious. On the US side alone, the airport would offer both a passenger and a light-cargo terminal, the former connected by a passenger bridge to the terminal at Rodríguez Field. Meanwhile, an underground conveyor system would move light cargo between customs warehouses in each country and to private carriers such as DHL, UPS, and FedEx. There was also to be a Free Trade Zone established at the border to handle larger cargo.

This plan, too, failed, in part because SANDAG had moved on to another airline proposal, one to turn either the Marine Corps Recruit Depot or the Naval Air Station Miramar into a replacement for San Diego Airport. The Pentagon turned down the two proposals. SANDAG tried again with a second binational airport proposal—even to the point of visiting Mexico City armed with an eight-page booklet entitled "Tijuana-San Diego International Airport," filled with illustrations of the proposed airport with its three runways.

Unfortunately, two of those runways would have required moving Tijuana Airport's passenger terminal and one of its runways. That was something the Mexican government was not willing to do—after all, it already had an excellent airport. Why should it be punished for the Americans' failure to plan for the future?

The Mexican government did make a counterproposal: Why doesn't San Diego just develop a cross-border terminal with a bridge link to the Tijuana Airport? SANDAG turned down the idea as too limited.

It would come to regret that decision.

Later that year, in 1990, there would be one last attempt to build a Tijuana-San Diego binational airport. This was led by San Diego councilman Ron Roberts, who happened to be an architect. On his own initiative, he, too, developed a plan to build a binational airport on the Mexican border. Roberts's Twin Ports proposal also involved building on the Otay Mesa, but this time just west of 3,572-foot Otay Mountain. On the US side of the border, San Diego would build a 12,000-foot runway running parallel to the existing long runway on the Tijuana side, with shared taxiways and control tower. In Roberts's vision, the resulting complex would function as a giant international airport, with American passengers landing on the Mexican runway, then taxiing to the US terminal.

As always, the response in San Diego was enthusiastic—and as often happened, it failed. But in the process, it did, in the words of San Diego's *City Beat* magazine, "draw the ire of some local leaders, determined to push their own airport sites through." It was not well received either by federal authorities in Mexico City, who chafed at the short memories and perceived arrogance of its proponents.

Roberts would later say: "Of all the things I've ever worked on that didn't happen, probably most disappointing would be the Twin Ports plan, because I think the future of this community is going to be impacted greatly." In retrospect, however, even if the plan had been more realistic and gained political support in both countries, 9/11 and the fight over illegal immigration in the new century would have killed it.

Some of the alternate ideas for an airport site, then and in the years that followed, were the stuff of science fiction. *City Beat*:

> "One weird proposal in the eighties," remembers Congressman Bob Filner [then a member of the San Diego City Council and subsequently a disgraced mayor of the city convicted of sexually assaulting women], "was someone suggested that we should have planes land at Lindbergh Field and take off at North Island. [T]hey never explained how you get between the two." Another suggestion cited most often on the list of the outlandish [was] the idea of a floating airport—dubbed "fantasy island" by some legislators—off the coast of Point Loma.

The ludicrous nature of these proposals underscores San Diego's desperation about finding a solution to its growing need for a true international airport. As *City Beat* wrote at the time: "An airport, like a lot of big planning projects, becomes an emotional issue as much as a planning issue." It also reflected the unwillingness of city residents to have an airport in their backyards. Further, it captured something else: civic pride and the weight of history. San Diegans, from the city's leadership to everyday citizens, might imagine sharing an airport with Tijuana but couldn't imagine using an airport that existed exclusively in—and was owned by—Tijuana. That still, in their minds, was a bridge too far.

AN EQUITABLE SOLUTION

But by 2006, the world had changed. Tijuana had not only grown to become a city nearly the population of San Diego, but relations between the two cities—politically, commercially, and culturally—were better than they had ever been. Meanwhile, even as Tijuana Airport had thrived—further expanding its facilities in 2002, becoming part of the twelve-airport Pacific Airport Group (Grupo Aeroportuario del Pacífico), and adding international flights to Japan and China—San Diego International, despite endlessly improving its efficiency, was only feeling the pinch even more. Moreover, the success of the new passenger-crossing programs at the border points of entry was proving daily that the movement of citizens across the border could be made both efficient and safe.

San Diego would need to swallow some of its pride and accept first that Tijuana International Airport would play an important role in its future, and second that it was time to dust off the old Mexican solution, now featuring the latest air transportation and cross-border technology.

This new program, which would at last achieve San Diego's enduring dream of enjoying the benefits of a true international airport, would ultimately be called Cross Border Xpress (CBX). The project would begin with a low-key announcement in 2006 (the year that SANDAG had predicted—back in 1988—that San Diego International would reach full capacity) by the San Diego Regional Airport Authority that it would investigate building a cross-border airport terminal to give passengers access to Tijuana International Airport and thereby relieve pressure at Lindbergh Field.

That was it. It seemed just one more proposal in decades of such failed efforts. But however humble its start, this initiative succeeded—not least because the time was right. San Diego was desperate, Tijuana triumphant, and teamwork between the cities was the greatest ever. Civic leaders like Malin Burnham, used to thinking both big and boldly, solidly backed the proposal, community leaders like Cindy Gompper-Graves propelled it forward, and veteran border proponent Alan Bersin was chair of the Airport Authority. The vision would take nearly a decade to realize, but when it was complete CBX would become a historic milestone, making Tijuana International the world's first functionally binational airport, with a San Diego terminal in the United States and its main passenger terminal and runways in Mexico.

Cross Border Xpress (CBX) San Diego Terminal and bridge to Tijuana International Airport.

That said, San Diego International Airport still has no physical or financial connection with CBX. There aren't even organized shuttle services between the two locations, keeping the two airports from reaching their potential as a connecting hub for Mexican and Latin American travelers to Northern California, Las Vegas, and the Pacific Northwest. The visionaries' next dream is to build a monorail connection between San Diego International and CBX, and thus to Tijuana International. Time will tell, but the history of commercial aviation in

San Diego doesn't lead to much optimism that this will happen anytime soon.

PRIVATE PLAYERS

Once San Diegans accepted the idea of using Tijuana's airport as its own for flights south to Mexico and Central and South America (and increasingly west over the Pacific to Asia), the next challenge was finding the capital and gaining the governmental go-aheads to build such an unprecedented terminal and passenger bridge facility. After all, despite the nearly unbearable congestion at San Diego International, San Diego's citizens had long proven themselves wary of paying for anything using public funds. Decades of voting down bond issues dampened any hopes that the public would fund a facility likely to cost more than $80 million. As a proposed cross-border facility, it was a federal responsibility anyway—and the federal government was not likely to pay for a new class of border crossing at a site not even on its list of infrastructure priorities.

Then, a breakthrough: federal authorities appeared to be open to a public-private partnership (a P3), and seeing a business opportunity in CBX, a consortium of investors from both sides of the border—including Chicago real estate and newspaper magnate Sam Zell—formed a new company, Otay-Tijuana Venture LLC. The company bought the targeted land on the north side of the border for $30 million and set about raising funds for construction. Realizing that its longtime dream just might finally come true, the city of San Diego jumped in with both feet, embarking on a major advocacy campaign in both Mexico City and Washington, DC, to gain support for the initiative. The bigger challenge—partly because most of CBX would be on the US side but also because of the enduring concern over international terrorism—was with the US government.

The timing proved to be perfect. US-Mexican relations, tense a few years before (and destined to be tense again a few years later), were experiencing a thaw, and both sides were looking for signature partnerships to promote the renewed amity. CBX fit the bill, and to the surprise of many, the US State Department agreed. It approved the project in 2010 and granted the presidential permit necessary for cross-border facilities. Showing how anxious San Diego was to get things done, the city took only two years, until 2012, to grant all the permits for land use and construction at the site. The negotiations with the federal government over operations and costs were arduous to be sure but adroitly handled by Enrique Valle, CEO of Otay-Tijuana Venture, and Ben Rohrbaugh for Customs and Border Protection (working under Alan Bersin, who was then CBP commissioner). Just two years later, in 2014, construction began.

Constructing a cross-border bridge would come with its own challenges. Valle explains: "The length of the Mexican bridge from the Tijuana Airport to the border is 150 feet." That portion would be built by a Tijuana team. "And there's another portion, of six hundred additional feet, to get to the building on the US side." That portion would be built by a San Diego team. Not only did this mean translating all plans from the American system of measurement to the Mexican system, it meant the Mexican team would need to build their portion of the shared bridge to California building codes, some of the strongest regulations in the world. But the challenges did not stop there.

When it came to assembling the structural beams on the Mexican side of the border, says Valle, "There was no room for that." The structure would cross "one of the main highways in Tijuana." To close the highway would be too disruptive. To authorize Mexican workers and a Mexican company to work on the US side of the border would have been a bureaucratic nightmare. So Valle sought an unlikely third option: "We spoke with CBP, and CBP agreed to move the border." A testament to the amity of the times, the US agreed to move a 450-foot length of border fence fifty feet into US territory, so the Tijuana team could construct their side of the bridge on what was now, temporarily, Mexican soil.

Incredibly, in December 2015, a mere three years after US government approval, Cross Border Xpress opened for the first US passengers to cross over to Rodríguez Field and fly out of Tijuana International Airport. It was the first bridge west of Texas, where bridges and tolls across the Rio Grande River were common, to charge a fee to travel over the border. The CBX arrangement was a new form of public-private partnership, where all construction capital and operating expenses were funded privately (including the cost of CBP officers) but operated by Customs and Border Protection as an official port of entry and exit between Mexico and the United States.

The official ribbon cutting, in April 2016, was attended by the mayors of Tijuana and San Diego. At the time the facility's name was officially changed from the Tijuana Cross-Border Terminal to CBX (Cross Border Xpress). The award-winning, postmodern facility (which had ultimately cost $120 million thanks to cost overruns) was created—again in the spirit of cross-border amity—by the famed Mexican architect Ricardo Legorreta, who worked with a premier architectural firm, Stantec Inc. of Canada. From the beginning, the CBX facility was lauded not just for its simple and elegant design but also for its appropriateness: its airiness and its garden, featuring desert plants, evoking the old Tijuana Valley of the mission era, before its urbanization.

But more important, CBX was designed to be efficient, eventually to serve as many as 2.5 million passengers per year, more than a third of the overall traffic at Tijuana International. To do that, each component of the CBX facility had to work well and in harmony. In the official description:

> Passengers departing from the US park on CBX property, enter the building, check in, walk over the border using the new bridge, and literally descend into [Tijuana International] to reach their flights. Returning passengers land at [Tijuana International], take the bridge across the border, enter the US through the new [US Customs and Border Protection] facility, and emerge from the CBX to take their preferred form of transportation.

This formal description doesn't capture the singular experience of using CBX. In practice, travelers park in a lot in suburban Otay Mesa contiguous to Tijuana Airport and, showing their boarding passes and passports (and paying $16 to the private investors for the opportunity), and pass through the 65,000-square-foot US terminal. Then they cross the signature, purple 390-foot bridge over the border, with its black fence, and then down into the terminal at Tijuana International. It all looks simple, but the entire structure was something of a prodigy of engineering, including an extensive retrofitting of the terminal on the Tijuana side to serve as a pier to the bridge and as a portal to five thousand or more new arrivals crossing the border every day. These travelers from the US side arrive both day and night. Unlike its counterpart in San Diego, which is subject to a curfew, Tijuana International is open twenty-four hours a day. Not to mention the cost of plane tickets out of Tijuana can be as much as one-third cheaper than out of San Diego International.

The new facility has received generally glowing reviews, including even from Ron Roberts, the councilman who proposed the Twin Ports solution. Having used CBX multiple times, he has publicly stated that it is "working super."

So successful has CBX been in its few years of existence that it is already experiencing growing pains. The biggest is parking: the original CBX parking capacity was overwhelmed within a matter of months, forcing a quick expansion. But even that hasn't proven sufficient; so the city of San Diego, ever anxious to keep this outlet growing, has already approved permits for a new parking garage—and even a hotel—adjacent to the CBX facility.

Ironically, given the concern on the US side about surrendering the future of the area's commercial aviation to another city in another country, the presence of CBX and its connection to Tijuana International hasn't reduced usage of San Diego International. To the contrary, demand by commercial passengers in the region has grown so strongly that San Diego International usage has continued to expand—albeit perhaps slightly less than it might have. Of course, San Diego International Airport (the name was changed from Lindbergh Field in 2003) can barely handle the passenger and flight traffic it has now.

It all proves that, rather than a threat to San Diego's commercial aviation program, the new connection to Tijuana's airport likely averted an air transportation catastrophe. Travelers now have a choice of two airports from which to travel, with many more destinations to which they can fly nonstop. Once again, Tijuana helped spare San Diego from the consequences of its own limitations—and in the process had found another way to grow rich on American dollars. Air traffic to Tijuana since CBX has increased 33 percent.

As San Diego's mayor Kevin Faulconer, who presided over the grand opening of CBX along with Tijuana's mayor Jorge Astiazarán Orcí, would tell Politico, "We breathe the same air, we use the same watershed . . . [T]he story of San Diego is the story of its relationship with Mexico." It remains for San Diego to figure out how to capitalize on CBX from its end.

RAINMAKER

Carlos Bustamante, 74, is a man who gets things done. He got a running start early. His father, Felix, has been called the founder of modern Tijuana: his twin towers, only recently joined by other high-rises, defined the Tijuana skyline for a generation.

Carlos was schooled in the United States, attending high school at the Army and Navy Academy in Carlsbad and college at the University of San Diego. As a young man, he worked as the Baja California state distributor for his family's oil and propane gas company. By twenty-eight, he was elected chairman of the Chamber of Industry of Baja California. He also helped with the construction of his father's twin towers in 1981:

> My father liked the hotel business. He had already built one hotel; now across the street he wanted to build another, bigger one. It was supposed to be 200 rooms. It ended up being 430.
>
> He didn't stop there. With the one tower, he wanted to build another, this one full of offices and medical facilities for what he predicted would be a major medical-tourism industry here. That tower took a little longer because Mexico started having problems in its banking industry and the government nationalized the banks.

Carlos did not just stick with the family business. Even in his twenties, his growing involvement with various industry associations had given him a taste for local politics, and he started getting involved. "I noticed that lots of people like to complain about things. But nobody tries to fix those things."

Bustamante had long been a supporter of the PRI. Now the governor, a fellow party member, asked him to form a business council to promote the region internationally. In the process, Carlos made good friends in China: "They ended up doing business with me at the center we have at the Tijuana Airport."

From there on, his career would follow two paths. On one path, the PRI asked him to become a candidate for Tijuana mayor in 2010. Carlos entered the race twenty-one points behind. Meanwhile his opponent from PAN was the groom in a much-publicized wedding, attended in Tijuana by Mexican president Felipe Calderón. Nevertheless, a few weeks later, Bustamante won the election by five points. How? "God only knows," he says with a laugh. "I like to think it was a lot of hard work. But maybe it just was that the people were sick of all the corruption and violence—remember, this was during the drug wars—and figured maybe a businessman could fix things up. In the end, we did fix a lot of things."

In fact, Bustamante's tenure is often credited with reducing Tijuana's annual murder rate—from eight hundred to four hundred—and launching the city on its current era of prosperity. That has made him one of the most consequential Tijuana mayors of the modern era. Carlos is proud of that achievement, but he notes ruefully that it wasn't permanent: at this writing, Tijuana is bloodier than ever.

At the same time, Bustamante set out to sell Tijuana to the world. He worked his network in the Far East for investment, and he encouraged US corporations to participate in the maquiladora movement. He became close friends with San Diego mayor Jerry Sanders, establishing the strongest mayoral relationship in the history of the two cities. They launched the US-Mexico Border Mayors Association together, hosted the inaugural meetings in Tijuana and San Diego to develop consensus policy platforms, and supported its expansion to involve functions today, and Carlos and Jerry remain good friends. Bustamante built a similar friendship with CBP Commissioner Alan Bersin who proposed the idea of a border mayors' association to him to advocate for the border in both Mexico City and Washington. "We all agreed that what's good for Tijuana is good for San Diego and vice versa, and the same is true along the entire border," Bustamante says with a glint in his eye.

Those friendships proved crucial because, during Bustamante's tenure as mayor, the US embarked on a massive, $750 million renovation of its border crossing at San Ysidro, and Mexico built a completely new facility on its side. "It was obviously going to affect traffic, so we worked very closely together to make sure we weren't obstructing construction schedules, while still getting the cars and people through."

Those same friendships proved pivotal in the creation of CBX. Bustamante, who already had a thriving business at the Tijuana Airport, was initially resistant to the plan. As mayor he did not want to antagonize Tijuana taxi drivers who stood to lose business carrying passengers from the airport to the US border crossings if CBX were built. "But Alan made a very convincing argument that it would work," Bustamante recalls.

> He said, "I don't think there's another one like this in the world." And he mentioned to me, "It rarely happens that you get the US president and the Mexican president to agree on something like this at the border." That importance made me reflect a little bit. And that's mainly why I did it.

In the end, Bustamante became a major supporter. "I'm glad he changed my mind, because it really has been a boon for everyone. Even I use it."

Parallel to all this was Carlos's pursuit of the dream that would become Matrix, Tijuana's new air-cargo operation. It took him thirty years.

> There was a British gentleman named Len Dunning who was living in Hong Kong and was director of the Hong Kong Trade Development Council. I've never forgotten what he said when he landed in Tijuana: "My God, this is a green field. Where else can you find an airport that is just a stone's throw from the United States?"

I approached the Mexican government of President Carlos Salinas Gortari and convinced them to give me a concession for sixty acres inside the airport to create an aircraft-maintenance operation, because that's how they started at [Hong Kong's] airport. President Salinas agreed, and we opened the facility in 1995. We also slowly added air-freight services.

Then, a few years later, the federal government privatized Mexico's airport. Now the new operator (GAP) wanted to take away my concession. I took them to court.

It took eleven years, but I won, and I started the air freight terminal. It has a long Spanish name, but we just call it Matrix.

The facility, to be known as Matrix Air Cargo and Logistics Park, would begin operations in Bustamante's airplane-repair hangar. As planned, it would include an on-site Mexican Customs inspection area and a bonded distribution center, with plans already in the works to add a US Customs facility. Bustamante's strategy was to first capture the air freight currently being processed at the airport and then to capture US express carriers and freight forwarders who would find the quick border crossing far less cost- and time-intensive than their current practice of using Los Angeles International Airport.

In June 2018, Bustamante publicly announced Matrix. With Tijuana's Abelardo Rodríguez Airport already an important passenger hub in Tijuana Valley, Bustamante and his son, Matrix president Carlos Bustamante Aubanel, now were proceeding to make it the dominant cargo hub as well, both for domestic and international routes. Even the *San Diego Union-Tribune*, once wary of life across the border, now cheered the location:

Just west of the cargo facility is the Cross Border Xpress, a privately operated skywalk between San Diego and the Tijuana airport. About two miles to the east is the planned Otay East Port of Entry, envisioned as a toll facility planned and operated jointly by the United States and Mexico. Farther east in Tecate is a project for a future cross-border commercial rail crossing.

Matrix is a cargo and commercial game changer for the region. Almost from the day of his announcement, Bustamante was inundated with contacts from near and far. Nearby, in Tijuana and northern Baja California, the maquiladoras were looking for a reliable delivery source for the components—from medical to aircraft—they needed from Asia, Europe, and the United States to keep their assembly lines moving. From Asia, the interest was in getting a quick and reliable delivery source for fresh fish and produce from Baja California and elsewhere in Mexico.

On the US side, there is already talk of recreating the success of the CBX bridge with an aerial tram system, a "freight shuttle," that would originate at a revitalized Brown Field Municipal Airport, which is located on the Otay Mesa about 1.5 miles from the border, and move containers of cargo across the border to the Matrix facility.

As for those (on both sides of the border) skeptical about his plans, Bustamante told the *San Diego Union-Tribune* in words that might serve as the epitaph of the story of transportation and much else that has happened in the Tijuana Valley: "I'm stubborn. I said I'm going to see it through, though they told me I was crazy."

Bustamante smiles at the memory. Everything he predicted has come true. "Today, we host UPS, FedEx, DHL, and all the Mexican carriers. And we are about to transport goods to the Orient. Mexican Customs has moved to our terminal as well. So the future looks pretty promising."

It looks pretty great for Tijuana too, Bustamante believes:

> If you look around Tijuana, you're going to see a lot of condos being built. A *lot* of them. Why? Because in San Diego a two-bedroom apartment will run you $3,000 a month. In Tijuana? $800. That's why Americans, particularly Mexican-Americans, are moving here— especially if the border gets easier to cross, so they can get to their jobs in San Diego. The trained workforce is

here, with access to the US market. That's why companies from other parts of Mexico are moving here.

It was Jerry Sanders who first called us "two cities,
one region." I think that's where we are now, and it's
great for both of us. We're becoming real sister cities.
And why not? We breathe the same air; we look out
on the same ocean. We increasingly share the same
future.

"Of course, I'm always optimistic," Bustamante says with a broad
smile and sparkling eyes. "That's how I get things done."

TROLLEY TALES

Compared to the multiple victories in ground and air transportation
in Tijuana, the third transportation form—rail—has been a mixed success, despite the fact, as already noted, that San Diego had been pursuing the dream of a continental rail connection for more than a century.

One form of rail transportation that has proven wildly successful
is light rail: the legendary San Diego Trolley.

San Diego Trolley Inc. (SDTI) is a subsidiary of the San Diego
Metropolitan Transit System (SDMTS) and has been in service since
July 1961, making it the oldest "second-generation" system in the US.
But, in fact, it has been in existence far longer, as a descendant of the
San Diego Electric Railway, which was installed in 1891 by civic leader
and businessman John Spreckels. Before that, starting in 1886, a horse-
drawn, open-air streetcar ran up and down Fifth Avenue, eventually
replaced by a cable railway.

The original, nineteenth-century electric railway, the first in the
western US, initially served both new and old downtown San Diego
with just five routes totaling about twelve miles of track. In the years
that followed more track would be laid, with the number and length
of the routes jumping after 1905, when Spreckels built a new electrical power plant to support the line. In 1910, following a ballot initiative that gave him control of the railway for another quarter century,
and the construction of a second power plant, Spreckels embarked on

another expansion, to a total of eighty-four miles of light rail in the city and into its suburbs. The 1915 Panama-California Exposition spurred yet another expansion, notably to Balboa Park.

But World War I brought a halt to the golden age of the San Diego Electric Railway. Construction costs rose nearly three-fold, floods wiped out part of the line, and the first gasoline buses arrived on the scene as competition. By 1920 the situation had become dire, prompting Spreckels to shut down lines and sell one of his power plants. By 1930, buses were replacing the rail lines' perpetually popular beach routes.

Yet, even as light rail companies were folding, their tracks replaced by roadways in cities throughout the United States, San Diego's Electric Railway somehow hung on, always on the brink of going bankrupt, long enough to see a second life.

That resurrection came in 1942 with World War II. Suddenly, between sailors and defense workers, San Diego was one of the busiest cities in the country—and all were on the move, either on leave and wanting to hit the town, or going to work at the port or defense-industry factories. Ridership jumped 600 percent during those years. In 1942 alone, the combined streetcar and bus lines carried 94 million riders, and by 1944, 146 million. So desperate did the Electric Railway become for rolling stock that it brought in scores of cars on loan from as far away as New York City and Pennsylvania.

These boom times didn't last long after VJ Day. As early as 1946, there were only three streetcar lines remaining. New owners, beginning in 1948, focused on buses in lieu of rail. Indeed, by May of that year, crews began to remove the overhead electrical lines and pull up tracks. By the end of 1949, San Diego was the first major city in the US Southwest to eliminate all its streetcars, many of which were sold to Mexican cities (though not Tijuana) or donated to museums.

But by the 1980s, the world had again changed. As traffic congestion and commute times grew, interest in mass transit returned. Belying its conservative reputation in this instance, San Diego led the way, becoming known in later years as the city that launched the light rail craze in the United States.

Championed by State Senator James Mills, the San Diego Trolley began service in July 1981. It would eventually expand to a total of fifty-four miles and fifty-three stations, and it is still growing rapidly forty years later.

From the beginning San Diegans took the Trolley to heart, and its parent company, SDMTS, went to great lengths to assure they did. It not only installed the latest-generation European streetcars on its three primary lines (Blue, Orange, and Green) but also restored historic trains for special use, notably on the downtown Silver Line, which operates on weekends and holidays.

Today, the San Diego Trolley is a vital part of the city's transportation network. In the final quarter of 2014, with 120,000 riders each day, it was the fifth-most ridden light rail system in the United States. Apparently, that is just the beginning. Working with the cities of SANDAG, an extension of the Trolley's Blue Line is currently being built in the eleven miles between San Diego's Old Town Transit Center and UC San Diego to the north. It is expected to be completed in 2021 and will more closely tie the university and its surrounding neighborhoods with downtown. In an interesting irony, studies are currently underway to restore the electrified railway from city center to Balboa Park, possibly using vintage cars. Another plan would extend the Orange Line from downtown to San Diego International Airport.

But the most interesting future plan for the San Diego Trolley would take place along what is being called the Purple Line. This streetcar line would run from Kearny Mesa, just inland from Old Town San Diego, due south twenty-three miles to the border crossing at San Ysidro. That alone would be a measure of how much the border has become integrated into the daily life of San Diego. But the planning doesn't stop there. Already this vision includes plans to continue the Purple Line across the international border—with a fast customs-crossing program similar to SENTRI—and into Tijuana. This would take considerable pressure off the endless traffic crowding the roads across the border.

If such a line were completed—and there is no reason to doubt it will be—the San Diego-Tijuana Trolley Line, like so many other binational collaborations between the two cities, will be the only system of its kind in the world.

TRACKS OF TEARS

Unfortunately, the same good news and optimism does not extend to the region's other mass transportation system, the Binational Railroad.

Because of their shared location in the Tijuana Coastal Plain, San Diego and Tijuana have always found mass transport of goods and people unusually challenging. The endless, frustrating attempts to build a real railroad from the canyons and mesas north to Los Angeles and beyond were described earlier in this book. John Spreckels may have been brilliant at building a streetcar line, but even he consistently failed at creating a permanent, profitable railroad line out of his city.

So has it been true ever since. The recurring floods and complex topography to the north make building a reliable rail line a daunting, expensive proposition. More promising is the path to the east, but because of the location of mountain ranges there, any such track would not only need to vault steep river valleys but—and this has been the biggest obstacle—any such line would necessarily have to swing back and forth across the border, with all the questions of sovereignty, ownership, security, and custom duties that entails.

As a result, San Diego and Tijuana are among the few major cities on earth that are not hubs of extensive railroad networks. Because rail remains the most efficient means of transporting large manufactured goods and foodstuffs in volume, this imposes a major limitation on the two cities. Therefore, the dream of a railroad remains alive today.

Currently that dream takes the form of a proposal by Baja California Railroad (BJRR) to construct a state-of-the-art, binational railroad line. The Desert Line would exit east out of the Valley, crossing the border near Campo, California, and connecting with the Union Pacific in Imperial County. Will it finally happen? Perhaps, though the odds are probably worse than they were a decade ago.

Still, Roberto Romandía, CEO of BJRR, is not giving up:

> We're looking to do a joint venture with a well-established company. We are already getting close to a Utah company, and we are in conversation with two others. One stipulation we are making is that they

handle different commodities—like natural gas, diesel, and jet fuel—that can be the anchor to the Desert Line.

At the same time, all of the big maquiladoras—Toyota, Samsung, Sanyo, and Hyundai—have signed letters of intent to bring raw materials to the region on the railroad when it is finished. The Port of Ensenada wants to use the railroad to transport raw materials that arrive via ship.

Romandía admits that many people call such a rail line impossible—indeed, its nickname for more than a century has been the Impossible Railroad—but he argues that the latest studies and technologies suggest that it can now be done.

The critical year, he says, is 2020. All the players—the Mexican and US governments, BJRR and whoever becomes its partners, engineering companies, and all the other stakeholders in the project—will be holding regular meetings to determine what needs to be done, who will do it, and who will pay for it. If they all agree, construction on the Desert Line will begin. Until then, it remains the Impossible Railroad.

Meanwhile, the lack of a great rail system to San Diego and Tijuana will remain a century-old congenital defect in the economies of both cities. One that even Matrix, the Port of San Diego, and the region's massive highway network and giant fleet of trucks won't quite ever heal.

CHAPTER NINE

Making It Personal—
The Rise of the World's Most
Dynamic Cross-Border Community

One of the most important features of the San Ysidro Point of Entry are the pedestrian crossings on the west and east sides of the auto lanes, a massive $741 million undertaking finished in 2019. Thanks largely to Jason Wells, CEO of the San Ysidro Chamber of Commerce, the pedestrian lanes feature their own SENTRI/Global Entry program for trusted travelers crossing the border on foot. This has proven exceptionally useful to shoppers in Tijuana, who come across the border by the thousands each day to take advantage of the many retail stores that have opened nearby to cater to them. The result is a singular mix of the two cultures that could only exist in The Borderland.

Iris and José are married and live in Tijuana. They have come to the Las Americas Premium Outlets to "buy some pants sets from Aéropostale. Dark blue. Oh, and we've gone to Gap and Old Navy. We came to shop for family," says Iris in Spanish. Iris is a certified public accountant; José is an engineer. They estimate that they have spent $200 today.

Automobiles line up at the world's busiest land border crossing.

Why did they come to this mall in particular, instead of driving further north? "It's closer to us, and for the quality and prices. We are registered in the stores here, too, so we get sales coupons in the mail in Tijuana. Like 20 percent off an item or even the whole purchase.

Sometimes we come here every week; other times of the year, once a month."

The couple say they tend to buy the same type of items on both sides of the border, but typically they cross to San Diego to buy here. "For example, if I go to Nike in Tijuana, the price is double for the same shoes as here. And both stores are about the same distance from where we live—a couple miles." However, they admit, making the crossing adds another forty minutes—but for now it is worth it. It is worth it, too, to come to San Diego even for household incidentals. And they certainly need those: Iris and José have five children, from age thirteen to six months.

Estefania Gonzales, 22, and her daughter Ximena, 4, are from Rosarito Beach, the coastal neighbor of Tijuana. Estefania wears a Tommy Hilfiger ski jacket; Ximena wears a pink Old Navy sweatshirt with a matching pink bow in her hair. Estefania is a business student at the Universidad de Mexicali and works for the government.

"I am here today to buy Christmas presents for a gift exchange," Estefania says in Spanish. "I also came to buy some clothes for Christmas." The pile of bags beside Ximena's stroller confirms that she's shopped at Burlington, Ross, Marshalls, Gap, and Old Navy. Estefania estimates that today she has spent $500 so far.

"I come to buy here regularly because it's just across the border and also the closest mall. I came by car, but it stays on the other side because it is easier to come on foot. I come every month or so. Right now, I'll be coming more because of the season." On this trip, she says she's mostly bought socks, sweaters, and other winter garments.

Estefania says that on other shopping trips to the US she also buys toys, shoes, and even food. Why, when the same items can be purchased in Tijuana? "I think the quality is much better here. And the prices are better too. For example, I can purchase two items here for the price of one there. In Rosarito [Beach] I mostly buy food."

Wandering the mall, speaking another language, mixing with a different culture, does Estefania ever feel unwelcome?

She says with a laugh, "Actually it is more comfortable here. In Mexico they treat you like you're a delinquent when you are shopping. [Security] constantly follows you around and watches your every move. Shopping in Mexico is very uncomfortable, especially when you want to try clothes on. I understand the crime rate is just a little higher there, but not *that* much. It's better to shop here."

Then she considers a different angle: "It feels safer in Mexico than San Diego when you are shopping." How so? Because, she says, though the store security in Mexico annoys her, she feels nervous in San Diego where there is less visible law enforcement. "I think Americans don't think that people are going to steal stuff." She seems amused by the apparent contradiction in what she just said.

She shrugs, adding that Mexican salespeople are more personable, while American ones are more serious and professional. "We Mexicans try to be happy at all times, and we always greet others with happiness."

A WELCOME FLOOD

With the development of new public and private programs at the turn of the twentieth century, crossing the border between San Diego and Tijuana became much easier. Indeed, for residents on both sides of the border, the opposite city became "el otro lado," the other side of town. San Diegans and Tijuanenses began treating the once-endless crossing as little more than another stretch of road congestion.

Initially, this binational experience was reserved primarily for the well-to-do shuttling between primary and vacation homes, mostly on weekends, or between home and school on weekdays. But within a few years, border crossing became incorporated into the lifestyles of ordinary people, even US military personnel who live on one side of the border and work on the other. On the Tijuana side, the biggest attractions for Mexican citizens (and increasingly, Americans) were the highly competitive real estate prices, in close proximity to the better-paying professional jobs to the north, in San Diego. On the San Diego side (where a growing number of increasingly prosperous Mexicans were also making their homes), the equivalent appeal was greater security and the attraction of superior infrastructure and premium products, prices, and services.

The result was a quotidian mixing of populations and cultures never before experienced in the two cities, even in the days when crossing the border was all but unrestricted. Now, not even the imposing wall that casts its shadow over the border could stop this growing interpenetration of the two societies.

Of course, this mixing produced some unlikely phenomena. For example, the governor of Baja California made his home in Chula Vista. Meanwhile, each day, California doctors made the drive to Tijuana to their offices and clinics, where they often administered care to patients from the United States. Students who lived in apartments on one side of the border crossed each day to attend universities on the opposite. On both sides of the border people listened to radio shows emanating from the other side. What the San Diego Dialogue discovered in the 1990s about locals making up the vast majority of border crossers has grown beyond even the prognosticators' wildest predictions: each day, nearly seventy thousand cars pass through the San Ysidro Point of Entry alone, and thirty-two million pedestrians make the crossing each year.

A sizable fraction of this extraordinary number doesn't travel far, either. The areas abutting the border on both sides have seen the greatest growth since 2000, such that nearly a half million people, in 150,000 households, now live within ten miles of the San Ysidro Point of Entry. Like the families shopping at the Las Americas Premium Outlets, they confine much of their shopping to nearby stores, to the tune of $5 billion per year. In a telling turnabout, the amount of shopping by Tijuanenses in San Diego stores now far exceeds that of San Diegans shopping in Tijuana. Alan Bersin:

> Once we cracked the heart of the matter and created a safe and efficient means and—mostly—predictable time of crossing the borderline at the ports of entry, the potential for "one community in two countries" became possible. After all, it is difficult to manage professional or personal and social relationships and calendars if meetings are missed because of multi-hour delays in border crossing. Making the border predictable totally altered the calculus in this respect for hundreds of thousands of people who responded accordingly. Bringing border corridors under control, and improving the security there, created the

possibility for neighborhoods in what previously had been a "no-man's-land." Houses and schools and shopping centers were built, and the people came.

Of the effort to open the cities to one another, says C. Samuel Marasco, president of LandGrant Development and developer of La Plaza de las Americas: "We're turning two back doors into two celebrated front doors."

Despite all these advances, the cross-border situation remains fragile. Though it is unlikely it could return to the difficult days of the two cities staring warily across their common border, the current boom will remain vulnerable to some of the same forces that have threatened amity in the past: crime in Mexico, economic recessions in the United States, and perhaps most of all, the enduring problem of vast swings in the currency exchange rate that have troubled the two countries forever, as well as the business fortunes that are deeply affected by those swings.

Even as Tijuana and San Diego begin to look more and more like one metropolis, when even language becomes—slowly—less of a barrier, the fact that they will continue to operate with separate monetary systems will present a giant risk. Yet even that is beginning to change, as Tijuana becomes more "dollarized," with some financial institutions, retailers (such as José B. Fimbres at Calimax), and landlords (like Lorenzo Berho, industrial park developer at Vesta) accepting payment in both currencies, even as many still trade (and, when appropriate, offer stock) in pesos.

MR. SAN DIEGO

Malin Burnham may be the single most consequential private citizen in the story of a single major American city in the last century. It is impossible to understand San Diego—and its relationship with Tijuana—without appreciating his role in the two cities over the last forty years. At 92, he remains as active as ever.

Burnham was born in San Diego, and he has devoted all three of his lives to making the city great. In his first life, despite having a degree in industrial engineering from Stanford, he worked for his father as a real estate developer, mortgage lender, and banker. He worked diligently at his job until his father abruptly, at age fifty-six, announced his retirement and Malin's appointment, at just thirty-two, as the firm's new CEO. Three years after that, Malin's father, who had moved up to chairman, retired completely from the business world to spend the rest of his life powerboating with Malin's mother.

Malin was stunned: "His retirement came as something of a surprise to the company and even to me. We never really believed he'd do it. But he had always been a man of his word, and this time was no different."

Now, at just thirty-five, Malin Burnham found himself running a multimillion-dollar firm, one of the youngest financiers in the region. This experience led him to the first of his famous aphorisms: Start early.

In fact, Burnham had already lived that motto for a long time. When Malin was a child of ten, his mother used to take him and his brother to the beach on San Diego Bay. Malin would sit for hours, entranced by the sight of the sixteen-foot "junior" sailboats passing back and forth. Then, on one unforgettable day, one of those sailboats came close to the shore, and the young pilot shouted, "Hey, want to go sailing?"

"I couldn't get out in the water fast enough," Malin recalls. "My parents, bless their hearts, saw my enthusiasm and took out a family membership at the San Diego Yacht Club."

Before long, little Malin was spending every spare moment sailing. He quickly became obsessed:

> When you are sailing and out there on the water, there is no guarantee that you will return. You have no motor, and getting back to the dock is dependent upon your skill with sail and tiller. Once you've succeeded at that task twenty or thirty times, you have complete confidence that you will always be able to sail home. That's a very big deal for a thirteen-year-old boy. It's a belief in [your] own abilities that you carry throughout your life.

With this new confidence, young Malin began to compete with his peers, and soon he was beating them all. At fifteen, he graduated to the twenty-two-foot Star class, and he began to beat the adults. Before long, even San Diego had become too small for his sailing talents. So in August 1945, the seventeen-year-old high school graduate, along with his fifteen-year-old crewman, headed by train to Stamford, Connecticut, for the Star class World Championship.

Malin returned the youngest world champion in that class, ever. It is a record he still holds.

Upon his return to San Diego, Burnham had planned to join the Navy. But on the trip home, the train suddenly stopped at a lonely spot in the middle of Kansas, and the crew and passengers jumped out and celebrated. The news had come of VJ Day: World War II was over. When Malin arrived at Union Station in Los Angeles (San Diego's train dilemma also existed then) and told his father of his plans, the older Burnham nixed them. "The war is over," he told his son. "There'll be no future in the Navy. I've arranged instead for you to be admitted to Stanford University."

Within a week after graduating, in 1949, Malin was back in San Diego, working for his father and about to get married. He was moving fast for someone pursuing such a stable career. But Malin had other, private plans. Even as he was learning his profession, not only was he still sailing whenever he had a chance but he was beginning to test the waters in his third career by joining the boards of various nonprofit organizations around the San Diego area.

On the sailing side, Burnham's life took on the nature of a myth. A young man he had known at the yacht club since the late 1950s, Dennis Conner, had grown into a superb sailor, one who crewed with Malin in several races. They had become fast friends, Conner the avid student and Burnham his mentor. Conner went on to sail in the America's Cup, the world's oldest sports trophy still in competition. Then disaster struck. In 1983, the American team lost the Cup to Australia, the first such loss in more than 150 years for the New York Yacht Club.

Realizing that the Australians had won using a revolutionary new keel technology, Burnham, age sixty-two, stepped in and took over America's team, resolving to meet the Australians on their own terms. He was successful, and, representing the San Diego Yacht Club, the

Conner-Burnham team won the America's Cup in 1987. Invited to the White House to celebrate the victory, Malin was given an etched-glass memento from President Reagan that read:

To Malin Burnham:
There is no limit to what a
man can do or where he can go
if he doesn't mind who gets the credit.

This counsel has proven to be Malin Burnham's guiding philosophy. His team would go on to lead the Stars and Stripes team to a second America's Cup win a year later, with this race bringing international attention to his beloved San Diego. For those successes, he was elected to the America's Cup Hall of Fame.

In the years since, Burnham has never been far from the ocean and sailing. Remarkably, two weeks before his eighty-eighth birthday, Malin entered the International Masters Regatta and won. In doing so, he became the youngest and oldest world sailing champion, with the longest interval between victories.

In 1981, having successfully navigated his company against the arrival of national banks and mortgage companies trying to capture the booming San Diego market, Malin Burnham, when he might have been enjoying the fruits of his longevity and success, did the unexpected: he handed the company over to his subordinates, and, like his father, he retired. Why retire when he was only in his late fifties? He had found his third career, one that would define the rest of his life: philanthropy.

Burnham had always given money and energy to charity and civic improvement. As early as 1965, he had joined a consortium of five investors who created the San Diego Transit Corporation to buy the company for the city. It would eventually become the San Diego Metropolitan Transit District, which would build the city's celebrated trolley line.

Now, at the dawn of the eighties, Malin wanted to devote himself to philanthropy full time.

He set out to change the face of San Diego, to leave a positive mark on his hometown. At first, he was almost too enthusiastic: at one point early on, he sat down with a pad of paper and listed all the charitable organizations with which he had a connection. It took him four days to remember all of them, and when he was done, he counted:

> The list totaled thirty-five organizations, for which I chaired or co-chaired fourteen. Frankly, I was shocked. I knew I was heavily committed, but I had no idea I was that committed. Looking at the list I wondered how I managed to do it all.
>
> The truth was, I realized that I couldn't do it all. No one human being could do justice to that kind of load.

Malin concluded that he had to prioritize his commitments, stay involved with those organizations where he could have an impact, quit those where he couldn't, and leave the job to someone who could. He also realized that most of his contributions were not only too small to make much of an impact, but for those that did, there was no way to measure their real impact. Then, thanks to an old investment that returned ten times the money, Malin and Roberta, his wife, found themselves with an unexpected new body of wealth.

The Burnhams decided to create their own foundation. Moreover, they agreed to commit time and money only to initiatives where they would play a decisive role in the initiative's success. That meant more than just money; often, it meant Malin's direct involvement at the very top.

Over the last forty years, Malin Burnham has executed this strategy and in the process has changed the face of San Diego more profoundly than anyone since Alonzo Horton and John Spreckels. Remarkably, he has done much of this with other people's money. Perhaps no one in the modern US has been more successful at using the power of leverage. Malin, a wealthy man but never a true tycoon, learned early on that if he was willing to put up first money on a project—and follow Reagan's dictum about keeping his ego out of the way—he could almost always find someone far richer than he to put up many times that amount. He also learned never to involve himself in any initiative where he didn't have some hands-on control over its direction and operations.

What he never mentions, even in his autobiography, *Community Before Self*, is one other factor that sets him apart: he is a man of rock-solid integrity and fairness. His word is his oath, and his handshake his guarantee. When Malin invites a billionaire to join him on a project, that investor knows the project will get done, on budget, and with the investor's name, if he or she chooses, first over the door.

Over the decades, this process has enabled Malin Burnham to make a decisive impact on a mind-boggling list of important improvements in the life and culture of San Diego: he has helped to save the Padres baseball team; brought the carrier USS *Midway* to become a museum in the harbor; built the San Diego Yacht Club a new sailing center; sat on committees of all three of the city's great universities—UC San Diego, San Diego State University, and the University of San Diego (where he established the Burnham-Moores Center for Real Estate); led the creation of the First National Bank of San Diego; and helped build the elegant Le Meridien Hotel in Coronado.

Creative graffiti marks the Mexican side of the border fence at Friendship Park.

But perhaps Burnham's greatest contribution to his city has been in medicine and biotechnology, in which he has helped make San Diego a world leader. The nexus of this work can be found atop a hill in La Jolla—Torrey Pines—adjacent to the campus of UC San Diego, which, because of its connection to this and related centers, has itself become a world leader in the field.

It began with the establishment, in 1976, of what was then called the La Jolla Cancer Research Foundation (now Sanford Burnham Prebys Medical Discovery Institute). Essentially a laboratory, the Institute would occasionally spin out a new technology that would be commercialized. The Institute was a moderate success until, in 2004, Malin was contacted by a fellow real estate broker he had known in his past career:

> I received a telephone call from Bob Klein, in Palo Alto. Bob had a crazy idea about floating a large, state-wide bond issue to support stem cell research. Crazy or not, by the end of the phone call, I knew that this was something I needed to investigate.
>
> At the time, stem cell research was comparatively controversial, with several states going so far as to ban such research—not least because at the time it could only be done using fetal cells. [But] the more investigation I did, the more I believed such a program would not only benefit humankind but also greatly complement the greater San Diego medical research scene.

Burnham convinced the Institute to become the first of its kind in California to support the initiative. Then he formed a consortium of all the key players in biotech in San Diego to back the bond issue. Making this easier, all happened to be located on the Torrey Pines mesa: Sanford Burnham Prebys Medical Discovery Institute, Scripps Research, Salk Institute, and UCSD Medical. Their target was $50 million to be set aside by the state for the construction of new research laboratories.

But to earn that grant, the consortium had to raise a matching 20 percent in private donations. Here, Malin Burnham was on his own turf. He contacted a friend in South Dakota, Denny Sanford, also a philanthropist, and asked him to help. Because Sanford's home state had voted down stem cell research, he agreed to join Burnham's efforts. The result was a $30 million gift for what would soon become the Sanford Consortium for Regenerative Medicine. The bond issue passed, and San Diego received its funds.

Within a few years, thanks to Burnham's vision and his talent for what he calls exploiting "points of leverage," San Diego was a leader in stem cell research in the United States. In 2011, the La Jolla Institute for Allergy and Immunology became the fifth member of the consortium. By then, less controversial sources of stem cells had been found in adult tissue.

In 2014, Malin's leverage paid off again: Denny Sanford donated $100 million to underwrite the Sanford Stem Cell Clinical Center at UC San Diego Health. Sanford also increased his support of the Institute, which was now called—because Malin always gave top billing to the greater donor—the Sanford Burnham Prebys Medical Discovery Institute.

Today, those laboratories, all exhibiting innovative architectural design, and all blinding white in the bright sun, preside atop the mesa, dominating both the landscape below and the international field of tissue regeneration. Burnham:

> What I see is a twenty-year string of leverage points, each identifying a unique opportunity to improve on the status quo, to build something five or ten times larger, and to do that again and again.

In March 2020, now ninety-two years old, Malin Burnham announced his return to blue water sailboat racing. The event would be the Ocean Race 2021.

This time, as with his America's Cup wins, Malin would participate not as a sailor, but as a co-owner of the sixty-five-foot sloop *Viva Mexico* and as an investor in the campaign. Joining him would be the sloop's other owners, including Burnham's good friend and business partner, Lorenzo Manuel Berho Corona, founder and CEO of billion-dollar Corporación Inmobiliaria Vesta SAB, Mexico's leading developer of key industrial parks in Tijuana and elsewhere.

Viva Mexico's entry represented a historic binational cooperation between the Acapulco and San Diego Yacht Clubs. It commemorated the fiftieth anniversary of a Mexican yacht winning the first Whitbread

Round the World Race (the original name of the Volvo Ocean Race). Said Berho, "We share an ocean and need to share more of the solutions, and this is a great opportunity."

Adds Malin Burnham, as usual the man in the middle of such an initiative between the two countries, "Strengthening the relationship between the two clubs, the two countries, and then sailing—that's why I'm helping. It's an absolute natural for us because of our history."

SECOND CITY

One perhaps surprising facet of Malin Burnham's remarkable career is that, for someone so completely identified with the city of San Diego, he has a great love for Mexico. He owns a home in Los Cabos, at the southern tip of Baja California, and sails there often, but he has a particular affinity for Tijuana. He has, in fact, been a crucial catalyst in the four-decade rapprochement between the two cities.

Like some people of his age in San Diego, Malin started visiting Tijuana before WWII, and like most kids of that era, his trips were tightly chaperoned. But even then, he felt increasingly at home on the southern side of the border. As a young man, he often sailed down the coast and made friends with his fellow Mexican sailors.

Given his affection for Mexico, it makes sense that Malin's philanthropy also extended across the border. He initiated, then chaired the San Diego Symposium of the Kyoto Prize, the international award for global achievement, founded in 1985. Each year, the San Diego chapter awards six one-year college scholarships to high school seniors, three from each side of the border. Malin and Roberta found themselves so impressed by the winners from the Tijuana side that they have continued to support many throughout the rest of their college careers—even, for the winners most in need, personally helping them with travel and living costs.

Further, Burnham was a founding member of Chuck Nathanson's San Diego Dialogue and, true to his nature, a member of the inner circle that made its policy decisions. In 2007, James Clark, at the time Mexico Business Center director at the San Diego Regional Chamber of Commerce, proposed reviving the Dialogue's role in advancing the quality of movement across the border and restarting its ground-breaking work of accurately measuring and characterizing the millions of people each year crossing at the point of entry. Malin jumped on the idea.

Clark, a former magazine publisher and the former executive director of the United States-Mexico Chamber of Commerce, California Chapter (USMCOC), based in Los Angeles, had opened a San Diego/Tijuana office in 1999. He had devoted years to developing what is still among the most extensive networks (created by an American) of contacts among the power brokers of San Diego and Tijuana. These connections received their first great exposures in 2000, when the USMCOC hosted, in San Diego and Los Angeles, three debates among the three principal parties vying for the presidency of Mexico (PAN, PRD, and PRI), for an audience of US and Mexican citizens and businesses.

In 2003, Clark, who had been a member of the San Diego Regional Chamber of Commerce International Committee, was hired by the Chamber to establish a Mexico Business Center (MBC), to improve outreach to the academic, business, and civic communities of the San Diego-Tijuana metro areas. He also obtained permanent resident status in Mexico, and was named both the director general of the MBC and to the executive staff of the SDRCC. Now he began to link both sides of the border with a passion. On the Mexican side, he joined all the major Tijuana economic development organizations, adding them to his growing list of their San Diego counterparts. He also began to organize cultural events, like the annual International Tribute Awards, which honored a major Mexican leader, such as a member of the president's cabinet, as well as cross-border awards for business development and culture, and a San Diego-Tijuana Citizen of the Year award. (The first recipient of the Citizen of the Year award was Yolanda Walther-Meade.) With the Chamber he also helped lead annual policy missions to Mexico City and Washington, DC, to discuss cross-border issues with government officials in both capitals. By the end of the decade, James Clark, with his now-unmatched network of powerful business and political connections in both countries, had made himself the go-to person for just about anything regarding the evolving relationship between the two cities. Now it was time to make the boldest move yet.

In 2007, Clark and Burnham formed the San Diego-Tijuana Smart Border Coalition (SBC). Some of the names of the people who joined them in founding the Coalition will sound familiar: Salomón Cohen, José Larroque, Steve Williams, José Galicot, Mary Walshok, José B. Fimbres, Jeff Light, Rafael Carrillo, Dave Hester, Francisco ("Frank") Carrillo, and Russ Jones, among others. Their official aim was "to convene San Diego and Tijuana business, government, agency, and civic society leaders to advocate for an efficient and welcoming border at our ports of entry for both people and cargo."

Designed to be the successor to the San Diego Dialogue, SBC had a critical difference: it would be binational from the outset, with leading figures from both cities holding posts at every level in the organization, thus awarding Tijuanenses, for the first time, a full, formal civic partnership with San Diegans. Malin Burnham and Salomón Cohen were named as the first Smart Border Coalition co-chairs. They were followed by Steve Williams and Ascan Lutteroth, son of Hector, a leading and deeply respected trailblazer from the Dialogue years, who passed away in February 2020. SBC alternated the bimonthly board and stakeholders' meetings between the two cities.

In the years that followed, the Smart Border Coalition, along with the San Diego Regional Chamber of Commerce, organized the first North American Competitiveness and Innovation Conference in San Diego, with Canadian and Mexican attendees. It also established a Stakeholders Working Committee to bring together the leading NGOs from both Tijuana and San Diego to coordinate support of binational initiatives. Says SBC Tijuana co-chair, José Larroque:

> We're nimble. We don't create these massive structures. We're very flexible, and what we essentially try to do is build bridges so that there can be a communication engagement that's cross-border. If people see leaders engaging, then it makes it easier for other organizations to engage.

In 2014, the Smart Border Coalition, an independent, binational organization, left the San Diego Regional Chamber of Commerce and moved to a new home at the San Diego Foundation. Three years later, Clark stepped down as executive director of the Coalition but remained on its board as an honorary member (along with the consuls general of Mexico and the United States, as well as the mayors of San Diego and Tijuana).

Clark was succeeded by Gustavo de la Fuente, who in many ways embodies the new relationship between the two cities. A bilingual US-Mexican dual national, de la Fuente was born in Nogales, Sonora, Mexico, and educated at both Stanford University and Harvard Business School. A former entrepreneur and banker, from 2001 to 2010 he served as CEO of Omnicable, a private Mexican telecommunications company. He is a leader who moves effortlessly across the border, feeling utterly at home on both sides—truly, and appropriately, a cross-border citizen: *Un Fronterizo Norteamericano!*

EMPIRE BUILDER

When people call Salomón Cohen the "Malin Burnham of Tijuana," he quickly dismisses the idea: "No, no," he says. "Yes, I do many of the same things, but I'm not as big as him. I think Malin is the life of San Diego, and one of the best men I have ever known."

But the parallels are hard to dismiss. Like his San Diego friend, Salomón became a wealthy man, then retired early in order to serve his beloved city. For decades, he has sat on the boards of the defining cultural and political institutions of his city—and his reputation is that of a man who gets things done.

Over the course of sixty years, Cohen built the largest retailing empire in Northwest Mexico. Now, like his erstwhile competitor and good friend José Galicot, he is dedicating his retirement years to improving the life of Tijuana, as well as its border with the United States. Indeed, in that work, he has become a key board member in Galicot's organization, Tijuana Innovadora.

Cohen arrived in Tijuana from Mexicali as a boy, fresh out of secondary school, in 1953. He was seventeen years old and apprenticed to work for a merchant. When his own father opened a small dry-goods store in town, young Salomón went to work for him.

His father died young, in 1957, and Salomón took over the store. It turned out he had a natural gift for retail. So, just two years later, he was invited to join a consortium to found Tijuana's first department store, Dorian's.

> Why did I join [the founding team]? Because it struck me as a good idea. My background from my father was in retail—mostly clothing—and we didn't just have the store, but we also went door-to-door selling blankets and clothing.
>
> What I saw was that most people in Tijuana, when they wanted to shop, had to cross the border and go to San Diego. Tijuana just didn't have enough to offer. So we saw the opportunity to open a department store. And not a little one, but what seemed huge at the time: ten thousand square feet. Of course, at the time, Tijuana had a population of not even one hundred thousand people.

The timing couldn't have been more perfect. Over the next half century, Tijuana's population would grow to nearly two million citizens. Dorian's became, and would remain, the city's flagship department store. (Dorian's was purchased in 2004 by Carlos Slim and rebranded as Sears. Sears in Mexico remains much more prestigious and financially stable than the Sears group in the US, which has failed to adapt and fallen on hard times.)

Dorian's was just the beginning: between 1959 and 2005, the team's empire grew from that one store to seventy stores of three different types—department stores, specialty stores, and beauty-supply stores, under various names including La Bola, MAS, SAM, DAX, Extra, and Solo un Precio. "We were doing a pretty nice business," says Cohen, stating the obvious. Indeed, Salomón Cohen's stores represented a sizable fraction of all retail sales in the state of Baja California.

But it was at this point, at the height of his career, Cohen decided he was done. "Both of my partners had passed away, so I was alone. I decided to sell the business in 2005."

Though he stays heavily involved in his other business, real estate—buying and selling land and developing small shopping centers (he doesn't mention that he has played a central role in developing the city's new World Trade Center)—the primary focus of his life the last fifteen years has been philanthropy.

In this he was joined by Maria Juana Cohen, his late wife, a major figure in Tijuana in her own right. Together, they convinced San Diego's Mostly Mozart Festival to come to Tijuana—something that has continued for fifteen years. This program served as a launchpad for the Cohens to support other music programs in the city, notably children's choirs, which are now operating in more than twenty of Tijuana's schools, training as many as one thousand students annually. Cohen continues to underwrite them all.

In addition to music programs, he is involved in numerous other charities, including the Mexican Red Cross, the Castro-Limón Foundation, the El Trompo Interactive Museum, and of course Tijuana Innovadora.

Cohen was the key player in bringing the Tijuana business community into the San Diego Dialogue, and his commitment to the two cities' relationship and the border remains deep. Today, he stays involved in the Smart Border Coalition, which he sees as continuing the Dialogue's work. Cohen:

> The border is the key. It has always been the key to the relations between the two cities. And so we need to keep working to improve the crossing. We are doing a lot better, but there are also twice as many people crossing today as there [were] thirty years ago.
>
> That's the reason I was so interested in joining the Smart Border Coalition. I think we have made some great progress. But we can't stop. The borders are always going to have problems, and we will keep working to solve them.
>
> That means working with governments on both sides of the border to help them understand both the problems and the solutions.

As the population increases, the problems are going to increase as well. For example, San Diego did a great job with SENTRI and the express lanes on the US side. But on our side, we haven't yet built such a lane, even though our population is now bigger than San Diego's. This is our responsibility, and it is going to cost money. We need to convince our government to pay for it, or we'll be back to the same traffic crisis at the border we had twenty years ago. We need to have a plan, and then work toward achieving its goals.

It will take some time. The Mexican government usually isn't as fast as the US, which isn't so fast itself. So we need to get going, and we need to push. To persist.

Beyond the border, Cohen sees security as the other great challenge facing Tijuana:

The federal government always thinks everything is okay, but it's not. If we don't secure our industrial areas, we won't have future investments from the United States and other countries. I already think a lot of foreign companies are holding back their investments until they see certain parts of Tijuana more secure.

Even so, we're still having a lot of investors coming into Tijuana to build factories, no? I just think if we give them more secure areas, they would expand operations here even further. After all, we have such a good labor force here. We have to push our government to do more.

Cohen muses about his six decades working in Tijuana, from a young apprentice to becoming one of its most powerful leaders:

My dream for Tijuana? We hope to have a much better life. We have to work on more security. We need to have more safe streets and safe cities. The crime is very high in Tijuana, as you know. We all just want to have a good place to live.

As for our relationship with San Diego? We have to be more close to them. We both need the same things. I think the organizations in San Diego are very good. They are able to put things together with our organizations over here. We need to do that too. We need to be willing to work with them, all the time. We have a strong neighbor in San Diego; they need a strong neighbor in Tijuana.

In the Dialogue and Smart Border [Coalition], I've learned how well things are working here versus what you read in the mainstream media in the US, where all people hear about is conflict. We need to tell the positive story of Tijuana and San Diego better: that we have never been closer—or stronger—than today.

I think we have a very unique relationship with the two nations, between Tijuana and San Diego. We have to take advantage of that.

The people of Tijuana are different than the people from the interior of Mexico. We have a mélange, we have a mix, no? And we always fight to be a good city. Yeah, we have problems like any other town in the world, but we work very hard to have a much better place to live for us and for our children and for the people who visit us.

We are a place of opportunity, where you can make a start, as I did. Do you know that today in Tijuana, we have no unemployment? We need more labor than any other places in Mexico. We need people to come to work here. Workers don't have to leave our country and cross the border illegally; they can stay right here and find a job.

THE END OF DEPENDENCE

Once upon a time, the story of Tijuana was one of dependence—providing for the needs and desires of Americans, especially San Diegans, and in particular, those needs and desires they couldn't fulfill at home, legally or illegally. This was true of the curio shops and bullfights early in the twentieth century, through Prohibition and World War II, to the cheap labor of the maquiladoras at the century's end.

Beginning at the turn of the twenty-first century, Tijuana faced a new challenge: What did the Americans want now? Most of the services the city had provided over the previous century—from alcohol to abortions to drugs to divorce—had now been adopted and legalized in recent years in the US, reducing demand for them all. The maquiladoras made a huge contribution to Tijuana's economy and employment, and they tied the city even closer to the US.

"But is it enough?" the city leaders asked themselves. How long must their city be dependent upon its northern neighbor? How many more decades must it settle for San Diego's scraps and serve San Diego's vices? Was there nothing Tijuana could do better than San Diego, nothing that would make the gringos look south in admiration?

What was becoming clear was that Tijuana is a place of innovation. In the words of José B. Fimbres, CEO of the Calimax chain of supermarkets that dominate Tijuana and Northwest Mexico:

> I think Tijuana has always been an incubator of some sort. It's always been, if you try things here, and especially in commerce, especially in retail, if you try things here, they might work in the rest of Mexico. Not entirely true, but most people use this region [this way]: "If we can make it here, I'm pretty sure we can make it somewhere else in Mexico and Latin America." It's always been like a test bed; we've always been the guinea pig in a way.

Calimax is itself an example of this philosophy. Founded in 1939 by José's father, José Fimbres Moreno, it is today, with 117 stores and a joint venture with the US grocery chain Smart & Final, one of the largest businesses in the region. The concept engineered by the Fimbres family—to bring food products from the US and sell them in Mexico—turned the usual model of border business on its head. The idea was simple, but its practical implementation at scale required deep border savvy, not least in dealing with the endless roller coaster of the peso-dollar exchange rate. Not surprisingly, the younger José Fimbres has followed in the footsteps of his father (who was a trail-blazing member of the Dialogue), becoming a principal leader of San Diego-Tijuana's next generation.

He describes the ups and downs of doing business on the border:

> There are economic cycles and devaluations, so you have to adapt your business to be able to survive. My father would always joke that [my generation] was raised in crisis. I was born in 1970. We had a banking crisis in 1976 and another one in 1982 and then we had the peso crisis in the 1990s and then I lived through the huge recession in 2008. So it's crisis after crisis, the Mexican ones and the global ones. We were raised in crisis, and adaptability is part of our DNA. We're fight-ers. At the end of the day, surviving in business on the border, you have to be tough as well as smart.

SAINT BETTY

One of the most remarkable stories of the rise of the modern, independent Tijuana can be found in the most unlikely place: a small hospital clinic in the city's industrial district, just a few yards from the border, run by an ex-patriot nurse-turned-doctor who is Canadian.

In 1955, a twenty-one-year-old from Calgary, Elizabeth "Betty" Jones, decided to celebrate the completion of her degree in nutrition from the University of Alberta by taking a vacation in sunny San Diego. There, one day, she joined in a grunion hunt, which entails snatching up the silvery fish as they strand themselves on the beach to spawn. Joining her in the hunt was a young veterinarian, Robert Jones.

The two fell in love, and Betty moved to San Diego. "I came down to find out if it was for real and decided, yes, it was for real," she told *Banderas News* in 2007. In the years that followed, she earned postgraduate degrees at San Diego State and the University of San Diego. Then, in 1976, now Dr. Betty Jones, she was approached by a Catholic sister from an organization called Project Concern about volunteering at a tiny pediatric clinic a few miles south of Tijuana. Her job would be to teach nutrition not just to the patients and their parents but to the doctors as well.

Dr. Jones fell in love a second time, this time with Mexico. She says, "Once I got bitten by Mexico, it was infectious. It's the feeling that, in many ways, you can actually make a difference."

In the two days per week she volunteered at the clinic, Dr. Jones didn't settle merely for teaching nutrition; she also began to introduce revolutionary childcare techniques, most famously "kangaroo care"—a technique in which infants are tightly swaddled and held closely against their parents' (and doctors' and nurses') skin. The procedure proved to help underweight and unhealthy babies survive. Word got out, and soon mothers in Tijuana proper were bringing their babies to the clinic. Medical professionals north of the border also took notice: something interesting was going on in a shack-turned-clinic in the barren landscape of the remotest part of the Tijuana Valley.

Dr. Jones continued to volunteer at the facility until the early 1980s, when the Mexican economic crises led the clinic to close. It was donated to the Baja California state government, which converted it to a full medical clinic. Suddenly, the children of Tijuana and its environs once again had to go to the city's general hospital, a facility regularly short of supplies, equipment, and nurses. "We just thought this was terrible. The kids weren't getting anything," Jones recalled.

Joining with a Mexican partner, Dr. Gabriel Chong King, Dr. Jones set out to build a new clinic, a process that would lead her to spend a decade in the world of fundraising, a field about which she knew nothing at the beginning and had become an expert by the end. Ultimately, the state of Baja California donated a barren, gravel-strewn vacant lot in Tijuana's industrial district. Meanwhile, Dr. Jones managed to raise $50,000 from US donors. It wasn't much, but it was enough to construct a 2,000-square-foot day clinic (the size of a suburban home in San Diego) on the lot.

Dr. Jones had her clinic again, but she was not content to stop there. *Banderas News*:

> Jones had bigger plans, an expanded facility that could provide everything from dental care to ophthalmology services to orthopedic surgery. So she began knocking on the doors of wealthy Californians, often driving executives to Mexico to see the hospital firsthand.

Eventually, after a process that she described as "lots of blood, sweat, and tears," she found support from John Moores, owner of the San Diego Padres, and from Toshiba and Mattel, which operated factories in an industrial park not far from the clinic. Some of her fundraising techniques in these early building stages were unorthodox:

> To raise money, we got thirty-eight big oil drums and painted them with "Buy Me a Smile" and placed them around the city. We collected money for the day, and we had a connection to the Televisa Network. A lot of our success is thanks to Televisa. It was the first telethon in Mexico. All day long they announced this. People were putting money in barrels and coming to the station with their pesos. A bank sent tellers, and they counted the pesos live on television. We collected $100,000 in grassroots money in one day.

She also found donors from her old home country, making the new $2.4 million, 20,000-square-foot clinic, which opened in 2001, the only "trinational" medical facility in Mexico, with supporting foundations in Canada, the US, and Mexico. Dr. Jones commissioned a Canadian architect to design the building and received a donation from McGill University to make it "green." Even her old classmates at the University of Alberta formed an endowment to support the clinic. As she told the University of Alberta alumni magazine, "It's a collaboration of three countries working together, which to me is amazing and wonderful."

The Hospital Infantil de las Californias proved to be an instant, and enduring, success. By 2010 it had served more than a quarter-million patients and performed five hundred surgeries, all on an annual budget of less than $2 million. One in ten patients was so poor that the hospital provided their medical care for free; others paid just $15 for a consultation. How was this possible? Only 25 percent of the hospital staff is paid. Most of the 250-person staff of aides, nurses, and doctors volunteered their services.

Yet Dr. Jones still wasn't done. Despite being long past retirement age, she continues to devote her talents to her life's mission. Today, thanks to her American, Canadian, and Mexican supporters, the hospital is now a 56,000-square-foot operation, featuring an $8 million surgical center. In July 2017, the hospital reached the milestone of five hundred thousand children served. Today, the hospital conducts more than one hundred surgeries per month, ranging from cross-eye correction, hernioplasty, hip surgery, and endodontics, for a total of more than nine thousand surgeries since the center's founding. Currently, four-fifths of all its patients cannot afford to pay for their medical expenses. In response, the hospital created a program, Programa de Apoyo a Pacientes Indigentes (PAPI), to help them pay for surgical care. In 2016, the Foundation for the Children of the Californias (an organization funded by the San Diego Foundation) established a fund that, in its first year, distributed $540,000 in medical-assistance aid to families.

In 2018, Dr. Betty Jones was honored with the Hero Award of the World of Children Foundation. From a tiny clinic, she had built a world-class operation that had become a model for the world and equal to anything found north of the border. As such, she had shown Tijuana the way into its next era.

THE WORLD LEADER

The modern collaboration in healthcare between San Diego and Tijuana began with the establishment in 2001 of the US-Mexico Border Health Commission, with its twelve commissioners from each side of the border and chaired by the US secretary of Health and Human Services. As with many breakthroughs in border relations, it, too, grew out of the work of the San Diego Dialogue and was incubated by Mary Walshok's UCSD Extension.

Malin Burnham with his biotech institutions in La Jolla and Betty Jones with her Tijuana clinic were pioneers in their respective cities, but the ingredients were already in place for their efforts to spark a regional revolution. While observers at the turn of the century might have looked at La Jolla and predicted a healthcare explosion there, few would have predicted the transformation that made Tijuana into the medical tourism and supply leader of the world.

Long before Jones's children's hospital, Tijuana had been a mecca for Americans searching for pharmaceuticals and surgical procedures banned in the United States, from narcotics for pain to abortions to controversial cancer cures (such as Laetrile). A few doctors also ventured down from San Diego a day or two each week to serve Mexican patients. But these had been largely isolated efforts, just more services in the overall mix Tijuana provided to the northern neighbors.

But as the border became more porous to regular, approved travelers after SENTRI and subsequent initiatives, the nature of healthcare in Tijuana began to change fundamentally. A number of factors came together for the first time: growing prosperity in Mexico, an economic boom in the US that enabled a new class of citizens to consider elective and cosmetic surgery for the first time, and a population of young doctors and other medical professionals graduating from Mexico's own medical schools. All that was needed was a catalyst.

It came in 2000, with the Sistemas Medicos Nacionales SA de CV (SIMNSA) Health Plan. Founded by Francisco "Frank" Carrillo, who became its president and CEO, SIMNSA, headquartered in Tijuana, had already made a name for itself as a full-service healthcare plan (HMO) with clinics, hospitals, laboratories, and pharmacies throughout Mexico.

But Carrillo had bigger plans. In 2000 he achieved the seemingly impossible by making SIMNSA the first Mexican medical organization to earn regulatory approval in the United States (a Knox-Keene license), to offer its program in the state of California. This was the culmination of a two-year effort by Carrillo, which included joining the effort to gain passage of an unprecedented amendment to California law, allowing cross-border health plans. By creating a brand-new beachhead market for SIMNSA in the US, Carrillo opened the door to other ambitious Mexican healthcare companies.

Frank Carrillo was uniquely suited to be a cross-border medical pioneer. Born in Mexico, the son of migrant workers, he had come to the United States as a child. Seeing the crude conditions in which his parents and other migrants worked in the fields, as a young adult Carrillo dedicated his career to assisting progressive agricultural employers who wanted to provide Mexican workers and their families with healthcare plans.

Before Carrillo expanded his services through SIMNSA, he spent twenty years working as a consultant with unions and other organizations seeking to institute trans-border healthcare programs. The California certification of SIMNSA thus was the culmination of a life-long dream for Frank.

SIMNSA was founded with the specific charter of providing quality healthcare for the growing number of workers in the southwestern US who preferred to receive their healthcare coverage in Mexico. Why? Because of the range of available services, but even more: cost. In Mexico, the prices of almost everything medical—drugs, doctor visits, surgeries, hospital stays—was a fraction of their counterparts' prices north of the border. Americans were willing to accept what they may have perceived as inferior services for those kinds of savings.

As it turned out, they wouldn't need to compromise for long. Within a decade, SIMNSA had put into place a network of more than two hundred physicians along the US-Mexico border. It opened corporate offices in Tijuana, San Diego, and Mexicali, and affiliated with or opened scores of clinics, dental offices, laboratories, and surgical centers in those cities. At those facilities it established standards equal to any in the US, including the requirement for board-certified physicians, continuing education, and peer-review programs. Further, all clinics had to belong to the National Hospitals Association and meet their standards for operation.

Carrillo didn't stop there. He built a home for children with cancer and their families, then created fundraising events to help them meet their medical costs.

But SIMNSA's greatest innovation, one that wasn't planned, was in service. When American patients began to rave about the quality of service provided by the program's personnel, Carrillo looked at the matter more closely. He discovered that the secret ingredient was something he had always taken for granted: the Mexican tradition of hospitality. American patients were unaccustomed—and thrilled—by the level of attention, cultural sensitivity, and personalized care they received. For their Tijuanenses nurses and orderlies, delivering this level of care was second nature, not just because it was part of the national culture but because, after all, had not the people of Tijuana spent the last century making Americans comfortable and happy to visit?

Walking through the door Frank Carrillo had opened, next into the US market was the healthcare network MediExcel Health Plan. Founded by cardiovascular and thoracic surgeon José Hernández Fujigaki, who came to wide public attention when he performed Baja California's first open-heart surgery, the health network had been serving the cities of north Baja California for twenty years.

In 1991 MediExcel was successful enough to build Tijuana's third-tallest building, which by 2018 would grow to twenty-two stories. This hospital would become the centerpiece of the Excel Medical Center, located in the commercial heart of the city. At this writing, the hospital is being joined by an even taller, thirty-four-story building that will house doctors' offices, parking, and support services, making it the largest multispecialty hospital in Tijuana. Though it remains best known for its cardiac services, it has also met the growing demand for elective surgery by adding everything from hip and knee replacement to gastric bypasses, breast augmentation or reduction, and cosmetic surgery.

But not all of Tijuana's medical services began with an eye on San Diego. The city also had a homegrown medical pioneer who would become world-famous.

The practice of modifying the shape of the eye to improve vision dates back to pioneering work in the 1950s by an ophthalmologist in Colombia. Until the development of precise lasers, though, it was done through risky surgical techniques. The first ultraviolet excimer laser was developed in 1980 at IBM, and the first papers on using it for radial keratotomy were published in 1985.

That very year, a young, second-year surgical resident at the Instituto de Oftalmología Conde de Valenciana in Mexico City, Dr. Arturo Chayet, conducted his first refractive surgeries. To improve his skills, he took a fellowship in cornea and refractive surgery at the UC San Diego Department of Ophthalmology, which resulted in him incorporating that type of surgery into his regular clinical practice. Over the years that followed, as new practices and new laser types appeared, he was consistently asked to participate in their field tests. As a result, he was one of the first doctors in the world to see the new excimer laser. Enthusiastic about its prospects, he performed the first LASIK surgery in western North America, in 1994. Then, in 1997, Chayet invented Bitoric (or all-laser) LASIK for the correction of complex astigmatisms. It has since become the standard procedure to address that malady.

Then, in 2001, Dr. Chayet perfected the technology using the new femtosecond laser. It is still considered the premiere procedure for refractive surgery.

Patients streamed to Dr. Chayet's Tijuana clinic not just from San Diego and the rest of the United States but from around the world, confident that they were receiving not second-rate care but rather the finest eye surgery from the best in the world. The penumbra of Chayet's reputation extended to other medical-tourism operations throughout the city. His impact on the city's reputation in healthcare is incalculable.

IN THE FAST LANE

The consequences of these pioneering healthcare operations on Tijuana were quick (as business shifts have always been there), stunning, and extensive.

In just four years, from 2014 to 2018, the number of medical tourists traveling to Tijuana jumped from eight hundred thousand to 2.4 million. They came for everything from dentistry and blood work to major surgery. Most of them came through the US, and so great were their numbers that as early as 2011 Mexico instituted a special Medical

Lane at the San Ysidro Point of Entry to facilitate border crossing for US patients and Mexican doctors.

Like all efficiency initiatives at the border, it was immediately popular. It was also immediately abused by others desperate to escape the wait.

When the Medical Lane first opened, the passes were available only to patients who came to Tijuana for medical procedures. Doctors and patients loved the new ease of crossing, which measurably bolstered Tijuana's medical-tourism industry. But within three years, under pressure from other interest groups, the city of Tijuana modified those passes to include tourists. Now, resorts, hotels, and restaurants began to purchase the passes to hand out to their clients and customers. Meanwhile, with medical tourism itself booming, the number of bona fide medical passes jumped as well.

By 2018, Tijuana's secretary of economic development, Arturo Pérez Behr, said there were 288,000 Fast Lane passes issued, of which he believed 90 percent were still issued for medical reasons. This volume has slowed the "fast" lane considerably. Still, it remains an improvement over regular border-crossing lanes, so most hospitals and clinics continue to offer the passes as part of a patient's stay. They enhance that stay with other offerings as well, such as all-inclusive packages that include recovery accommodations in nearby hotels, recovery nurses, medications, a special diet menu, and an escort who uses the Medical Lane pass to drive the patient back and forth across the border.

The economic spillover of medical tourism in Tijuana has spread across the entire region. According to Baja California tourism officials, the entire state has enjoyed an additional $785 million in revenues. In the Zona Rio, Adrian Bustamante, Carlos Bustamante's nephew and a skilled businessman in his own right, manages the Grand Hotel Tijuana Medical Complex, which encompasses the eleventh floor of the city's flagship hotel (the hotel his grandfather built). There the accommodations have been converted into private hospital recovery rooms, under a program called Grand Care. It is regularly fully booked.

The nature of medical tourism has evolved as well, separating into different niches based on the type and quality of care.

Now there are hospitals for the budget-minded patient who wants to enjoy the 40 to 65 percent cost savings versus the US. But other hospitals cater to those who want the highest levels of service, even if it costs more. The first hospital to serve high-end customers, the Hospital Angeles Tijuana, opened in 2006. It is located in a busy retail district that features restaurants and cafés, as well as a movie theater where American films are played with Spanish subtitles. Part of a national chain in Mexico, Hospital Angeles Tijuana does its best not to look like a hospital but more like a resort, featuring patient suites with private entries and private dining areas.

The incredible growth of Tijuana's medical-tourism industry also has had an extraordinary impact upon San Diego. For perhaps the first time in the history of the two cities, the tables have turned, and the northern neighbor has moved to capture some of the success of the southern: San Diego is now seeing the birth of its own medical-tourism industry. Even as millions of Americans have headed to Tijuana for medical care, an estimated one hundred thousand US citizens living in Baja California have chosen to travel to Chula Vista, just seven miles north of the border, to take care of their medical needs at Sharp Chula Vista and Scripps Mercy Chula Vista. The biggest reason for heading north? Not the quality of care, but the fact that those two facilities accept Medicare patients, which Mexican hospitals thus far cannot under US law.

Construction cranes punctuate the skyline of the Tijuana district closest to the San Ysidro Point of Entry, offering a glimpse of where medical tourism goes next. The NewCity Medical Plaza is part of a larger complex of five high-rises designed to house Tijuana's new professional class. The medical plaza itself represents two of those high-rises, one a twenty-six-story tower with doctors' offices, a medical laboratory and surgery center, a 1,000-plus-car garage, and the adjacent 140-room Quartz Hotel & Spa, much of it to be used by recovering patients. On the ground floor, the Plaza offers a full range of restaurants and shops. It is a basically a city within a city and purposefully placed just yards from the US border. San Diego has nothing like it. Developed and built by the Abadi family, whose patriarch, Moisés, died in a tragic traffic accident in Panama City in early 2020, NewCity seems the personification of modern Tijuana.

The NewCity Medical Plaza and Quartz Hotel are a part of Tijuana's medical tourism industry.

Says Isaac Abadi, son of Moisés, the dynamic CEO of NewCity:

> When you cross the border, the first thing you see is our building. We see it as our responsibility to show the visitor what Mexico is about. We know that if they have a good experience with us, they will wander in a little more. We do have the responsibility of giving them a great experience not just for ourselves and our companies but for the entire Mexican Republic.

TO THE HEART

Coincident—and partly related—to the rise of medical tourism in Tijuana has been a parallel rise in medical-device manufacturing. The existence of these factories and assembly lines in Tijuana can be credited to the maquiladora movement, but the nature of those businesses has necessarily been impacted by the presence of so much medical care in the vicinity, just as life-science companies have swarmed around the Torrey Pines mesa in La Jolla.

San Diego mayor Kevin Faulconer has publicly stated that the San Diego-Tijuana region has become the "the largest hub of medical-device manufacturing in the world," responsible for the creation of 110,000 jobs in San Diego.

The Medical Device Cluster of the Californias, centered in Tijuana and including companies in San Diego and Baja California, claims to be the current world leader in medical-device manufacturing, with forty-two thousand workers at seventy affiliated companies. Some of these are divisions of the largest medical and healthcare companies in the world, including, in Tijuana alone, Welch Allyn, Medtronic, Baxter Healthcare, and Honeywell. It is not rare to see new technologies that emerge in the laboratories in La Jolla eventually commercialized and manufactured in volume at a plant in Tijuana. The technology transfer is smoothed by the fact that 70 percent of Tijuana's medical-device makers are US-owned.

The United States also has become deeply dependent on Tijuana's medical devices. Mexico is now the leading supplier to the United

States of $43.9 billion in medical devices purchased each year (30 percent of the nation's total consumption of those products). For some devices the market dominance is even greater: according to the *New York Times,* nearly every pacemaker in the United States is partly manufactured in Tijuana. Other items produced in Tijuana include feeding tubes, orthopedic devices, thermometers, blood-pressure cuffs, and the stent rings inside heart valves.

One of those stent rings ended up in the heart of Tijuana businessman José Galicot. In 2009, Galicot sought help from his San Diego doctor: "I was feeling bad because I had problems with my heart. I went to the doctor and he said, you need a valve. I said okay." When the doctor told Galicot where that valve would come from, he was surprised: "In Tijuana? They don't make such sophisticated things in Tijuana." At seventy-two years old, Galicot emerged from surgery with a repaired heart and a new vision: to showcase Tijuana's innovations and industries for the world to see.

FAST TALKING

In times of great change, even tiny things can be amplified to enormous effect. It is possible that much of the medical-tourism revolution and the other developments that transformed Tijuana might never have happened but for a change in the local telecommunications.

As late as the 1990s, a telephone call from Tijuana to San Diego, and vice versa, was billed as an expensive, long-distance international call. In other words, a person standing on one side of the San Ysidro border crossing could call someone they could see on the other side and be billed the same as if they were calling someone in Singapore or Cape Town. This put a serious crimp in any transactions taking place across the border, from business deals to everyday citizens inquiring about an item in a store in the other city. This particularly hurt Tijuana businesses and professionals because part of the appeal of goods and services south of the border was their lower cost, and that margin diminished every time a San Diegan made a call there.

Some clever—and desperate—people living near the border took to using walkie-talkies to communicate with their cross-border counterparts. As binational business collaborations grew, the situation was becoming absurd. Cheryl Hammond of AT&T remembers, "What companies would do when they needed to get data across the border was make a copy of the tape, put the tapes in a car, and drive them across the border. That was 'data transmission.'"

One of the collateral benefits of José, Rafael, and Gregorio Galicot's operation, BBG Telecommunications in Tijuana (which was joined by a sister company, BBG Communications in San Diego, in 1996), was that it established local telephone connections, at local telephone prices, between the two cities. The timing was perfect, not just because it caught the binational economic boom between the two cities but also because the network went into place just in time for the Internet. That meant businesses and citizens in the two cities didn't miss a beat as they added e-mail and messaging to their means of cross-border communication. This, in turn, proved immeasurably valuable for US patients talking to doctors, setting up appointments, and arranging medical-tourism packages at hospitals and hotels in Tijuana. Now, they could tour websites, pay online, and—importantly—circumvent the usual language challenges. Most of all, having a regional broadband communications network meant this experience was scalable—enabling the medical, hospitality, and retail industries to enjoy their explosive growth in the new century without constraints in the communications infrastructure, even when the volume approached a billion voice and data transfers monthly.

THE NEW MUMBAI

As with every structural change, the arrival of low-cost international telephony to Tijuana inspired its own set of ambitious entrepreneurs, nowhere more so than in the call-center industry. The city offered low-cost labor, access to a modern telephone network, an increasingly binational culture, and a shared time zone—all this, plus Tijuana's growing population of accent-neutral English speakers (many of them deportees from the US), made the city's call centers a perfect match for US companies' needs. Tijuana soon featured more than sixty such centers.

Redial BPO, one of the most progressive of the call centers, was founded by two brothers, Jason and Chris Heil, who had grown up in San Diego and had often visited Tijuana and Baja California. After college, they decided to open their own company.

Jason recalls:

> We started off in San Diego. We were a merchant service doing credit card processing, providing point-of-sales systems to brick-and-mortar businesses, restaurants, and other clients.
>
> We started off paying our employees a minimum wage of $7.50, which then went up to $8 a handful of years ago. We could handle that. But then a bill was passed in Sacramento that threatened to move the minimum wage up to $15 per hour over the course of the next few years.
>
> With that, it no longer made sense for us to run our business. At the time, we had twenty people working for us in San Diego. So now the question became: What do we do now? Do we shut our doors and lay off everyone, or do we make a lateral move? And to where?
>
> We had a friend and silent partner who lived in Mexico. He convinced us to establish a business down there. He basically enabled us to get into the Tijuana market and to change our business by opening a call center. We've been doing that now for three years.
>
> So you can say that the best thing that ever happened to us was getting priced out of the San Diego economy.

The minimum wage in Mexico is about five dollars per day. Redial BPO pays more than that, enabling employees, many of whom have only known poverty, to earn a comfortable living. Meanwhile, the company is profitable enough to have already grown to sixty employees with plans in the works to build out a hundred more seats.

What surprised the Heil brothers was the quality of the workers. The Heils had been raised in a world where Mexican workers were

considered hardworking but low-quality workers. "I think most uninformed companies in San Diego don't much like Mexican workers at
all," says Jason. "We found just the opposite of that stereotype."

What surprised the brothers even more was the abundance of
Mexican citizens, often the children of undocumented immigrants,
who had been raised in the United States, then deported. Ironically,
many of these individuals were having trouble adapting to life in
Mexico because they were *too* American. The Heil brothers realized
that they had discovered an untapped resource: Mexican citizens, desperately needing employment, who spoke English with an American
accent, and were perfectly comfortable talking with Americans about
life and culture in the US. Deportees make up 90 percent of Redial
BPO's employees.

"They don't just speak English, but *American*, which is very different," Jason told the *Los Angeles Times*. Wrote the *Times:*

> Deportees are valuable because they know a lot about
> American culture. In sales, they can use that knowl-
> edge to engage in small talk, find shared interests, and
> quickly establish rapport to close a sale.

In other words, Redial BPO's agents know to talk to San Francisco
callers about the Niners and Houston callers about the Astros. Such
rapport instantly raises the callers' trust and comfort levels.

To make these employees feel more at home, the Heil brothers have
imported the American corporate culture to their Tijuana operation.
Unlike some of their counterparts, Redial BPO's employees are each
given a wide desk featuring two monitors. The company celebrates
American holidays, even hosting an in-house Thanksgiving dinner.
Jason says, "There's times when everybody's hitting their goals and
their metrics and we're nailing our KPIs and we're doing great, and
then I will just show up with In-N-Out burgers," a beloved American
fast food not yet available in Tijuana.

"Tijuana has become like the new [Mumbai]," one employee, José
Salvatierra, told the *Los Angeles Times*. "India is no longer the first
option."

But the Heils haven't forgotten the vital role of Mexican culture at their company. For example, the entire company is given time off during the World Cup. They watch the games at the company headquarters, while enjoying a buffet provided by the brothers.

Recently, other Tijuanenses call centers have begun to notice Redial BPO's unique recruiting, and the demand for American-speaking deportees has grown. This has driven up wages for these workers, a benefit for them, but still not enough to threaten the Heil brothers' business.

"Sometimes I forget that Tijuana is in another country," Chris Heil says. "It's just like another neighborhood for us, besides this fence."

Figure 1: San Diego Major Companies with Manufacturing in Tijuana and Environs

- Solar Turbines (a Caterpillar company) / Turbotec Tijuana
- Kyocera International / Kyocera Mexicana
- Cubic Corporation / Cubic de Mexico
- Taylor Guitars
- DJO Global (Vista/Tijuana)
- Hunter Industries—industrial irrigation
- Thermo Fisher Scientific—life sciences
- CareFusion—medical devices producer

GETTING IN TUNE

One company has become emblematic of both the effectiveness and the inversion of stereotypes of the maquiladora movement: the celebrated Taylor Guitars, a world leader in the design, building, and marketing of acoustic guitars. The story of Taylor's Mexican manufacturing operations captures both the burden of historic expectations and the freedom of being largely invisible.

Compared to most guitar makers (Martin, for example, was founded in 1833), Taylor is a surprisingly young company. It began as American Dream, a tiny guitar-making shop in El Cajon. In 1974, a twenty-year-old employee named Bob Taylor teamed with fellow employee Kurt Listug, bought the business, renamed it Westland Music Company, and set out to build their own designs. Before long, the two owners divided up their tasks—Taylor working on guitar manufacturing and Listug handling the business operations. They also settled on a new name, Taylor Guitars, because it sounded more American than *Listug.*

The early years were a struggle. As Bob Taylor has written, "Nobody knew who we were, and we were only one step away from going out of business every day."

By 1976, the company had begun selling standardized guitar models in retail stores. Sales soon skyrocketed—today it is an $80 million company, having sold more than one million guitars—not just because of Taylor's new distribution model, but because it was quickly recognized as one of the most innovative designers the acoustic guitar industry had seen in generations. The most famous of these innovations was the patented "Taylor neck," considered the industry's first major innovation in a century. It consisted of a bolt-on, continuous length of wood that simplified realignment and service. Taylor also pioneered an innovative electric pickup to amplify their guitars. Further, the company experimented with the use of sustainable (and responsible exotic) woods. Bob Taylor even, famously, built a guitar out of an old oak pallet from his warehouse floor.

But in the guitar business, a reputation for innovation and one for superior quality are often two very exclusive matters—and often desired by two very different audiences. Taylor Guitars wanted to be both, believing it possible to build a radically different product, using state-of-the-art computerized tooling, while producing finished guitars that would be the epitome of the luthier's art.

Being headquartered in El Cajon was propitious for Taylor; just across the border in Tijuana a manufacturing revolution was taking place. The maquiladora movement was offering the potential to grow US companies using domestic design, marketing, and sales, while moving manufacturing to Tijuana, with its more competitive costs and young, hungry workforce.

Still, there was one obstacle: the perception of American consumers. Products made in Mexico still bore the long-standing stigma of

being of lesser quality. That was not a problem for most other maquiladoras, especially those that assembled components for industrial
products. But in the acoustic guitar world, where build and finish are
everything, the myth that Mexico made second-tier goods was hard to
shake off, a belief only reinforced by Fender, America's most famous
electric guitar company, whose "Made in Mexico" budget products
were rated a distant third behind its products built in the US and Japan.

But Taylor Guitars wasn't intimidated. If the company was going
to grow—and take advantage of its singular creativity—it was going
to have to move beyond the limited production of expensive handmade guitars. Its competitive advantage, the company decided, was its
unequalled skill of putting automated manufacturing technology to
work to make its guitars both cheaper *and* better.

In 2007 Taylor opened a new factory in Tecate, twenty-two miles
from downtown Tijuana (its finished products are shipped through the
latter city). Here, in a three-hundred-employee operation that resem-
bles more a clean-room fabrication laboratory than a woodshop, Taylor
builds its Academy series of guitars. The Academy line is Taylor's least
expensive, priced between $300 and $1,300 (compared to as much as
$10,000 for the company's other guitars), but buyers can find little dif-
ference between the Academy guitars and the rest of the Taylor family,
save one: the California-made models have solid backs and sides, while
the Mexican models use laminates.

Cheaper products, cheaper components—it sounds like the usual
image of "Made in Mexico." But here there is a fundamental difference:
the Academy line also features Taylor's most creative designs, and
the Mexican factory applies far more advanced technology to achieve
those competitive prices. As such, Taylor turns the old image on its
head.

For example, the Academy line may feature laminates, but that
wood is carefully formed, and then the interior walls are milled away
by a computer-controlled cutter. In the words of *Guitar* magazine,
"The cutter rotates at around 12,000 RPM, moving slowly for a clean
cut, and the clever design allows for a process that takes four hours
on the company's higher-end instruments to be automated—and takes
just a couple of minutes as a result."

At the same time, to save costs, instead of the traditional lining, the Academy guitars use larger pieces of mahogany—left over from the neck-making process—which is machined down to create a combination lining and armrest. "The result," says *Guitar*, "is not only more functional and comfortable but reveals its component parts and structure in an elegant, understated manner, much like an Eames chair."

For now, Taylor's handmade guitars built in El Cajon still dominate the company's revenues. But with guitar prices rising and demand growing, the handwriting is on the wall: if the company is going to remain in the ranks of elite guitar makers—a lofty position it has struggled to reach—it will need to keep its costs under control while multiplying its production rate. That means its destiny, increasingly, will lie beyond the US border.

Figure 2: Non–San Diego Major Manufacturing Companies in Tijuana

- Welch-Allyn
- Samsung
- Sharp
- Toyota
- Hyundai
- Panasonic
- Poly (Plantronics)
- Delphi
- Lockheed Martin
- Greatbatch
- Smith Medical
- Bose (speakers)
- Honeywell
- Medtronic

Taylor isn't the only iconic American or international company that has joined the maquiladora movement. Others include Honeywell, Coca-Cola, Samsung, Hyundai, Welch Allyn, Schlage, Daewoo, and PepsiCo. There are currently more than three thousand maquiladoras in Mexico (the program is now officially known as IMMEX, though the old term endures) employing more than one million Mexican workers.

Of these, an estimated six hundred companies operate in Tijuana and its environs. Since its creation in the 1960s—and especially after the passage of NAFTA in 1994, after which the number of maquiladoras skyrocketed—the impact of the movement on Mexico's economy has been profound. Today, 80 percent of Mexico's exports go to the US, making it the largest trading partner of the United States.

In fact, Taylor Guitars, for all its influence, is a relatively small example of cross-border manufacturing by US and international companies with plants in Tijuana. The size of these plants, and their impact on the US economy, often surprises both Americans and Mexicans. For example, Prime Wheel, a US aluminum company with 3,700 employees, produces five million wheel rims annually in Tijuana. Japanese giant Toyota manufactures a Tacoma truck (the second-most popular pickup truck in the US) every two minutes in Tijuana. That adds up to 166,000 units per year, mostly for export to the American market.

But perhaps the most stunning production statistic comes from South Korean Samsung's television factory in Tijuana. It assembles 100,000 sets per day—which, during periods of high demand, can be increased to 140,000—totaling twenty-six million television sets per year. In other words, nearly every Samsung television sold in Mexico, the United States, and Canada was shipped from the company's Tijuana plant.

Figure 3: Prominent Maquiladoras in Tijuana

- Aldila de Mexico S.A. de C.V.—golf equipment
- Amex de Mexico, S.A.—office desks
- Berthamex S.A. de C.V.—communications network integrator
- Bourns de Mexico, S. de R.L. de C.V.—electronics components
- Clayton Industries—industrial steam oilers
- Comair Rotron de Mexico—fans and blowers
- Ensambles de Precision de las Californias, S.A. de C.V.—electronics and communications components and subsystems

- Hitachi Consumer Products de Mexico, S.A. de C.V.—wireless speakers, automotive products
- Imperial Toy de Mexico S.A. de C.V.—toys
- Levimex de Baja California S.A. de C.V.—lighting control systems
- LLCDouglas Furniture de Mexico—furniture
- Maxell de Mexico, S.A. de C.V.—gaskets, packing and sealing devices
- NSK Safety Technology Inc., S.A. de C.V.—ball and roller bearings
- Pioneer Speakers, S.A. de C.V.—stereo speakers
- Pulidos Industriales S.A. de C.V.—surface finishing
- Rectificadores Internacionales—rectifiers
- Sanyo E&E Corporation—major household appliances
- Sony de Tijuana Este S.A. de C.V.—broadcast and communications Equipment
- Tecnología del Pacifico, S. A. de C.V.—energy lab

THE TEST

The relationship between San Diego and Tijuana has enjoyed enormous—and hugely lucrative—growth since the 1960s, especially in the 1990s. But skeptics might note that it was not hard to do well in those boom years, which marked one of the most extensive economic expansions in history. Good times lift all boats, so every enterprise was more likely to succeed, and every businessperson more likely to appear a genius.

San Diego and Tijuana were no exceptions. Even as the two cities celebrated this relationship, there was a gnawing sense that it had not really been tested. When it was, would their new bond hold up, or would the old animosities and fears reemerge and break it apart?

The answer came at the end of 2007. Both cities were about to face their own separate demons. San Diego and Tijuana were about to discover their relationship did not just make good times better; it was vital to surviving hard times.

San Diego's crisis in 2008 was one shared by the entire United States. The business cycle, a loss of traditional manufacturing jobs to other competing nations, and the tipping point, a subprime mortgage crisis in which millions of people purchased homes they couldn't afford, created a perfect economic storm. The US economy spiraled downward into what would be called the Great Recession, its worst fall since the Crash of 1929. The stock market dropped precipitously, banks were menaced and many closed, Americans stopped buying high-ticket consumer goods, which threatened to bankrupt the automobile industry, and hundreds of thousands of homes were abandoned to foreclosure.

San Diego was not spared this calamity. To the contrary, as one of the fastest-growing major US cities over the previous decade, it had enjoyed more than its share of new housing developments and subprime loans. A hot stock market had attracted large investments from many local citizens. As a high-tech center, it found many of its most important companies hunkered down trying to survive the collapse of customers, strategic partners, and stock prices.

Mexico was not spared the Great Recession either—it rippled around the world—but the economic damage was less extreme there. That said, assembly plants in Tijuana saw demand from their US parent companies abruptly dry up as the US raced to reduce inventories. Tourist shops and destinations suffered reduced demand as well, but not as steeply as other places, since US international vacationers opted to visit nearby Mexico over, say, Europe.

However, Tijuana was destined to suffer its own nightmare: for much of the next three years, a bloody and vicious gang war would paralyze the city, radically reducing the quality of life for everyone forced to live through it.

The crusading reporting of *Zeta*, the new extradition laws between the US and Mexico, and the joint law enforcement efforts between the two countries—particularly the task forces in Northern Mexico created in the 1990s under Alan Bersin's leadership as US Attorney and border czar—had paid off. By the early 2000s, gang operations, especially those of the AFO, had been dampened considerably. There were a few shocking acts of violence—such as the assassination of *Zeta* cofounder and editor Francisco Ortiz Franco in 2004—but for the most part gang activity muted in the city, as most organized-crime leaders were in prison. In 2006, when cartel boss Javier Arellano Félix was arrested by the US Coast Guard on a boat off the coast of Baja California, it seemed as if the AFO was finally defeated.

But this loss of leadership was only temporary, and the celebrations of the gang's demise premature. Struggling to fill its vacuum at the top, the AFO devolved into internecine warfare as two different factions fought for control. One, led by Teodoro Garcia Simental (El Teo), specialized in kidnappings; the other, led by Luis Fernando Sánchez Arellano (El Ingeniero), who had the benefit of the family name, sought to dominate the city's drug trade and control the so-called Plaza territory leading up to and across the US-Mexico border in Tijuana.

Their battles for dominance might have spilled into the outlying districts of Northern Mexico, but for two countervailing forces. One was the bigger cartels in the region, which constrained the spread of the Tijuana gangs. The Sinaloa was immediately to the east, and the Gulf Cartel was mostly farther east but also spawned a particularly vicious splinter group called the Zetas (obviously not related to the Tijuana newspaper). As Andrew Selee describes it in his book *Vanishing Frontiers*:

> As these groups began to fight over territory, Mexico went through a spiral of violence. From 2007 to 2011, the nation's homicide rate tripled, from a modest eight per 100,000—not far above the US homicide rate at the time—to more than twenty-four per 100,000, among the highest in the world. More than 45,000 Mexicans died in organized crime violence in those five years, with some cities, including Tijuana and Ciudad Juarez, outpacing some of the war-torn cities in Afghanistan and Iraq in the sheer numbers of deaths each day. Ciudad Juarez was, for three years, the world's most violent city, and Tijuana was not far behind.

Beyond the turf wars, the power vacuum in Tijuana also presented an opportunity to the gangs. The many arrests of gang leaders a few years earlier also had exposed a level of corruption in Tijuana (especially connected to the AFO), particularly among the police. The resulting arrests of law enforcement officers and their leaders so compromised the city's ability to enforce the law that Mexico City sent thirty-three hundred troops to Baja California (out of a total of twenty-six thousand sent to gang-controlled regions throughout the country) to restore order in Tijuana.

As a result of these pressures, the two factions of the AFO were bottled up together within Tijuana, and they soon began to interfere with each other's business. In particular, El Ingeniero's faction wanted to continue its day-to-day low-key crime business selling drugs, shaking down businesses, and engaging in other traditional criminal activities. But El Teo had bigger dreams: he set out to kidnap and ransom the leading citizens of Tijuana, from the wealthy to the professional elites to white-collar entrepreneurs at the maquiladoras and other emerging industries, including medical tourism.

Sánchez Arellano demanded that Garcia Simental and his gang lay off the kidnappings—or at least reduce them to a manageable level—because they were not only starting to paralyze life in the city and drive out many of the city's leading citizens but also bringing focused law enforcement scrutiny on Tijuana from both sides of the border. (One place where the AFO could still operate beyond city and national limits was in Southern California and Nevada, where a spin-off group, Los Palillos—the Toothpicks—operated as an enforcement wing.) El Teo refused: there was too much money to be made from kidnap ransoms. A full-scale vicious and bloody gang war resulted.

The AFO, in various forms, had been part of Tijuanenses life since the early 1980s, and by the early years of the twenty-first century it was not uncommon to see top gang members hobnobbing with the rest of the city's elite at restaurants and nightclubs, their armed bodyguards ostentatiously waiting by their expensive automobiles outside. While never viewed as a benign force, they were tolerated, as long as they restricted their most violent activities to the poorer, outer neighborhoods and conducted their other crimes, such as drug smuggling, on the down low.

But in the early hours of Saturday, April 26, 2008, all that changed. Throughout the city, the predawn hours echoed with the sounds of gun battles and screeching cars. As dawn came up, police found seventeen

AFO members dead, killed by rifles and machine guns. Fourteen of the dead were discovered on a single road in the maquiladora district, many of them riddled with bullets and dishonored by having their faces obliterated. Six other men were wounded and another six arrested by police.

Of the dead, just two were hit men from the Sánchez Arellano faction; the rest were from the Garcia Simental gang. The hit men were identified by their large gold rings bearing the image of gang icon Saint Death, which was supposed to protect them. It had been an ambush: El Ingeniero had had enough.

Rommel Moreno Manjarrez, Baja California's attorney general, held a news conference, telling reporters: "Today shows we are facing a terrible war never seen before on the border."

He wasn't wrong. The first four months of 2008 had already seen nearly two hundred people murdered in Tijuana alone. It was about to get much worse.

A Reuters reporter, Lizbeth Diaz, captured the mood of a city already terrified about the growing chaos:

> Police cordoned off the surrounding roads, forcing workers at a nearby maquiladora to walk through the crime scene to get to work.
>
> "Another shoot-out," said a woman who gave her name only as Lisa. "There are just too many. We are so afraid."

It was as if a dark cloud had descended upon Tijuana, turning it into a populace of frightened citizens increasingly benumbed to violence and death, furtively looking over their shoulders when outdoors, hunkering down in their homes whenever possible, and looking for a way to escape. Most who could escape did, as always throughout Tijuana's history, across the border into the sanctuary of San Diego: business executives, politicians, judges, almost anyone wealthy or prominent. Many took up permanent residence in the southern districts of San Diego and have never fully returned. By year's end, 844 Tijuanenses had been murdered, up from 337 the year before.

SCRIBE

In 1994, Sandra Dibble had moved to Tijuana to work at that city's bureau of the *San Diego Union-Tribune*. She had been working as a journalist in Washington, DC, and had taken the new job because it was a chance to immerse herself in another culture and write about it. She even chose to live in Tijuana, rather than commute daily from San Diego. "I wanted to be embedded, so to speak," she recalls. She would end up living in an apartment downtown for seven years.

The bureau employed just two reporters, and Dibble's counterpart mostly focused on law enforcement, so she expected to cover cultural stories.

Nothing turned out quite as she planned. Almost at the moment she arrived, Tijuana (and Mexico) was swept by a paroxysm of violence:

> I got there in 1994 right after they killed the presidential candidate, [Luis Donaldo] Colosio, in Tijuana. Then a couple weeks later, they killed the police chief. There was a high-profile kidnapping of a maquiladora executive, and federal officials were being killed too. All of these big, dramatic crimes. It was sort of my baptism by fire. I ended up having to help report those stories.
>
> It was usually the Arellano-Félix [Organization]. They would be trying to get rid of a guy who had crossed them or wasn't collaborating or was collaborating with someone else. All I know is that we'd run out and cover the shooting. There would often not be many immediate answers, so you never really knew exactly why that person was killed. I think the big thing was that the Arellanos were just exerting their power.

In time, the violence settled down again, and Dibble could report on the good side of Tijuanenses life: the cultural events, the arts, the social whirl. But then, in 2006, the violence again began to ramp up. A burst of kidnappings in 2006 had stunned the city—citizens even marched against the growing gang violence. In response, newly elected

Mexican president Felipe Calderón ordered federal troops to Baja California in early 2007. The Army immediately confiscated the weapons owned by the police department, "and started arresting bunches of cops that were believed to be corrupt."

By this time, Dibble had moved to San Diego, but she still commuted every workday to Tijuana, into the thick of the troubles. Yet she still tried to maintain a social life there—though it was severely shrunken:

> It was spooky. It was the only time I'd ever experienced Tijuana like that. You'd see these caravans of dark cars racing by. Maybe it was federal police, maybe it was the narcos. Just speeding down the highway. The Avenida Revolución, the tourist strip, was like dead, dead.
>
> It was also spooky because you'd go out into the neighborhoods and you'd see police on patrol with high-caliber weapons—but they all had ski masks on because they didn't want to be recognized and set up for assassination.
>
> I think there were a lot of restaurants that lost clientele because people were not going out after dark. I think there was even a movie theater in a nice area in which somebody was shot.
>
> There were a couple instances where the gunman stormed into a restaurant and made everybody get on the floor and took their wallets and purses. Everybody tried to keep the story quiet because if it spread, nobody [from Tijuana, or San Diego] would go out to restaurants. It was also the recession, so that, with the crime, made it not a good time for Tijuana.

The burden of recording for history this dark era in Tijuana's history now fell entirely on Sandra Dibble's shoulders. Newspapers all over the US were shrinking in the face of the Internet boom, and many were offering buyouts to senior reporters as a prelude to larger layoffs. Dibble's partner at the Tijuana bureau took one of those layoffs and wasn't replaced. Even the bureau office was closed. Sandra Dibble was now the *Union-Tribune*'s sole "international" correspondent in Tijuana. She struggled to find stories that would help her readers understand what was happening, that captured the resistance and resilience of the city's citizenry. Sandra:

> I did a story about people who were doing a night bike ride on one of the busy thoroughfares. You'd have a couple hundred bikes going down at 7:00 at night in the winter, riding through the city. It was an act of defiance. They were getting police escorts. Still, there was one time when they had to turn back because there was a shoot-out up ahead.

Businesses in Tijuana soldiered on. None was hit harder than those industries—tourism and medicine—that catered to visitors from the US. They tried innovative solutions that offered more security to travelers, such as well-guarded tours on special red buses. But for the most part, the visitors did not come, and the Tijuanenses economy began to slide into its own recession.

LOST YOUTH

Other than the victims of crimes, this era may have come down hardest on the children of Tijuana. An entire period of their lives was severely circumscribed. Young children, once living in relative freedom, weren't allowed to walk to friends' houses or school or the local store unaccompanied, even in daylight. At night, they and their parents locked (and sometimes barricaded) themselves in their homes, and when the gunfire became especially intense, prayed for morning.

Tijuana's teenagers, young adults today, remember this as a lost period in what should have been an exciting time of their lives. The enduring traditions of Mexican teenagers—dances, parties, promenades, courtship—were put on hold. Just the idea of kids going out on a Saturday night, driving around with friends, would strike terror in their parents. Recalls Rene Perez, now with the Tijuana Development Commission:

During those years, we almost never went out at night, even on the weekends. It was like we had no social life. And if we did go out, our parents would be terrified. It was a very lonely few years—right at the time of your life when you want to be out and meeting girls and hanging out with your friends.

For Alfredo Angeles, who today is a business development specialist at the Tijuana Economic Development Corporation, was a seventeen-year-old high school senior during the troubles, a period he describes as a "scar" on the city.

I had some classmates that didn't go to school for months. Some of them went to live in different places like San Diego. But I didn't want to see it like that. We stayed.

I still wanted to go out in the night, you know, on weekends and stuff like that. But at a lot of the parties, these young guys would show up that were involved in narco and other things—we called them Narco Juniors. They could cause trouble. We called them *mangueras*—fire hoses—because they would suddenly pull out their guns and just start spraying bullets, killing people.

I was still able to go out, but I was careful not to get involved with them.

I learned that they were usually at house parties. Some of the parties were so big that they took up the whole block, which meant roaring cars, and loud music, and people drinking in the street. I went to two or three of those parties, but I realized they were so dangerous that I started going downtown instead. There were only three or four bars still open. Tourism was dead, even from Mexico, and even if Americans wanted to visit, the border crossing took forever because of the increased inspections. But for me, it was safer there. My parents were still afraid for me. That led to a lot of fights with them. And my friends didn't want to come by my house and pick me up because they were afraid to go into my neighborhood.

We had a neighbor that we didn't even know was in the narcos until he got killed.

Why didn't we leave? I often ask myself that. All I can say is that in Mexico, we are very familial. We take decisions as a family—and as a family, it's what the uncles, the brothers of my parents, wanted for us. My uncles were here, and my cousins were here. My grandparents were here . . . Where are we going [to go]? We don't have a job waiting for us.

The worst, I think, was the holiday season. Nobody went outside. The streets were almost empty. Normally, you'd see the streets filled with families celebrating, eating in restaurants, shopping . . . now there was none of that. It really was hard times.

Finally, it got so bad that the police officers began wearing ski masks so they couldn't be identified. They also started painting out the numbers on their patrol cars for the same reason. One of my cousins was a police officer—it was very dangerous for him. We all worried about him.

He was in the special forces for kidnappings. There were a lot of them. My dad worked for a construction company, and probably 70 percent of the management hired private security to protect them.

For Alfredo Angeles the low point came when Tijuana police, supported by Mexican soldiers, attacked an elegant old home that happened to be a cartel safe house near Alfredo's own home. Alfredo's ex-girlfriend lived next door. The resulting gun battle lasted fourteen hours, with thousands of rounds fired.

That gun battle was the beginning of the end. The election of Felipe Calderón and the arrival in Tijuana of the Army had signaled the change. Within a couple of months, just two years after it began, the drug wars in Tijuana settled to a dull roar.

Alfredo:

> I remember my graduation from high school was a joyous time. The party afterwards was very good. My family was there. My father had just gotten a new job with a San Diego construction company that had decided to come back to Tijuana. They had been very tough times, but now they were over.

Alfredo Angeles chose to remain in Tijuana to attend the Universidad Autónoma de Baja California. And he still lives in Tijuana.

About those difficult years, José B. Fimbres of Calimax supermarkets remembers:

> I got married in '98, and I had three boys at the time the trouble started. I was starting to build my house here at Tijuana. And all of a sudden, you get a little antsy, especially in my family, because we already had experienced a kidnapping—of my uncle—in the 1970s. I was in the fifth grade when that happened.
>
> So you always had that in the back of your head, and we always had security since then. Luckily, he was rescued. But we knew it could happen again one day, especially as our family name became more recognizable.
>
> Fast forward to the 2000s. Murders and kidnappings once again were becoming everyday occurrences. So I went to my dad [José Fimbres Moreno] and I said, "Dad, I think it's easier, I think I want to live in the States to minimize my risk."
>
> He just looked at me very solemnly—he would talk in a way that you would always listen—and he said to me, "You're going to go where?"
>
> "Dad, I'm going to go to San Diego, probably live in Coronado or somewhere nearby."
>
> And he just looked at me again.
>
> "Where are you going to go?"

"Coronado or San Diego." That was the second time.

He asked again. "Where are you going to go?"

"San Diego. Dad, this is really difficult."

And for the fourth time he asked, "Where are you going to go?"

I finally understood. That when the good guys leave, the bad guys win. If you're a presence in the community, if you are providing jobs, you're providing solutions to your customer base, you're here, you're part of the community by economy, socially, and culturally. It represents more than just the name. It represents more than just a brand name or a family name. So I said, "No, I'm going to stay right here."

"Good," my dad said. "I didn't raise cowards."

THE FIGHTER

No individual in the Tijuana Valley has had more impact on his community than Hugo Torres. He not only played the central role of carving the district of Rosarito Beach out of the city of Tijuana, but in the region's darkest days, he fought the criminal gangs to save his town. Today, at eighty-three, when Rosarito Beach is home to not only tens of thousands of Mexicans but also thousands of Americans, he remains the city's biggest booster and economic force.

Hugo Torres arrived in Rosarito in 1943 as a seven-year-old. A city boy who only knew the urban life of Mexico City, he was stunned by Rosarito, a dusty little beach village with fewer than five hundred residents. "[It was] like if you were from New York City going to some tiny place," he told the *San Diego Union-Tribune*.

When young Hugo's father died and his mother remarried, the boy found himself in an increasingly tense relationship with his new stepfather. To maintain domestic peace, he was sent to live with his aunt in Rosarito. It was the turning point of his life: not only was Aunt Maria Luisa Chabert—a retired opera singer—welcoming but she was also the wealthiest person in town. She owned the venerable Rosarito

Beach Hotel, and she lived next door to the hotel in an eight-bedroom mansion.

The Rosarito Beach Hotel had begun, in 1924, as a cluster of tents by the ocean for hunters and fishermen. It had proven so successful that five years later, Aunt Maria Luisa and her husband had bought twenty-five acres and begun construction of a real hotel.

By the time Hugo moved in with his now-widowed aunt, the hotel had grown to fifty rooms featuring brilliant Mexican tilework and ocean views. It had also become a draw for Hollywood glitterati. Torres loves to recount that the former Tijuana citizen Rita Hayworth arrived with new husband Aly Khan and an eighteen-person entourage. As he tells it, the prince purchased a seventy-five-cent beer and paid for it with a $100 bill, saying, "Keep the change." Percentage-wise it remains the largest tip ever by a customer of the Rosarito Beach Hotel.

In the early 1950s, Hugo left home to attend a military boarding school in Mexico City. He then moved to Monterrey to earn a degree in accounting. Then it was back to the capital to work for nearly a decade at Arthur Andersen's Mexico City office.

It wasn't until the mid-1960s that Hugo's aunt called him home to Rosarito Beach. By now the hotel was owned by a corporation, but Aunt Maria Luisa still had enough pull to award management of the operation to her nephew.

Hugo hit the ground running with a massive growth strategy. It had long bothered him that the hotel, with its fifty rooms, was failing to take advantage of its valuable twenty-five acres of land. So he began a major building program that continues to this day. Then, to fill the new rooms, he embarked on an unprecedented promotional program for the hotel in Mexico and the US. "I wanted to make it profitable," he told the *Union-Tribune*.

By 1968, his efforts had been so successful—and his ability to obtain financing so strong—that Torres was able to bring the hotel back into the family: he bought the Rosarito Beach Hotel.

For the next three decades, Hugo Torres continued to grow not only his hotel but also his influence over his beloved Rosarito Beach. Most famously, weary of the town being little more than a forgotten corner of Tijuana—the town had no sewage system, only a handful of streetlights, and a single police officer—Torres embarked on a campaign to make Rosarito Beach an independent city. He formed a working committee. "We started in March and thought we'd finish in December," Torres has said. "It took twelve and a half years."

When Rosarito finally gained its independence in 1995, it was only natural that Hugo—not only the leader of the committee but the wealthiest man in town—was appointed to the newly created town council. The council, in turn, elected him council president. Characteristically, Torres donated his salary to a breakfast program for local schoolchildren. And when he found the city's coffers empty, he bought computers for the city government. He stepped down in 1998 after a three-year term. "Looking back, it was a relatively peaceful time," he says. "We had no idea what was coming."

So it might have remained in the years that followed: Hugo Torres dividing his time between the hotel and his boosterism of Rosarito Beach. Indeed, he even started two newspapers, the Spanish language *Ecos de Rosarito*, and a good-news, English-language paper, the *Baja Times*, targeted at the expatriates living in the region—a population that was approaching ten thousand residents. It looked like a graceful ride to a well-earned retirement.

Then everything fell apart. The cartel wars had begun in Tijuana and Northern Mexico, and still-tiny Rosarito Beach eventually would be one of the communities hardest hit. Its tourist orientation, comparative isolation, and small police department made it an ideal spot for criminals to operate with impunity. Within months, the town began to fall under the control of organized crime. "The criminals came here like it was Disneyland," he recalls.

Hugo Torres couldn't allow this to happen to his hometown, so he jumped back into politics with both feet. In 2007, he ran for mayor on a platform of weeding out corruption in the police force and arresting criminals. "People really wanted something done about security, so I guess that's why they picked me to govern. For the most part, Rosarito was still a pretty peaceful area with few security problems, but the growing threat from the area in general prompted the people's concerns."

He was elected just in time. Seen as Rosarito Beach's last hope, Torres earned a landslide victory—two-to-one over his opponent— that earned headlines throughout the region. The crusading Tijuana weekly *Zeta* named him "Man of the Year," noting that he had won the election "by earning the trust of citizens at a time when the political profession lacks prestige."

Once again, he moved fast and decisively. One of Torres's first moves was to disarm the town's police force until, through hours of lie-detector tests, he could determine which officers were on the cartels' payrolls. Seventy percent of Rosarito law enforcement professionals failed their tests and were summarily fired. Says Torres, "I assumed at least some of our policemen had cartel connections, but having more than half definitely surprised me. I'm just glad that we combed through the ranks the way we did."

Torres also hired a new police chief, a former Mexican Army captain named Jorge Montero. Considered incorruptible, Montero was tasked to rebuild the police department.

Not surprisingly, the cartels did not take these changes lying down. Just weeks after Montero came on board, hired assassins burst into the police station, killed one of Montero's bodyguards, and wounded another. The assailants escaped. Learning that a former Army officer had nearly been murdered, the Mexican Army general in charge of security for the region sent eighty soldiers—with Torres's permission—to patrol the town's streets.

Torres, for his part, began to receive death threats. "I knew it was bad; but I didn't know it was that bad," he said later. Hugo hired his own team of bodyguards.

As in Tijuana, the drug wars got worse before they got better. In 2008, the violence only increased. That year, there were sixty-one homicides in the small town, making Rosarito Beach per capita among the most violent places on earth.

As the news spread north, the tourist business, the lifeblood of Rosarito Beach and Hugo's hotel, began to disappear. Rosarito Beach risked an economic collapse that would turn its control permanently over to the cartels. At the Rosarito Beach Hotel, the vacancy rate sometimes reached 97 percent. Yet even in the darkest times, Torres never laid off his employees.

Remarkably, beneath this troubled surface, Hugo and his town were slowly winning. By the end of 2010 and Torres's term as mayor, Rosarito Beach had turned the corner. That year, the murders fell to thirty-three—not great, but a vast improvement. American tourists began to return.

Hugo Torres was universally credited with restoring the town to its former glory. But the victory had come at a cost. With the credit came controversy: Hugo's methods, though ultimately successful, were also seen as authoritarian. Some hard feelings still remain. However, as crime has begun to rise again in recent years, many Rosarito Beach citizens look back fondly on Torres's autocratic years as mayor. "He attacked the insecurity in the city with all his might," said Víctor Loza Bazán, president of a statewide association of Baja California real estate agents, to the *Chicago Tribune*. "He did a great job on that."

Though his heavy footprint on Rosarito Beach remains, in the years that have followed, Hugo Torres, now the grandfather of six, has turned away from politics. He focuses his energy on his hotel (now approaching its second century), promoting the town, working to achieve a greater economic base beyond tourism, and perpetually fighting the media whenever it writes a remotely negative story about the place. Rosarito Beach is now a full-blown city of more than seventy-thousand citizens, and the Rosarito Beach Hotel today features nearly three hundred suites, many of them in a new nineteen-story tower. On any given day, occupancy usually approaches 100 percent.

Historic Rosarito Beach Hotel has delighted guests since 1924.

AFTER THE STORM

Tijuana's nightmare ended in 2010 as the gang war seemed to burn itself out. What precisely ended it remains an open question. Some credit newly elected mayor Carlos Bustamante of the PRI, or his predecessor, Jorge Ramos Hernandez of PAN, whose administration labored under the gang war for its entire duration.

Adela Navarro, editor of *Zeta*, gives much of the credit to SEDENA, the Mexican Army, and its still-controversial commander in Tijuana, General Alfonso Duarte. Duarte seemed instinctively to understand that he could never put down the gangs unless he worked in close coordination with the people of Tijuana: the police, the press, and the citizenry. Regarding the police, instead of circumventing their efforts, he actually invited the state prosecutors and the police chief of Tijuana to work out of offices at his Army base, the better to keep them safe. Meanwhile, he worked with the city government to recruit and vet new police officers to replace those who had been fired or arrested.

At the same time, General Duarte worked with the press, notably *Zeta*, which had become the go-to source for coverage of criminal activity in the city. Again, the Army provided protection and served as a news source. The ability of *Zeta*, in turn, to bring real news to the public without fear of intimidation or murder, empowered average citizens to rise up and protest against the destruction of their city and the disruption of their lives. Selee, describing Tijuana's finest hour in the twenty-first century:

> [C]itizens—armed with the knowledge they gained each week from reading *Zeta*—demonstrated in the streets against corrupt officials and businesses, shaming them and forcing authorities to arrest dozens of the cartels' accomplices. [Small-business people] and average citizens put together civic groups that pressured the government to improve policing and reform the judicial system, effecting massive changes in both the police and courts.

Still, beyond the contribution of Duarte and the citizens of Tijuana, the end of the violence in 2010 was so abrupt that it has led to considerable speculation about what really happened. Insight Crime, a journalistic organization that covers crime in Central and Latin America, has proposed that General Duarte, or officers in his Army, decided that the only way to end the violence was to pick and support a winner: a pact was created by which the Army would work with the Sánchez Arellano faction to eliminate Simental's group, thus creating relative peace in the city.

The US government took a slightly different view. A secret report on the situation, which appeared on WikiLeaks in 2009, suggested that it was, instead, Tijuana police chief Julián Leyzaola who had cut a deal with the Sánchez Arellano gang to bring relative peace to Tijuana. Says Dibble: "As long as you have a dominant drug organization, then there's less killing."

Whatever the real story, the arrest of "El Teo" Simental in January 2010—with the surviving members of his gang escaping to join the Sinaloa Cartel—effectively ended Tijuana's worst gang war. Thanks to the Army and the police, with the help of everyday citizens and a group of extraordinarily brave journalists (more than one hundred reporters had been murdered throughout Mexico during the decade), Tijuana had survived what Selee characterizes as three years of "bodies hung from bridges, shoot-outs in the streets, and executions on the main roads."

The citizenry, shell-shocked and suspicious, slowly rebuilt their lives. Nightlife gradually returned, families began again to visit parks, teens reasserted their lost social lives, and the economic engine of Tijuana—the maquiladora factories, the medical-tourism centers, the restaurants and resorts, all of which had operated as if under siege for three years, reemerged into the public eye. Leading Tijuanenses, who had sought sanctuary with the Mexican military or in San Diego, began to make their way home. Sandra Dibble was finally able to start covering Tijuana's resurgent culture. And San Diegans, who had watched warily across the border, fearful that the violence would spill into the United States, breathed a sigh of relief. The US's Great Recession was over as well, and San Diegans were ready to get back to work—and to Tijuana.

The Tijuana Renaissance, which had transformed the city over the previous two decades, had met its greatest threat and not only survived but emerged stronger than ever, ready to reach even greater heights.

CHAPTER TEN

Darkness to Light

After the dark years of the gang wars, the resurrection of Tijuana was highlighted by the most unlikely source: a culinary revolution—and the San Diego food bloggers who celebrated its inventors.

By 2012, the economy of Southern California—and San Diego in particular—was starting to prosper once more. Foreclosed homes were being snapped up, corporations were again humming (and more important, hiring), the freeways were as jammed as ever, the convention center was bustling, and nightlife was alive with revelers. The US economy overall was slowly ramping toward the biggest boom in the nation's history.

A new generation had grown up as well. Gen Xers in the US were now entering middle age and enjoying their new prosperity and disposable income. Behind them came the millennials who had grown up in San Diego, or attended its universities, and had made trips to Tijuana a regular feature of their lives.

Mostly they had stayed away from "TJ" during the gang wars—after all, not only was the city dangerous, but most of the entertainment they had enjoyed in earlier years was muted, if not entirely gone. Why risk crossing the border if the nightlife you sought had all but disappeared?

San Diego Bay, showing convention center and Petco Park.

But another phenomenon had emerged in the intervening years: Internet culture. These two generations, especially the millennials, had grown up with the Web and now lived their lives submerged in it. It had transformed American culture, especially with the arrival of social networks, and one of its side effects was to turn millions of Americans into amateur gourmands.

Unlike previous generations, these TJ visitors were not hedonists in search of sensation and transgression but epicures, obsessed with health and experiencing the very best. Nowhere was this truer than in "foodie" culture: the endless search for the most authentic, most creative, and healthiest cuisine to consume. These foodies' guides were other people like themselves, who posted their discoveries on social sites like Facebook. Even more influential were the army of amateur writer-reviewers who used the combination of low overhead and potentially infinite access to readers to offer their opinions to the world: bloggers.

Because writing about any discovery differentiated them from the competition, these food bloggers engaged in a perpetual search for the next great food outlet, the newest exciting cuisine. Because there were already a dozen or more food bloggers based in the San Diego region alone by 2010 (and more than one hundred today), intense competition for readers sent these writers, despite the apparent danger, across the border to Tijuana, a city not known (with the one exception of the Caesar salad) for world-class food.

Simultaneously, something important was happening in Tijuana's kitchens. The city's own next generation had emerged. Hidden behind the stories of gunfights and murder that filled the news, these young chefs were experimenting with something exciting: a cuisine that combined indigenous ingredients and traditional foods with radical experimentation in preparation and presentation. The San Diego bloggers took notice, and the pilgrimages south began.

THE FOOD SUPERSTAR

In particular, the bloggers found the scion of a famous restaurant family: Javier Plascencia. Plascencia, nicknamed by *Pacific San Diego* the "Mexican George Clooney" for his good looks, had enjoyed a classic cross-border upbringing. Born in Tijuana, Plascencia had been raised and schooled mostly in San Diego. There he worked in his family's award-winning restaurant, Romesco, in that city's suburb of Bonita. But his heart remained in Tijuana's open-air markets and his favorite food: carne asada tacos.

With the gang wars of 2008, the Plascencia family had packed up and moved north. Javier Plascencia:

> When the situation started in Tijuana, a lot of people left the city. Even us, as a family. We were scared of getting kidnapped and so on. We had too many clients that we knew that got kidnapped or some family member did. So, as many other families that were able either to pay rent or buy a home in San Diego, we moved. But there [were] a lot of people that couldn't and stayed in the city.
>
> We decided to move out of Tijuana. Restaurant sales went down by 50 percent. People weren't going

out at night. It was just a lunch kind of thing. So we had to let go a lot of employees and [that] was the worst thing. Even my father, who has been in the restaurant business for fifty years in Tijuana—he had never seen, never experienced anything like that. We were just real scared.

When we moved to San Diego, we decided we wanted to run a restaurant until things calmed down in Tijuana. That's when we opened Romesco in Bonita. It turned out we had a lot of clients from Tijuana that came across the border. So it became like Tijuana there. It felt like our restaurant in Tijuana, which is more family run. The service was very warm, and we had waiters that had that style of service from Tijuana and the food, so people really liked it.

As the violence eased, the Plascencias again began to move back south. In 2010, even with the gang war underway, the family purchased the iconic Caesar's on Avenida Revolución, in the middle of downtown Tijuana.

Caesar's, the city's most famous restaurant, had been founded in 1923 and was the birthplace of Mexico's most famous contribution to world cuisine in the twentieth century: the Caesar salad. But Caesar's had fallen on hard times in recent years, its reputation diminished. It was even rumored that waiters, in their famous at-table preparation of the salad, were now using supermarket Parmesan cheese. Mostly it was visited by nostalgic tourists who wanted more to say they had been there than to enjoy the food.

The Plascencia family changed all that. In restoring Caesar's to its former glory, they helped do the same to the Avenida Revolución, which, as Javier describes it, "was dead. It was like a zombie street."

Birthplace of the Caesar salad at Caesar's on Avenida Revolución.

Not surprisingly, given the endless bad news in the media, San Diegans remained wary. So Javier and his family took direct action.

> Me and my brothers, my dad would bring people in our own cars from San Diego to Tijuana to have them come and see that it wasn't what they were seeing on TV. I mean, it was bad, but the press made it a lot worse than what it was. So people were really scared, not just the locals, but especially the people [who] lived in San Diego or California. They were super scared of coming down. And that was really frustrating for us. And so we started doing these little tours and [bringing people] to dinners at our restaurant.

Caesar's was a revelation not only to its customers and to food writers but to Javier Plascencia himself. As a child, dining out in Tijuana usually meant fettuccine Alfredo: "We didn't have many Mexican restaurants in Tijuana, so all my food memories are Italian and Chinese." Now he saw in the growing crowds of diners at Caesar's a glimpse of the potential to transform his native cuisine into something world class:

> I decided to partner with some friends. They were putting up a new "green" building in Tijuana, which never had anything like it before. And they wanted to have the best restaurant in the city, just to make a statement that we as young Tijuanenses wanted the city to keep growing. So I said yes, and this is the first restaurant that I had opened without my family.

The result, which opened in 2011, was Misión 19, an upscale restaurant that combined his innovative cuisine with ingredients gathered within a 120-mile radius. Diners were greeted with the kind of service that had always characterized Mexican restaurants but had been lacking for decades up north. It did not take long for the food bloggers to find Misión 19, and their delirious reviews were posted, shared, and reposted around the US and the world. Writers dubbed the new food "Baja-Cali," "Tijuana Cuisine," and "Baja Mediterranean," but Plascencia prefers his own term, "Baja Cuisine."

Why *Misión*? In part because of Plascencia's love of old mission churches. But there's a deeper meaning to the word:

> I felt like we were on a mission. We hired a lot of the young cooks that were coming out of cooking school. And we started doing a [prix fixe] menu using all local products. We were feeling really proud of what we had locally, and we wanted to make a statement with that. We were telling Tijuana: we're here and we're opening this great restaurant so people will come back and probably won't leave, and they want to come back with their own businesses.

Soon, the *New York Times* and the *New Yorker* came calling—and their profiles made Javier Plascencia and his new cuisine famous.

For a chef like myself, being my age and my generation,
I think it couldn't have been a better moment. You
know, the times were perfect. I feel very fortunate to be
of this generation that started this whole movement. It
was fun. It was a very creative process for me, even for
myself. I discovered all these new ingredients as well.
And it's still happening, you know, I still discover a lot
of new things.

The US visitors who started frequenting Misión 19 and Caesar's
rediscovered one of the biggest selling points in Tijuana restaurants:
the legendary Mexican service. Plascencia has a simple explanation, one that involves both pride and commitment. Mexican cooks
and servers don't see their work as a short-term job, but as lifetime
employment:

We have servers that have been with us for more than
twenty years. So you're talking to servers that are going
to do that job for their entire lifetime. They take a lot of
pride in what they do. The cooks, too: I have amazing
cooks who have been with me for more than twenty
years as well. And they feel very proud of what they
do. People are very loyal down here. And diners love
having the same waiter every time they visit—for years
and years.

At the same time, another legendary Mexican phenomenon—the
food truck—was finding its own celebrity, morphing into high-quality,
foodie-oriented trucks that could now be found in the parking lots of
upscale office parks and shopping centers throughout the West Coast
of the US.

A born entrepreneur, Javier quickly leveraged his new celebrity. In
short order, he opened a number of restaurants and cafés in Tijuana
and throughout Baja California (he even, in recognition of his childhood meals, opened Villa Saverios, an Italian restaurant). Just as
importantly, he bolted the food truck and Baja Cuisine trends together
to create food service on the streets of Tijuana as good as that found in

any restaurant in the region. Finally, he returned north across the border and opened a "Mexican roots" restaurant (Bracero Cocina de Raiz) in San Diego's Little Italy that quickly closed, but not before earning a nomination for a James Beard Award for Best New Restaurant in the nation.

But it was in Tijuana where Plascencia had the greatest impact. His revolutionary new cuisine set off an efflorescence of food culture in the city, which, in turn, seemed to set the stage for a cultural revival as well. After hiding in their houses for years, Tijuanenses were ready to enjoy a social life again. As *Pacific San Diego* wrote, "Tijuana got its mojo back." Fox News called Tijuana "a true foodie destination." *Travel + Leisure* magazine awarded Misión 19 its Best New Restaurant award.

No one seemed more surprised than Javier Plascencia himself: "I knew that Tijuana had something to offer. People used to come here to drink cheap beer and eat tacos and misbehave. Now they come for the arts and music and the better quality of beers and wines and restaurants."

What Plascencia does not mention is that, with him in the lead, for perhaps the first time in its history Tijuana had transformed itself in a particular field *not* with the leadership of San Diego business interests, but on its own. More generally, as Tijuana regained its balance this time, the rejuvenation of the city was not principally dependent on Americans but rather on the growing Tijuana middle class.

Today's Avenida Revolución offers fine dining, craft beer, and foreign films.

For example, Avenida Revolución, for the first time since it was Avenida Olvera at the turn of the twentieth century, was no longer totally dependent on the tourist bars and curio shops. Now it is oriented toward the Tijuanenses family. Zonkeys, the iconic burros painted with zebra stripes, still patiently pose with tourists, but they are more a nod to the past than a mainstay tourist attraction. On any given day, far more diners in Caesar's are now from Tijuana rather than elsewhere.

THE OTHER VALLEY

The revival of Tijuana after 2012—made possible by the end of the gang war and the stunning improvements in the ease of border crossing, then sparked by Javier Plascencia's revolution in Baja Cuisine—didn't stop with food. Young brewers in both San Diego and Tijuana were fashioning many styles of regional craft beer that would become well known across both countries and the world. Their names include Ballast Point, Stone Brewing, Mission Brewery, and Karl Strauss in San Diego, and in Tijuana, Border Psycho, Cervecería Insurgentes, Cerveza Norte, Cervecería Tijuana, and Mamut Brewery. Indeed, with more than 150 licensed craft breweries, San Diego has the most of any county in the United States.

But it has been the wine made in Northern Mexico that would take center stage in the region, and Tijuana would be in the middle of the story. Baja California had never been known for superior wines—though not for lack of trying. In the Guadalupe Valley, south of Tijuana, mission grapes, destined for sacramental wine at Baja's missions, were cultivated from the seventeenth century until the beginning of the eighteenth century, when Spanish King Charles II ordered all vineyards in the New World destroyed to protect the wine industry in Spain. Nevertheless, by the end of the eighteenth century, grapes were again under cultivation, and the Santo Tomás Mission (in Baja California) became the largest wine producer in Mexico.

The next century saw a series of winemakers in Valle de Guadalupe (located thirty miles or so south of today's border): the Dominicans, private owners (when the Church's land holdings were broken up), and—ironically—strict, abstemious Russian Molokan ("milk drinker") refugees. In the twentieth century, other winemakers arrived from both California and European countries such as Italy.

But for all the growers' and winery owners' varying degrees of skill, winemaking in Guadalupe Valley seemed doomed to remain forever marginal, for two reasons. First, Mexico was not a major wine consumer. Wine was the preserve of the elite; everyday Mexicans simply found beer more compatible with their fiery food. Second, even if the demand were there, Guadalupe Valley did not have enough water to support a robust wine industry. Average annual rainfall hovered right on the brink of being too little for grape vines, and the groundwater had a tendency to become salty, especially in drought years.

Still, the winemakers of Guadalupe Valley persevered. They tried different grapes, installed new irrigation systems, even pioneered the building of water treatment and desalinization facilities. Slowly the situation began to improve.

The 1980s saw the first big payoff. Just as the hipster foodies would do twenty years later, a new generation of Americans, educated on wine connoisseurship by the now-famous wines of Napa and Sonoma Valleys in Northern California, began to search for new wine-tasting experiences. In Mexico's Guadalupe Valley, they found undiscovered wineries—some of them, such as Adobe Guadalupe, founded by Americans and Europeans—and an incipient infrastructure of inns, restaurants, and resorts.

Unfortunately, the wine industry of the Guadalupe Valley nearly died just as it was about to take off. Mexico decided to open the market to foreign-made wines, and the long-protected domestic wines were unprepared to compete. Because of that, the number of wineries in the entire country fell from eighty-two to fifteen. Most of the survivors lasted only because they had other businesses as well. Perhaps the best known were Adobe Guadalupe—created by Anaheim banker Donald Miller and his business partner (and wife), Dutch-born Tru Miller— together with homegrown Mexican vineyards such L. A. Cetto, Monte Xanic, Chateau Camou, Casa Magoni, and Bibayoff.

In the end, the influx of new tourists saved Valle de Guadalupe's wineries. But those wine tourists were also demanding the highest quality. In response, the valley's wineries began upgrading their facilities, importing top-quality international winemakers, even setting up local winemaking training schools. Most of all, ambitious wineries—notably Monte Xanic, founded by Hans Backhoff—set out to produce Mexico's first world-class wine. By the end of the century, Valle de Guadalupe—now featuring eighty wineries, an award-winning restaurant (Guadalupe Inn), first-rate resorts, and even a leader in "luxury camping"—was on the world wine tour map, a must-visit for any true oenophile. Today, on the bucket list of many wine travelers is Valle de Guadalupe's annual summer harvest celebration, the Fiesta de la Vendimia.

When Tijuana's internationally acclaimed chefs, such as Javier Plascencia and Miguel Angel Guerrero, went looking for wines to complement their locavore menus, they found in Baja California's wines the perfect companions. Ultimately the innovators of Baja Cuisine discovered in the 2010s what the wineries of Valle de Guadalupe had known for two decades: the time had come for Tijuana and the people of northern Baja California to make the best use of their unique strengths to provide goods and services superior to those found north of the border. Be it in the quality products of the maquiladoras, the wine and food of Valle de Guadalupe and the restaurants of Tijuana, the medical services offered in state-of-the-art facilities, or the superior personal service provided by the Mexican people—Tijuana was no longer the entertaining-but-troubled little brother of San Diego. From now on, the two cities would be equal partners.

Another reminder of the shared topography, geography, and climate of the two cities: San Diego—where California winemaking was born—enjoyed its own celebrated, and even larger, wine industry. According to the San Diego County Vintners Association, the county was home, in 2020, to 142 wineries and vineyards, including thirty wineries in the Ramona and San Pascual Valleys. One of these, Bernardo Winery, founded in 1889, is the oldest continuously operating winery in Southern California. The magnitude of this local industry is matched by the county's craft-beer industry, which counts 130 breweries, the best known including Karl Strauss, Ballast Point, and Stone Brewing.

ONE CULTURE

In the second decade of the twenty-first century, with Tijuana at relative peace (at least downtown) and receiving some due respect, and with San Diego enjoying one of the biggest economic booms in its history, the floodgates opened. Suddenly binational cultural, educational, and sports programs, constrained from their full potential since the 1990s, exploded.

The cultural scene saw an extraordinary range of interplay between the two cities. One of the pioneering joint events, created in the mid-1990s, had been the INSITE Art Program. Organized at the border by San Diegan Michael Krichman and colleagues from Mexico City, it featured the work of renowned contemporary installation artists from both Mexico and the United States, integrated in an unprecedented way and positioned, pointedly, on or near the Border Patrol's fence.

Today, a million visitors per year from both sides of the border visit Centro Cultural Tijuana (CECUT) in the Zona Rio District, with its IMAX theater, museums, shops, and giant esplanade for public events. Each June they attend the Mainly Mozart Festival at the Balboa Theatre. These concerts, dedicated to the common language of music, are held around San Diego County throughout the rest of the year. Binational audiences crowd Tijuana's increasingly famous Opera in the Streets (Opera en la Calle), and the Orchestra of Baja California, a large orchestra made up of both Mexican and American musicians, regularly tours on both sides of the border.

Tourists and locals alike visit the San Diego Natural History Museum and join the throngs at the unmatched San Diego Zoo, or they tour the carrier USS Midway Museum in San Diego Bay, while others visit Tijuana's vast open market. Dancers from Tijuana's ballet schools train with the San Diego Ballet, Tijuana opera singers perform with the venerable San Diego Opera, and art galleries and museums on both sides of the border loan works to each other from their collections. The *San Diego Union-Tribune* publishes a full section of its newspaper in Spanish, catering to both the Mexican market in Tijuana and Baja California as well as Spanish speakers residing in San Diego.

Training fields at the Chula Vista Elite Athlete Training Center.

Between the two cities, sports, of course, have always been of binational interest, dating back to the bullfights and jai alai facilities in Tijuana and minor-league baseball in San Diego. It is an exchange that is now generations old. Children from Tijuana attend San Diego Padres games with their grandparents, who attended Padres games in the 1930s when it was just a Pacific Coast League team. The experience has even been institutionalized: Tijuanenses make up one of the most loyal fan groups for San Diego Padres' home games at Petco Park. Mexican alumni of San Diego's many colleges and universities attend countless numbers of NCAA and AAU sporting events held at those schools.

Tijuanenses, despite the national preference for *fútbol* (soccer), also filled the stands for the NFL's San Diego Chargers, until the team moved to Los Angeles in 2017, and even then, some still commute north to attend. Many others seem to have shifted their support to Rafael Carrillo's Tijuana Zonkeys, a championship team of the Pacific Coast League of Mexican professional basketball. The team, which plays at Tijuana's Unisantos Sports Center, has featured in its ten-year history

A blend of shopping and dining lend fun and sophistication to central Tijuana.

a number of American players. The Tijuana Toros, a homegrown AAA baseball team playing in the Mexican league, often finds its games sold out and counts among their fans a fair number of supporters from San Diego.

Meanwhile, San Diegans, many of them of Mexican heritage, routinely travel south of the border to attend uniquely Mexican sporting events in Tijuana—including bullfighting, professional "Lucha Libre" wrestling, and Club Tijuana (Club Tijuana Xoloitzcuintles de Caliente) Mexican League soccer, founded in 2007. The Xolos play at the twenty-seven-thousand-seat Estadio Caliente.

Both cities also offer world-class sports complexes. San Diego has numerous such facilities, including the Chula Vista Elite Athlete Training Center for Olympic-level athletes, which sits seven miles from the border. Tijuana offers its own enormous Centro de Alto Rendimiento Sports Complex near the Tijuana International Airport and the Universidad Autónoma de Baja California.

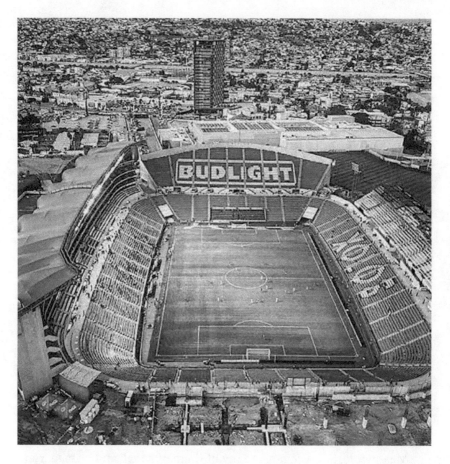

Tijuana's championship football (soccer) team plays at Estadio Caliente.

The Tijuana region's colleges and universities have played, according to Alan Bersin—who was not only the US border czar but also a former superintendent of the San Diego Unified School District and secretary of education in California—"a vanguard role in enlightening Fronterizos (Borderlanders) and residents of the two cities about the advantages of collaboration and cooperation. Students are flocking to the cross-border academic opportunities that continue to spring up in the region."

Centro de Alto Rendimiento Sports Complex trains world-class athletes in Tijuana.

LEARNING THE NEW RULES

Almost every major institution of higher learning in San Diego and Tijuana operates a research institute for cross-border relations. The California State University system offers MEXUS. Founded in 1980, it is an academic institute, located on multiple campuses in both countries to encourage binational research, faculty exchanges, and collaborative academic programs that typically offer dual degrees with partnering Mexican universities. The University of California operates a Center for US-Mexican Studies at its UCSD campus in La Jolla. Four of the luminaries central to the history of this academic collaboration are Paul Ganster of San Diego State, Fernando León-García of Centro de Enseñanza Técnica y Superior (CETYS), and Wayne Cornelius and Rafael Fernández de Castro of UCSD.

In Tijuana, CETYS, one of Mexico's highest rated educational institutions—accredited in the US by the Western Association of Schools and Colleges (WASC)—offers high school, undergraduate, and postgraduate courses and degree programs. Founded in 1961 in Mexicali, CETYS was encouraged by the Fimbres family (of Calimax fame) to establish a Tijuana campus in 1972. Led by the brilliant, internationally celebrated educator Fernando León-García, CETYS maintains reciprocal relationships and collaborations with nearly thirty US colleges and universities, including most of the major schools in San Diego. Increasing numbers of American students from San Diego cross the border daily to attend CETYS, or they live in Tijuana altogether to take advantage of the school's strong engineering and business faculties. The Universidad Autónoma de Baja California, part of the University of Mexico system, and with three campuses in Baja California, has a similar collection of relationships with US schools.

Among the most important examples of the new face of binational higher education in the region is the Southwestern College system, with campuses near the border in Chula Vista, National City, Otay Mesa, and San Ysidro. It specifically targets students from both sides of the border by offering courses in trans-border professions, including classes on international logistics and transportation and international business administration and training at the California Center for International Trade Development.

FOR THE GOOD OF THE ORDER

If there is one area in which Tijuana continues to trail San Diego, it is in philanthropy. San Diego has enjoyed the likes of Malin Burnham, with his transformative effect on the cityscape, and his biomed-giving partners Denny Sanford and Conrad Prebys. There have been many who have shaped San Diego over the generations. Among notable others, they include Darlene Shiley, widow of heart-valve coinventor Donald Shiley, who has supported everything from the University of San Diego to Scripps Health to *Masterpiece* on PBS; Ray Kroc, founder of McDonald's, and his wife Joan, who have underwritten National Public Radio among many other institutions; Joan and Irwin Jacobs (founder of Qualcomm); and the Copley family, who published the *San Diego Union-Tribune* for decades.

Why does San Diego lead Tijuana in philanthropy? First, San Diego benefits from more generations of wealth and therefore a deeper sense of noblesse oblige. Second, US national taxation laws encourage philanthropy. Third, enough successful San Diego entrepreneurs have cashed out of their companies and begun to give money away. That began happening in San Diego as far back as the turn of the twentieth century, and in other boomtowns in California—Hollywood, Silicon Valley—in later years. It stood to reason that the newly rich of Tijuana would, in a few years, migrate into philanthropy and good works.

However, working against these expectations was the fact that this sort of philanthropy had little tradition in Mexican culture. In fact, five centuries of a more stratified society had actually reinforced just the opposite behavior. But the emergence of closer cross-border ties had an additional effect: as the powerful figures of San Diego, such as Malin Burnham, increased cross-border interactions, they began to extend their philanthropic efforts into Tijuana and beyond.

A crucial institution in this process has been the International Community Foundation (ICF), founded in 1990 by Lucy Killea with support from the San Diego Foundation. Killea was succeeded by Richard Kiy and then Anne McEnany as ICF's third president. Headquartered in National City, the foundation is dedicated to "inspir[ing] international charitable giving by US donors with an emphasis on Northwest Mexico." The ICF's avowed goal is to strengthen civil society and promote sustainable communities, and it backs this up with annual grants across nearly two hundred projects for a total of nearly $11 million. The ICF also serves as a model (and a resource) to budding philanthropists in Tijuana. Christy Walton remains the driving force in this effort, particularly in matters affecting the regional environment.

Meanwhile, existing philanthropists and institutions on both sides of the border formed the US-Mexico Border Philanthropy Partnership in 2006, headquartered at the San Diego Foundation and run by Andy Carey. Its institutional members range from the Ford Foundation and Southwest Airlines to Wells Fargo and Univision television. One aim is to imbue the next generation of privileged Tijuanenses with the idea of charitable giving across a wide spectrum of interests, importantly including education. To hear José B. Fimbres, whose family has long supported CETYS, this can happen, and San Diegans can help serve as a catalyst:

I had a fundraising lunch two or three days ago because we are modernizing the [CETYS] campus completely. For the first time, I invited leaders from San Diego to join local leaders from Tijuana. I brought in Malin, Steve Williams, and Ted Gildred, another friend of mine whose family founded the Institute of the Americas [in La Jolla], to consider contributing. I thought: we're so intrinsically linked between the two [cities,] and these are very philanthropic people . . .

We need to expand their culture of giving in Mexico. We do have it, but not like in the States, where it's become part of the culture. Here people give, but we still don't have it in our DNA. I want to be able to change that . . .

San Diegans can help this happen by making contributions in Tijuana, for education and other good causes. They have industrial properties in Tijuana, and there are maquiladoras and multinationals. But where are the educated people going to come from to keep their businesses thriving and growing? So I wanted them to see CETYS as one example of a charitable investment in the future of Tijuana that is good for them as well as the city. And if they help set an example, that this is how you create a legacy . . . It is a precedent we need.

FIRST CITY

The second decade of the twenty-first century for the Tijuana Valley began, literally, with a bang. In 2010, a 7.2 earthquake centered in Baja California's capital, Mexicali—109 miles from Tijuana by car or eighty-eight miles as the crow flies—created blackouts on both sides of the border. It was symbolic of what was to come.

In 2010, the city of San Diego had a population of 1.3 million people; Tijuana, thanks to its much faster growth, had at last passed its northern neighbor, with 1.4 million citizens. That trajectory would continue through the decade, so that by 2019 San Diego would enjoy a population of 1.5 million, Tijuana more than 2 million. Tijuana was now the larger member of the pair. Despite a smaller footprint, it was also more populous than the other cities of Baja California. Historians Piñera and Rivera:

> The municipality of Tijuana [723 square kilometers or 279 square miles] is only larger than Rosarito and is dwarfed by the huge municipalities of Ensenada, Mexicali, and Tecate. Tijuana has only 1.7 percent of the land of the state of Baja California, but with [2] million residents in [2019] had about [63] percent of the state's population [3.16 million].

On the other hand, San Diego had not lost its economic dominance. Per capita income was now more than $80,000 per year. By comparison, the average salary in Tijuana was $37,000—impressive for Mexico, which had a lower cost of living, but still less than half that of its neighbor to the north.

Nonetheless, Tijuana was catching up fast, thanks to a number of factors: the maquiladoras, the medical-tourism industry, tourism, and the sheer number of Tijuanenses commuting across the border each day to jobs earning San Diego salaries. It was not hard to imagine that wealth on both sides of the border would, within a decade or two, approach parity.

But then, just as everything seemed to be moving smoothly ever-upward, a series of events between 2015 and 2020 again threatened to tarnish what had been accomplished by the two cities over the previous quarter century.

The two sources of this unexpected chaos were those old curses of crime and unlawful migration. The gang wars of the beginning of the decade in Tijuana had not returned, but after a brief respite mid-decade that allowed the renaissance of Tijuana's cuisine and culture, the crime rate again began to rise. This time it was the Sinaloa Cartel, which had moved into a power vacuum and was now clearing out the opposition to its narcotics trade. That trade was now even more dreadful and deadly than ever, with opioids like fentanyl added to the staples

San Diego Central Library.

of cocaine and heroin. (Cross-border trafficking of marijuana had virtually disappeared with its legalization in several states in the US.)

By 2017, the homicide rate in Tijuana had climbed nearly to the levels seen in the dark years of the previous decade. This time, though, it was different in several ways. First, the problem seemed more intractable, with solutions hard to find. Unlike the Arellano-Félix cartel war, in which one side could be played against the other, this time the problem was almost monolithic. Now there was just a single, dominant regional gang, the Sinaloas, doing most of the killing to keep down ever-present challengers, such as the Jalisco New Generation Cartel (Cártel Jalisco Nueva Generación) from Central Mexico, which was trying to get traction in the highly lucrative drug corridor or "plaza" leading into the United States through Tijuana and San Diego.

Second, this time the killings were largely restricted to the poverty-stricken outer neighborhoods, mostly in the southern and eastern parts of town, where drug marketplaces were springing up everywhere—not in the heart of the city, where it would scare local professionals and international visitors. Mexico was no longer just a transit zone for narcotics channeled to the United States but, increasingly and more worrisomely, a consumer of drugs itself, particularly in lower-income neighborhoods. To the upper and middle classes of Tijuana, ensconced in their vibrant, undisturbed downtown, the new Tijuana was bigger and brighter than ever before, the streets brimming with people and commerce, social life uncompromised. If one did not look too closely, Tijuana seemed as safe as any big city in North America.

Nevertheless, the murders continued to climb until they could no longer be ignored. In 2018, Tijuana was declared to have the world's worst homicide rate: 138 murders per 100,000 citizens. At more than 2,500 total murders, this was a 40 percent increase over 2017, which was itself a record year, and three times as many killings as the city had suffered in the dark period from 2008 to 2010.

"It's devastating what is happening here," a Tijuanenses man (who understandably asked not to be named) told *The Guardian*. "It is out of control."

SINALOA

In late 2019, the situation took another turn for the worse. In February of that year, Joaquín Archivaldo Guzmán Loera, El Chapo, the head of the Sinaloa Cartel, the man called the most powerful drug trafficker in the world, extradited by Mexico and tried in New York, was convicted of numerous crimes ranging from drug distribution to murder and sentenced to life in prison plus thirty years. El Chapo had been imprisoned twice before in Mexico but had managed to escape both times. This time, however, was different: the conviction was not only in the US (Mexico, which has no provision for capital punishment in its law, allowed his extradition once the US agreed not to execute Guzmán), but El Chapo was to be incarcerated at Colorado's ADX Florence, the US's most secure supermax prison.

Although this conviction was considered a game changer in the drug wars, soon Mexico was wracked by a bigger wave of violence— not least by the Sinaloa gang, which quickly reconfigured itself after the loss of El Chapo, to be led by his four sons known as Los Chapitos and advised by his longtime deputy, Ismael "El Mayo" Zambada. The so-called kingpin strategy—which through close Mexico-US law enforcement cooperation over the previous fifteen years had decapitated and fragmented Mexico's largest drug cartels—had neither slowed the demand for narcotics nor significantly weakened the capability of criminals on both sides of the border to traffic in them. The drug flow continued unabated, along with the rampant violence attendant to it.

Aggravating the situation, it was claimed, was the "strategy for peace" of Mexico's newly elected president, Andrés Manuel López Obrador (AMLO), who took office in December 2018. López Obrador's strategy, *abrazos no balazos* ("hugs not bullets"), was to offer amnesty to all Mexican citizens involved in drug production and trafficking, as long as they weren't involved in violent acts. The idea was to allow those individuals to escape the drug industry and return to normal lives—a situation, AMLO believed, that was the result of the great disparities of wealth in the country. He also reorganized parts of the nation's military and police into a National Guard to implement these new policies.

With El Chapo off to prison two months later and a vacuum resulting at the top of Mexico's largest remaining drug cartel, López Obrador's approach to security was quickly tested. On October 17, 2019, the new National Guard, not yet fully organized, captured one of El Chapo's sons, Ovidio Guzmán López, in the western Mexican city of Culiacán, in the state of Sinaloa, the cartel's homeland. Initially the operation succeeded, but when news of the arrest reached the cartel, gang members launched a full-scale attack on the city to free the prisoner.

The resulting "Battle of Culiacán" was a catastrophe for Mexican government forces, who were quickly outnumbered and outgunned by an estimated seven hundred cartel gunman armed with bulletproof vests, .50-caliber machine guns, rocket and grenade launchers, and armored pickup trucks. They were led by Ovidio's brothers, Iván Archivaldo Guzmán and Jesús Alfredo Guzmán Salazar, the sons El Chapo had personally groomed to take over the family business. The cartel gunmen not only attacked the Guardia Nacional but, because many of the soldiers were locals, also attacked the housing units where their families lived, taking hostages. Through it all, Mexico's premier antidrug military force, Secretaria de Marina's Naval Special Forces, remained in their barracks, not having been included in the operation.

In one of the more discouraging events in modern Mexican history, the Army retreated, releasing Guzmán López, essentially surrendering the city to the cartel. By the time the shooting stopped, thirteen people were dead. President López Obrador justified his decision to release Guzmán López by arguing that it prevented further loss of life, but he admitted that the National Guard had underestimated the manpower (and firepower) of the cartel. He also immediately ordered eight thousand troops and police officers to Culiacán to maintain the peace.

In the meantime, news of the battle sent shock waves across Mexico and the United States. For the first time, a drug cartel had not only taken on the government directly but defeated it. Was the long-standing fear of Mexico becoming a narco-criminal state about to be realized? Would hordes of refugees from this war now stream north, begging (or demanding) sanctuary in the US? Would all of Mexico's gains over the last half century now be lost? Though these fears were dramatically overstated, mutterings about "a failed state" started up again, after they had been put firmly to rest in the decade before the Battle of Culiacán.

Tijuana was no more immune from these fears than any other city in Mexico. In some ways, the fears were even greater. After all, the Sinaloa Cartel, with its local associates, controlled the underworld in most of Tijuana's back streets, and the gang war with the Cártel Jalisco Nueva Generación was intensifying significantly. Sinaloa had long used Tijuana (most infamously via secret tunnels on Otay Mesa) as a portal to ship drugs into the US, and they would continue to do so. In early 2020, Mexican authorities found the largest and most sophisticated tunnel burrowed deep into the ground and reaching across to San Diego. If the uncontrolled violence seen in Culiacán ever broke out on a similar scale across Tijuana, it could reverse all the city's advances, crush trade (medical tourism, the maquiladoras, the airport) with San Diego, and once again force the city's most successful and influential people to flee for their lives to the north, leaving the rest of the city to the predations of gangs. While, all things considered, this did not seem at all likely to unfold in Tijuana, the possibility did exist and remained uncomfortably in the back of people's minds.

Then another shocking cartel crime hit Northern Mexico. In the town of La Mora, members of a Mormon sect, practicing polygamy according to their religion, had lived for generations as dual-nationals. In November 2019, a caravan of their vehicles was intercepted on the highway by La Línea, an armed wing of the Juárez cartel. Some say these sicario gunmen from the neighboring state of Chihuahua, challenging the Sinaloa Cartel in its home base in Sonora, may have confused the Mormons' convoy of large black SUVs with similar vehicles driven by the rival gang. Other observers differed, seeing the attack as a deliberate effort to intimidate the residents of La Mora and clear them out of a principal narcotics-trafficking corridor. Whatever the case, when the smoke cleared, three women, four children, and eight-month-old twins had been murdered. Others among their children were wounded, and all of them were, of course, severely traumatized.

In the United States, news of the massacre was met with revulsion and anger. President Trump mused publicly about officially designating Mexican drug gangs as "terrorist organizations," considering the damage they inflicted. In Congress, there were a few calls for the White House to send an army to Mexico to take on the cartels once and for all before they destroyed Mexico and then perhaps attacked the Southwest United States. Cooler heads soon prevailed, especially after the situation in the states of Sinaloa and Sonora quieted down, and several suspects in the massacre were arrested. In addition, President López Obrador intervened personally, and very publicly, to attend to the needs of the Mormon community in Mexico, which also helped calm both the fears and tempers that the atrocity had aroused.

But as 2019 turned to 2020, the situation in Tijuana and across Mexico remained tense, and people in the US wary, as both populations awaited the cartels' next move, wondering how their respective populist presidents, Andrés Manuel López Obrador and Donald Trump, would respond.

THE CARAVAN

The flow of "undocumented persons," "irregular and unauthorized migrants," or "illegal aliens" (even the term is subject to endless, angry debate) has changed its composition over the years. The number of migrants, particularly Mexicans, decreased significantly, though it never really ended. Even as Tijuana-San Diego managed to get local illegal border crossings under control starting in the 1990s, its success only rerouted the flow of migrants elsewhere, first to the less-populated border regions of the Sonora Desert, along the eastern California border and Arizona, and then after 2011, dramatically into the Rio Grande River region in Texas.

These vast, remote tracts were difficult to guard, even with the Border Patrol having grown from three thousand agents in the 1990s to more than twenty-one thousand by 2010, the level where it has mostly stayed through the present. However, unlike the Tijuana-to-San Diego or Juarez-to-El Paso crossings—that is, urban crossings featuring considerable infrastructure—the Sonoran and Rio Grande crossings were and remain especially arduous and very dangerous. Even reaching the isolated crossing points was a huge challenge, forcing most undocumented migrants to hire coyotes to bring them to the border, often with far too many people jammed into the backs of trucks along the way. At the border, summer temperatures could soar over 110 degrees—lethal for travelers without access to shade and water. Moreover, many of the coyotes were professional criminals, indifferent to the fate of their customers. Any whiff of risk might lead them to abandon the people they were transporting in the desert or on the river, or to leave them to die locked in the back of a tractor trailer. This has happened on all too many occasions, with grisly and tragic results.

Even before the turn of the twentieth century, Americans found themselves in a deep moral quandary over what to do about illegal immigration. On the one hand, the United States prided itself on being a nation of immigrants—after all, the Statue of Liberty beckoned refugees to the American Dream. With its citizenry growing older and the rate of population growth slowing, the nation's leaders and corporate executives also recognized that the country's labor market needed an influx of new citizens to remain competitive. Those millions of undocumented immigrants also contributed billions to the US economy each year—not least their social security payments, which they had to sacrifice and could never collect as benefits because they had to remain in the shadows.

On the other hand, many Americans chafed at the idea that millions of people were sneaking into their country illegally and, whenever they could, taking advantage of the nation's largesse, while legal immigrants from other countries were responsibly taking the proper channels and often forced to wait years for approval because of long delays in the US immigration system. As stories began to appear in the media about the continued scale of illegal immigration, the conflict between these points of view widened, roiled by rhetoric and reaction from across the political aisle.

From time to time, throughout American history, this undercurrent had burst into restrictive immigration legislation and resulted in migrant roundups and deportations, including the anti-immigrant Palmer Raids in the 1920s and the "zoot suit riots" in Los Angeles in the 1940s. In 1994, California aimed Proposition 187 at Mexican migrants, and in 2010, Arizona replicated the initiative with Senate Bill 1070.

Historically, following the Mexican-American War in the 1840s, there were no legal restrictions on immigration, with citizens from both countries moving back and forth across the border without limitation. The first federal nativist legislation was directed not to Mexico, but against China in the Chinese Exclusion Act of 1882. According to historian Rachel St. John, associate professor at UC Davis, "One of the ways that immigrants from China would try to get across the border [was] to learn a few words of Spanish and disguise themselves as Mexican." According to St. John:

> Restrictions on the movements of Mexican citizens were not particularly enforced by the US government until the decade of the Mexican Revolution in the 1910s, when large numbers of refugees came to escape the war and there was a large demand for Mexican labor. Following Mexican revolutionary Pancho Villa's deadly raid on Columbus, New Mexico, in 1916 and the subsequent publication of the Zimmerman telegram proposing a World War I military alliance between Mexico and Germany, the United States tightened border security and deployed soldiers to patrol the

boundary along with the Texas Rangers and government-sanctioned "home guards."

By 2000, it became obvious that the rate of unauthorized immigration had exploded—with migrants a major force in Southern California, and a presence now in every state of the union. Rising voices began to call for improved border security, including physical barriers and electronic sensors, along the length of the 1,900-mile Mexico-US border.

Then came 9/11. A traumatized United States, fearful of more terrorist attacks, worried that the porous southern border might provide a pathway for Al-Qaeda and other Islamic terrorist groups to sneak in camouflaged within migrant groups. While this threat has never materialized beyond a few isolated arrests, the perceived risk added to the sense of urgency and the clamor for border security.

What was as yet unknown was just how many former Mexican citizens, now undocumented immigrants, were now living in the United States. An accurate census was nearly impossible, not least because those immigrants were reluctant to talk to any authority for fear of being deported. Initial estimates put the number at a few million, but as the years passed, demographic researchers conducted more detailed studies, with some surprising results. For example, a 2019 study by Pew Research agreed with the US government that the number of unauthorized immigrants in the US was about eleven million, and that approximately eight million of them were from Mexico.

As the twenty-first century unfolded, the dispute in the United States over undocumented migration at the southern border continued to divide the country even more sharply into two opposing camps. But the actual boundaries of those two camps were, in reality, not that clear. For example, labor unions (including, paradoxically, Cesar Chavez's United Farm Workers) lined up largely against undocumented migration because its potential for cheap labor threatened to undermine many of the gains they had made for their members over the previous generation.

Meanwhile, many traditionally conservative institutions, including the US Chamber of Commerce and the *Wall Street Journal*, came out on the side of enhanced legal immigration, not just for moral reasons but also to boost the US workforce with low-income workers. By the second decade of the century, the two political parties had staked out opposing positions: the GOP for tighter border control and greater internal enforcement with no amnesty of any kind for those illegally in the country; the Democratic Party for strengthened border control to be sure, but accompanied by relaxed entry requirements, a focus on family reunification, and steps toward earned citizenship for the undocumented.

Of course, both parties accused the other of bad faith—Democrats accused Republicans of racism and nativism, of trying to keep brown people out of their white country. Republicans accused Democrats of cynically conspiring to replace existing Americans with a new population of voters it could easily manipulate to vote Democratic. The polarization along these fault lines hardened as the years passed.

As for Mexico, the idea that millions of their fellow citizens were choosing to leave their home country to live in El Norte always seemed humiliating to a proud people. When Yankees described these migrants—the vast majority of whom were economic migrants trapped in situations beyond their control—as criminals, it was both infuriating and too much an echo of the anti-Mexican bigotry of the last century. Further, the border deaths in the deserts and mountains were heartbreaking, to the point that the Mexican government published maps and easy-to-read comic books to help the migrants safely cross the border.

That further infuriated many Americans: to them it showed that Mexico, while mouthing platitudes about helping to control the border, was in fact complicit in illegal migration, no doubt to protect the billions of dollars in remittance payments being sent each year from migrants north of the border—payments that were a major factor in Mexico's economy. The shooting of Mexicans—not infrequently young Mexicans—by US Border Patrol agents added combustible fuel to the clashing attitudes on both sides of the border. Ironically, cooperation between officials in the two nations, particularly those involved in law enforcement, had grown enormously from the 1990s forward. But the border remained a potentially lethal "third rail" in the politics of both countries. For that reason, the broad and deep extent of US-Mexico cooperation, though not a secret, remained pretty much an "inside baseball" matter. Public opinion in Mexico and the United States alike remained vulnerable to political exploitation, including pandering and demagoguery, when it came to the border.

The situation boiled over during the 2016 American presidential campaign. Donald Trump ran an insurgent campaign built largely on taking stands on subjects that traditional politicians would not dare touch, infuriating not just Democrats but establishment Republicans as well. One of the pillars of Trump's campaign was a promise to build an "impenetrable, physical, tall, powerful, beautiful southern border wall" from the Pacific Ocean to the Gulf of Mexico, and to make the Mexican government pay for it. With his unexpected election, President Trump immediately set out to fulfill this pledge. After three years of fighting with congressional Democrats over funding, the Trump administration found some of the money it needed to begin the work.

Initially, talk about the wall focused on San Diego, because of its accessibility to media, because much of the wall there already existed, and because President Trump chose that stretch for his media events. There was no little irony in his choosing to start in San Diego—along the entire length of the southern border, likely no place had more control over border crossings than San Diego, nor less need for the new wall. Nearly twenty years earlier, Operation Gatekeeper, including the existing fence, had proven largely effective.

Like many political spectacles in the US, at the point when they reach peak hysteria—by the time there are congressional calls for action and presidential orders for intervention—the actual crisis has either passed or fundamentally changed. Such was the case with the latest iteration of the border crisis: undocumented migration had largely topped out before the Great Recession, declined in the immediate years thereafter, and never came all the way back. Americans, who still saw the border through the lens of those "running family" freeway signs in San Diego, did not realize those signs were now historic collectibles. Meanwhile, the growing prosperity in Mexico had convinced most would-be migrants to stay home or look for jobs in now-booming Mexican cities such as Tijuana. A study by the Pew Foundation in 2018 documented that fewer Mexicans were entering the United States, legally and illegally, than were departing from the US, voluntarily and involuntarily (via deportation).

While politicians rhetorically were fighting the last war, on the ground meanwhile, the officials who had to deal with the border crisis pragmatically and on a day-to-day basis were encountering a far different reality: the one depicted in the Pew study. For one thing, the classic undocumented migrant—a Mexican campesino from the country's poor central highlands or southern villages looking for a better life—was disappearing, replaced by a new wave of even more desperate migrants from the Northern Triangle of Central America. These people were fleeing both extreme poverty and gang violence in Guatemala, Honduras, and El Salvador. They were joined, albeit in fewer numbers, by people from across the globe, anxious to participate in the US economy at any cost—from the Caribbean to the Middle East, and from Africa to South and East Asia.

The biggest test came in 2018 and 2019 when organizers in Honduras began forming caravans of several thousand migrants, who made their way up from Central America through Mexico to assault the US border, having been taught by smugglers and migrant rights advocates how to ask for legal amnesty—asylum—under American law. Both groups knew the US asylum system was thoroughly broken and that its loopholes and disrepair made it vulnerable to wholesale manipulation. The first place chosen by caravan leaders to force the issue was Tijuana—mimicking Trump's preferred site to promote a wall—since media attention would be plentiful and CBP resources on the San Diego side sufficient to process thousands of asylum claims.

Migrants arriving in the caravan did not try to evade capture at the border but, to the contrary, actively sought out CBP officers in order to initiate the asylum process. Once in custody, the asylum applicants would be administered a "credible fear" interview. This examination set a relatively low standard, which a large majority of the applicants could pass. When the migrants met this standard, they were paroled into the Unites States, where they were able to live and work until the immigration courts resolved their asylum petitions. The catch is that this legal status turned out to be neither short nor temporary because the court dates were scheduled years into the future on account of massive backlogs on the immigration court docket.

Complicating further the government's ability to manage the situation was a federal court order that strictly limited the amount of time juveniles and families could be detained pending their proceedings. Thousands of migrant families, accordingly, were released into the United States on little more than a "promise to appear" downstream in immigration court. Rather than security weaknesses per se, these systemic dysfunctions and glaring loopholes, along with strife in the migrants' home countries, brought the caravans to the doorstep of San Diego at Tijuana. The problem, in short—particularly in San Diego-Tijuana—was not one of border security but rather one of migration management.

The new Mexican government looked upon all this refugee theater with some amusement and no little hypocrisy. The amusement came with many Americans getting their wish: fewer Mexican migrants. Instead, the US was getting a far bigger problem: 53 percent of the undocumented immigrants were Central Americans with less education and financial means, who could not be easily transported home across a contiguous border. The hypocrisy came from the fact that, while Mexico discounted the ever-mounting attempt by the US to seal its border against illegal migration, since 2015 it had been guarding its own southern border from migrants, initially under pressure from the Obama administration. Now, in a turnabout, Mexico's President López Obrador was letting Central American migrants and refugees through on a free pass, as long as they kept going to the US border.

It was not long before amusement and hypocrisy turned to dismay and anger. The dismay came when the United States proved successful at turning back the caravans. First, caravan organizers instigated a migrant rush at the border, which backfired badly when rebuffed by teargas from CBP officers equipped with military-like armor and high-caliber weaponry, a level of ferocity rare if not unprecedented at San Ysidro. No serious casualties resulted, and the ensuing media coverage handed the Trump administration a public-relations victory.

Second, and more significantly, President Trump soon brought Mexico back to the border enforcement table by threatening tariffs on Mexican exports to the United States. It was, to be sure, a strong-arm approach to one of America's most important partners. But it may have been the only way to get President López Obrador's attention and obtain action from the Mexican government. López Obrador promptly resumed his predecessor's enforcement efforts by deploying the newly created National Guard to Mexico's southern border. Ultimately, twenty thousand guard personnel were positioned directly on that border, and soon nearly twenty-five thousand Central Americans each month were being detained and repatriated by Mexican authorities to their home countries.

In the meantime, the thousands of Central American refugees who already had made the caravan journey north became Mexico's problem. The so-called Migration Protection Protocols (MPP), implemented by the Trump administration around the same time as Mexican enforcement ramped up, mandated that migrants who passed the credible-fear test would no longer be admitted into the United States but rather would be compelled to wait in Mexico for their immigration court dates. Opponents decried the administration's lack of empathy and challenged its policies requiring Central Americans to remain in Mexico against their will.

By the end of the first quarter of 2020, more than sixty-two thousand Central Americans had been shuttled back across the border after their initial processing in the US. Many settled into squatters' camps, unable to go forward and unwilling to go back. In desperate need of food, medicine, and other services, they became a burden on their host cities, not least Tijuana. The Central American migrants were now Mexico's problem.

The irony was that, even as the government of Mexico was decrying its predicament, Tijuana had a different response. The local economy was good; the maquiladora, medical-tourism, and hospitality industries were thriving; and these industries needed employees. Numerous enterprises in the city were willing to hire and train—even though it would take a major investment—any refugee who wanted a job. Indeed, in 2016, three thousand Haitians had migrated to Tijuana after their construction jobs ended along with the Olympics in Rio de Janeiro. Blocked from entering the US, the Haitians settled down in Tijuana, quickly becoming contributing members of society there, opening restaurants and working in the factories.

In Tijuana at least, the border crisis had become a border opportunity. Some of the Central American migrants took up the offer. Unfortunately, most of them did not, preferring to get across the border into the United States, in many cases to reunite with family members already there. For these people, the Mexican federal government established a large, safe, and sanitary shelter on the outskirts of Tijuana. But most of the Central American migrants chose not to stay there, instead opting to remain on the streets, or to pay smugglers to sneak them into the United States farther east along the border.

In May 2019, the border saw the highest level of irregular migration in almost two decades: 144,116 people. By the beginning of 2020, the number of migrants encountered at the border had shrunk to a fraction of that.

How did the situation change so dramatically in a few months? The answer is straightforward: the Trump administration stopped treating the crisis as an American border-security issue and began to handle it as a regional problem of migration management. The Migration Protection Protocols were implemented, and a series of "Safe Third Country" agreements were imposed on Guatemala, Honduras, and El Salvador, denying access to the American asylum system if the applicant had not sought refuge along the way. This changed the calculus, making it much more difficult for those who wanted to leave the Northern Triangle. For the first time since Trump took office, in 2017, the Trump administration had created an effective deterrent to unlawful migration—which its earlier policies, including an ill-conceived and ill-fated decision to separate children from their families, manifestly had not accomplished.

By the end of 2019, although it was unclear how long it might last, the Central American migrant wave had receded, as had the remnants of Mexican migration before it. Trump supporters claimed that administration policies had been the reason. Mexico had indeed built President Trump's wall—not on the US border but on the border between Mexico and Guatemala, and not a giant steel fence, but one of soldiers and police officers put in place by the Mexican Guardia Nacional. Others pointed to changing demographics and the improving economy in Mexico convincing citizens and some migrants to stay in the country. In the end, it simply may have been that the migration problem was about to move elsewhere—just as it had when San Diego gained control of its border in the 1990s—and the message was conveyed back, via cell phones and smuggling networks: *Don't come because you won't get through.*

But in March 2020, the situation was thrown into limbo again by a judicial ruling in the Ninth Circuit invalidating the administration's Migration Protection Protocols, which, like them or not, had stemmed the earlier uncontrolled migrant flows from Central America by forcing asylum applicants to wait in Mexico. As the decision headed for review in the US Supreme Court, uncertainty prevailed, and President Trump ordered further troops to the border—including at San Diego-Tijuana—to support existing civilian enforcement by agents and officers of US Customs and Border Protection.

The border wall, as imposing as it is, has been in place in Tijuana and San Diego long enough that it has now become largely invisible to residents from both sides. In the maquiladora district, it passes from horizon to horizon just across the street from factories and car-choked employee parking lots. On the Otay Mesa and near the ocean at Friendship Park, it runs along the crest of a hill, like a geological formation of black rock. At the San Ysidro border crossing, it seems to play hide-and-seek as it tracks between government buildings crowding both sides of the border, and, as at CBX, it passes like a monorail track under the cross-border pedestrian passageways. In the Las Americas Premium Outlets, which snubs up against the fence, it suddenly appears at the end of streets, just beyond the Ghirardelli Chocolate shop and the Ralph Lauren store, seemingly keeping shoppers in rather than keeping Mexicans—who just happen to be about half the shoppers in Las Americas—out.

On the rare occasions when the fence does reenter the consciousness of San Diegans and Tijuanenses, it seems to draw an irritated shrug: it just seems so superfluous here. At least for now.

INNOVADORA

José Galicot, 82, has seen it all since his family arrived in Tijuana in July 1946. Tijuana in those days was a city of twenty thousand citizens, a third the size of San Diego, and very much in its shadow.

> My father told me, "You are a free man; you can live
> in two worlds." In those days we had our depression

cards. We received things from Mexico or from the
United States with those cards. We used them for oil,
for butter, for shoes.

The story of his upbringing—his career as a tailor, as a department-store magnate, and, after the collapse of his empire, as a telecommunications giant—has already been told. But history is likely
to remember most what Galicot did after his retirement. Like Malin
Burnham, a good friend to whom he is often compared, and his neighbor in Tijuana, Salomón Cohen, José Galicot has devoted the third
phase of his life to transforming his beloved city, burnishing its image,
and making its presence known on the world stage.

When José walked out of his doctor's office that day in 2009, after
the doctor informed him that his new heart valve had been made in
Tijuana, he had an epiphany:

> I realized that I had no idea what was being manufac-
> tured in my own city, what contributions they were
> making to the larger world. The maquiladoras were
> all closed to the public. I wanted to know what all of
> them were doing. And I wanted them to show the peo-
> ple of Tijuana the impressive things they were doing. I
> thought, "Let's do something to show the world that."

Being a natural impresario, Galicot decided the best way to present
all these innovations would be some sort of trade show or an international forum and exposition open to the general public. To test the
idea, comparable to the Panama-California Exposition that had introduced a young San Diego to the world nearly a hundred years before,
he contacted sixty Tijuana companies, asking if they would be willing
to put up $25,000 each to sponsor such an event. In a testament to the
appeal of this idea, as well as Galicot's reputation as one of Tijuana's
greatest entrepreneurs, all sixty companies agreed.

By then, Galicot's dreams were already growing. Remember, this
was 2009, the height of the AFO's drug war in the streets of Tijuana—
gun battles, bodies hung from bridges, frightened citizens huddled in
their homes. Tijuana's image had never been lower. Only José Galicot,

with a Tijuana-made valve in his heart, would decide that this was an ideal moment to celebrate the city's future.

> I decided it was time to remind people what was great about the city. Its energy. The fact that it is constantly changing. That we are a city of immigrants—the kind of people who work hard and do their best to make a better life. People who left their homes and took great risks to come here. I had been here long enough that I knew Tijuana. I knew the life of the city, its stories, its people, its soul. I wanted to tell that story. To show that despite the recent setbacks, life in Tijuana was getting better and better—and would continue to do so.

The seed of the Tijuana trade-show idea had grown into a full-blown promotion of Tijuana on the world stage. The two-week Tijuana Innovadora event would bring together global celebrities, leaders, and thinkers to address the future of various attributes of modern life, to show the latest technologies, and to restore a sense of optimism in a battered city. In the face of the violence on the city's streets, all citizens of Tijuana would be invited to hear the talks, tour exhibits, enjoy food and crafts, and, in an unforgettable moment, join a massive dance mob celebrating the occasion.

The first Innovadora took place in October 2010. Speakers rolled in from around the world—talk-show host Larry King, Wikipedia founder Jimmy Wales, former US vice president Al Gore, Mexico's richest man, Carlos Slim, and Mexico's then-president Felipe Calderón—conferring a legitimacy on Tijuana it had rarely known. But the crowning moment was the street dance: sixteen thousand revelers showed up to dance in the plaza, joined by a crowd at Las Americas Premium Outlets across the border, within earshot of the music.

Innovadora I was a genuine cross-border—indeed transnational—triumph, a vindication of José Galicot's vision and a thumb of the nose to the gangsters and the cynics about Tijuana's future. Galicot was ebullient. He told *La Prensa*, "[I feel] total gratitude and satisfaction . . . It was a clear example of what can be achieved with care, imagination, discipline and love."

He was already planning for the future of Innovadora:

> I had said this could happen every two years, but now
> I think I would like to have something of the same
> magnitude but different spirit. For this year's event the
> stars were aligned in our favor in order to show what is
> being done in Tijuana, but I believe our next endeavor
> should be with a different focus . . .
>
> As many as two hundred businesses that did not
> participate in the Innovadora now are first in line for
> our next effort.

Some of those companies are in San Diego. As for involving San
Diego and its businesses in future Innovadoras, Galicot agreed but
also bluntly expressed a view held by many Tijuanenses, but rarely
verbalized:

> San Diego has long believed it has been living with a
> toad called Tijuana, but in reality, Tijuana is a prince
> waiting to be discovered. The truth is we are sleeping
> in the same bed, whether they know it or not . . . I'm
> convinced 99 percent of us living in Tijuana are hon-
> est, interesting, hardworking people. It is only a small
> group that insists on terrorizing us.
>
> So I strongly believe those events can only be
> answered by doing exactly what we have been doing,
> working from the cultural standpoint and letting the
> police and military take care of the violence because
> that's their job.

Over the next decade, Tijuana Innovadora grew into a global phenomenon and a defining cultural event of Tijuana life. Malin Burnham
joined its advisory board as co-chair with Galicot, raising the event's
prominence in San Diego.

Every two years, the event has drawn not only the best of the city
but visitors and speakers from around the world. The themes of the
Innovadora have grown ever-more ambitious: in 2010 it was "The

Smart Frontier," in 2012 "Heading to Greatness," in 2014 "The Mexican Diaspora," in 2016 "Creative," and in 2018, no single gathering was held, but a series of special events took place throughout the year. Galicot contemplated a culmination of sorts and began to plan for the "big one" in 2020.

But he wasn't content to settle for a biannual celebration. He wanted a continuous initiative in Tijuana—what would in time be a "citizen platform that integrates creative proposals for social innovation (creative innovation) to raise the quality of life of Tijuana"—punctuated by the actual celebration every two years.

Toward that end, Galicot and his growing team began to create a number of programs that filled the many months in between the showcase events. All of this resembled a distinctive combination of think tank, TED conference, and public forum—and as the years passed, the Innovadora slowly began to encompass almost every aspect of Tijuana's commercial and cultural life. For example, the InnovaModa event focused upon the fashion industry and was held at the Quartz Hotel & Spa. It comprised panel discussions featuring leading fashion designers, training sessions on marketing and sales, and a film contest, and it culminated in a "Great Catwalk" of regional fashion design.

Ongoing Innovadora initiatives, each of them led by dedicated teams of volunteers, have included:

- Industrial Arts: A continuing art installation program targeted at Tijuana's seniors, in particular social security recipients, these exhibitions in 2019 were seen by nearly six hundred thousand visitors.
- Casa de las Ideas: A small, award-winning facility located in the Camino Verde neighborhood (notorious for its crime and flooding), this digital library was designed to improve the neighborhood's quality of life.
- Tijuana Youth Orchestra: As reported by KCRW television, "You don't typically associate classical music with Tijuana, but Tijuana Youth Orchestra gives the lie to that assumption." In recent years, the Tijuana Youth Orchestra has begun to perform regularly with various San Diego–based youth orchestras (notably Mainly Mozart). The

best-known such occasion took place in 2018, when the
two orchestras joined together, with a thousand-voice
children's choir, to perform at the Palenque auditorium in
Tijuana's Parque Morelos.

- The Tijuana chapter of the International Foundation of
Young Leaders: This group features programs in entrepre-
neurship, volunteering, robotics, and networking.

- Tijuana Paseo de Fama: Designed to celebrate the best
of Tijuana and its people, this program includes installations on a special walkway in the middle of the city, as
well as a traveling exhibition continuously showing at
various public facilities and cultural centers around the
city. The Paseo de Fama ("Walk of Fame"), at the end of
2019, had celebrated 185 individuals and organizations
for their contributions to Tijuana's culture, arts, science,
technology, sports, business, and academics. Those
honored were not just Tijuanenses but also a number of
Americans who have influenced the progress of the city.
Among the honorees are many individuals who appear
in this book, including Deborah Szekely, Sandra Dibble,
Javier Plascencia, Mary Walshok, Malin Burnham, Jerry
Sanders, James Clark, Salomón Cohen, Denise Ducheny,
and Alejandro Bustamante.

- Tijuana Verde ("Green Tijuana"): This initiative focuses
on projects and programs that improve environmental
quality and support sustainable development. Tijuana
Verde does its work by bringing together industry, government, and nongovernmental organizations (NGOs)
through congresses, workshops, and fairs that feature
international speakers and exhibitions of university
environmental projects. Green Tijuana also has refor-
ested eight acres of barren Tijuana landscape.

In 2018 alone, Tijuana Innovadora conducted nearly 550 different
programs in Tijuana and its surrounding region, directly affecting, it
claimed, more than one hundred thousand individuals and indirectly

more than four hundred thousand, with a total of more than two million direct beneficiaries since its founding in 2010.

That last figure includes a number of San Diegans. Despite José Galicot's initial reservations, he has come to embrace the binational model for his Innovadora. The most telling example of this is the addition to the Innovadora's extensive Tijuana-based board of directors and staff of a San Diego Advisory Council, presided over—not unexpectedly—by Malin Burnham. The Council also includes Jerry Sanders, Mary Walshok, and James Clark, as well as various San Diego–area mayors and city council members; Jim Fitzpatrick, publisher and CEO of *San Diego Magazine*; and Rafael Fernández de Castro, director of the Center for US-Mexican Studies at UCSD.

The creation of this San Diego Advisory Council foretold how José Galicot is preparing Tijuana Innovadora for its next step, timed for its tenth anniversary in 2020. Indeed, he is swinging for the fences this time, his goal being to put the Innovadora—and by extension, Tijuana—on the world map as one of the most innovative and progressive events and cities on the planet. The theme, typically grandiose, is "Tijuana Is the Future."

"This is going to be more than an event," the Innovadora's director of institutional development, Flavio Olivieri, has announced. "It will be a whole platform for social innovation."

For Tijuana, the decade of the 2010s began in blood and violence. It ends with José Galicot's Innovadora, in the words of *ANA Noticias* (paraphrased from the Cuban revolution), "a cry of struggle to demonstrate the skills and talents of Tijuanenses." Despite the challenges of the intervening years, the city and the Innovadora will conclude the decade in triumph. José Galicot has succeeded in making the world take notice, and Tijuana is ready to be seen for the extraordinary city it has become at the side of San Diego.

MORNING

Locals call it June Gloom. The first hot days meet cool, humid nights, and the thick fog, always sitting just beyond the horizon over the Pacific, sneaks eastward, obliterating the moon and stars.

By morning, the citizens of San Diego and Tijuana arise to a monochrome world under gray, wet overcast skies. Despite it being the eve of summer, they eat breakfast under the lights in their kitchens and pull on sweaters and jackets as they head out the front door. Outside, the air is moist and chilly, and as they climb into their cars, they sometimes turn on the heater and briefly run the windshield wipers to clear away—and more likely streak—the fine spray on the glass.

At Imperial Beach, Ocean Beach, and Playas de Tijuana, the white sand is gray and damp and clumps underfoot, the ocean sullen and the color of lead. At the Naval anchorage at North Island and across the bay from the USS Midway Museum, the aircraft carriers are dark silhouettes, their tall superstructures fading upward into the gloom. At Mission Bay, only a few locals in hoodies trot along the sand. And at the Hotel del Coronado, the wooden seats along the lawn are deserted and wet.

At the border, the wall, tall and black, drips water from every one of its thousands of posts from where it rises from the gray foam of the ocean to where it disappears over the horizon miles inland. At Friendship Park, the metal netting between the posts seemingly turns the wall solid; at the Las Americas Premium Outlets, it squats dark and malevolent at the end of side streets, and on the Otay Mesa, it races along, thin and horizontal like the black strata of an ancient great catastrophe.

In the San Diego Zoo, the African plains animals stand listlessly, impossibly out of place under the gloom, while the musk oxen and polar bears seem never more at home. At Mission San Diego de Alcalá, the roof tiles are a shade darker, and in the tower, the bell has the slightest sheen—as do the outdoor images of the famous at the Tijuana Hall of Fame and the huge ball of CECUT's IMAX theater. Drops run down the flagpole of the preserved wooden San Diego Union building in Old Town.

The cars with hundreds of thousands of commuters—and college students heading to summer classes—now fill the streets of Tijuana and stream up and down the freeways—the 5, the 15, the 805—to San Diego, long filaments of white and red lights. At the border, the stream of those cars passes almost in equal measure in both directions.

The US-built fence heads into the Pacific Ocean at Playas de Tijuana.

Planes lift off from San Diego International Airport and Aeropuerto Internacional de Tijuana and quickly disappear into the clouds.

Some people are already in their offices. In a high-rise overlooking the airport in San Diego, and at another in downtown Tijuana, two elderly men, with the dreams of young men, have already been at their desks for hours. Malin Burnham, 92, and José Galicot are hard at work on their latest plans for their respective, beloved cities.

In their hotel rooms in San Diego and Tijuana, tourists and visiting businesspeople are just getting out of bed. They stumble to their windows and pull open their curtains—to be greeted by gray gloom and damp streets. *This isn't what I was promised,* they say to themselves.

But outside, the commuters driving by in their cars or quickly striding down the crowded downtown streets look up—and detect just the slightest lightening of the overcast. *It's burning off,* they tell themselves. It's going to be a warm, sunny day for the two great cities of the San Diego-Tijuana Coastal Plain.

EPILOGUE

On January 7, 2020, a California Border Patrol contractor's bulldozer appeared at Border Field State Park—Friendship Park—and proceeded to plow up the park's most popular feature: a garden, filled with native flora, that had been planted on both sides of the fence to foster friendship between the two countries.

The garden was first planted in 2007 by Border Encuentro ("Border Encounter"), a binational group that had maintained the site ever since then. It was members of this group who first spotted the bulldozer destroying the garden on the San Diego side of the fence and alerted the local media.

Contacted by reporters, San Diego sector Border Patrol chief Douglas E. Harrison issued a formal statement:

> Traffickers cut the legacy border mesh and were using the binational garden to cover illegal activities. We had to take measures to eliminate the vulnerability. I contacted Friends of Friendship Park and will meet with them to discuss the next steps.

In the past, such a justification—allaying fears of San Diegans about illegal activities at the border—might have been the end of the story. But the world—at least along this stretch of the US-Mexico border—had changed, as Harrison quickly discovered.

The garden's destruction further irritated nerves still raw from CBP's decision, a year before, to suspend the hugely popular Opening the Door of Hope program, also held at Friendship Park. In that program, conducted annually for six years, the Border Patrol had opened a gate between the two countries and allowed a dozen preselected families to walk through and meet face-to-face for three minutes. That program was shut down when it was discovered one of the men selected to participate in a much-publicized (three-minute) wedding between a US citizen and his Mexican fiancée, had been charged with drug smuggling.

This recent history made the painful symbolism of the Border Encuentro garden bulldozing that much sharper. That it happened in the midst of an ever-warming relationship between Tijuana and San Diego—and at Friendship Park, of all places—made it even worse.

In the resulting outcry from both sides of the border, Chief Harrison felt compelled to apologize. As he wrote on Twitter:

> I met with [Friends of Friendship Park] today & apologized for the unintentional destruction of the garden. The original intent was to have the garden trimmed. We take full responsibility, are investigating the event, and look forward to working with FoFP [Friends of Friendship Park] on the path forward.

This was not the US Customs and Border Patrol of old. Nor was the outcry by San Diegans characteristic of their historic attitude exhibited over two centuries, which fluctuated between indifference and fear, between disrespect and contempt for Tijuana and the border. In the three decades since the San Diego Dialogue brought the original trailblazers together in search of a new relationship for these two cities, something had changed, profoundly.

USMCA

While local attention was focused on Friendship Park, a much larger event was taking place in Washington, DC, and Mexico City—one that promised to continue the transformation of both countries' economies, and nowhere more than in the integrated, cross-border economy of San Diego and Tijuana.

Notwithstanding the pending impeachment hearings against President Donald Trump, the majority of Democrats in the House of Representatives, unexpectedly, voted to pass one of President Trump's signature pieces of legislation: the US-Mexico-Canada (Trade) Agreement (USMCA). In 2016, the president had run on the promise to end NAFTA, which had been a bonanza for the Mexican economy and the engine behind the vast expansion of maquiladoras and cross-border trade that had occurred since 1994.

In his campaign, President Trump had characterized NAFTA as too heavily weighted to Mexico's advantage. He declared he would scrap it unless it was renegotiated. Now, even as he faced impeachment, Trump had his victory. Just months prior, passage of USMCA had seemed unlikely. House Ways and Means Committee chairman Richard Neal had predicted "a very hard" path to ratification because of Democrats' concerns regarding inadequate protections for US unions, workplace discrimination, and adverse environmental impacts.

But these worries were allayed by modifications expedited through President López Obrador's administration in Mexico, and House Speaker Pelosi was able to push the measure through her caucus in the US Congress. The Republican-controlled Senate, already strong supporters of USMCA, took advantage of this breakthrough and quickly passed the agreement on January 16, 2020.

In a January 29 ceremony on the South Lawn of the White House, surrounded by workers in hard hats, President Trump signed the agreement into law, announcing, "Today, we are finally ending the NAFTA nightmare and signing into law the brand-new US-Mexico-Canada Agreement." He was joined at the signing ceremony by Mexico's foreign minister, Marcelo Ebrard.

The Mexican Senate, not surprisingly, moved quickly. Faced with an offer it couldn't refuse from its largest trading partner, Mexico had ratified the initial agreement in June 2019, with only three dissenting votes. It then passed the revised treaty on December 12, 2019, by a vote of 107–1. In a crucial concession to Mexico (and Canada), the US accepted the demand that steel and aluminum tariffs, earlier imposed by the Trump administration, would be dropped.

In March 2020, Canada, the lone holdout, ratified the USMCA treaty. The ratification delay occurred largely because, in Canada's October 2019 federal election, Prime Minister Trudeau's Liberal Party lost the majority in Parliament, although he retained his leadership position through a coalition government. As a result, legislative deliberations had to start over—a process that began in early December. Unfortunately, in the interim between the reintroduction of the bill and its ratification, the COVID-19 pandemic swept North America, closing down international travel, paralyzing the economies of all three countries, and postponing much of the new agreement's implementation.

Just how USMCA is an improvement over NAFTA remains a subject of debate. The truth likely will not be known for years. For San Diego and Tijuana, the significance of the "new NAFTA" was the continuity it ensured for the region's cross-border, integrated economy. USMCA meant that national politics in both countries would remain aligned with this local development. Businesspeople in both cities would not need to swim against adverse policy currents in either country. For Tijuanenses and San Diegans, the results of NAFTA had been outstanding over the years; it appeared as though USMCA would enable further economic growth.

San Diego continued to win big in America's economic boom, notwithstanding the shrinking inventory of affordable housing and the growing problem of homelessness that has plagued it and other large California cities. In 2019, the city gained 34,800 jobs, the most of any city in Southern California. It also added eighteen hundred new hotel rooms. Three thousand five hundred new apartments were expected to open in 2020. Indeed, so robust was this current and expected local growth that there were calls for new legislation—even in the face of rising real estate prices and a pronounced need for affordable housing—to curb runaway development in some of the county's more pristine, less dense districts.

San Diego skyline and cruise ship terminal as seen from Coasterra restaurant.

Tijuana's economic boom continued as well into early 2020, partly due to increased business with San Diego and the US but also because of its own internal development. But the news was also mixed, thanks to resurgent crime. The drug cartel wars between Sinaloa and the Cártel Jalisco Nueva Generación had returned—as had the murder rate, which continued to exceed that of the dark days a decade before. This sustained high crime level was further complicated by the controversial Migration Protection Protocols (MPP) program—nicknamed "Remain in Mexico"—an unwritten US-Mexico agreement to which the López Obrador administration had acquiesced.

Pursuant to the MPP, migrants, who previously had been allowed to enter the US to await adjudication of their asylum petitions, would instead be forced to remain on the Mexican side of the border (potentially for years) while their claims were processed. Thousands of Central American migrants from Honduras, Guatemala, and El Salvador were returned to Tijuana from San Ysidro during 2019, in accordance with the program. Their fate, as well as the viability of the program itself, however, was thrown into limbo in late February by a judicial appellate ruling invalidating the MPP under federal law. As of March 2020, utter uncertainty reigned, with the case unquestionably heading to the US Supreme Court.

A month earlier, the *San Diego Union-Tribune* had reported that cross-border tourism to Tijuana from San Diego and the rest of the US—contrary to earlier predictions—was dropping unexpectedly. Much of this was blamed on a growing perception by Americans that Tijuana increasingly was becoming—once again—a dangerous place to visit.

What made these numbers particularly perplexing was that everyday commuting between the two cities continued to grow, as did specialty visits to Tijuana for medical tourism and other purposes. Moreover, as noted, Tijuana itself was enjoying its own economic boom. Some Americans might be absent from the city's restaurants, hotels, and cultural sites, but their missing numbers were being replaced, and then some, by visitors from Mexico and elsewhere in Latin America. Additionally, regular visitors to the city understood that nearly all the organized-crime violence was taking place in the outer neighborhoods (colonias) of the city and that the prospering, bustling downtown districts remained as safe as any major city anywhere. These regular border crossers were only increasing their back-and-forth activity between San Diego and Tijuana.

Hidden in the border-crossing and tourism numbers was another, remarkable new reality: after two centuries of dependence upon San Diego and the United States for its survival, Tijuana had at last begun to become not just a border town, with all of the term's pejorative connotations, but an economically independent city. That said, as long as the city's crime rate continued to grow—and especially if it spilled out into the more prosperous districts—the danger to Tijuana's economy and well-being remained high.

This was not a new situation for Tijuana, which, ever adaptable, had confronted and overcome similar threats time and time again in the course of its history. The close relationship Tijuana was developing with San Diego—and the unified community emerging between them—was a source of both additional resilience and confidence that Tijuanenses would again bounce back stronger than ever. This synergy now worked both ways across the border.

SHARED RESPONSE

A prime illustration of these reciprocal benefits arose during the first quarter of 2020 with the media explosion over the pandemic involving a novel coronavirus: COVID-19. The threat was met with growing apprehension worldwide. It rocked global financial markets as they had not been since their near-collapse in 2008. The first two cases of the virus appeared in San Diego in early February, leading county officials to declare a local and public health emergency out of an abundance of caution and to enable the region to tap into state and federal emergency funds.

By mid-February, dozens of Americans, taken off airlines under suspicion of exposure to the infectious disease, were being quarantined at Marine Corps Air Station Miramar for a fourteen-day observation period. Seven patients exhibiting coughs or fevers had been taken to the UC San Diego Medical Center or Rady Children's Hospital. Meanwhile, local public health authorities in both San Diego and Tijuana remained in close consultation as they had been in 2009 in successfully confronting the H1N1 virus (thought to have originated in the region) and the SARS outbreak originating in China six years before that epidemic. Together, San Diego and Tijuana had modeled cross-border health-protection protocols for their countries, and they were prepared to do so again amid the uncertainty in the current crisis.

On March 1, 2020, the White House announced the first death in the United States from COVID-19—the beginning of an exponential curve of fatalities that within the next six weeks would kill more than forty thousand Americans, with no end in sight.

Unlike most other places on earth, San Diego, thanks to its global biomedical leadership, possessed the potential to control its own fate. Local labs were racing to develop a vaccine to fight COVID-19. Meanwhile, Tijuana—the preeminent maker of medical devices, a major source of medical supplies, and a leading site for medical tourism—stood by, ready to contribute to and benefit from its partnership with San Diego with a flood of respirators and other devices and personal protective equipment.

As the pandemic—potentially the greatest since the Spanish Flu a century before—spread in early March 2020, the number of cases in the United States far exceeded those in Mexico. If this trend continued, some speculated, perhaps the ultimate irony in the long story between the two nations would be that Mexico might close its border to its northern neighbor.

The Mexican government dismissed such speculation. But when asked about the possibility of closing its border to Americans, Deputy Health Minister Hugo López-Gatell Ramírez reluctantly held a press conference to say, "The possible flow of coronavirus would come from the north to the south. If it were technically necessary, we would consider mechanisms of restriction or stronger surveillance."

Few people on either side of the border believed a full closure would ever happen, especially at San Ysidro. San Diego and Tijuana were now too deeply interconnected—culturally, economically, socially—for that to happen. "Mexico cannot survive without goods crossing the border," said Duncan Wood, director of the Mexico Institute at the Woodrow Wilson International Center for Scholars think tank. "Last year, the only thing that kept the Mexican economy even close to 0% growth—it ended up with a 0.1% or 0.2% contraction—the only thing that kept it close to positive territory was demand from the US." Meanwhile, a break in the supply chains from the Tijuana maquiladora enterprises and some of the most important US companies would only further damage the stalled Mexican economy.

Nonetheless, the uncertainty and fear that gripped the world that March placed the previously unthinkable on the table regarding the border and much else in everyday life as much of the United States and the world shut down in a frenzy of "social distancing." On the US-Mexico border, for the first time, the security problem was not, in Alan Bersin's analogy about managing the border, finding a (high-risk) needle in the haystack of lawful travelers. The threat of contagion from a pandemic had made the *entire* haystack itself a problem. While the outcome in the early days of the national emergency declared by the two presidents remained unknown, it seemed likely that Tijuana and San Diego would be the crucible for any cross-border situation—and potential solution—that might emerge from the crisis. Moreover, the pandemic seemed destined to become a measure of what the two cities had accomplished together and become—for better and for worse.

Then, in early April, Mexico announced that COVID-19 had now hit that country as well. By April 21, the nation had experienced 686 deaths, with 8,261 infected, and the peak of the crisis was expected to hit in early May. Mexico City was the worst hit, but Baja California—especially Tijuana—had the second-highest number of cases in the nation. As in San Diego, Tijuana, too, began to shut down: offices and (many, but not all) maquiladoras closed, and the citizens hunkered down, quarantined in their homes.

But something unprecedented in the long history of the two cities—and the two countries—had occurred. Here is how Alan Bersin described it in a post from the Woodrow Wilson International Center for Scholars in Washington:

> In the midst of this global economic shut-down, there was a silver lining . . . in the pragmatic, sensible way the governments of Canada, Mexico, and the United States have reacted thus far to the crisis.
>
> The situation clearly could have led policymakers to recommend a complete and extended border closure—and it would not have been surprising were such a sweeping security measure imposed unilaterally by the United States, as so many have been in the wake of 9/11.
>
> But that is not the way it has unfolded. Instead, the North American response emerged following close and coordinated consultation. Although conducted in "parallel bilateral fashion" (between the US and each of its neighbors), a trilateral result was reached among the three governments: to limit spread of the coronavirus, non-essential travel was curtailed while cross-border trade ($3.4 billion daily) remained unconstrained . . .
>
> That these actions were taken by leaders in the three countries who do not really trust one another—in an era of counter-globalization to which two of them subscribe—leaves the lesson even more undeniable and compelling.

By early April 2020, despite the COVID-19 pandemic still raging on both sides of the border, the economic traffic across the border between Tijuana and San Diego had returned to nearly the same level as before. Even more remarkably, in the face of this extraordinary distraction of a continent-wide health crisis, the three nations still pressed on and began their implementation of USMCA. It was a statement of defiance: no crisis, not even a global pandemic, could impede this new relationship between the three countries—a relationship that, in important ways, had begun with the pioneering work of private citizens in San Diego and Tijuana.

PASSINGS

The death of two prominent citizens saddened Tijuana at the beginning of the new decade. The lives of both men charted the transformation of the city, and both men played key roles in creating and nurturing warm and constructive relations between Tijuana and San Diego.

In early February, developer Moisés Abadi died tragically in a motorcycle accident in his native Panama. He was just sixty-two.

Educated in Mexico, Abadi had left Panama in 1988, just before the US invasion of that country to unseat its president–drug dealer, Manuel Noriega. In 1998, for safety reasons, Abadi moved his family from Mexico City to San Diego and set up his firm, Grupo Abadi, in Tijuana. Betting that many Tijuanenses and San Diegans would like to live as close as possible to the border, in 2004 Abadi bought an eight-acre site within walking distance of the border for $14 million and embarked on the creation of NewCity.

Abadi's death sent shock waves through not just Tijuana but San Diego as well. As much as anyone, he was responsible for the modern Tijuana skyline, most famously for his massive but stylishly elegant $170 million NewCity development, with its five towers and medical campus. One of those high-rises, Diamond Tower, is the tallest edifice in the city. At twenty-seven stories, the building is visible even from downtown San Diego, nearly twenty miles away.

Abadi was well known in San Diego as well. A resident of Del Mar, he was deeply involved in the region's Jewish community and part owner of multiple restaurants in San Diego County. But he was best known on both sides of the border for his tenacity.

In 2007, with just two of his towers built, the recession hit and construction halted. Meanwhile, 140 of the two hundred people who had put down deposits on the luxury condominiums the towers would house walked away from their commitments. But Abadi persevered. Then, in 2017, even as it was being completed, the NewCity development again nearly went broke. But, instead of bailing out, Abadi fought on, and the project survived. Today, NewCity has more than one thousand residents and continues to grow rapidly, especially now, with the completion of the fifth tower.

"Thank God I never walk away from anything," Abadi told the *San Diego Union-Tribune* at the time.

After announcing the news of his father's death, Abadi's son, Isaac, CEO of Grupo Abadi, said, "He was always looking to make a change and help people, and create something different than what there was. He had an amazing vision."

Less of a surprise, but no less mourned or impactful a loss, was the February 10 death of Hector Lutteroth at ninety-three, after a long illness.

Lutteroth was an early and prescient binational pioneer. He devoted countless hours to his support of the Orchestra of Baja California, Iberoamericana University, CECUT, and the San Diego Natural History Museum, in addition to many other civic and business groups in the region.

It was *San Diego Evening Tribune* editor Neil Morgan who first brought Lutteroth to a community board meeting in the late 1980s, as part of his efforts to knit the two cities closer together. Lutteroth soon became a leading figure in the San Diego Dialogue and helped Chuck Nathanson bring other leading Tijuana citizens into the organization.

Said Mary Walshok, "He helped create a community of leaders that were looking to the issues together—talking about what a certain idea can mean to each city, trying to find what to do to make things work better."

Lutteroth was born in the state of Sonora and came to Tijuana in 1961 to help his father run the Country Club Hotel. In time, his Grupo AFAL (Asociación Familia Lutteroth) would become a major force in real estate, sports, and restaurants in Tijuana. As for himself, Lutteroth became known for his leadership of the local PRI party and for his many philanthropic endeavors—including donations of sports uniforms and equipment and school tuitions to the young people of Tijuana.

THE THIRD COUNTRY

For all their achievements, perhaps the greatest legacy of both Lutteroth and Abadi was to strengthen and help set Tijuana on its trajectory into the twenty-first century, and to do so in concert with San Diego. They were quintessential Borderlanders-Fronterizos who lived and worked in both cities and helped knit a border fabric of interdependence at the national margins of the two countries. While the border was often an occasion for collision at the federal level, to Hector Lutteroth and Moisés Abadi, and to the others chronicled in this book, it remained a place of synthesis, where cultures, economies, and families have blended and meshed. This is why, in Mexico, the border is known as El Tercer País, "the third country"—something distinct and special. It is what Bayless Manning characterized as "intermestic," simultaneously international and domestic. As globalization proceeds through increased trade, travel, and technological advances, the line between international and domestic issues becomes more blurred. Nowhere is that more true than along the US-Mexico border at its westernmost reach in San Diego-Tijuana. As Alan Bersin has observed:

> Borders today are as much about flows of goods and people, north and south, as they are about east-west sovereign boundary lines. Living where cross-border commerce flows and binational communities thrive, the San Diegan-Tijuanenses Fronterizos are well positioned to offer important guidance to their countries at large about integration and collaboration. Much of modern border management pertaining to security and the expedited handling of lawful cross-border flows originated in Tijuana-San Diego. This is the technical base of skill and knowledge that, coupled with

community understanding and support, could gener-
ate a dynamic of economic and social integration not
only involving Mexico and the United States but along
the entire north-south axis of North America, from
Colombia to the Arctic.

The "one border community" that San Diego and Tijuana are
crafting together might just prove to be the gateway and bridge to that
continental future. The mantle of cross-border leadership likely shall
pass to the sons and daughters of the Mexican trailblazers—José B.
Fimbres, Carlos Bustamante Aubanel, Alejandra Mier y Teran, Ascan
Lutteroth, Isaac Abadi, Rafael Galicot, Gregorio Galicot, Alvaro Luken
Luna, Simón Somohano, Yolanda Selene Walther-Meade, and others—to carry forward this work over the next generation. In light of
the story that has been told here, this development should be neither
surprising nor unwelcome. These "next-gen" individuals, in their lifestyles, careers, capabilities, and choices, embody and exemplify the
emergence of the new cross-border, North American citizen: fully
bilingual, entirely binational, and completely bicultural. In the words
of Pedro Romero, himself a Tijuana-San Diego trailblazer and today
President López Obrador's "northern border" adviser, they are the "3-B
Generation"—equally comfortable and at home in the two cities and
both countries, no longer marginalized in a diversifying United States
or ignored by an inward-looking Mexico.

Raymundo Arnaiz, the real estate developer and a founding
Mexican member of the San Diego Dialogue, captures this sense of the
future in the context of his own family:

> I was born in San Diego in the 1940s. I renounced [my
> US citizenship] when I turned eighteen because hav-
> ing a dual nationality then wasn't a possibility. I had
> to pick one, and I chose to be Mexican. [Today] all my
> family is binational. I have three daughters and one son
> and eleven grandchildren. They all own two passports.
> They have both nationalities . . . [They] have the best of
> two worlds in the shared community that Tijuana and
> San Diego have built.

Since its beginning, time and again, it has seemed as if Tijuana would fall apart. But it never did, in part because of the toughness José B. Fimbres describes, the tenacity and courage Carlos Bustamante possesses, and the resiliency that José Galicot embodies. Tijuana has survived and prospered as well because of San Diego, which, historically, it looked to and relied upon, sometimes as a refuge, often as a model, and always as a neighbor and customer to be served and cultivated.

As a result, Tijuana-San Diego has prospered as a region, such that, in the future, it may become a model for the evolution of an interdependent, economically thriving North America—a collaboration not mandated by government but built by civic, business, and community groups, one fueled by the opportunities offered to its people and by the trusting, confident relationships between their leaders.

AGAINST THE ODDS

In its half century of existence, half-acre Friendship Park had suffered many insults and assaults, from border jumpers to smugglers to a massive steel fence cutting it in two, from cynical media events to the bulldozing of its garden on the US side.

Yet through everything, the park had somehow continued to grow in its spiritual value to the two great cities that surrounded it on opposite sides.

Said park architect James Brown, who has been commissioned to redesign Friendship Park for even greater cross-border interaction, "Our culturally rich border region is ultimately made stronger and safer through cooperation instead of fear. The best security that we can attain is not achieved by force, but by friendship . . . Our nations need a symbol of solidarity at this moment in our shared histories."

This was particularly true on the Tijuana side of the park. Whereas to San Diegans, the border fence was an ugly scar to be largely ignored, to Tijuanenses, it was something more: an insult, an embarrassment, a reminder of the arrogance and power of the United States and of the weaknesses of their own country. Many of their fellow citizens had abandoned their country crossing the border there; too many had died in the process. For all those reasons, from the Tijuana side the giant border fence couldn't be ignored; the pain it represented could only be salved, defanged for now in hope of a better future, when its iron bars were pulled down forever.

On the American side, visitors mostly pass through the park, barely giving it a second glance on their way toward the beach. For those few who do stop, the experience is typically solemn. But on the Mexican side, the experience is very different: it has become a gathering place for celebration, contemplation, and reverence, with that characteristic Mexican combination of vivid colors and uninhibited exultation. And much of it has been organized in concert with Americans.

On a given weekend day, one is likely to find on the Mexican side of the fence the black bars painted with brilliant reds, yellows, and blues—a staccato mural or a simple cross. The activity on this side of the park appears in a memorable photo-essay by Ariana Drehsler, a photographer for *San Diego Magazine*: a church service, food vendors, weddings and family reunions, and musicians—from a junior high school chamber orchestra to a lone accordion player. On both sides of the fence, the Mexican and US volunteers of Border Encuento tend their binational garden, a riot of flowers, shrubs, and vegetables, demarked by painted automobile tires sunk into the earth.

Against all odds, Friendship Park has lived up to its name. If on the American side the gates to the park are open only a couple of hours each day, on the Mexican side the park is open day and night—and those who flood its contiguous space are just as likely to be Americans who have crossed the border to visit from the Mexican side.

Some of these Americans have come from hundreds of miles away. Some have come in anger or dismay at the very idea of borders and fences. Some have come in solidarity with the people of another nation, a proud nation that has faced endless challenges. But others have come to honor the name of the park itself—to celebrate an enduring relationship that has evolved through thick and thin for more than two centuries, one that now seems to grow stronger by the year, with a momentum toward friendship and interdependence that is no longer denied but rather embraced by people on both sides of the border they share.

AFTERWORD

The story of how Tijuana and San Diego became a single metropolitan area, intimately linked by deep economic, cultural, and social ties, is an unusual one, and it makes for a great read—partly a history, partly a thriller.

It's the story of how two tiny hamlets, one originally a mission and the other a ranch, grew into two great cities, among the largest in their own countries, and eventually discovered each other, at first reluctantly and later enthusiastically. But first they had to live through gangsters, international political intrigue, economic booms and collapses, profound cultural misunderstandings, and the constant presence of a border that both kept them apart and tied them together like a seam.

Cities along the US-Mexico border often have complex but closely tied histories, and most of them have historically embraced their relationship, but San Diego and Tijuana were different. They were both large enough to think of themselves as independent from each other, and culturally and economically different enough to be able to believe that they didn't need each other. They developed identities almost at odds with each other: a fun-loving, relaxed beach town to the north, and a gritty industrial town, with a touch of danger, to the south. In many ways, they defined themselves in contrast to the other.

But over time these distinct identities began to blur. Both gradually became a single integrated economy based largely on the production of high-end technology, including medical and audio equipment. Both also became hotbeds for culinary and cultural innovation, with chefs, musicians, and artists creating cultural repertoires that defied and reinterpreted the border between them. Soon they started to discover that this interdependence was actually a source of profound strength and that they could each make a bigger mark in their own countries and on the global stage if they worked together and built a shared identity that could unite them.

The recognition of this interdependence did not come easily nor is it yet complete. There are forces in each country that still pull them each in the other direction, away from each other. But it has been surprising to watch how two cities that once tried their best to define each other against the other have embraced the idea that they are now a single metropolitan region with a common future ahead of them, with everything from joint urban planning exercises to shared cultural activities that seek to tie them closer together.

The human stories in this book are fundamental because they compel us to look more closely at new and different angles of a border that defies simplistic categorizations or an outdated narrative describing just customs and immigration checkpoints. A big-picture look at the region allows us to realize that when we talk about the border, we are also talking about us. We are talking about friends and families in Tijuana and San Diego that move, invest, shop, and socialize across the boundary line. When we talk about the border, we talk about railroad builders, miners, investors, and migrant men and women whose work ethic and dignity have made them an essential component of the success of both countries.

In many ways, this remarkable and still evolving relationship between San Diego and Tijuana is a microcosm of what is happening between the United States and Mexico writ large. Two countries that once saw each other as deeply dissimilar have been discovering— sometimes slowly and unevenly—that they are, in fact, deeply intertwined and that they are stronger together than apart. Shared supply chains, deep family ties, and increasingly strong cultural bonds are turning what used to be two distant nations into intimately linked neighbors who depend on each other for their future prosperity. The border that once defined their difference from each other now also ties them together in their mutual interdependence.

This does not mean that Mexico and the United States are one country, any more than Tijuana and San Diego are one city. The unique characteristics that each have, and their proud histories, are part of what makes the relationship so rich and meaningful. But much as these two cities have become a single metropolitan area, enriched by their differences but bound together by their shared economies, personal and family ties, and ability to learn from each other's cultural histories, so too the United States and Mexico are finding that their differences only strengthen a partnership anchored in deep economic, social, and cultural ties. And this holds true even when the politics of divisiveness sometimes tries to tear them apart.

This book is a testament to two cities that overcame and embraced their differences to create a common space and a shared future, building a bridge over the wall that separated them. It is also a testament to this larger relationship between Mexico and the United States, which is also growing day by day, as people in both countries embrace their differences as an asset and build multiple bridges—through investment, shared production, film, music, art, food, family and personal relationships, and even the choice to live in the other country, as millions of US and Mexican citizens have—that span the walls that once separated them.

We salute the many people who have made this possible. This includes the consuls general who have served their countries, representing Mexico in San Diego and the United States in Tijuana; the civic, political, and business leaders who have actively sought to bridge the divide between the two countries; the artists, musicians, chefs, writers, and others who have created a new vision of the shared space between the two cities and our two countries; the journalists who have reported on these changes; and, above all, the citizens of both cities— and both countries—who have had the courage to imagine a different relationship in which our geographical proximity is an opportunity to be explored, reimagined, and celebrated.

Martha Bárcena Coqui, Ambassador of Mexico to the United States

Dr. Andrew Selee, author of Vanishing Frontiers *and President of the Migration Policy Institute*

SELECTED BIBLIOGRAPHY

San Diego Reader: https://www.sandiegoreader.com/news/1988
    /feb/25/baja-rebellion/

Library of Congress, Hispanic Reading Room: https://www.loc.gov
    /rr/hispanic/mexico/timeline.html

US-Mexico Borderlands: Historical and Contemporary Perspectives by
    Oscar Jáquez Martínez

Research Data Library UCSD: Neil Morgan collection

The 1982 Mexican peso devaluation and border area employment:
    https://www.bls.gov/opub/mlr/1985/10/art3full.pdf

Golden Door: goldendoor.com

Tripsavvy: https://www.tripsavvy.com/godmother-of-modern-spas
    -deborah-szekely-3089670

The *San Diego Union-Tribune*: Neil Morgan Obituary, 2/1/2014

The National Review: The Long, Long Depression: https://www
    .nationalreview.com/2012/01/long-long-depression-matthew-lynn/

Maryland Journal of International Law, Volume 33, Issue 1, Article
    10: "Extradition as a Tool for International Cooperation: Lessons
    from the US-Mexico Relationship" by Emily Edmonds-Poli David
    Shirk

San Diego Reader: Mexican revolution and the role played by Tijuana
    by Bob Owens, Feb. 25, 1988

Southern California Quarterly, Vol. 35 No. 4, December 1953:
    "US-Mexico Law Enforcement and Border Security Cooperation:
    An Institutional-Historical Perspective" by Guadalupe Correa-
    Cabrera and Evan D. McCormick

Politico: https://www.politico.com/magazine/story/2017/02/san
    -diego-bridge-border-wall-airport-tijuana-214788

Banderas News: http://www.banderasnews.com/0712/hb
    -drbettyjones.htm

The *San Diego Union-Tribune*: https://www.sandiegouniontribune
    .com/news/border-baja-california/sd-me-tijuana-mayors
    -20170206-story.html

Quartz.com: https://qz.com/947305/this-is-free-trade-nearly-every
    -pacemaker-used-in-the-us-is-partly-made-in-tijuana-mexico/

The *San Diego Union-Tribune*: https://www.sandiegouniontribune
    .com/news/border-baja-california/sd-me-tijuana-mayors
    -20170206-story.html

Tijuana EDC: https://tijuanaedc.org/

DVID Inc: https://www.dvidshub.net/video/722206/border-wall
    -system-construction

BiopharmaGuy.com: https://biopharmguy.com/links/state-ca-all-geo
    .php California Biotech, Pharmaceutical & Life Sciences
    Companies

The *Brownsville Herald*: https://www.brownsvilleherald.com/violence
    -the-result-of-fractured-arrangement-between-zetas-and-gulf
    /article_84acae85-f39d-53f4-ad50-fd4cfebd8115.html

The New Yorker: https://www.newyorker.com/magazine/2012/01/30
    /the-missionary-dana-goodyear

Pacific Magazine: https://www.pacificsandiego.com/magazine/pac
    -chef-javier-plascencia-baja-story.html

CETYS: https://www.cetys.mx/en/international-collaboration/

Universidad Autónoma de Baja California: http://www.uabc.mx/en/

International Community Foundation:
    https://3i9i2q3n686v427cr941c7do-wpengine.netdna-ssl.com
    /wp-content/uploads/2015/11/Shared_Destiny_English.pdf
    Shared Destiny: Shaping a Binational Agenda for Health Priorities
    in the San Diego—Baja California Region

Ibid: https://3i9i2q3n686v427cr941c7do-wpengine.netdna-ssl.com
    /wp-content/uploads/2015/11/Blurred_Borders_2004.pdf Blurred
    Borders: Transboundary Issues and Solutions in the San Diego/
    Tijuana Border Region

The Guardian: https://www.theguardian.com/world/2019/nov/04
    /bloody-tijuana-mexico-murderous-border-city-week

TJVisitor.com http://www.tjvisitor.com/new-city-medical-plaza

NBCI: https://www.ncbi.nlm.nih.gov/pmc/articles/PMC2234298/
  "Medical Tourism: Globalization of the Healthcare Marketplace"
The Border, by Don Winslow (New York: William Morrow, 2019)
San Diego Foundation: https://www.sdfoundation.org/news-events
  /sdf-news/why-medical-coverage-meaningless-at-only-pediatric
  -hospital-in-tijuana/
Banderas News: http://www.banderasnews.com/0712/hb
  -drbettyjones.htm Tijuana's Poor Get Rare Care Courtesy of
  Canadian Expat
Smart Border Coalition: https://smartbordercoalition.com/
San Diego Chamber of Commerce: https://sdchamber.org/?s=mbc
San Diego City Beat: https://www.sdcitybeat.com/news-and-opinion
  /news/things-change../
Politico: https://www.politico.com/magazine/story/2017/02/san
  -diego-bridge-border-wall-airport-tijuana-214788
SANDAG: https://www.sandag.org/uploads/publicationid
  /publicationid_1257_5883.pdf
International Wastewater Treatment Plant: https://www.ibwc.gov
  /Mission_Operations/sbiwtp.html South Bay International
  Wastewater Treatment Plant (SBIWTP)
World Gazetteer: *"America: metropolitan areas,"* 2011
World Gazetteer: "San Diego," 2007
Compact.org: "San Diego Dialogue," https://compact.org
  /resource-posts/the-san-diego-dialogue/
UCSD News: https://ucsdnews.ucsd.edu/archive/newsrel/general
  /C%20Nathanson.htm
*Vanishing Frontiers: The Forces Driving Mexico and the United
  States Together*, by Andrew Selee https://books.google.com
  /books?id=oDI4DwAAQBAJ&pg=PT42&lpg=PT42&dq
  =jose+galicot+telecommunications&source=bl&ots=
  VDpYFYPTZl&sig=ACfU3U1ecl7cSFLw389BTb1rZ3BK
  dZctSA&hl=en&sa=X&ved=2ahUKEwjR4_KQvP_kAhUTJjQ
  IHWvyBjwQ6AEwEnoECAgQAQ#v=onepage&q=jose
  %20galicot%20telecommunications&f=false
Semantic Scholar: "San Diego Dialogue," https://www.semanticscholar
  .org/paper/The-San-Diego-Dialogue%3A-Reshaping-the-San-

Diego-Christensen-Rongerude/518b2667dd86aba04e12dfc
    18c40a287e1e905fd
Redial Inc.: Reaganista.blogspot.com: https://reaganista.blogspot
    .com/2012/01/beloved-wife-philanthropist-cuban.html
Times of San Diego: https://timesofsandiego.com/
Co-Production International: "Getting Started In Mexico," https://
    www.co-production.net/nearshore-solutions/get-started-in
    -mexico/mexico-manufacturing-news/plantronics-mexico
    -manufacturing.html
US Customs and Border Protection: https://www.cbp.gov/newsroom
    /local-media-release/cbp-reminds-sentri-users-lane-has-moved
    -gateway-americas-bridge-juarez
Sandler, Travis & Rosenberg, P.A.: "Trusted Trader Program
    Could be Operational This Year" https://www.strtrade.com
    /news-publications-trusted-tader-CTPAT-importer-self
    -assessment-CBP-020618.html
San Diego Magazine: https://www.sandiegomagazine.com/features
    /one-sunday-in-friendship-park/article_df14eeec-477a-11ea
    -a444-dfb4d6e20c7b.html

PHOTO CREDITS

Page 7: Photo courtesy of Las Americas Premium Outlets

Page 13: Photo courtesy of Poly/Plamex

Page 25: From a painting by H.M.T Powell done in 1850

Page 36: Andre Williams Collection, courtesy *Tijuana in History: Just Crossing the Border*—David Pinera/Gabriel Rivera

Page 52: Photo courtesy: San Diego History Center

Page 61: Photo courtesy: San Diego History Center

Page 63: Photo courtesy: San Diego History Center

Page 65: Photo courtesy: San Diego Natural History Museum

Page 66: Photo courtesy of the *San Diego Union-Tribune*

Page 69: Andre Williams Collection, courtesy: *Tijuana in History: Just Crossing the Border*—David Pinera/Gabriel Rivera

Page 70: Andre Williams Collection, courtesy: *Tijuana in History: Just Crossing the Border*—David Pinera/Gabriel Rivera

Page 72: Andre Williams Collection, courtesy: *Tijuana in History: Just Crossing the Border*—David Pinera/Gabriel Rivera

Page 82: Historical Archive of Tijuana IMAC, courtesy: *Tijuana in History: Just Crossing the Border*

Page 85: Andre Williams Collection, courtesy: *Tijuana in History: Just Crossing the Border*—David Pinera/Gabriel Rivera

Page 87: Photo Courtesy: Caliente Casino Hipódromo

Page 89: Andre Williams Collection, courtesy: *Tijuana in History: Just Crossing the Border*—David Pinera/Gabriel Rivera

Page 90: Andre Williams Collection, courtesy: *Tijuana in History: Just Crossing the Border*—David Pinera/Gabriel Rivera

Page 91: Andre Williams Collection, courtesy: *Tijuana in History: Just Crossing the Border*—David Pinera/Gabriel Rivera

Page 96: Andre Williams Collection, courtesy: *Tijuana in History: Just Crossing the Border*—David Pinera/Gabriel Rivera

Page 97: Rebeca Herrera de Laveaga Collection, courtesy: *Tijuana in History: Just Crossing the* Border—David Pinera/Gabriel Rivera

Page 108: Photo courtesy: San Diego History Center

Page 109: Photo courtesy: San Diego History Center

Page 113: Photo courtesy: San Diego History Center

Page 115: Photo courtesy: San Diego History Center

Page 120: Photo courtesy: San Diego History Center.

Page 134: Photo courtesy of Rancho La Puerta

Page 215: Photo courtesy of the *San Diego Union-Tribune*

Page 241: Photo courtesy of Cross Border Xpress

Page 257: Photo courtesy of Club de Empresarios in NewCity

Page 266: Photo courtesy of James Clark

Page 288: Photo courtesy of NewCity

Page 314: Photo courtesy of Rosarito Beach Hotel and Tower

Page 319: Photo courtesy of the *San Diego Union-Tribune*

Page 322: Photo courtesy of Grupo Plascencia

Page 325: Photo courtesy of Julio Rodriguez

Page 330: Photo courtesy of CVEATC and City of Chula Vista

Page 331: Photo courtesy Julio Rodriguez

Page 332: Photo courtesy of Caliente

Page 333: Photo courtesy of the City of Chula Vista

Page 338: Photo courtesy of the *San Diego Union-Tribune*

Page 360: Photo courtesy of James Clark

Page 366: Photo courtesy of Henning von Berg

ABOUT THE AUTHOR

 Michael S. Malone is one of the world's best-known high-technology/business journalists. He is the author or coauthor of nearly thirty books, including such award-winning works as *The HP Way*, *The Intel Trilogy*, and *The Virtual Corporation*. He has also been the host or producer of several public-television series (notably the award-winning PBS miniseries *The New Heroes)*, editor of *Forbes ASAP* magazine, and is Dean's Executive Professor at Santa Clara University. He is a Distinguished Friend of Oxford University. Malone lives with his wife and younger son in Sunnyvale, California.

CPSIA information can be obtained
at www.ICGtesting.com
Printed in the USA
LVHW010339191220
674577LV00001B/1/J

9 781733 959148